Regional Approaches to Affordable Housing

STUART MECK, FAICP, REBECCA RETZLAFF,
AND JAMES SCHWAB, AICP

TABLE OF CONTENTS

Acknowledgments

The authors would like to express their appreciation to all of the individuals and organizations that provided information for the preparation of this Planning Advisory Service report, and to the project sponsors, the U.S. Department of Housing and Urban Development (HUD) and the Fannie Mae Foundation. In particular, we would like to thank our two project officers in HUD's Office of Policy Development and Research, Edwin A. Stromberg and Dale E. Thomson, now with Wayne State University in Detroit, and Jamie L. Holtzclaw, Stephanie A. Jennings, AICP, and Kris Rengert at the Fannie Mae Foundation. Marya Morris, AICP, senior research associate at APA, contributed to the research design of the project. John Bredin, Esq, a former research fellow at APA and now a practicing attorney in Chicago, assisted in legal research for the project and the completion of an initial draft of chapter 2 of this report.

The project got off to a good start in with the enthusiastic help of all of the participants of the symposium on regional affordable housing held at the APA offices in Chicago on October 29-30, 2000: Alex Amoroso, AICP, Association of Bay Area Governments; Professor William Baer, University of Southern California; Caren Dewar, Metropolitan Council; Tasha Harmon, AICP, affordable housing activist in Portland, Oregon; Thomas Kemper, builder/developer in Portland Oregon; Roberta Longfellow, AICP, Montgomery County Community and Economic Development Department; Professor Rolf Pendall, AICP, Cornell University; Peter Reinhart, Hovnanian Builders; Jennifer Twombly, National Low Income Housing Coalition; symposium facilitator Joseph Whorton, Georgia Rural Development Council; and project officers, Dale E. Thomson, HUD, and Stephanie Jennings, Fannie Mae Foundation.

iii

The following people responded graciously and generously to the authors by providing interviews, loaning photographs, and reviewing report drafts: Ray Brewster, Twin Pines Housing Trust; James Cordingley and Sean Thompson, New Jersey Council on Affordable Housing; Nancy Firfer, Metropolis 2020; Professor Sharon Perlman Krefetz, Clark University; Nan Merritt, Columbus and Franklin County Affordable Housing Trust; Joan Friedman, Association of Bay Area Governments; Andrew Michael, Bay Area Council; Arthur Sullivan, A Regional Coalition for Housing (ARCH); Paul Carlson, ARCH Citizens Advisory Board; Richard Conrad, City of Mercer Island; Terry Shirk, AICP, City of Redmond, Washington; David Wood, Affordable Housing, Education, and Development; Beverly Fretz-Brown, Sacramento Housing and Redevelopment Agency; Brian O'Connell, AICP, and Vanessa Baker-Latimer, City of Ames, Iowa Department of Planning and Housing; Linda Wheaton, Karen Westmont, and Robert Maus, California Department of Housing and Community Development; John Papagni and Mitra Basu, Maryland Department of Housing and Community Development; Jacob Lieb, Southern California Association of Governments; Susan Baldwin, AICP, San Diego Association of Governments; Polly Nichol, Paul Hannan, Larry Mires, and David Weinstein, Vermont Housing and Conservation Board; Gerry Uba and Rex Burkholder, Metro Council, Portland, Oregon; Allan Mallach, AICP/PP, a New Jersey planning consultant; Werner Lohe, Massachusetts Affordable Housing Appeals Committee; Derry Riding, Rhode Island Statewide Program; Judy Jones, Rhode Island Housing and Mortgage Finance Corporation; Professor Terry Tondro, University of Connecticut School of Law; Dave Bennett, Metropolitan Mayors Caucus; Theresa Huntsinger, Coalition for a Livable Future; Steve Krohn, Real Estate Analytics; Steve Torsell, Homes on the Hill Community Development Corporation; Bruce Mayberry, planning consultant in Yarmouth, Maine; Jeffrey R. Hayes, AICP, North Country Council; Ben Frost, New Hampshire Office of Planning; Ed Stretch, Gilman Housing Trust; Ed Sullivan, land-use attorney with Garvey Schubert & Barer in Portland, Oregon; Brenda Torpy, Burlington Community Land Trust; Adam Zoger, Pacific Coast Capital Partners; Matthew Walsh and Laura Scott, Central New Hampshire Regional Planning Commission; William Ray, New Hampshire Housing Finance Authority; Professor William Morrish, University of Virginia School of Architecture; Joy Sorenson Navarre, Metropolitan Interfaith Council on Affordable Housing; Guy Peterson, Metropolitan Council; Mayor Karen Anderson, City of Minnetonka, Minnesota; and Steve Heuchert, Nashua Regional Planning Commission.

Additional photographs and information for the report were provided by Shannon Taylor and Brad White, LR Development Company, LLC; Jason Wittenberg, Minneapolis Planning Department; Rebecca Davis, San Diego Association of Governments; and Deb Wenig, County Corp.

Stuart Meck, FAICP
Rebecca C. Retzlaff
James C. Schwab, AICP

December 31, 2002
Chicago, Illinois

CHAPTER 1

Affordable Housing as a Regional Planning Priority

The United States in the twenty-first century is a swirling eddy of demographic change. Nothing today seems as simple as it once did in the folk songs of the 1960s. Idealistic musicians then dreamed of a society that conquered poverty, eradicated discrimination and inequality, and brought white and black, rich and poor together in a utopian search for justice. Generally implicit in those dreams was the notion that everyone should have access to decent housing and fair employment, regardless of race, religion, or ethnic background, and that somehow we could all live together as one happy American family.

At the time, there were obvious challenges to this ideal, but racial discrimination seemed to be yielding to the straightforward attack of civil rights laws. Throughout the 1960s and 1970s, federal, state, and local legislation sought to guarantee equal access to public facilities, open housing, and a wider range of opportunities for all Americans. Many communities passed open housing resolutions while experimenting with programs to neutralize blockbuster tactics in the real estate industry.

But during this period cities also metamorphosed into highly suburbanized metropolitan areas, with governance spread among an increasing number of local authorities. Faced with this fragmentation of local government, several communities believed regional cooperation could produce equitable solutions to the challenge of distributing housing for the poor. In Minnesota, the Metropolitan Council emerged as an innovative regional governance tool for the Twin Cities area, while Oregon created Portland Metro. Other areas of the country experimented with the consolidation of city and county government or joint service provision and, in some of those places, coordination of housing policy was a consequence.

But trouble loomed on the horizon. Already, wealthier communities were using their local land-use control authority prerogatives to create levels of economic homogeneity and segregation that had never existed in central cities. Concurrently, the growth of poverty in central cities exceeded all expectations. Differences were widening, and if governmental action were to resolve the problem, state and federal government had to act quickly. The federal government responded with a war on poverty and a growing array of incentives for regional planning.

FIGURE 1-1
OWNERS AND RENTERS FACE SEVERE AFFORDABILITY PROBLEMS

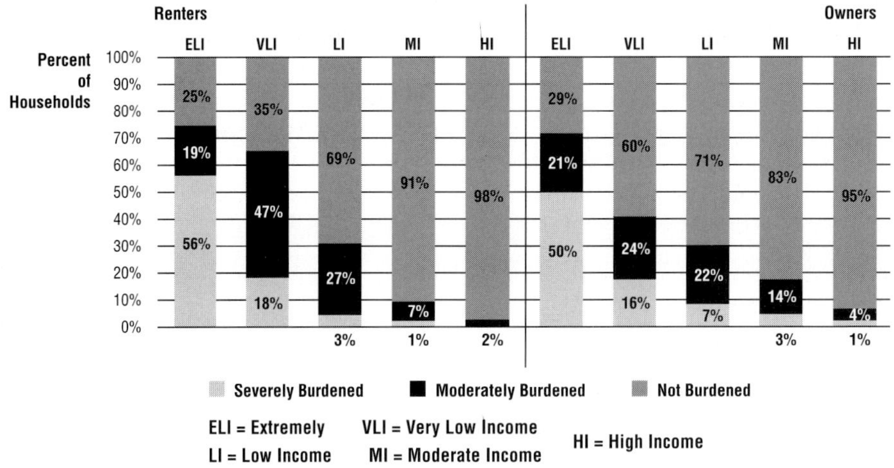

Source: Millenial Housing Commission (2002, 15)

In the three decades that followed, we have become a nation of contrasts. These contrasts, however, are no longer simply between black and white, between big cities and small towns, or even between central cities and evolving suburbs, although all of those disparities persist to varying degrees. These contrasts have been complicated by the surge in new immigrant minorities who now, unlike in the 1960s, populate central cities. The once familiar nuclear family has also begun to disappear. Defined as households that contain a married couple with children, nuclear families fell from 45 percent of the population in 1960 to slightly less than 25 percent in 2000. These and other demographic changes have produced profound development changes, both in suburbs and central cities, often at the expense of the less advantaged. The poor who live in inner-city neighborhoods often watch helplessly as gentrification produces benefits for new, wealthy residents while it eliminates access to affordable housing within commuting reach of the jobs long-time residents hope will rescue them from poverty.

Today, a number of governmental initiatives seek to resolve the dilemma of providing affordable housing, although primarily in locations where regional or state-level housing programs were created years ago out of a sense of fairness are in place. These programs often grew because of unique timing and circumstances that produced the critical balance of forces needed to effect such change, through either the courts, public opinion, or remarkable political leadership, or some combination of these. For instance, few courts have come close to taking the stance of the New Jersey Supreme Court in its *Mount Laurel* anti-exclusionary decisions. These decisions, described in Chapters 2 and 4, interpreted the state constitution to ensure that local governments used their authority to zone to provide realistic opportunities for low- and-moderate income housing and to remove barriers to their construction. Successful experiments that have produced affordable housing do exist; but many metropolitan areas have yet to find a balance of forces capable of creating institutional structures and financing mechanisms that can sustain effective programs.

ABOUT THIS REPORT

This Planning Advisory Service (PAS) Report examines the results achieved to date in those regions or areas of the country where equity in housing opportunity is a planning priority. It is intended as a source book that identifies and analyzes regional strategies that encourage the provision of a full range of housing types across metropolitan areas or areas that are multijurisdictional in nature. This PAS Report is an attempt to shine a spotlight on the mechanics of success in order to make successful regional approaches to affordable housing more feasible and more common. The report analyzes statewide programs that have regional impacts and subregional programs that involve multiple jurisdictions.

The study was completed by the American Planning Association (APA) Research Department with funding from the U.S. Department of Housing and Urban Development, the Fannie Mae Foundation, and PAS.

The key questions addressed by this report include:

- What are the most successful and promising approaches to retaining or developing affordable housing from a regional perspective? What factors contributed to their success, and can those factors be replicated?

- What are the principal barriers to providing affordable housing?

- Which institutional structures work better than others? How effective are public/private partnerships? How effective are private approaches?

- How can regional approaches to affordable housing be successfully translated into housing production? What must be present for affordable housing production to occur?

- What types of inducements can be offered to local governments so as to orient their policies toward consideration of regional housing needs?

- What are alternate ways of providing financial assistance for affordable housing on a regional basis (e.g., housing trust funds)?

These issues are addressed in the following chapters, summarized below.

Chapter 2 covers the historical development of regional planning for affordable housing in the U.S. until the 1980s. It addresses the emergence of housing planning from a series of technical studies on housing conditions to regional and state-level systems that identify local obligations for the provision of affordable housing.

Chapter 3 describes the "big picture" issues associated with regional approaches to affordable housing. These include the questions of what affordable housing is, what a region is, and what authority regional planning agencies have. This chapter examines what has been termed the "chain of exclusion" in local land-use regulation: the impact of local land-use controls and their administration on the supply of affordable housing.

This PAS Report is an attempt to shine a spotlight on the mechanics of success in order to make successful regional approaches to affordable housing more feasible and more common.

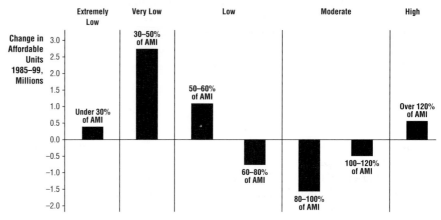

FIGURE 1-1
AFFORDABILITY PRESSURES ARE MOUNTING
AS THE MODERATE-INCOME RENTAL SUPPLY PLUMMETS

Note: HUD Income limits are adjusted for inflation and real income growth for both 1985 and 1999.

Source: Millenial Housing Commission (2002, 19)

Chapter 4 describes and evaluates a variety of fair-share programs in New Jersey, California, New Hampshire, and Portland, Oregon. It also includes evaluation of an incentive program in Minnesota's Twin Cities region. The emphasis in this chapter (and in Chapters 5 through 7) is whether the programs described are producing affordable housing, to whatever extent that can be determined, regardless of the structure of the program.

Chapter 5 describes and evaluates a variety of statewide and regional affordable housing trust funds programs, including the Vermont Housing and Conservation Board; A Regional Coalition for Housing (ARCH) in suburban Seattle, Washington; the Sacramento Housing and Redevelopment Agency; the Columbus and Franklin County, Ohio, affordable housing trust fund; and the Montgomery County (Dayton), Ohio, housing trust fund.

Chapter 6 describes and evaluates three state-level housing appeals laws in Massachusetts, Rhode Island, and Connecticut.

Chapter 7 describes and evaluates private sector approaches to encourage the production of affordable housing in the San Francisco Bay Area and Chicago. Also included are approaches used in Maryland, New Hampshire, and Ames and Story County, Iowa, that do not easily fall into a single category.

Chapter 8 sets forth a series of second-best and best approaches to affordable housing on a regional basis. The first is a collection of programs that are distinctly less action-oriented and whose likelihood of measurable results is slim to none but that may offer a starting point for regions contemplating the problem of affordable housing for the first time. The second group is a collection of elements that would improve the provision of affordable housing if assembled as a package for a region.

Appendices to this report include a bibliography of major sources consulted, a bibliographic research note on the techniques of housing forecasting and the design of fair-share allocation formulas, a list of state statutes describing local housing elements, and relevant excerpts on local and regional housing planning from APA's *Growing Smart Legislative Guidebook, 2002 Edition*, which contains model enabling statutes for planning and land-use control.

HOW THIS STUDY WAS CONDUCTED

This study was conducted using primary source data and personal interviews on a variety of state, regional, and local programs from around the nation. Secondary sources, including articles from planning, housing, and law journals, were also consulted. The initial research effort involved compiling a bibliography of materials on such programs, particularly sources emphasizing program activities beginning from the early 1990s. Some of the material is historical in nature and available only in hard copy. More recent information on these programs is available on the Internet but requires careful analysis.

The APA Research Department staff identified these programs through a variety of measures. These included revisiting well-known, long-established programs, such as the New Jersey Fair Housing Act, and identifying lesser-known programs through a survey of PAS members, who submitted a variety of documents, some of which are included in the case studies in Chapters 4 through 7 (such as the case study from Ames and Story County, Iowa, in Chapter 7).

Other approaches were also used. A review of state statutes, for example, resulted in the decision to investigate the New Hampshire program of regional housing needs assessments, about which relatively little has been written. Similarly, when bibliographic research turned up information on a variety of regional housing trust funds, the research team decided to look into such programs further; the result is the discussion in Chapter 5 of the multijurisdictional trust funds in Eastern King County; Washington (ARCH); the City and County of Sacramento; Montgomery County (Dayton), Ohio; and the City of Columbus and Franklin County, Ohio.

In addition, APA conducted a symposium in its Chicago office on October 29–30, 2000. Participants included public officials, academics, housing policy specialists, professional planners, and representatives of constituency groups (see Appendix C for a complete list). The purpose of the symposium was to assess past efforts at regional planning for affordable housing, factors that contributed to the success or failure of such planning, and promising new approaches. Based on a literature search, APA provided participants with a draft of a working paper describing a variety of programs and obstacles to regional affordable housing. Portions of the findings from the symposium have been incorporated in Chapters 3 and 8.

PREVIOUS STUDIES ON THE TOPIC

There have been a number of national studies proposing or evaluating regional approaches to affordable housing. These form the backdrop to this report and are described below.

National Commission on Urban Problems (Douglas Commission)

In 1968, the National Commission on Urban Problems issued its report, *Building the American City*. This commission was also known as the Douglas Commission, after its chair, Senator Paul Douglas. The commission's charge, among other responsibilities, was to examine "state and local zoning and land-use laws, codes, and regulations to find ways by which [s]tates and localities may improve and utilize them in order to obtain further growth and development" (NCUP 1968, p. vii). The wide-ranging scope makes it one of the most comprehensive and thorough studies to date in terms of examining the authority of governments to plan and regulate development.

The commission called for broadening housing choice through two regional approaches:

1. Enactment of state legislation requiring multicounty or regional planning agencies to prepare and maintain housing plans. These plans would ensure that sites are available for development of new housing of all kinds and at all price levels. The commission proposed that in the absence of a regional planning body—given the broader-than-local nature of the plan and the importance of political approval of such plans—the state government should assume responsibility for the necessary political endorsement of the plan.

2. Amendment of state planning and zoning acts to include, as one of the purposes of the zoning power, the provision of adequate sites for housing persons of all income levels. The amendments would also require that governments exercising the zoning power prepare plans to show how the community proposes to carry out such objectives in accordance with a county or regional housing plan. This would ensure that, within a region as a whole, adequate provision is made for sites for all income levels (p. 242).

The American Bar Association's *Housing for All Under Law*

The American Bar Association (ABA) Advisory Commission on Housing and Urban Growth published a far-reaching report in 1978, *Housing for All Under Law: New Directions for Housing, Land Use, and Planning Law* (ABA 1978). Funded with a grant from the U.S. Department of Housing and Urban Development, the report proposed a series of measures to increase housing opportunity and choice and to promote a more rational growth process.

The advisory commission took the position that, insofar as housing planning is concerned, local governments, at a minimum, have an affirmative legal duty to:

1. plan for present and prospective housing in a regional context;

2. eliminate those local regulatory barriers that do not make it realistically possible to provide housing for persons of low and moderate income; and

3. offer incentives to the private sector in this regard (p. 445).

The report went on to review a variety of state and regional programs for housing planning, many of which are covered in this study, and also described the steps in devising a regional fair-share housing allocation plan. It recommended housing planning at the local, regional, state, and federal levels that "should be coordinated to effectively achieve a hierarchy of established goals and objectives" (p. 479). Local housing planning, it emphasized, should consider "regional housing circumstances and needs" and "must be assessed in the context of the region in which it is situated, to determine whether the community is responsive to housing needs of poorer households" (p. 479). Local governments, nonetheless, "should retain the major control over housing as long as local control is not abusive to overall state goals and regional responsibilities" (p. 479). Local governments, it said, must "deal with impediments to housing opportunity that are within their respective spheres of influence (e.g., land-use controls, building codes, etc.), and then cooperate in a metropolitan or regional effort to assess and balance the needs of neighboring jurisdictions" (p. 480). Adequate implementation of such housing planning, the advisory commission concluded,

"requires government and private sector cooperation at all levels, sufficient funding, and technical assistance" (p. 480).

Advisory Commission on Regulatory Barriers to Affordable Housing

In 1991, the Advisory Commission on Regulatory Barriers to Affordable
Housing, appointed by HUD Secretary Jack Kemp and also known as the
Kemp Commission, issued its report, which reiterated many themes in earlier federal studies (Advisory Commission 1991). The Kemp Commission
report called for the establishment of state and federal "barrier removal
plans" for which the federal government would provide funding. The report noted that a number of states reviewed local regulations as part of a
housing element or comprehensive planning requirement. It also favored
state review of local barrier removal plans and HUD support for such efforts. The report also advocated that, where states required localities to
submit barrier-removal plans to meet state housing or planning goals, federal law should be modified to permit HUD to accept, if substantially
equivalent, the same barrier-removal submission required by the state in
its own Comprehensive Housing Assistance Strategy (CHAS) review process (p. 6-3). (The CHAS process is required for receipt of federal Community Development Block Grant funds.)

While the report did not address regional approaches in any detail, they
surfaced in a set of recommendations for state zoning reform:

> The Commission strongly recommends that, as part of their overall bar-
> rier-removal strategy, [s]tates should thoroughly review and reform their
> zoning and land-planning systems to remove all institutional barriers to
> affordability. Reforms that [s]tates should consider include: a requirement
> that each locality have a housing element subject to [s]tate review and ap-
> proval; effective comprehensive planning requirements; modification of
> zoning-enabling authority to include affordability and housing opportu-
> nity as primary objectives; [s]tate authority to override local barriers to
> affordable housing projects; *[s]tate-established housing targets and fair-share
> mechanisms*; and requirements of a variety of housing types and densities.
> (p. 7-8; emphasis added)

Although it did not recommend their endorsement, the report noted the
existence of state housing trust funds, about 20 at the time, which provided loans for the construction or rehabilitation of affordable rental housing. The report observed that housing trust funds could potentially generate incentives for regulatory reform in two ways: (1) by conditioning the
authorization of such loans to local governments in exchange for undertaking specific regulatory reforms; and (2) by structuring the number and
size of grant and loan packages to be contingent upon a program of regulatory reform, "with the most cooperative municipalities receiving the most
help" (p. 7-14).

Regional Housing Opportunities for Lower-Income Households

A 1994 study prepared for HUD by the Rutgers University Center for Urban Policy Research (CUPR), *Regional Housing Opportunities for Lower-Income Households*, was intended to provide researchers and policy makers
with a sampling of tools across the U.S. to promote regional mobility and
housing affordability (Burchell, Listokin, and Pashman 1994). It defined
"regional mobility programs" as those that "allow lower-income households more freedom to pursue housing choice at a greater distance from
their existing urban neighborhoods" (p. vi). The study grouped regional
mobility and affordable housing programs into two main categories, with
the second category divided into two subcategories: (1) planning need estimates, which include (a) required local housing plans and (b) local hous-

*The Kemp Commission
report called for the
establishment of state and
federal "barrier removal
plans" for which the federal
government would provide
funding.*

ing allocation; (2A) implementation activities related to housing production, which include (a) specialized access to appeals or rewards, (b) inclusionary zoning, and (c) regional public superbuilders[1]; and (2B) implementation activities for housing funding and assistance, which include (a) affordable housing finance strategies and (b) portable certificates and vouchers. Within these categories, the report described both historical programs (those that no longer existed) and current ones.

The report did not offer up a model program, but did note that, within the various program categories it examined, there were "remarkable similarity and conceptual convergence. This is due to the fact that common difficulties affecting states and localities have led to an informal exchange of ideas and strategies" (p. 50). Many programs used private developers as the catalyst of regional affordable housing production via a requirement or incentive. As a consequence, the programs were market-driven; thus "[t]hey flourish in good economic times and wane in bad times" (p. 50). Almost all of the programs, the report said, used HUD Section 8 income guidelines (low- and very low-income).[2] Sometimes median income was determined for a region that was different from the HUD region of which the implementing jurisdiction was part, the report found, and, as a result, "housing is often provided at the top rather than throughout the Section 8 income range," meaning that very low-income persons were less able to participate (p. vii).

After inventorying and assessing these programs, the report predicted that "[s]tates and localities not already involved in affordable housing will be pushed unwillingly into affordable housing delivery by the pressures of unanswered housing demand" (p. ix). State strategies, the report concluded, "appear more durable . . . if they actively encourage rather than mandate local participation. Head-to-head confrontations with the home-rule prerogative of municipalities typically culminate in de facto compliance or program rejection" (p. ix). (It should be noted that not all states give home-rule authority to municipal governments.)

ENDNOTES

1. The report defines "regional public superbuilders" as "public agencies acting in the capacity of a housing developer unaffected by local zoning, having the ability to override local zoning, condemn land, or all three. Public superbuilders may build affordable housing at the request of another government or on their own" (p. 37). An example of such an agency is the New York Urban Development Corporation, which had zoning override powers but was stripped of them by the New York legislature in 1973 (p. 38).

2. The U.S. Department of Housing and Urban Development's Section 8 program provides vouchers that allow lower-income recipients to live in market-rate units. Vouchers can be used for rent charges at any level. Very low-income families and certain other families or individuals apply to a local public housing agency (PHA) that administers the Section 8 program. When an eligible family comes to the top of the PHA's housing voucher waiting list, the PHA issues a housing choice voucher to the family. The PHA pays the owner the difference between 30 percent of adjusted income and a PHA-determined payment standard or the gross rent for the unit, whichever is lower. The family may choose a unit with a higher rent than the payment standard and pay the unit's owner the difference. ("Tenant based vouchers," http://www.hud.gov/offices/pih/programs/hcv/tenant.cfm, accessed December 12, 2002)

CHAPTER 2

Historical Development of Regional Housing Planning in the U.S.[1]

The first manifestation of planning activity specifically related to housing took the form of studies focused on the improvement of housing conditions for lower-income persons. The earliest of these studies were nineteenth-century exposés of living conditions in slum areas that employed personal experience and anecdotal evidence more than scientific surveys or analyses. These included such works as *How The Other Half Lives* by Jacob Riis (1890), which described living conditions in New York's tenement houses, and *The Shame Of The Cities* by Lincoln Steffens (1904), which deals in the main with exposes of corruption in city government but also vividly depicts conditions in urban slums. A more organized examination of slum housing conditions came with the 1900 report of the New York Tenement House Commission (DeForest and Veiller 1903; see also Fairbanks 2000).

Regional planning, albeit by nongovernmental organizations, arrived with the twentieth century (Meck 2002, 6-5 to 6-22). The famous 1909 Plan of Chicago, prepared by Daniel Burnham and Edward Bennett for the Chicago Commercial Club, focused on the city proper but had much to say about facilities and amenities, especially transport and forest/recreational lands, throughout the Chicago region (Burnham and Bennett 1970). However, it touched little on housing conditions beyond a few paragraphs that claimed broad streets and open parkland, combined with good sanitation and transportation, would improve living conditions in slum areas. Noted the plan's authors:

> Chicago has not reached the point where it will be necessary for the municipality to provide at its own expense, as does the city of London, for the rehousing of persons forced out of congested quarters; but unless the matter shall be taken in hand at once, such a course will be required in common justice to men and women so degraded by long life in the slums that they have lost all power of caring for themselves. (p 109)

The Chicago Plan was both the descendant and the progenitor of many other sweeping plans prepared at the behest of civic organizations (Wannop 1995). The Russell Sage Foundation financed the *Regional Survey and Plan of New York and its Environs*, completed in 1931 (Committee on Regional Plan 1931; Adams and Heydecker 1931; see also Kantor 1973). In contrast with Burnham's plan for Chicago and similar "city beautiful" plans, this work directly examined housing and the economic and social problems that were both the cause and effect of substandard housing. For example, the Regional Plan devoted an entire chapter to housing and neighborhoods, with a series of eight specific recommendations for a housing policy for New York City and its environs. These included slum clearance, ongoing surveys of housing conditions, methods of renovating slum areas and promoting housing development within them, and regulation of overcrowding through zoning (Committee on Regional Plan 1931, 204).

The Regional Planning Association of America was formed in 1923, and by the late 1920s states were creating (or at least authorizing) county- or metropolitan-wide planning bodies by statute (Wannop 1995, 276-77). These bodies were also encouraged by the Standard City Planning Enabling Act, a model state statute from Herbert Hoover's Department of Commerce which expressly authorized regional planning commissions and the adoption of regional plans.[2]

STATISTICAL STUDIES OF HOUSING CONDITIONS

Statistical regularity in the study of housing was encouraged in the 1930s by the Federal Housing Administration and the Home Owners Loan Corporation, which created a methodology that evaluated more accurately the value of land securing mortgage loans. In 1945, a committee of the American Public Health Association (APHA) developed criteria that better analyzed the condition and livability of housing (Hodge 1963; see also Baer 1986, 174).[3] Both methodologies scored a particular property or neighborhood on a standardized scale, which allowed comparison to other properties or neighborhoods. A property's score was based on objective factors (age of the building, indoor plumbing, central heating, number of bathrooms, number of exits, etc.) and more subjective evaluations (e.g., the state of repair of a building, scored on a scale from 1 to 10 or A to F). Both methodologies also required users of each evaluation system to be trained in its standards and methods to ensure their uniform application and therefore statistically valid, broadly comparable scores.

Planner Carl Feiss, writing in the *Journal of the American Planning Association*, credits the APHA inventory techniques with having "a direct effect on the identification of the condition of cities and the conditions of slums and blight" (Feiss 1985, 177). These techniques were later incorporated into Title I of the federal Housing Act of 1949 to meet program verification requirements.

But these techniques also sanctioned racial discrimination in lending. The appraisal studies done by or for lending institutions included not only a property's physical condition and livability factors but also the racial or ethnic composition of the neighborhood, with lower ratings given to housing in neighborhoods dominated by racial minorities. This practice did not cease until the early 1960s, when President John F. Kennedy ordered government agencies to stop practicing racial discrimination.[4]

Madison Park Place; affordable housing in Springfield, Illinois.

The planning and construction of the interstate highway system from the 1940s through the early 1960s led to recognition of the important planning and land-use issues raised by these new highways (Allaire 1960; ASPO 1955). Both the federal government and state and local officials acknowledged the need for regional or metropolitan bodies to plan the transportation needs of the wider areas served by highway systems, needs that had not been sufficiently met by the previous practices of coordinating transportation investments at the state level (which had too broad a perspective for metropolitan issues) or through individual local governments (with their too-narrow focus).

The Highway Act of 1962 required that, as a prerequisite to receiving federal highway dollars, states and local governments cooperate in areawide transportation planning (ACIR 1973, 70). The act also required the designation of metropolitan planning organizations (MPOs) for the regional planning of highway transportation (23 U.S.C., Section 134), and subsequent amendments laws carried this requirement through to other types of transportation receiving federal funding, such as mass transit (49 U.S.C., Section 5303). It is not unheard of, however, for a region or metropolitan area to have a regional planning body separate from its formal, transportation-oriented MPO. This was the case, and still is, in Boston and Chicago (e.g., the Chicago metropolitan area has the Chicago Area Transportation Study (CATS) as its MPO and the Northeastern Illinois Planning Commission (NIPC) to address nontransportation planning). Elsewhere, metropolitan councils of government (COGs), which are voluntary alliances of local governments formed to undertake planning or any type of joint governmental activity that its members could agree upon, or a regional planning commission often assumed the transportation planning function.

FEDERAL PROMOTION OF LOCAL AND REGIONAL HOUSING PLANNING

The earliest federal role in planning was the Standard City Planning Enabling Act of 1928, but this model law did not expressly address issues of housing. A New Deal federal planning agency, the National Resources Committee (later the National Resources Planning Board), published in 1939 the report "Urban Planning and Land Policies." In 1940, it also produced a document, "Federal Aids to Local Planning," listing all assistance available from the federal government for planning activities. That assistance, however, did not include grants to fund local planning. What little headway the National Resources Planning Board had made ended in 1943, when it was terminated by Congress (Feiss 1985).

Pre-war studies and analyses of housing eventually resulted in the Housing Act of 1949 . The Act provided federal funds for the redevelopment of depressed urban areas and required local governments applying for such funds to have a "general plan of the locality as a whole" as well as a redevelopment plan consistent with that general plan It also required that "the adoption, improvement, and modernization of local codes and regulations relating to land use" be examined in evaluating eligibility to receive such funds (The Housing Act of 1949, Chapter 338). The federal money, however, could not be used for the preparation or revision of the local general plans. This oversight was corrected with the Housing Act of 1954. Section 701 of the act authorized grants to cities and counties to be spent on planning activities. The program was expanded to include regional councils of governments in 1965.

The Housing and Urban Development Act of 1968 amended Section 701 to require federally funded local comprehensive plans to include housing elements considering regional housing supply and needs. Also, in 1969, Circular A-95 of the U.S. Office of Management and Budget gave to states and regional agencies that were designated as areawide clearinghouses the authority to review applications for federal assistance, including federally assisted housing projects, for consistency with local and regional plans. This circular implemented Title IV of the federal Intergovernmental Coordination Act of 1968 (for a history, see ACIR 1973, Chapter 5); the circular is no longer in effect.

The Housing and Community Development Act of 1974 required local governments applying for federal grants to adopt a Housing Assistance Plan (HAP) that included both a comprehensive assessment of the housing needs of low- and moderate-income households and an action plan for meeting those needs. Regional consideration of housing needs was further promoted by the Housing and Community Development Act of 1977, which authorized the adoption at the regional or metropolitan level of Areawide Housing Opportunity Plans (AHOPs) (see discussion of regional housing plans below). AHOPs were especially valuable as comparative tools. They were often used to evaluate a local government's HAP so as to determine whether the HAP provided adequate affordable housing. AHOPs and HAPs were thus required to be generally consistent (Mandelker 1981, 485). In addition, because these plans set goals for low- and moderate-income hous-

The Housing and Urban Development Act of 1968 amended Section 701 to require federally funded local comprehensive plans to include housing elements considering regional housing supply and needs.

TABLE 2-1
INCOME LEVELS AND OCCUPATIONS

Percent of Median Household Income (MHI)	Size of Household and Occupations
Less than 30% MHI	• 1 person: fast food worker, service station attendant • 4 people: preschool teacher with 3 children
30–50% MHI	• 1 person: home health aide, hairdresser, receptionist • 4 people: dental assistant with 3 children; fast food worker and a service station attendant with 2 children
51–80% MHI	• 1 person: emergency medical technician, computer operator • 4 people: full time registered nurse or social worker with 3 children; teacher's aide and bank teller with 2 children.
81-120% MHI	• 1 person: computer programmer, corrections officer, carpenter • 4 people: electrical engineer or health services manager with 3 children; dental assistant and a maintenance worker with 2 children

Source: Metro Council (2000, 10)

ing, a regional agency that was designated as an areawide clearinghouse under OMB Circular A-95 could evaluate applications for federal-assisted projects against the goals. By the spring of 1980, there were 31 HUD-approved AHOPs in the nation (Shafor and Longfellow 1980, v). In 1981, the Section 701 program was terminated as part of a policy shift aimed at allowing more local flexibility and requiring less federal oversight in the redevelopment funding process.

Since 1990, the Cranston-Gonzalez National Affordable Housing Act has also required local governments seeking assistance under that act to prepare a "comprehensive housing affordability strategy," update it annually, and submit the strategy and updates to HUD for its approval (42 U.S.C., Sections 12701 et seq.). The strategy must include a detailed analysis of housing need in general and for various categories (low-income, moderate-income, elderly, disabled, etc.), public policies that affect the supply and affordability of housing, and the various methods the local government will employ to provide that housing (42 U.S.C., Section 12705). This document also goes by the name "consolidated plan" and covers several HUD programs (24 CFR, Part 91).

REGIONAL FAIR-SHARE HOUSING PLANNING[5]

The problem of exclusionary zoning—that a local government may, deliberately or not, exclude affordable housing through its land-use decisions—has been recognized for some time. The perception that some local governments avoid affordable housing and therefore pass the problem on to neighboring communities is also not new. However, knowledge of this problem did not translate into regional approaches to address it until the 1970s.

The Miami Valley Regional Planning Commission (MVRPC) in metropolitan Dayton, Ohio, adopted the first fair-share regional allocation plan for low- and moderate-income housing in 1970.

The first regional allocation of affordable housing goals to local governments was voluntary—that is, not required by either state or federal law. The Miami Valley Regional Planning Commission (MVRPC) in metropolitan Dayton, Ohio, adopted the first fair-share regional allocation plan for low- and moderate-income housing in 1970. The plan quantified the need for housing in each of the five counties in the region. The need was then allocated to each of the counties by planning units (municipalities or townships in the respective counties), thereby establishing common housing goals for local governments. A detailed housing policy package accompanied the plan, which was revised in 1973, and then again in 1978. Over time, the plan resulted in the dispersal of low- and moderate-income housing outside Dayton to the surrounding counties and townships as local governments provided sites for affordable housing. It received a great deal of national attention (Meck and Pearlman 2002, 21). MVRPC, however, no longer maintains the plan.

The Metropolitan Council in Minneapolis/Saint Paul adopted a fair-share strategy in 1971, replacing it with a more detailed document for the seven-county region in 1973.[6] Similarly, the Metropolitan Washington Council of Governments adopted a fair-share plan in 1972. The Delaware Valley Regional Planning Agency, the regional planning body headquartered in Philadelphia whose authority extends to four New Jersey counties and five Pennsylvania counties, adopted a fair-share plan in 1973 (Listokin 1976, ch. 3). These early regional affordable housing allocation systems gave rise to the federal policy that created the AHOPs, described above, and their use in evaluating local HAPs and federally assisted housing projects. This policy in turn encouraged more metropolitan areas and regions to consider housing allocation systems.

California, faced with affordable housing issues in multiple metropolitan areas in the state, adopted fair-share regional allocation by statute in 1980 (Cal. Government Code, Secs. 65580 et seq.). Under the statute, the mandatory housing element in local comprehensive plans must be founded on an assessment of housing needs derived from a Regional Housing Needs Assessment (RHNA), which is prepared by the regional council of governments or, in its absence, the state Department of Housing and Community Development. A local government is accommodating its fair share of affordable housing only when its comprehensive plan and land development regulations include enough land zoned at the right use classification, adequate density, etc., to allow such housing to be built. Permit caps do not reduce the fair-share obligation, and residential moratoria must be justified on the basis of public health or safety. On the other hand, the statute allows a local government to reduce its fair-share allocation if another local government within the same county agrees to take up the difference.

New Jersey, like California, has more than one large metropolitan area and therefore also needs a statewide approach to regional housing allocation. However, in New Jersey the regional allocation system was established by statute after a series of judicial decisions: the *Mount Laurel* anti-exclusionary zoning cases decided by the New Jersey Supreme Court in 1975 (*Southern Burlington Co. NAACP v. Twp. of Mount Laurel*, 67 N.J. 151, 336 A.2d 713, appeal dismissed and cert. denied, 423 U.S. 808, 96 S.Ct. 18 (1975); hereinafter, *Mount Laurel I*) and 1983 (*Southern Burlington Co. NAACP v. Twp. of Mount Laurel*, 92 N.J. 158, 456 A.2d 390 (1983; hereinafter *Mount Laurel II*)). In New Jersey, the Council on Affordable Housing—a specialized state agency created by the State's Fair Housing Act of 1985 (New Jersey Statutes Annotated, Sections 52:27D-301 et seq (2002))—oversees the affordable housing effort. The act was upheld by the New Jersey Supreme Court in 1986 (*Hills Development Co. v. Twp. of Bernards*, 103 N.J. 1, 510 A.2d 621 (1986) hereinafter *Mount Laurel III*).

In the *Mount Laurel* rulings, the New Jersey Supreme Court held that the state's local zoning statutes had to be read in the context of a state—not federal—constitutional requirement to legislate "for the general welfare" (*Mount Laurel I*, A.2d 713, 726). Local governments that enacted zoning had an obligation to provide realistic opportunities for low- and moderate-income housing. Any zoning ordinance that denied reasonable opportunities to meet the local government's fair share of a region's low- and moderate-income housing need thus failed the state's constitutional requirements.

In 1969, Massachusetts became the first state to create a state-level housing appeals board empowered to provide for a direct appeal and override of local decisions that reject or restrict proposals for low- or moderate-income housing. Under the Massachusetts law (Massachusetts General Laws Ch. 40B, Sections 20-23 (2001)),[7] an applicant for an affordable housing development applies to the local board of adjustment for a single comprehensive permit to authorize development; the permit consolidates all other local development approvals. If the board denies the permit or imposes conditions that are financially prohibitive, the applicant may appeal that decision to a state administrative body, the Housing Appeals Committee, which can overturn or modify the local decisions. Two other states, Connecticut and Rhode Island, subsequently adopted variants of the Massachusetts law (Connecticut General Statutes Annotated, Section 80-36g; General Laws of Rhode Island, Sections 43-53-1 to 53-2). The Connecticut law provides for an appeal to a court rather than to a state-level board.

The California and New Jersey fair-share programs are discussed in more detail in Chapter 4 of this report, and the housing appeals statutes from Massachusetts, Connecticut, and Rhode Island are discussed in more detail in Chapter 6.

TECHNICAL MANUALS SUPPORTING REGIONAL HOUSING PLANNING

Two technical manuals were published in the early 1970s, one by the Federal Housing Administration (FHA) and HUD, and the other by the American Institute of Planners, a predecessor organization to APA, under contract to HUD. Both publications crystallized approaches to regional analysis of housing needs and regional planning for housing. In addition, a third monograph by a Rutgers University researcher documented the methodology behind fair-share allocation approaches used in the regional fair-share plans described above.

The first publication was *FHA Techniques of Housing Market Analysis* (U.S. HUD 1970). FHA developed the manual to train new analysts in its offices and to improve the quality and uniformity of its market analysis work, which it used to provide its insuring and central offices with information to evaluate the acceptability of individual projects.

The manual was not a planning document per se. Rather, it provided guidelines for estimating housing demand in quantitative and qualitative terms for the nation's housing market as a whole or for major geographical submarkets, including specialized submarkets like those in regions with military bases, colleges, or seasonal tourism. The manual outlined a six-part analytical framework:

1. Delineation of market area: the area within which dwelling units are competitive with one another.

2. Area economy: principal economic activities, basis resources, economic trends.

3. Demand factors: employment, incomes, population, households, family size.

In 1969, Massachusetts became the first state to create a state-level housing appeals board empowered to provide for a direct appeal and override of local decisions that reject or restrict proposals for low- or moderate-income housing.

4. Supply factors: residential construction activity, housing inventory, conversions, demolitions.

5. Current market conditions: vacancies, unsold inventory, marketability of sales and rental units, prices, rents, building costs, mortgage defaults and foreclosures, disposition of acquired properties.

6. Quantitative and qualitative demand: prospective number of dwelling units that can be absorbed economically at various price and rent levels under conditions existing on the "as of" date. (p. 5)

The FHA manual also acknowledged its own limitations, especially with respect to planning.

The FHA manual also acknowledged its own limitations, especially with respect to planning. For example, FHA market analysis was not concerned with such factors as land use, public works, and transportation by themselves. Such a market analysis, according to the manual, should only look at those factors if they have an important or significant impact on the area under consideration. In addition, the projections are only intended to go out one to three years, with five years as a maximum, because, as FHA argued, a longer projection would be of questionable guidance in making local mortgage insurance decisions (p. 6). But the manual does discuss considerations for undertaking market analysis for subsidized housing, as the federal programs existed in 1970 (pp. 179-82).[8]

Beyond its comprehensiveness, what is noteworthy—but also problematic—about the FHA manual is its attention to the metropolitan area or the region as its primary analysis unit. As Baer (1986, 75) has pointed out, the manual ignores the role of local jurisdictional boundaries in determining market demand and supply: "This disregard for the importance of local jurisdictions reflected the technicians' judgment that local elected officials were unwilling (or only barely willing, in the case of large central cities) to be responsible for housing in their communities. Certainly, it reflected the technicians' judgment that politicians were unwilling to engage in the requisite coordination of housing matters between local governments that a metropolitan perspective would entail."

The second publication was *Regional Housing Planning: A Technical Guide*, published in 1972 and prepared by a consulting firm under the aegis of the American Institute of Planners (Hammer, Greene, Siler 1972). It focused on the analysis and forecasting of requirements for new housing projection on a regional basis and provided a series of worksheets to develop the forecasts. In contrast to the FHA manual, *Regional Housing Planning* was aimed at planners and public officials concerned with evaluating and developing public policies, programs, and regulations to achieve housing goals. Its projections also reached farther into the future: 10 years instead of FHA's one to three years. As part of its identification of new housing production requirements, the *Regional Housing Planning* approach broke down new housing projection needs in two ways: basic production output, which assumed no additional government programs or subsidies , and potential unmet needs, including additional housing for the elderly and low- and moderate-income families. The guide also included units needing rehabilitation in its projections.

However, neither of these manuals addresses the allocation of regional needs for low- and moderate-income housing to individual local governments or planning units within a region or county. The technical basis for doing so was assessed by David Listokin, a researcher with the Rutgers University Center for Urban Policy Research. Appendices A and B in Listokin (1976) summarize a variety of allocation formulas and strategies, and identify their strengths and weaknesses. Listokin documented a variety of techniques, including statistical formulas in which various allocation factors are converted into weighted location quotients or Z-scores (which compare planning area data against similar regional or county data) and summed. The allocation of need is then made on a percentage basis using a distribution index. A second technique Listokin identified is a point-factor system: each planning subarea is individually evaluated against a set of numerical criteria and the numbers summed into a score. This score is then converted into a percentage of the total regional scores and used as a basis for allocating need.

ENDNOTES

1. This section owes a great deal to Baer (1986) and draws on his research extensively. John Bredin, a Research Fellow with APA, also contributed to an initial draft of this chapter.

2. The Standard City Planning Enabling Act did not mention "housing" or "housing conditions" as such as part of the "master regional plan," but it did refer to a "zoning plan for the control of the height and area, or bulk, location, and use of buildings and premises, and the density of population" (Advisory Committee 1928, Title IV, Section 28).

3. Discussing the criteria by the American Public Health Association, Hodge (1963, 116) notes studies in Boston and New York where "shabby physical conditions mask a viable social structure" and suggests that "social factors also have to be considered in order to define completely the dimension of *sub-standardness*" (emphasis in original). Baer (1986, 174–76) discusses the appraisal methodology of the Home Owners Loan Corporation.

4. Baer (1986, 182) describes the issuance in 1962 by President John F. Kennedy of Executive Order 11063, prohibiting discrimination in housing that received public assistance, including the Federal Housing Administration, Veterans Administration, and public housing. Polikoff (1978, 16–19) also describes the Federal Housing Administration's race-based underwriting practices.

5. Listokin (1976, ch. 1) provides an excellent introduction to, and discussion of, this topic.

6. Goetz, Chapple, and Lukerman (2000) conclude that the 25 years after its enactment, fair-share housing legislation in Minnesota (Minnesota Statutes, Section 473.859), which is part of the Minnesota Land Use Planning Act of 1976, has yielded minimal changes either in the planning or implementation of the housing elements of municipal land-use plans. This law's implementation is discussed in Chapter 4 of this PAS Report.

7. The state and federal constitutional validity of the Massachusetts statutes has been affirmed in several Massachusetts decisions. See, for example, *Mahoney v. Bd. of Appeals of Winchester*, 366 Mass. 228, 316 N.E.2d 606, appeal dismissed 420 U.S. 903 (1974); *Bd. of Appeals of Hanover v. Housing Appeals Committee in Dept. of Community Affairs*, 363 Mass. 339, 294 N.E.2d 393 (1973).

8. The FHA manual apparently did not consider locational diversity of affordable housing a priority. It states: "The location factor is of especial importance in the provision of new units at the lower-rent levels. Families in this user group are not as mobile as those in other economic segments; they are less able or willing to break with established social, church, and neighborhood relationships, and proximity to place of work frequently is a governing consideration in the place of resident preferred by families in this group" (pp. 181-82).

CHAPTER 3

The Big Issues

In May 2002, the Millennial Housing Commission, appointed by the U.S. Congress, released its long-awaited report, *Meeting Our Nation's Housing Challenges*. Its conclusions were not surprising. "Affordability," it asserts, "is the single greatest housing challenge facing the nation" (Millennial Housing Commission 2002, 14). The study points to a number of ongoing problems with housing affordability. In 1999, one in four households (almost 28 million) reported spending more on housing than the 30 percent of household income that the federal government considers affordable. One in nine households reported spending more than half its income on housing. The report also estimates that, on any night, hundreds of thousands of people go homeless. Wide gaps also remain, it finds, between the homeownership rates of whites and minorities, even those with comparable incomes (p. 2).

The gap between the available supply of rental units affordable to the poorest households and the demand for them stood at 1.8 million in 1999, according to the commission. Federal support in the housing sector has been insufficient to cover growing needs and to fill the gaps in availability and affordability. In particular, the commission pointed to the lack of resources in protecting the nation's investment in federally subsidized housing (p. 2).

The amount of multifamily housing created during the 1990s was only half that in each of the previous two decades (p. 2). This stalled growth, paired with developers' increased focus on more expensive apartments, meant that "rentals affordable to low- and moderate-income households fell by 9.5 percent between 1985 and 1999, further shrinking the supply of affordable housing" (p. 2). In 2000, for example, only 13 percent of all completed two-bedroom apartments in the U.S. were affordable to renters earning the median income for the metropolitan area in which they lived (p. 19). This gap, the commission argues, demonstrates that, in most regions of the U.S., the private sector is unable to produce apartments that households with incomes under 70 percent of the area median can afford without a subsidy (p. 19). Rental units for working families with incomes between 60 and 120 percent of area medians "are disappearing at an alarming pace," and, as a result, "a potentially important source of rentals that might later become available to lower affordable ranges is being lost" (p. 2).

The commission attributes this loss of affordable housing to a variety of factors: rising housing production costs in relation to family incomes, inadequate public facilities and subsidies, restrictive zoning practices, local regulations that discourage housing development, and the decreasing number of federally subsidized housing units. Rural areas and native lands, it notes, have "especially difficult environments for affordable housing because of the higher costs of providing infrastructure and the dearth of well-paying jobs," and, it adds, despite civil rights and fair housing guarantees, "the housing shortage hits minorities hardest of all" (p. 2).

These brief highlights of the Millennial Housing Commission's findings set the stage for the topics covered in this chapter: working definitions of affordable housing and the provision of—and obstacles to—affordable housing at the regional level. It should be noted at the outset that these obstacles can have distinct regional variations, with the most severe problems occurring in areas of rapid job growth or where the structure of local government (as in the New England states) makes it difficult to expand quickly the supply of *all* housing, not just affordable housing, when the economy booms.

DEFINING AFFORDABLE HOUSING

In normal parlance, "affordable" is a word with elastic meanings. For most people, however, it translates into a simple question: Do I have the money to pay for it? "Affordable," in other words, is linked fundamentally to income. *Webster's New Universal Unabridged Dictionary* makes this link clear: it defines "afford" as "to be able to meet the expense of; have or spare the price of: *He still can't afford a car.*"

These common sense or dictionary definitions of the term are important because they reflect the general public's understanding of the issue and hence affect public support for affordable housing programs. However, the dictionary oversimplifies the concept of affordability by excluding the idea of the substitution of goods. He may not be able to afford a car, in other words, but he can instead afford public transportation. This substitution is roughly equal: the fixed schedules and unvarying routes of buses or light rail are less convenient than a car but still provide access to work and shopping. Yet there are few satisfactory substitutes for housing. The most drastic result of not being able to afford housing is homelessness. Other undesirable substitutions include building overcrowding or the occupation of substandard housing. "[B]ecause they could afford nothing better," the Millennial Housing Commission estimates, "1.7 million lower-income households lived in severely inadequate households [in 1999] , placing their heath and safety at risk" (p. 2). Although some housing may come in luxu-

In normal parlance, "affordable" is a word with elastic meanings.

rious forms, the public generally views basic shelter as a necessity that has no substitutes.

Using these perceptions of housing affordability and the basic need for shelter, public agencies and politicians build support for a variety of programs to ensure the availability of housing to lower-income households. Still, a host of other factors can influence political support for (or opposition to) such programs, including the effectiveness and efficiency of the delivery mechanisms and the fairness of the burdens imposed to achieve a program's goals. But almost no program would survive without the underlying belief that our society has an obligation to provide some measure of equity in access to housing. It is necessary, therefore, that regulatory definitions embody the basic sense of fairness and compassion that undergirds public support.

The relationship of the cost of housing to income is central to the definition of affordable housing. The need for programs to redress the shortage of affordable housing for those defined as lower- or moderate-income households depends on the market's ability (or inability) to provide adequate amounts of housing at prices that stay within prescribed guidelines. Thus there are two basic types of affordable housing, unsubsidized and subsidized, whose proportions may vary widely from one region to another due to economic and political circumstances.

Unsubsidized housing is housing that is inexpensive enough to allow low- and moderate-income families to pay for it without spending a disproportionate share of their income. When this housing meets the existing needs within a region, the market has succeeded largely without governmental intervention, although it is also clear that land-use regulations can determine the market's success.

More often, there is a need for the second type of affordable housing, *subsidized housing*. Such housing requires federal, state, or local subsidies.

River West affordable/mixed-income housing in Peoria, Illinois.

The relationship of the cost of housing to income is central to the definition of affordable housing.

If the housing is built or rehabilitated as affordable housing, it is subject to a deed restriction or covenant that restricts its sale price or rent to affordable levels for a certain time (e.g., 20 to 30 years) and provides eligibility criteria. The details of many of these subsidized housing programs appear in the case studies in chapters 4 through 7.

The definition of affordability varies among federal, state, and local governments. From a national perspective, the most important definitions are those used by HUD in its Section 8 and Community Development Block Grant (CDBG) programs. These standards grant eligibility for Section 8 benefits to those whose income does not exceed a certain percentage of median income in the region. For example, HUD considers households whose income is 80 percent of the area median to be a low-income family eligible to receive certain subsidies.[1] The HUD definition of affordable housing therefore assumes that housing costs should be no greater than 30 percent to household income (in other words, $300 monthly rent for a family with a total monthly income of $1,000).[2]

States tend to follow HUD definitions in their own programs, including the categorization of income levels. The California Department of Housing and Community Development, for example, uses the following income levels:

- *very low:* under 50 percent of area median

- *low:* 50 to 80 percent of area median

- *moderate:* 80 to 120 percent of area median

- *above moderate:* above 120 percent of area median (Burchell, Listokin, and Pashman 1994, 76)

Oregon shares California's highest two income categories, but it uses the HUD Section 8 income limitations for households below 80 percent of the area median. Both also calculate median income on a regional basis (p. 78). In contrast, Vermont, a largely rural state, uses the *county* median income to identify low- and very low-income families through HUD Section 8 requirements (p. 86).

But state and local definitions that accompany affordable housing programs sometimes deviate from the HUD definitions, usually because of specific needs and problems addressed by the legislation creating the programs. They may separate different categories of income levels served by various types of affordable housing and may also broaden income ranges. For example, the Connecticut Fair Share Compacts, an experimental state program of negotiated housing goals for the Hartford and Bridgeport regions that existed from 1988 to 1997, had affordability definitions that departed from HUD definitions. For the Capitol Region compact, centered in Hartford, participating communities assigned a specific percentage of fair share to each of four income groups, with moderate-income households defined as those earning 81 to 100 percent of the areawide median (Burchell, Listokin, and Pashman 1994, 106–7). This definition is broader than HUD's for the CDBG program, which only extends to 80 percent of the median.

Drawing on the HUD definition and New Jersey Administrative Code (see 24 CFR, Section 91.5 and New Jersey Administrative Code, Title 5, Section 5:93-1.3), the American Planning Association's *Growing Smart^SM Legislative Guidebook* defines affordable housing as follows:

> **Affordable Housing** means housing that has a sales price or rental amount that is within the means of a household that may occupy middle-, moderate-, low-, or very low-income housing. . . . In the case of dwelling units for sale, housing that is affordable means housing in which mortgage, amortization, taxes, insurance, and condominium or association fees, if any,

constitute no more than [28] percent of such gross annual household income for a household of the size which may occupy the unit in question. In the case of dwelling units for rent, housing that is affordable means housing for which the rent and utilities constitute no more than [30] percent of such gross annual household income for a household of the size which may occupy the unit in question.[3] (Meck 2002, 4-79)

In all of these efforts to define affordable housing, however, there remain several important and persistent gaps concerning qualitative issues:

- How do we determine if families spending more than 30 percent of their income on housing are doing so willingly in order to obtain greater housing quality? Or do they do so out of necessity because they have few other options? What is their level of satisfaction with housing services received?

- The 30 percent figure is a flat percentage that may not reflect significant differences between the very low-income and low- or moderate-income housing consumers in their ability to pay.

- The 30 percent figure also does not account for the combined impact on household budgets of housing and transportation expenses. If affordable housing is not accompanied by geographically accessible jobs, the combined expenses may be untenable. This problem is also a key issue (in addition to traffic congestion impacts) in the debate over jobs/housing balance. (Nelson et al. 2002, 3–4)

THE REGIONAL DIMENSION OF AFFORDABLE HOUSING

Like "affordability," "region" is a term that in common usage is somewhat elastic. For political purposes, however, the term has been defined largely through legislation that designates areas within the jurisdiction of specific regional planning commissions as regions. For statistical purposes, a region is often tied to the Metropolitan Statistical Areas (MSAs) used by the Bureau of the Census. MSAs are in large part derived from analysis of commuting patterns. They are, however, by definition built around urban cores, whereas many regional planning commissions represent multicounty rural areas.

From its inception in the U.S., zoning has raised the question of whether a single local government is the proper locus of land-use regulation. In many states with planning and zoning enabling legislation still based on the Standard City Planning and Zoning Enabling Acts of the 1920s, published and promulgated by the U.S. Department of Commerce, the municipality remains the primary decision maker, but growth management and planning legislation in some states (e.g., California, Florida, Oregon, Washington, Minnesota) has shifted review and approval power, if not actual land-use authority, toward counties, regional authorities, and even the state itself.

But what is a region? The urban historian and critic Lewis Mumford defines it as "any geographic area that possesses a certain unity of climate, soil, vegetation, industry, and culture" (quoted in Scott 1969, 221). His definition suggests that a region is an organic, self-evident whole. Yet this conceptualization fails to acknowledge that, in everyday practice, regional unity is rarely self-evident but is instead *created* by government. This creation of what he calls "a certain unity" remains a political problem to this day, one that ultimately can be managed only through constant negotiation, accommodation, and a certain amount of arbitrary line-drawing that often conveniently matches existing political boundaries, such as those of counties.

From its inception in the U.S., zoning has raised the question of whether a single local government is the proper locus of land-use regulation.

What is the size of the "community" that must be considered if a local zoning ordinance is going to serve the welfare of the community? Is that community simply the land within the boundaries of the individual municipality that is adopting the land-use regulations?

Transportation remains the one feature of a region that consistently challenges local political boundaries, not least because it is linked to the relationship between the demand for affordable housing and job availability. Because labor markets are regional in nature, the problem of getting to those jobs is regional as well. But planners have only recently begun to understand these connections. Thus, just as certain directional features of the landscape have been identified as watersheds, so too have planners chosen to identify what they call "traffic sheds." While traffic sheds have long been one of the defining features of metropolitan areas, which produce concentrations of employment opportunities, they are also a valuable descriptive tool that, by registering the regional link between housing and jobs, can define the unity of a region better than Mumford's five features. But managing traffic has frequently bedeviled regional governance because it is an interjurisdictional challenge. It demonstrates that boundaries that make sense for transportation purposes may not always be the most logical ones for economic, growth management, or environmental purposes.

Assumptions about the relationship between employment and housing have long been at the core of efforts to define a housing region. Burchell et al. (1983, 23) define such a region as "a geographic area in which units at the same price are in mutual competition." They argue that people usually choose locations for housing units based on a reasonable commuting distance to work. These preferences can be quantitatively studied, they claim, and they offer two methods of analysis that incorporate monetary and time costs to define a housing region. The first employs concentric circles drawn around employment centers with their dimensions based on commuting time and distance. For practical reasons, this method can become complicated because most metropolitan areas today are multimodal. The second "join[s] geographic areas together that are linked by cross-commuting from place of residence to place of work." Interestingly, Burchell et al. refer to these as "commuting sheds" (p. 23). Their methods inevitably involve some statistical manipulation but yield useful building blocks for defining a region that capture at least a few distinct economic characteristics.

If housing choice is not merely a matter of choosing a single municipality within which to live and work, and if in fact most commuting patterns are intermunicipal, what is the size of the "community" that must be considered if a local zoning ordinance is going to serve the welfare of the community? Is that community simply the land within the boundaries of the individual municipality that is adopting the land-use regulations? If an affluent community provides low- to moderate-income jobs in its commercial sector but adopts residential zoning that allows only for housing that is economically unattainable for those employees, what definition of community is actually at work? Earlier rationales for large-lot zoning that served exclusionary purposes would face much tougher scrutiny today for environmental reasons unrelated to the debate over affordable housing. For instance, Listokin (1976, 12) observed that some communities justified large-lot zoning on the assumption that they would reduce the costs of municipal infrastructure extension, for example, by using septic systems instead of municipal sewers. Today, however, there is a far greater awareness that onsite residential septic systems pose a number of significant environmental problems, while higher densities will more likely reduce the unit costs of extending sewer lines and other types of infrastructure.

Starting in the 1960s, some courts ruled that municipalities were obligated to consider the welfare of the entire region, and not just of the present inhabitants of the municipality, when designing their land-use regulations for residential development. It is interesting that the majority of these cases arose in eastern and northeastern states, such as Virginia (*Board of County Supervisors of Fairfax County v. Carper*, 200 Va. 653, 197 S.E. 2d 390 (1959)); Pennsylvania (*In re Appeal of Kit-Mar Builders*, 439 Pa. 466, 215 A, 2d765 (1971)); New Hampshire (*Wayne Britton v. Town of Chester*, 134 N.H. 434, 595 A.2d 492 (1991)); and, most significantly, New Jersey with the *Mount Laurel* cases (*Southern Burlington County NAACP v. Township of Mount Laurel*, 67 N.J. 151, 336 A. 2d 713, appeal dismissed and cert.denied, 423 U.S. 808 (1975); *Southern Burlington County NAACP v. Township of Mount Laurel*, 92 N.J. 158, 456 A. 2d 390 (1983)).[4] Indeed, in the 1991 *Britton v. Town of Chester*, 134 N.H. 434, 440, 595 A.2d 492, 495, anti-exclusionary zoning decision, the New Hampshire Supreme Court, interpreting the state zoning enabling act (N.H.R.S.A. Sec. 674:16) held that the term "community" in its phrase "[f]or the purpose of promoting the health, safety, or *the general welfare of the community*" (emphasis supplied) could have broader meaning than just the town itself:

> The possibility that a municipality might be obligated to consider the needs of the region outside its boundaries was addressed early on in our land use jurisprudence by the United States Supreme Court, paving the way for the term "community" to be used in the broader sense. In *Village of Euclid v. Ambler Realty Co.*, 272 U.S. 365, 47 S.Ct. 114, 71 L.Ed. 303 (1926), the Court recognized "the possibility of cases where the general public interest would so far outweigh the interest of the municipality that the municipality would not be allowed to stand in the way." *Id.* at 390, 47 S.Ct. at 119. When an ordinance will have an impact beyond the boundaries of the municipality, the welfare of the entire affected region must be considered in determining the ordinance's validity. *Associated Home Builders v. City of Livermore*, 18 Cal.3d 582, 557 P.2d 473, 487, 135 Cal.Rptr. 41, 55 (1976); *see also Berenson v. Town of New Castle*, 38 N.Y.2d 102, 110-11, 378 N.Y.S.2d 672, 681, 341 N.E.2d 236, 242-43 (1975).

The state's supreme court concluded that "community" in the enabling act was not limited to a municipality alone and thus a municipality may need to consider the interests of the region outside its boundaries.

These cases indicate that the time has passed when the law or public policy could justify allowing individual local jurisdictions to obstruct the achievement of a major policy objective like the adequate provision of affordable housing within and throughout a metropolitan area. Moreover, this shift accompanied an even wider realization, which was expressed through state-level growth management legislation, that local zoning and planning had regional or interjurisdictional impacts that required some form of accountability beyond the municipality itself (Meck 2002, 5-47 to 5-68). But at the core of these planning reforms is the belief that an adequate supply of affordable housing is too important and too dependent on regional cooperation to allow individual communities to opt out of their obligations through exclusionary zoning.

THE WEAKNESS OF REGIONAL PLANNING AUTHORITY

The impacts and residue of decades of exclusionary zoning policies with varying degrees of explicit discriminatory intent remain in many jurisdictions (Pendall 2000). In most areas, regional authority to challenge or override such practices is weak—or in some cases nonexistent—despite the existence of regional planning commissions and other entities of regional governance. Most regional planning commissions serve an advisory function, available to assist municipalities with planning and to provide data and analysis, but are not empowered to reject local plans or zoning ordinances that fail to meet regional expectations. Faced with intense opposi-

Pendall's findings suggest that any regional planning body that fails to account for the prevalence of low-density zoning and permit caps will only contribute to the problems they create.

tion from local municipal officials and their organizations, most state legislatures choose not to create strong regional authorities with the power to insist that local plans and zoning ordinances conform to specific fair-share expectations of accommodating affordable housing. Added to this problem is that of membership interests. Typically, the members of a regional planning agency are the local governments themselves, who pay dues to maintain, in full or in part, the agency, which then becomes a creature of local government. As a practical matter, angering a dues-paying member is problematic and it is unlikely that an agency beholden to its members for its financial existence will risk offending those members by adopting strong standards to monitor the production of affordable housing and by insisting that members provide realistic opportunities for such housing to be built (see Meck 2002, 6-4 to 6-15).

THE "CHAIN OF EXCLUSION"

Working against the provision of affordable housing is what Pendall (2000) called, in a landmark article on land-use practices, housing affordability, and their impact on minorities, the "chain of exclusion." Traditional land-use tools and policies can affect housing prices in a number of ways: by altering the costs of construction and infrastructure, by making the community more attractive, by limiting the supply of attractive residential locations, and by shifting consumer expectations. These variables interact to form Pendall's chain of exclusion, which links housing supply, type, and tenure to affordability. To determine the links in this chain, Pendall conducted a survey that asked 1,510 cities, towns, and townships in the 25 largest metropolitan areas in the U.S. to describe their land-use regulatory practices. Using regression analysis, he found that low-density zoning—which he defined as zoning that restricts residential densities to fewer than eight dwelling units per acre—consistently reduces rental housing. This reduction in turn limits the number of Black and Hispanic residents. Building permit caps, which are featured in a number of so-called growth management systems around the nation, are also associated with lowered proportions of Hispanic residents.[5]

Pendall's findings suggest that any regional planning body that fails to account for the prevalence of low-density zoning and permit caps will only contribute to the problems they create. His chain-of-exclusion theory thus makes it clear that regional approaches must minimize, if not eliminate, the restrictive impacts that certain land-use regulatory techniques have on affordable housing and on racial and ethnic diversity in communities.

THE NIMBY PROBLEM

Related to Pendall's chain of exclusion is the Not-in-My-Backyard or NIMBY problem documented in the 1991 report of the Advisory Commission on Regulatory Barriers to Affordable Housing. The commission defines it as "opposition by residents and public officials alike to additional or different kinds of housing units in their neighborhoods and communities" (Advisory Commission 1991, 1-1).[6] The translation of NIMBY sentiments into codes and ordinances, the commission argues, "effectively burden[s] development and constitute barriers to affordable housing. The results are excessive growth controls, exclusionary zoning ordinances, unnecessarily drawn-out permit and approval processes, and arbitrary restrictions against special types of housing units that combine to make housing less affordable for many households" (p. 1-1). Although the commission found that costs varied widely and that regulatory barriers and the NIMBY syndrome did not account for all regional variations in affordability, its study cites evidence that 20 percent to 35 percent jumps in housing prices were attributable to excessive regulation, especially in the most severely affected areas of the country, including Boston, Los Angeles/Long Beach, and San Francisco/Oakland (p. 1-1).

The NIMBY problem has an interjurisdictional impact, the advisory commission concludes. While communities that suffer from it may sense the compelling need for affordable housing, they expect other communities to satisfy that need. "Instead of dealing with the negative side effects of growth and the infrastructure financing problems," the commission asserts, "they take the expedient course of declaring their communities off limits to most development. Yet communities where the NIMBY syndrome is most entrenched are quick to invite those households seeking affordable housing to search in neighboring jurisdictions." When many jurisdictions in a metropolitan area refuse to take responsibility for affordable housing, the commission concluded, "households seeking affordable housing may find themselves shut out of the entire metropolitan area. As a result, everybody suffers in one way or the other" (p. 1-9).

ENDNOTES

1. Depending on the federal program, however, HUD uses different terminology to describe income levels. HUD Section 8 income definitions appear at 24 CFR 5.603 and are as follows:

   Low-income family. A family whose annual income does not exceed 80 percent of the median income for the area, as determined by HUD with adjustments for smaller and larger families, except that HUD may establish income ceilings higher or lower than 80 percent of the median income for the area on the basis of HUD's findings that such variations are necessary because of unusually high or low family incomes.

   Extremely low-income family. A family whose annual income does not exceed 30 percent of the median income for the area, as determined by HUD with adjustments for smaller and larger families, except that HUD may establish income ceilings higher or lower than 30 percent of the median income for the area if HUD finds that such variations are necessary because of unusually high or low family incomes.

   Very low-income family. A family whose annual income does not exceed 50 percent of the median family income for the area, as determined by HUD with adjustments for smaller and larger families, except that HUD may establish income ceilings higher or lower than 50 percent of the median income for the area if HUD finds that such variations are necessary because of unusually high or low family incomes.

   Yet these terms change to moderate-income family, middle-income family, and extremely low-income family in HUD's regulations for the federal Community Development Block Grant (CDBG) Program at 24 CFR 91.5:

   Middle-income family. Family whose income is between 80 percent and 95 percent of the median income for the area, as determined by HUD with adjustments for smaller and larger families, except that HUD may establish income ceilings higher or lower than 95 percent of the median for the area on the basis of HUD's findings that such variations are necessary because of prevailing levels of construction costs or fair market rents, or unusually high or low family incomes.

   Moderate-income family. Family whose income does not exceed 80 percent of the median income for the area, as determined by HUD with adjustments for smaller and larger families, except that HUD may establish income ceilings higher or lower than 80 percent of the median for the area on the basis of HUD's findings that such variations are necessary because of prevailing levels of construction costs or fair market rents, or unusually high or low family incomes.

   Extremely low-income family. Family whose income is between zero and 30 percent of the median income for the area, as determined by HUD with adjustments for smaller and larger families, except that HUD may establish income ceilings higher or lower than 30 percent of the median for the area on the basis of HUD's findings that such variations are necessary because of prevailing levels of construction costs or fair market rents, or unusually high or low family incomes.

2. See 24 CFR 5.628, which defines the total tenant rent payment as not exceeding 30 percent of the family's monthly adjusted income for Section 8 purposes. Other means of calculating the total tenant rent payment are included in this definition. See also 24 CFR 91.5, which, for CDBG purposes, defines "cost burden" to be "[t]he extent to which gross housing costs, including utility costs, exceed 30 percent of gross income, based on data available from the U.S. Census Bureau."

3. The *Growing Smart^SM Legislative Guidebook* offers these model definitions for its four levels of housing:

> **Low-Income Housing** means housing that is affordable, according to the federal Department of Housing and Urban Development, for either home ownership or rental, and that is occupied, reserved, or marketed for occupancy by households with a gross household income that does not exceed 50 percent of the median gross household income for households of the same size within the housing region in which the housing is located. For purposes of this Act, the term "low-income housing" shall include "very low-income housing."

> **Middle-Income Housing** means housing that is affordable for either home ownership or rental, and that is occupied, reserved, or marketed for occupancy by households with a gross household income that is greater than [80] percent but does not exceed [*specify a number within a range of* 95 *to* 120] percent of the median gross household income for households of the same size within the housing region in which the housing is located.

> **Moderate-Income Housing** means housing that is affordable, according to the federal Department of Housing and Urban Development, for either home ownership or rental, and that is occupied, reserved, or marketed for occupancy by households with a gross household income that is greater than 50 percent but does not exceed 80 percent of the median gross household income for households of the same size within the housing region in which the housing is located.

> **Very Low-Income Housing** means housing that is affordable, according to the federal Department of Housing and Urban Development, for either home ownership or rental, and that is occupied, reserved, or marketed for occupancy by households with a gross household income equal to 30 percent or less of the median gross household income for households of the same size within the housing region in which the housing is located. (Meck 2002, 4-81 to 4-83)

4. The first case, now known as *Mount Laurel I*, declared an affirmative obligation on the part of the local government to consider the regional, not just the municipal, welfare in zoning for housing. It also established the local government's obligation to provide for a fair share of affordable housing, but it did not establish a specific remedy. The second case, *Mount Laurel II*, resulted from the failure of the local government to produce a remedy to meet those obligations, and in this case the court initiated a process of prescribing a remedy. That remedy culminated in the 1985 legislative solution that produced the Council on Affordable Housing as an administrative arm of the state with the responsibility to define what a community's fair share of affordable housing should be. See the discussion of *Mount Laurel* in Chapter 4.

5. Interestingly, certain growth management techniques—urban growth boundaries, adequate public facilities ordinances, and development moratoria—had limited effects on housing prices and racial or ethnic distribution, according to Pendall (2000). Pendall comments that his research "confirms the long-known connection between low-density-only zoning and racial exclusion" (p. 35). He goes on to point out that it is no coincidence that land-use controls with the most exclusionary effects on Blacks predominate in the northeastern and midwestern U.S. while the controls with the most exclusionary effects on Hispanics are most common in California, where these are, respectively, the predominant minority group in these areas.

6. For a statistical analysis of NIMBY-based opposition to projects in the San Francisco Bay Area, see Pendall (1999). Pendall found that projects opposed by neighbors tended to be next to single-family housing, not multifamily housing. Projects that included affordable housing also generated more NIMBY protests than projects that didn't, although few citizen complaints explicitly mentioned affordable housing. Antigrowth and NIMBY protests were both more common in jurisdictions with lower median incomes. But institutional structures, Pendall found, tend to shape protest against affordable housing. He found that affordable housing projects with streamlined approval processes generated less controversy than the average project, even though one might expect affordable projects to draw more opposition. Pendall also remarks that nonprofit groups who build affordable projects in the Bay Area are more professional and sophisticated than similar groups elsewhere; these groups often conduct substantial background research and meet with neighborhood residents and elected officials. They also avoid jurisdictions in which elected officials, harassed by irate constituents, would be more likely to kill a project through delay or denial. These practices, he argues, can help to ensure the building of affordable housing projects that are embraced by local communities.

CHAPTER 4

Fair-Share Programs
and an Incentive Program

This chapter evaluates a variety of fair-share programs and an incentive program that establish regional approaches to affordable housing. It describes fair-share programs in New Jersey, California, New Hampshire, and Portland, Oregon. This chapter also includes a discussion of an incentive program in the Twin Cities, Minnesota. The analysis in this chapter, and in Chapters 5 through 7, focuses on whether the programs described are facilitating the provision or production of affordable housing, to the extent that can be determined, regardless of the structure of the program.

FAIR-SHARE PROGRAMS

NEW JERSEY

Title: New Jersey Fair Housing Act

Inception: 1985, but prompted by New Jersey Supreme Court's 1975 and 1983 *Mount Laurel* antiexclusionary zoning decisions.

Administration: The act established the New Jersey Council on Affordable Housing (COAH) as an administrative alternative to the courts, which had previously overseen the implementation of the *Mount Laurel* doctrine on a case-by-case basis using special planning masters. The act charges COAH with determining housing regions for the state and estimating the present and prospective need for low- and moderate-income housing at the state and regional levels. COAH is to then allocate a fair share to each municipality in the housing region and can make adjustments to the allocation. The act also allows COAH to grant "substantive certification" to local housing plans and related development regulations; this certification gives municipalities an affirmative defense against *Mount Laurel* lawsuits.

Key objectives: Establish for local governments numerical goals that describe affordable housing needs consistent with *Mount Laurel* doctrine.

Accomplishments: Forty-eight percent of cities and towns were participating in the program as of 2001. Since the state began monitoring progress, opportunity has been made available for 60,731 affordable units. New unit construction totaled 28,855 as of 2000.

Caveats: Local government participation is not mandated by the Fair Housing Act. Some critics believe the act needs a major overhaul, with a different, less complicated approach to calculating fair-share obligations.

New Jersey is an example of a state that has adopted a top-down approach to affordable housing as a consequence of a series of state supreme court decisions.

New Jersey is an example of a state that has adopted a top-down approach to affordable housing as a consequence of a series of state supreme court decisions. The New Jersey Supreme Court, in the case of *Southern Burlington County NAACP v. Township of Mount Laurel* (67 N.J. 151, 336 A.2d 713 (1975), appeal dismissed and cert. denied, 423 U.S. 808, 96 S.Ct. 18 (1975), hereinafter *Mount Laurel I*), ruled that developing municipalities have a constitutional obligation to provide a realistic opportunity for the construction of low- and moderate-income housing. In *Southern Burlington County NAACP v. Township of Mount Laurel* (92 N.J. 158, 456 A.2d 390 (1983), hereinafter *Mount Laurel II*), the state supreme court expanded the *Mount Laurel I* doctrine, holding that all municipalities share in the obligation to provide the opportunity for the development of affordable housing. In this decision, the court provided specific judicial remedies for municipalities to meet their constitutional obligation (COAH 2001a, 5). The two *Mount Laurel* rulings held that the state's local zoning statutes had to be read in the context of a state—not federal—constitutional requirement to legislate "for the general welfare" (*Mount Laurel I*, at 726). Local governments that

enacted zoning had to provide realistic opportunities to meet their fair share of their region's low- and moderate-income housing need. Any zoning ordinance that denied reasonable opportunities to meet the local governments fair share of a region's low- and moderate-income housing need thus failed the state's constitutional requirements.

Two single-family infill affordable housing units in Wall Township, New Jersey.

In 1985 the New Jersey Fair Housing Act was passed (New Jersey Statutes Annotated, Section 2:27D-301 *et seq.* (1986 and Supplement 1999)). It established the New Jersey Council on Affordable Housing (COAH) as an administrative alternative to the courts, which had previously overseen the implementation of the *Mount Laurel* doctrine on a case-by-case basis using special planning masters. A subsequent New Jersey Supreme Court ruling upheld the constitutionality of the Fair Housing Act itself.

COAH is an 11-member body appointed by the governor on the advice and consent of the state senate. The members of COAH represent local government, providers and users of affordable housing, and the general public. The Fair Housing Act charges COAH with determining housing regions for the state and estimating the present and prospective need for low- and moderate-income housing at the state and regional levels. COAH then allocates a fair share to each municipality in the housing region and can make later adjustments to its allocation (Section 52:27D-307c(1)).

After COAH assigns its fair-share obligations for affordable housing in a specific region (see below), it offers "substantive certification" to municipalities that choose to address the fair share of their region's need for affordable housing. Municipalities may voluntarily elect to complete housing elements and fair-share plans (Section 52:27D-310). In a fair-share plan, a municipality must show how it will address the present and prospective need figures calculated by COAH and identify techniques, including subsidies and amendments to zoning codes and site-specific rezonings, for providing low- and moderate-income housing. A municipality may then petition COAH for substantive certification of its housing element and fair-share plan (Section 52:27D-314). COAH grants such certification if it finds that the petitioning municipality's housing element and fair-share plan "make the achievement of the municipality's fair share of low- and moderate-income housing realistically possible" (Section 52:27D-314(b)). The certification may also be linked to the adoption of ordinances, such as rezoning to higher densities, that implement the fair-share plan. The primary value of substantive certification is the protection it offers municipalities from the "builder's remedy" described in the *Mount Laurel II* decision. The builder's remedy is a legal mechanism by which builders or developers can petition the courts for permission to proceed with an affordable housing development in communities that have previously failed to authorize such housing or have approved only minimal amounts.[1] Substantive certification granted to a municipality by COAH provides a statutorily created presumption of validity against any claim made against the local government in an exclusionary zoning lawsuit brought against it (Section 52:27D-317). In the first two allocation rounds, covering 1987–1999, substantive certification lasted six years; the next round will be 10 years. Certification may be withdrawn if a municipality fails to ensure the continuing realistic opportunity to address its fair-share housing obligation.

To provide the realistic opportunity for the construction of new units, municipalities may also zone specific sites for residential development by the private sector.

New Jersey Council on Affordable Housing

The Fair Housing Act also introduced the concept of the regional contribution agreement (RCA) (Section 52:27D-301; see also Chapter 93 of the New Jersey statutes). Under an RCA, a sending municipality may transfer up to one-half of its low- and moderate- income housing obligation to a receiving municipality within its housing region, at a negotiated per-unit cost to the sending municipality (COAH 2001b). Originally, the minimum amount for the transfer of one unit of housing was $10,000. The minimum was raised to $20,000 in 1993, and to $25,000 in 2001.

Most municipalities can meet a portion of their fair-share obligations through the rehabilitation of existing units. To provide the realistic opportunity for the construction of new units, municipalities may also zone specific sites for residential development by the private sector. Developers who are interested in building on these sites must agree to build a fixed percentage of affordable housing—usually 20 percent—of the total number of units constructed on the site; they must also market these units to low- and moderate-income households and maintain their affordability for 30 years. These units are also subject to deed restrictions intended to preserve their affordable sales price or rent.[2] Other methods of meeting the fair-share obligation include participation in regional contribution agreements; municipally sponsored construction using for-profit or nonprofit builders; the purchase of existing units for sale or rent to eligible households; the creation of accessory apartments within existing structures, a buy-down program, or the provision of alternative or congregate living arrangements including group homes for the physically handicapped or developmentally disabled (COAH 2002a).

COAH derives its fair-share obligations from population projections developed by the Center for Urban Policy Research at Rutgers University. They are calculated by multiplying a headship rate (the propensity to form a household) and population growth in an age group. Like population, household growth is projected by county. Headship rates are determined by age cohort and projected at one-half the rate of change observed from 1980 to 1990. The estimated aggregate growth in low- and moderate-income households is then summed at the county level and included in a regional pool to be subsequently distributed to municipalities in a region via allocation factors. There are six regional pools based on six groups of three to four counties.

The formula used to allocate the total fair-share need for affordable housing can seem complicated to persons not familiar with the process.[3] The formula consists of (1) *present need*, which is the sum of indigenous need and reallocated present need, and (2) *prospective need*, which is the share of total projected households that will qualify for low- and moderate-income housing (COAH 2001a, 9).

Present need is composed of *indigenous need* and *reallocated present need*. As defined in the New Jersey Administrative Code (Section 5:93-1.1), indigenous need is the number of deficient housing units occupied by low- and moderate-income households within a municipality. Certain urban centers have a disproportionate number of substandard housing units occupied by low- and moderate-income families. Under the COAH rules, these are currently the 45 Urban Aid cities—such as Newark, Trenton, and Bayonne—although this figure may fluctuate.[4] Where these cities' deficient housing, calculated as a percentage of all occupied housing units, exceeds the average for the region, their excess need is sent to a housing pool for subsequent redistribution in that region. The housing in that pool is called *reallocated present need,* and an individual municipality's responsibility is limited by this percentage. For example, if the regional average is 2 percent, and a specific municipality within that region has 3 percent of its substandard housing units that are occupied by low- and moderate-income households, the responsibility of that municipality is capped at 2 percent and the remaining obligation becomes a regional obligation assigned to other municipalities in the region (COAH 2001a, 9–10).

Prospective need is a projection of new low- and moderate- income households that are likely to form over the next projection period. In 1986, COAH adopted prospective need for its 1987–1993 cycle. Much of this projected growth did not occur and, therefore, during its second-round allocations (1993–1999 cycle), COAH modified the first round prospective need obligations based on its best estimate of actual growth.

The number that results from this retroactive modification is *prior-cycle prospective need*. Prior-cycle prospective need is the recalculated prospective need for the prior period, which has been recalculated because more accurate census data are available in subsequent cycles than was available when the need was initially calculated. Once present and prospective need are totaled, then prior-cycle prospective need is added into the allocation formula. Next, demolitions (increases need), filtering (reduces need), con-

COAH derives its fair-share obligations from population projections developed by the Center for Urban Policy Research at Rutgers University.

version (reduces need), and spontaneous rehabilitation (reduces need) are factored into the sum of the total need and the prior-cycle prospective need to determine the precredited need. *Demolitions* are a source of secondary housing demand because they eliminate housing opportunities for low- and moderate-income people; they *increase* municipal need. *Filtering* describes the process whereby the housing needs of low- and moderate-income households are partially met by sound housing units that were formerly occupied by people with higher incomes; increases in filtering reduce need. *Residential conversion* is the creation of dwelling units from already existing residential structures; it *decreases* need. *Spontaneous rehabilitation* measures the private market's ability to rehabilitate deficient affordable housing units so they meet applicable state and local code standards; it also *decreases* need.

The reallocated present need and the prospective need, both calculated on the regional level, are distributed to the municipal level on the basis of four factors: (1) the municipality's share of regional undeveloped land; (2) equalized nonresidential valuation; (3) change in equalized nonresidential valuation; and (4) aggregate household income differences. Undeveloped land is weighted by the *State Development and Redevelopment Plan* planning areas (COAH 2001a, 10). Nonresidential ratables are all land and buildings that are not residential uses for property tax purposes, such as commercial, industrial, retail, and office activities. These serve as a proxy for job holders who require housing (Cordingley 2002). COAH uses this measurement because it is an excellent indicator of employment in specific municipalities, and therefore, the nonresidential ratable factor is sensitive to the link between jobs and housing need. The income factor reflects COAH's belief that wealthier communities have a greater responsibility and financial capacity to provide affordable housing (COAH 2001a, 10).

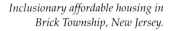

Inclusionary affordable housing in Brick Township, New Jersey.

New Jersey Council on Affordable Housing

To arrive at the allocation for present need, factors (1), (2), and (3) are summed and then averaged. The resulting figure is the present need allocation factor, and it is applied to the present need total for the region. To arrive at the allocation for prospective need, factors (1), (3), and (4) are also summed and averaged, and the result is applied to the prospective need total for the region.

Although Urban Aid municipalities are exempt from the regional reallocated need and prospective need obligations, they are still eligible to receive aid that is otherwise restricted to COAH-certified municipalities or municipalities that have received a judgment of repose from the Superior Court (a court-issued judgment approving a municipality's plan to satisfy its fair-share obligation).[5]

The municipalities that provided housing during COAH's first round of obligation assignments received a credit for each housing unit built, with rental units receiving greater credit; for units transferred via regional contribution agreements (discussed below); and for each unit provided through inclusionary zoning. Therefore, the calculated need is the precredited need minus any credits. The obligations assigned during the second round are lower for municipalities that addressed their housing needs during the first cycle because the calculations are cumulative.

Figure 4-1 represents COAH's calculation of a fair-share affordable housing allocation for Atlantic City in Atlantic County. Note: the numbers used here have been rounded by COAH, which may affect some calculations.

Program Results

Table 4-1 shows information about the COAH process from its inception in 1980 to 2000. The first column shows the name of each county in New Jersey. The second column shows the population of that county in 2000 (U.S. Census Bureau 2002). The third column shows the number of municipalities that are located in that county. COAH has calculated the need for affordable housing in each of these municipalities. The fourth and fifth columns indicate the number and percentage (as a percentage of the entire county) of municipalities that are voluntarily participating in the COAH process in the first and second rounds, respectively. The sixth column shows the number and percentage (as a percentage of the entire county) of municipalities that are involved in a court-ordered affordable housing process. These court-ordered municipalities do not necessarily participate in the COAH process, but they are nonetheless participating in an affordable housing process. The seventh column, precredited need, shows the cumulative (1987–1999) base calculation of affordable housing needed in the county before any credits have been subtracted. The eighth column, calculated need, shows the current cumulative calculated need for affordable housing, which is the precredited need minus any credits that have been subtracted from the base calculation for housing units that have already been built or rehabilitated, or for zoning that is already in place. The ninth column, built/under construction, is the cumulative number of housing units that have been built or are under current construction in that county. The next column, zoned/approved, shows the cumulative number of units of affordable housing for which inclusionary zoning is in place. The eleventh column indicates the cumulative number of units that the municipalities in the county have transferred via regional contribution agreements. Finally, the twelfth column indicates the cumulative number of affordable housing units that have been rehabilitated (COAH 2001b).

As Table 4-1 indicates, Hunterton County, located in western New Jersey, and Somerset, located just east of Hunterton County, had the highest participation in the first round, both with 62 percent of municipalities in each county taking part in the COAH process. In the second round, Morris County, in northeastern New Jersey, had the highest percentage of municipalities participating (90 percent). Burlington County, located east of Philadelphia, had the highest percentage of municipalities participating in a court-ordered affordable housing process at 25 percent. Hudson County, located near New York City, had the lowest participation in the first round,

FIGURE 4-1
COAH FAIR-SHARE AFFORDABLE HOUSING ALLOCATION FOR ATLANTIC CITY

Indigenous Need	343
Reallocated Present Need	+138
Present Need (1993)	= 482
Prospective Need (1993–1999)	+940
Total Need	= 1422
Prior-Cycle Prospective Need	+1538
Secondary Sources of Supply (−) and Demand (+)	
1. Demolitions	+220
2. Filtering	−302
3. Conversion	−75
4. Spontaneous Rehabilitation	−3
Pre-Credited Need	= 2799
Reduction	−0
Pre-1987 Credits	−0
20% Cap	−0
Calculated Need	= 2799

Source: New Jersey Council on Affordable Housing, Municipal Low- and Moderate-Income Housing Need, October 11, 1993.

TABLE 4-1
NEW JERSEY COUNCIL ON AFFORDABLE HOUSING ACTIVITIES 1987–1999

County	2000 Population	Number of Municipalities	COAH Participation First Round	COAH Participation Second Round	Court Involvement	Precredited Need 1987–99	Calculated Need	New Construction Built/Under Construction	New Construction Zoned/Approved	Regional Contribution Agreement Sending Municipality	Rehabilitation
Atlantic	252,552	235	5(20%)	4(17%)	1(4%)	6,568	6,350	61	281	0	399
Bergen	884,118	70	14(20%)	34(49%)	12(17%)	9,406	6,650	1,670	538	512	254
Burlington	423,394	40	10(25%)	19(48%)	10(25%)	6,677	4,438	1,322	1,957	578	385
Camden	508,932	37	11(30%)	13(35%)	2(5%)	5,848	4,662	1,289	385	0	632
Cape May	102,326	16	2(12%)	7(44%)	0(0%)	3,201	3,103	70	8	0	351
Cumberland	146,438	14	2(14%)	2(14%)	1(7%)	1,576	1,361	862	268	0	1,306
Essex	793,633	22	5(23%)	9(41%)	3(14%)	5,413	4,984	1,296	276	107	147
Gloucester	254,673	24	8(33%)	10(42%)	5(21%)	5,037	3,915	1,222	1,074	189	445
Hudson	608,975	12	1(8%)	3(25%)	1(8%)	6,267	5,634	534	159	0	302
Hunterdon	121,989	26	16(62%)	20(77%)	2(8%)	2,346	1,645	575	428	485	277
Mercer	350,761	13	5(38%)	10(77%)	2(15%)	6,039	4,098	2,251	805	503	1,121
Middlesex	750,162	25	12(48%)	15(60%)	4(16%)	9,408	5,143	4,603	2,103	362	1,150
Monmouth	615,301	53	9(17%)	16(30%)	8(15%)	14,809	9,300	2,187	1,135	2,153	499
Morris	470,212	39	14(36%)	35(90%)	0(0%)	6,557	1,862	3,851	813	673	907
Ocean	510,916	33	3(9%)	7(21%)	7(21%)	9,689	8,805	1,339	1,198	50	625
Passaic	489,049	16	2(13%)	9(56%)	1(6%)	6,177	6,112	652	760	567	346
Salem	64,285	15	2(13%)	4(27%)	1(7%)	1,248	1,180	0	0	0	157
Somerset	297,490	21	13(62%)	13(62%)	2(10%)	5,160	1,905	3,436	391	880	345
Sussex	144,166	24	10(42%)	16(66%)	1(4%)	1,356	1,304	115	181	0	359
Union	522,541	21	6(29%)	7(33%)	4(19%)	3,956	2,990	881	344	337	1,028
Warren	102,437	22	11(50%)	18(82%)	1(5%)	1,188	867	639	136	0	214
State Total	**8,414,350**	**566**	**161(28%)**	**271(48%)**	**68(12%)**	**117,935**	**86,308**	**28,855**	**13,231**	**7,396**	**11,249**

Source: New Jersey Council on Affordable Housing, COAH Options: COAH's 2001 Annual Report (Trenton, N.J.: New Jersey Council on Affordable Housing, 2001).

and Cumberland County, in the southwest corner of the state, had the lowest participation in the second round, with 8 percent and 14 percent of municipalities in each county participating, respectively. Cape May County, in southern New Jersey, had the lowest percentage (0 percent) of court-ordered participants.

Monmouth County, located to the south of New York City and in eastern New Jersey, had the highest precredited need (14,809 units) and calculated need (9,300 units). Salem County, located across the Delaware river from Wilmington, Delaware, had the lowest precredited need (1,248 units) and calculated need (1,180 units).

As of June 2001, 271 of the 566 municipalities in New Jersey were participating in the COAH process, approximately 48 percent of the state's municipalities. Additionally, there were some 68 municipalities that were under the court's jurisdiction (i.e., municipalities that have been ordered by a court to participate in an affordable housing program). These court-ordered municipalities do not report to COAH. Overall, some 339 municipalities in New Jersey—almost 60 percent—were participating in an affordable housing process as of June 2001 (COAH 2001b, 4).

The village at New Sharon affordable duplex units in Deptford Township, New Jersey.

New Jersey Council on Affordable Housing

Between 1980—the date when COAH started monitoring the progress of affordable housing development in New Jersey—and 2000, the opportunity has been made available for 60,731 low- and moderate-income housing units. This represents approximately 51 percent of the total precredited need and 70 percent of the calculated need. This total includes: 28,855 units that have been built or are under construction; 13,231 units that are the result of realistic zoning being in place or of approvals; 7,396 units that have been transferred via regional contribution agreements; and 11,249 units that have been rehabilitated (COAH 2001b, 4). These numbers reflect only the opportunities for low- and moderate-income housing created between 1980 and 2000 for COAH credit in municipalities that are participating in the COAH process, not the overall affordable housing opportunities in the state of New Jersey.

These figures show that the approximately 48 percent of the municipalities in the state that are participating in the COAH process are providing approximately 51 percent of the total precredited need and 70 percent of the calculated need for affordable housing for the entire state. In terms of actual affordable housing units constructed, 24 percent of the precredited need and 33 percent of the calculated need for affordable housing in the entire state have been constructed or were under construction in municipalities participating in the COAH process (COAH 2001b, 19).

Additionally, COAH has granted 5,372 rental bonuses, and seven municipalities have received 110 credits for substantial compliance. Rental bonuses are two-for-one bonuses awarded for the construction of rental units; for example, a municipality will receive two credits for the development of one unit of non-age-restricted rental housing. A credit for substantial compliance is a credit for municipalities that have substantially completed their construction obligations. For example, a municipality that has completed the construction of 90 percent or more of their obligation will receive a 20 percent reduction of their future obligation, a municipality that has completed between 80 and 89 percent of its obligation will receive a 10 percent reduction of their future obligation, and a municipality that has completed between 70 and 79 percent of its obligation will receive a 5 percent reduction of their future obligation (Thompson 2002).

Since 1987, 116 sending municipalities that have transferred part of their affordable housing obligations to 37 receiving municipalities through regional contribution agreements (RCA). A total of $145,086,736 has been transferred by RCA. New Brunswick/Middlesex County has accepted the most money, $17,875,000 from 11 suburban communities for 795 affordable housing units. The second highest receiver was Trenton/Mercer County, which accepted $15,758,500 from 13 municipalities for 801 units. The third highest receiver was Newark/Essex County, which received $13,581,500 from seven suburban municipalities for 740 affordable housing units (COAH 2001b, 20). The figures indicate that suburban municipalities are more often the senders of RCAs while urbanized areas are more often the receivers.

Project Freedom II affordable group home for physically challenged people in Washington Township, New Jersey.

New Jersey Council on Affordable Housing

A 1990 New Jersey Supreme Court decision, *Holmdel Builders Association* v. *Holmdel Township* (121 N.J. 550, 583 A.2d 277 (1990)), permitted the collection of mandatory development fees for affordable housing, and the deposit of those fees into a low- and moderate-income housing trust fund. The court mandated that development fees must be consistent with the 1985 New Jersey Fair Housing Act (Section 52:27D-301) and COAH regulations. To be able to use the funds from the trust funds, municipalities must have a spending plan that provides guidelines for how the municipality will spend funds from the trust fund, such as the requirement that only a maximum of 20 percent of all collected fees may be used for administration. The spending plan must also be approved by COAH. With a few minor exceptions, a municipality cannot impose a development permit fee ordinance unless it has petitioned COAH for substantive certification (New Jersey Administrative Code, Sections 5:93-8.1 et seq.). As of 2000, 112 municipalities had development fee ordinances that had been approved by COAH (COAH 2000, 27).

As might be expected, when it comes to affordable housing production under COAH, the devil is in the details. New Jersey planning consultant Alan Mallach, AICP, contends that COAH needs to revamp its regulations, which serve as its interpretations of the *Mount Laurel II* decision, in order to produce more housing. In particular, Mallach has recommended the following changes, which (as of November 2002) have not yet been acted upon:

- *Require inclusionary developments to have a mandatory affordable housing set-aside of 20 percent of the total number of units in the development.* Mallach has called for the revision of COAH rules that generally favor a 15 percent set-aside for developments built; that allow the set-aside to be reduced to less than four units per acre where density is reduced to the same figure; and that claim set-asides in excess of 20 percent "are clearly inappropriate under any circumstances" (Mallach 2002a, 3). A 20 percent set-aside, he states, would comport with a minimum standard set in *Mount Laurel II*. In his analysis, Mallach reviewed 77 different inclusionary developments that had been approved with set-asides below 15 percent. Had these 77 developments been built at an average set-aside of 20 percent, he determined, a minimum of 4,000 additional affordable housing units would have been built (p. 4).

- *Revamp the affordability levels in COAH's regulations, which establish the maximum rents or prices that can be charged and which establish a single affordability standard for the state.* The single standard impose a "widely disparate and unequal burdens on developers building in different parts of New Jersey." Mallach recommends that the regulations need to be modified to lower the average affordability level from the current (2002) figure of 55 percent to 50 percent and be adjusted on a regional basis to reflect the disparity in median incomes (pp. 8–9).

- *Amend COAH regulations that affect the use of residential and non-residential development fees by municipalities.* Developers often favor development fees, Mallach argues, because the fees relieve them of the obligation to construct affordable units; they thus do not have to use an internal subsidy to build the units as part of the development. Mallach favors new regulations that are based on a cost analysis of the mandatory 20 percent set-aside, with an appropriate premium—one which reflects the administrative costs associated with producing the lower-income units and the perceived impact of those units on the market value of other units in the development—to account for developers' preferences for fees in lieu of constructing lower-income units. Mallach also suggests that COAH conduct a nexus study to determine the lower-income housing impact of different nonresidential development types, and the appropriate level of development fee (pp. 13–15).

- *Require the expenditure of development fee proceeds within five years after they are received.* Exceptions may be made where funds have been formally committed to a specific project which, for legitimate reason, has been delayed, or will require more than five years for completion. Mallach recommends that any funds not so used or committed must be placed in a regional pool administered by COAH, to be provided to any municipality in the region for the provision of low- and moderate-income housing pursuant to regulations that COAH would adopt (p. 16).

- *Increase the required payment by a sending municipality in a regional contribution agreement from the 2001 level of $25,000 to $40,000, and increase the payment annually thereafter by an appropriate index.* Mallach maintains that the $25,000 level in effect in 2001 understates the subsidy cost of creating an affordable housing unit and that the amount of the unit cost in an RCA should reflect the full subsidy cost (p. 19).

CALIFORNIA

Title: California Housing Element Law; Regional Housing Needs Determination

Inception: 1980

Administration: The law requires each city and county to adopt, as part of its general or comprehensive plan, a housing element that meets state standards. The primary factor in the local government's housing needs assessment must be the allocation of regional housing needs prepared by regional councils of governments (COGs) under state supervision. To establish this allocation, the California Department of Housing and Community Development (HCD) determines each COG's share of state housing needs for four income categories (very low, low-moderate, moderate, and above-moderate), thus covering the entire spectrum of housing need. Based on data provided by HCD relative to the statewide need for housing, each COG must then allocate the existing and projected need for its region. Local governments must then include the COG's allocation of regional housing need in their individual housing plans. The statutes require that a local government's housing element identify specific sites to accommodate housing needs for all household income levels. The statutes also state that local governments must "provide for sufficient sites with zoning that permits owner-occupied and rental multifamily residential use by right, including density and development standards that could accommodate and facilitate the feasibility of housing for very low- and low-income households." Local governments must also revise periodically the housing elements as appropriate, but at least every five years. HCD has the authority to review local housing elements or amendments to determine whether they "substantially comply" with the statute prior to their adoption by the governmental unit. HCD may submit written comments that the local government may then incorporate into its housing element or amendment.

Key objectives: Establish for the state, regions, counties, and cities numerical goals that describe present and future housing needs.

Accomplishments: All councils of government have completed regional housing needs assessments. Approximately 52 percent of cities and counties have housing elements in compliance with state requirements. There is no statewide total of the number of affordable housing units provided that allows comparison with total need. Of the three regions analyzed, SANDAG, the regional council of governments for San Diego County, had the lowest rate of cities and counties with housing elements that are not in compliance (11 percent). Four cities in the SANDAG region have self-certified housing elements. SANDAG (59 percent) and SCAG, the COG for the Los Angeles region (54 percent), were far ahead of ABAG (15 percent), the COG for the Bay Area, in the number of cities and counties that had housing elements in compliance with the housing element law as of August 6, 2002.

CALIFORNIA *(continued)*

Caveats: The statute does not require the state or COGs to report on the number of all affordable housing units actually constructed in compliance with regional plans. Enforcement provisions are weak. The local government may adopt the draft element or amendment without changes recommended by HCD, provided that the legislative body includes in its adopting resolution findings that indicate why it believes the element or amendment "substantially complies" with the statute, despite HCD's findings. A 2002 state "Little Hoover" Commission criticized the housing element law for lacking "teeth" and "focusing on planning, not performance," but it did not propose substantive changes that would heighten enforcement.

California statutes require each city and county to adopt "a comprehensive, long-term general plan," with seven mandatory plan elements, one of which must address housing (California Government Code, Section 65302 (1999)). The statute contains detailed requirements for the housing element, which must include six parts: review of the previous housing element; existing and projected needs assessment; resource inventory; identification of governmental and nongovernmental constraints on housing; quantified housing objectives; and housing programs (Section 65583).

Mercado affordable rental apartments in San Diego, California. The density for this project is 37.3 dwelling units per acre.

Rebecca Davis

Under the statute, the primary factor in the local government's housing needs assessment must be the allocation of regional housing needs prepared by regional councils of governments (COGs) under state supervision. To establish this allocation, the California Department of Housing and Community Development (HCD) determines each COG's share of state housing needs for four income categories (very low, low-moderate, moderate, and above-moderate), thus covering the entire spectrum of housing need. The COG must determine, with HCD's advice, each city's or county's share of the regional total. The statute does not spell out the formula the COGs are to use in allocating the need, but instead provides a list of criteria that must be met. The COGs themselves design the assumptions and methodologies and submit them to HCD. (COGs can delegate this allocation responsibility to subregional agencies, although only five subregional agencies have requested such subdelegation and all in the Los Angeles metropolitan area.) The HCD has 30 days to review the COG's determination "to ensure that it is consistent with the statewide housing need" and may revise the need figure "if necessary to obtain consistency" (Section 65584). They also submit their draft allocations for local comment and conduct public hearings on them before they become final. Local governments can then propose revisions to their assessed shares of needs before the allocations become final.[7]

Local governments must then include the COG's share of regional housing need in their individual housing plans. The statutes require that a local government's housing element identify specific sites to accommodate housing needs for all household income levels and that the government "provide for sufficient sites with zoning that permits owner-occupied and rental multifamily residential use by right, including density and development standards that could accommodate and facilitate the feasibility of housing for very low- and low-income households" (Section 65583(c)(1)). Local governments must also revise periodically the housing elements as appropriate, but at least every five years.

HCD has the authority to review draft and adopted local housing elements or amendments to determine whether they "substantially comply" with the statute prior to their adoption by the governmental unit. HCD submits written comments identifying any provisions that would need to be revised or issues that would need to be addressed in order to comply with the state housing element law. Alternatively, the local government may adopt the draft element or amendment without changes, provided that the legislative body includes in its adopting resolution findings that indicate why it believes the element or amendment "substantially complies" with the statute, despite HCD's findings. Upon adoption, the local government must then send a copy of the element or amendment to HCD for a final review.

Village Crossing Apartments, funded by the Sacramento Housing and Redevelopment Agency.

Sacramento Housing and Redevelopment Agency

Up to 25 percent of a community's obligation to identify adequate sites for housing for any income category can be met with existing units that meet specified criteria, including committed financial assistance for affordability. The statute (Sections 65583.1(c)(4) and 65583.1(c)(7)) also requires that local governments report to the legislative body and the HCD during the third year of each five-year planning period. The report is required from local governments that have included in their housing element a program to provide such units with the local governments "committed assistance." The report must describe in writing the government's progress in providing such units.

The statute does not require HCD or COGs to report on the number of affordable housing units actually constructed in compliance with the regional housing needs assessments. Section 65588(a) stipulates that each local government shall review its housing element as frequently as appropriate and prepare, in the third year of the five-year planning period, a report on progress in providing housing units, which includes rehabilitation and new construction. Each city or county planning department must provide a copy of this report to HCD and the state Office of Planning and Research, but not all departments have done so, and the reports are incomplete for the state and have not been summarized.[8] Therefore, it is not possible to determine how many units of affordable housing have been constructed on a statewide basis as a result of the law. As is the case in other state programs, it could be that the law has been providing *opportunities* for the construction of affordable housing through inclusionary zoning and other techniques (as in New Jersey); however, these opportunities may not be translating into the actual construction of affordable housing units.

Beyond these reporting requirements, HCD and the COGs have no authority to enforce compliance with the law, beyond providing the advisory analysis of whether the element or amendment complies with the statute, and notifying the attorney general of jurisdictions with prolonged noncompliance. If the city or county disagrees with HCD's review of its housing element or amendment, it may adopt the draft without changes, provided it adopts findings that explain the reasons it believes the element or amendment "substantially complies" with the statute despite HCD's views to the contrary. Such findings do not, however, change HCD's representation of the compliance state of the housing element. Jurisdictions without a housing element found in compliance by HCD are also ineligible for or are disadvantaged in competing for allocation of certain state-administered funds. A local government whose housing element or amendment HCD has found to substantially comply with the requirements of state law does have one advantage: the statute grants a "rebuttable presumption of validity" in favor of the local government in any legal challenge to the element's validity (Section 65589.3).

TABLE 4-2
STATUS OF HOUSING ELEMENTS IN CALIFORNIA AS OF AUGUST 6, 2002

Status	Number of Cities
In Compliance	276 (52%)
Out of Compliance	153 (29%)
Plan Due	45 (8%)
Plan Under Review	52 (10%)
Self-Certification	4 (0.8%)
Total	**530 (100%)**

Source: California Department of Housing and Community Development, *Housing Element Compliance Report*, http://www.hcd.ca.gov/hpd/hrc/plan/he/status.pdf (accessed August 12, 2002).

Program Results

A total of 530 jurisdictions are required to have an adopted housing element as part of their local general plan (California HCD 2002; Section 65580-65589.8). As of August 6, 2002, 52 percent of those cities and counties that were required to adopt an approved housing element had adopted housing elements that were in compliance with California's housing element law; 29 percent either had adopted housing elements that were out of compliance with the law or had submitted draft housing elements to the HCD but had not adopted those housing elements (regardless of whether HCD found the draft housing element to be in or out of compliance with the state law). Another 8 percent of cities or counties had not yet submitted their housing element for that planning period, and 10 percent had submitted draft housing elements that were under HCD review (California HCD 2002b).

Less than 1 percent of cities or counties had been self-certified, which is a program that allows cities and counties in the San Diego region to self-certify the housing elements of their own general plans (see discussion below). Table 4-2 details the status of housing elements in California.

Housing element compliance figures from December 2000, when compared with the figures in Table 4-2, indicate that the number of cities and counties in compliance with California's housing element law has decreased by 11 percent while the number of cities and counties which have adopted housing elements not in compliance has increased by 18 percent (California HCD 2002b; California HCD Division of Housing Policy Development 2000).

While the California statutes (Section 65587(b) and (c)) do permit private action to compel a local government to meet its legal obligations, the state courts are often reluctant to intervene in local land-use decisions (Field 1993). According to an HCD housing policy analyst, lawsuits arise more frequently from housing advocacy groups than private developers (Maus 2000). Challenges to local governments' housing elements under Section 65587—made on the grounds that the elements did not "substantially comply" with the housing element law—have produced mixed results.[9]

Table 4-3 shows compliance with the housing element law in the Association of Bay Area Governments (ABAG) for the San Francisco region, the San Diego Association of Governments (SANDAG), for the San Diego region, and the Southern California Association of Governments (SCAG) for the Los Angeles region. HCD's *Housing Element Compliance Report* is updated often, and Table 4-3 may not reflect the most current information available. Readers of this report should check the HCD website (http://www.hcd.ca.gov) for the most current information on the status of housing elements in California.

TABLE 4-3
STATUS OF HOUSING ELEMENTS IN ABAG, SANDAG, AND SCAG REGIONS AS OF AUGUST 6, 2002

Region	In Compliance	Out of Compliance	In Review	Due	Self Certified	Total
ABAG	17 (15%)	45 (42%)	22 (20%)	24 (22%)	N/A	108
SANDAG	11 (59%)	2 (11%)	2 (11%)	0	4 (21%)	19
SCAG	103 (54%)	75 (39%)	14 (7%)	0	N/A	192

Source: California Department of Housing and Community Development, *Housing Element Compliance Report*, http://www.hcd.ca.gov/hpd/hrc/plan/he/status.pdf (accessed August 12, 2002).

SANDAG has the lowest rate of cities and counties with housing elements that are out of compliance (11 percent). Four cities in the SANDAG region have self-certified housing elements. The number of cities and counties in SANDAG (59 percent) and SCAG (54 percent) that have housing elements in compliance were far ahead of those in ABAG (15 percent). However, many of the housing elements in the ABAG region were under review (20 percent) or due (22 percent) as of August 6, 2002. Housing elements are reviewed by HCD on a staggered cycle, and housing elements from ABAG were recently scheduled for review, which may explain the high number of elements in that region that are in review or due. According to HCD, plans that are past due are considered in compliance once they are adopted, reviewed, and found in compliance. Meanwhile, if their old housing elements have expired, local governments are vulnerable to lawsuits (Westmont 2002).

A May 2002 report by the State of California's Little Hoover Commission has called for reform of the housing element law to ensure that local governments "effectively plan for and actually produce affordable housing." The report criticizes the housing element law for lacking "teeth" and "focusing on planning, not performance" (Little Hoover Commission 2002, 21–22). It notes that the state does not have a mechanism to track construction of new housing units so as to compare them to local and regional quotas, and that most local jurisdictions fail to complete required annual progress reports on their general plans, including the housing element. The report also states that some 2.4 million households (22 percent of the state) need some form of housing assistance and that the figure will likely rise to 3.7 million by 2022. "The housing element law has failed to ensure that the State's goals for housing--particularly affordable housing--are met," the report concludes. "The State can no longer simply encourage and hope that more than 500 local jurisdictions collectively do what is in the best interest of California and its most vulnerable citizens. It must assume a far more assertive stance than it has in the past" (p. 23). The report goes on to recommend a series of measures to strengthen the law:

1. *Strengthen and enforce the housing element law.* HCD, the commission asserts, should clarify what is required of local jurisdictions to ensure that the requirements of the housing element law are measurable. It should prepare a model housing element to assist local governments in complying with the law.

2. *Reform the housing needs allocation process.* The process "should better reflect local issues and trends. It should allow growth projections used by COGs for transportation and air quality plans to be used as the basis for housing growth projection and incorporate job projections" (pp. 23-24). (The commission did comment that HCD has opposed the use of projections generated by COGs and local governments, claiming that there is too much potential to inflict political bias into the process.) The commission advocates additional state resources and assistance from COGs to help local governments track building permits or occupancy permits and report the data to the state.

3. *Link fiscal incentives to housing production.* Observing that the state distributes a variety of funds such as federal Community Development Block Grant funds, transportation monies, and parks and open space grants, the commission proposes linking housing element compliance and housing performance in awarding state or federal grants and loans (p. 24). The state, it suggests, should pursue agreements with COGs and local governments in their regions on a set of incentives and penalties that are best aligned with local circumstances (p. 28).

Despite its tough language on the need for the state to be "more assertive" and the housing element law to have "teeth," the Little Hoover Commission stopped short of endorsing strong enforcement measures. It did acknowledge that some state policy makers advocated stiff penalties for jurisdictions that fail to comply with the housing element law. One of them, Senator Joseph Dunn, authored Senate Bill 910, which proposed penalties for noncompliance, including withholding a percentage of highway maintenance and repair funds from local governments that do not adopt a housing element and levying fines when a housing element is found by a court to be invalid. However, the commission did not lend its support to this bill. SB 910 was approved by the state Senate but did not reach an Assembly vote.

The following sections describe the individual regional housing plans prepared by the Association of Bay Area Governments (ABAG) for the San Francisco region, the San Diego Association of Governments (SANDAG), for the San Diego region, and the Southern California Association of Governments (SCAG) for the Los Angeles region. The sections also describe the status of local housing elements in those regions.

Despite its tough language on the need for the state to be "more assertive" and the housing element law to have "teeth," the Little Hoover Commission stopped short of endorsing strong enforcement measures.

Association of Bay Area Governments (ABAG), San Francisco

The San Francisco Bay region is composed of nine counties, 101 cities, over 5,600 square miles of unincorporated land area, and had a population of 6,783,760 in 2000 (ABAG 2001a, 9, Friedman 2002). ABAG (2001a, 9) estimates that the region's population will increase about 21 percent between 1990 and 2010, and the region is expected to add more than 1 million jobs in that period (ABAG 2001a, 11).

Only 16 percent of Bay Area households can afford a median-price home in the region, with that number dropping as low as 10 percent in San Francisco. . . . The housing shortage in the Bay Area means that workers will need to move farther from job centers to find affordable housing, resulting in dispersed development patterns and longer commuting times.

Only 16 percent of Bay Area households can afford a median-price home in the region, with that number dropping as low as 10 percent in San Francisco (ABAG 2001a). One reason for the Bay Area's housing crisis is housing growth's failure to keep pace with job growth. Between 1990 and 2000, the Bay Area produced approximately 500,000 new jobs but fewer than 200,000 new housing units (ABAG 2001a, 13). According to a recent independent study of housing issues and vacant or underused land in the Silicon Valley, "The number of new homes that Silicon Valley could produce based on its current residential land supply and average number of homes built per acre can only meet 50–66 percent of its projected demand based on household and employment growth projections for this region" (Strategic Economics 1999, 13).

The housing shortage in the Bay Area means that workers will need to move farther from job centers to find affordable housing, resulting in dispersed development patterns and longer commuting times. ABAG estimates that the region will see a 10 percent increase in the average travel time to work between 1990 and 2020 and an estimated 249 percent increase in congestion, measured as average daily vehicle hours of delay (ABAG 2001a, 17).

The Regional Housing Needs Determination (RHND) process for 1999—2006 began in March 1999, and ABAG first released its RHND housing allocations in December 1999. Following a 90-day review and revision period, ABAG revised its allocation methodology and released revised allocations in June 2000. Following the revision and appeals process, ABAG certified the final housing needs allocation numbers in March 2001 (Metropolitan Transportation Commission 1999).

ABAG's regional share of the state's housing need is 230,743 housing units, calculated by the HCD in accordance with California's housing element law (Section 65302), as discussed above. ABAG is responsible for using its own methodology to assign this allocation to Bay Area local governments and must divide the allocated housing units by income distribution categories (very low, low, moderate, and above-moderate). Once the distribution is determined, each city and county in the region must plan for the level of growth assigned by this process and update their general plan housing elements accordingly.

To determine RHND allocations, ABAG established an advisory committee to develop a methodology that incorporates the planning considerations required by state law and that fairly distributes the HCD-established housing need throughout Bay Area municipalities. The advisory committee developed the following set of methodology goals:

1. Base growth upon current city boundaries, as opposed to sphere of influence boundaries, when determining RHND allocations.

2. Address over- and under-concentration of low-income housing throughout the region.

3. Use the most recent, available, and up-to-date data source for total number of households in 1999.

4. Use *Projections 2000* to determine growth. *Projections 2000* is the report of ABAG's biennial forecast of population, housing, jobs, and income for the nine-county San Francisco Bay region.

5. Address state housing element law requirements.

6. Incorporate ABAG's smart growth policies.

7. Use methodology calculations that are simple, easy to understand and explain. (ABAG 2001a, 41)

ABAG's smart growth policies are based on its platform on growth management adopted by the ABAG general assembly in 1992. The platform addresses six primary subjects, including (1) a coordinated, integrated planning process; (2) local, subregional, and regional responsibilities; (3) consolidation of single-purpose agencies; (4) conflict resolution; (5) fiscal reform; and (6) housing. Each of these subjects contains several principles. The housing principle calls for restructuring needs assessments and the review process: "The housing-needs determination process should be restructured to better integrate overall regional and subregional growth management strategies. In addition, the housing-element review process should pay greater attention to performance and less to process. The state should delegate housing element review and certification to the regional planning body, if the governing board of the regional body elects to take on such a responsibility" (ABAG 2002b).

The ABAG Executive Board issued three policy directives to ensure that the goals identified by the housing methodology committee were implemented in the RHND methodology, as described below :

1. Incorporate a 50 percent jobs/50 percent household weighted ratio in the RHND methodology to address the jobs/housing issues in the region.

2. Assign 75 percent of the unincorporated SOI allocations to the cities, and 25 percent to the counties in order to promote development in urbanized areas rather than on unincorporated lands.

3. Establish guidelines that allow jurisdictions to redistribute the RHND allocations on a countywide basis during the 90-day review and revision period. (ABAG 2001a, 41)

To address these goals and directives, RHND methodology is based on each municipality's current household and employment growth and its current boundaries. The RHND methodology includes five components: household growth; employment growth; employment (jobs)/household ratio adjustment; an SOI allocation adjustment; and an income distribution calculation.

To determine household growth the RHND methodology uses two sources of data: the California Department of Finance (DOF) estimate of households in 1999, and ABAG's own forecast of households for 2006. Household growth is determined by subtracting DOF estimates of households in 1999 from ABAG's forecast of households in 2006. This household growth is then divided by total regional household growth, which derives that municipality's share of regional household growth. For example, as shown below, the DOF estimate of households in 1999 for San Francisco was 322,594, and the ABAG estimate for 2006 was 312,679. Therefore, the household growth for 1999–2006 is 9,915. The total regional household growth is 177,318, so San Francisco's share of household growth is 5.59 percent (ABAG 2002a).

The second component of the RHND methodology is the determination of each municipality's share of employment growth in the region. The methodology for determining employment growth uses ABAG's estimate of employment in 1999 and its 2006 forecasts (ABAG 2001a, 43). In the San Francisco example, the estimate for employment in 1999 is 614,948, which is subtracted from the 2006 forecast of 665,958, resulting in a figure for

ABAG's smart growth policies are based on its platform on growth management adopted by the ABAG general assembly in 1992.

Affordable housing in the Bay Area, California

employment growth of 51,010. The regional projection of employment growth is 422,754. Accordingly, San Francisco's share of the region's employment growth is 12.07 percent (ABAG 2002a).

The third component of the RHND methodology is the employment (job)/housing ratio adjustment. This component weights by 50 percent both the municipality's share of employment growth (as discussed above) and its share of household growth. The figure is then multiplied by the HCD-determined regional need to calculate the municipality's need (ABAG 2001a, 43). In the San Francisco example, the share of employment growth was 12.07 percent, which is then multiplied by 0.5 and added to the share of household growth, 5.59 percent after it is multiplied by 0.5. The resulting number is then multiplied by the regional need as determined by HCD (230,743), resulting in a jurisdiction need of 20,372 (ABAG 2002a).

The fourth component of the RHND methodology is the SOI allocation adjustment. Because the RHND allocations are based on current city boundaries, they exclude unincorporated areas that are within the city's SOI. The unincorporated areas of each county receive RHND allocations, which include those areas of a city's SOI. The methodology that determines these allocations assigns the county's unincorporated, mainly nonurbanized areas a RHND housing allocation that includes part of the growth being planned by nearby cities. However, in recognition of ABAG's smart growth policies, which seek to promote growth in urbanized areas, the RHND allocation for unincorporated areas is divided among the cities and counties. The amount of housing need associated with the growth in the SOI areas is calculated in the same way the cities' housing needs are calculated, and then subtracted from the unincorporated portions of each municipality. The allocation of the SOI housing need is based on each city's annexation and development plans and growth potential in that city's SOI for the next RHND allocation period (Amoroso 2002b). Each city is assigned 75 percent of this portion of the RHND allocation and the remaining 25 percent is assigned to each county. The resulting figure is the total projected need for each municipality (ABAG 2001a, 43). In the San Francisco example, there was no SOI need added to the jurisdiction need because there are no unincorporated areas surrounding it (ABAG 2002a).

Under the California housing element law, ABAG is also required to distribute the total RHND allocation for each local government by income category (very low, low, moderate, above-moderate). In order to reduce the concentration in cities and counties that already have disproportionately high proportions of lower-income households, ABAG's methodology shifts each local government's income distribution (based on the 1990 census) 50 percent towards the regional average. The distance of each local government's existing income percentage from the regional average determines the amount of adjustment applied (ABAG 2001a, 43). For example, in 1999, 31 percent of the residents in San Francisco and 20.5 percent of the residents in the ABAG region were categorized as very low income. When the San Francisco percentage is moved halfway toward the regional percentage, the resulting figure is 25.8 percent, which becomes the city's 1999 income percentage for the very low-income category. This means that 25.8 percent, or 5,244 housing units, of San Francisco's total projected need of 20,372 housing units should be for very low-income households (Amoroso 2002a). Figure 4-2 and Table 4-4 show the formula applied to the City and County of San Francisco, as discussed above.

Program Results

Prior to ABAG's adoption of its allocations, it reviewed comments and revisions proposed by 77 Bay Area jurisdictions. Twenty-nine jurisdictions requested changes to their RHND allocations, 20 of which provided an alternate figure. With the exception of one jurisdiction—ABAG staff supported the revision because it involved a shift in units from Santa Clara County to the city of Cupertino, due to an annexation—the ABAG staff recommended that all other requests for revisions to allocations be denied (ABAG 2001b). The rationale in most cases was that, in order to be granted, the revision had to comply with the requirements for a revision contained in the California housing element law: the revision must be based on available data and the same accepted planning methodology that determined the RHND allocations for the jurisdiction. Revisions, noted ABAG staff, must also consider the overall regional total assigned by HCD. The effect of these requirements is that one jurisdiction's allocation cannot be lowered without increasing the allocation of other jurisdictions. ABAG staff also recommended denials when the requested basis was a growth management ordinance or some other device that limited the construction of housing units. Under the housing element law, any ordinance, policy, or standard of a city that directly limits the number of residential building permits or of buildable lots that may be developed cannot be a justification for a reduction in the share of a city or county of the total regional housing need. This policy thus prevents local governments from adopting ordinances or policies that would frustrate the achievement of regional housing goals.

FIGURE 4-2
ABAG REGIONAL HOUSING DISTRIBUTION MODEL FOR CITY AND COUNTY OF SAN FRANCISCO 1999-2006 RHND ALLOCATION PERIOD

Households 2006	322,594
Households 1999	- 312,679
Household Growth	= 9,915
Regional Household Growth	177,318
Share of Household Growth	= 5.59%
Jobs 2006	665,958
Jobs 1999	- 614,948
Job Growth	= 51,010
Regional Job Growth	422,754
Share of Job Growth	= 12.07%
Share of Job Growth	(12.07%
Weight Factor	* .5
Share of Household Growth	+ 5.59%
Weight Factor	* .5)
HCD Regional Need	* 230,743
Jurisdiction Need	= 20,372
Unincorporated SOI Need	+ 0
Total Projected Need	**= 20,372**

TABLE 4-4
ABAG ALLOCATION OF TOTAL PROJECTED HOUSING NEED BY INCOME CATEGORY FOR CITY AND COUNTY OF SAN FRANCISO, 1999–20%

Income Category	1990 Income Percentage	1990 Regional Income Percentage	1999 Income Percentage	RHND Allocation
Very Low	31.0%	20.5%	25.8%	5,244
Low	10.0%	10.9%	10.5%	2,126
Moderate	29.0%	26.4%	27.8%	5,639
Above-Moderate	30.0%	42.3%	36.0%	7,363

Source: Association of Bay Area Governments "ABAG Regional Housing Distribution Model—San Francisco," http://www.abag.ca.gov/cgi-bin/rhnd_meth.pl (accessed July 22, 2002).

Consequently, ABAG adopted its RHND allocations for the 1999–2006 housing element cycle in March 2001. Table 4-5 summarizes the RHND allocations by county. As Table 4-5 indicates, Santa Clara County has the largest population and also has the highest number of affordable housing units allocated to it. In all counties, the allocation for above-moderate-income homes is larger than the rest of the income categories, and the allocation for low-income housing is smaller than the rest of the income categories.

TABLE 4-5
REGIONAL HOUSING NEEDS DETERMINATION BY COUNTY
IN ABAG REGION, 1999-2006

County	2000 Population[1]	Very Low Income	Low Income	Moderate Income	Above-Moderate Income	Total Projected Need
Alameda	1,443,741	9,910	5,138	12,476	19,269	46,793
Contra Costa	948,816	6,638	3,782	8,859	15,649	34,710
Marin	247,289	1,241	618	1,726	2,930	6,515
Napa	124,279	1,434	1,019	1,775	2,835	7,063
San Francisco	776,733	5,244	2,126	5,639	7,363	20,372
San Mateo	707,161	3,214	1,567	4,305	7,219	16,305
Santa Clara	1,682,585	11,424	5,173	15,659	25,735	57,991
Solano	384,542	3,697	2,638	4,761	7,585	18,681
Sonoma	458,614	4,411	3,029	5,879	8,994	22,313
Total	**6,783,760**	**47,258**	**25,090**	**61,079**	**97,579**	**230,743**

Source: ABAG, "Regional Housing Needs: 1999–2006 Allocation," http://www.abag.ca.gov/cgi-bin/rhnd_allocation.pl (accessed July 22, 2002).

1. Association of Bay Area Governments, "Bay Area Census," http://census.abag.ca.gov/ (accessed July 24, 2002).

ABAG attempted to collect data on housing production by jurisdiction for the period January 1, 1988, to December 31, 1998, by mailing two requests for housing production data (July 1999 and October 1999) to all of the Bay Area's cities and counties. After extensive follow-up, ABAG received responses from approximately 75 percent of the jurisdictions (Baird+Driskell 1999, 1). Although the data are questionable because of a lack of consistency and other problems (see below), the data collection process was important because it established a jurisdictional contacts database.

Following the data collection process, ABAG hired a consultant to complete and review the process. The consultant found that there was no consistent methodology for categorizing and counting housing units and that the majority of jurisdictions lack staff, time, and resources to keep regular housing production data. Also, the majority of jurisdictions did not keep records of housing units produced either through new construction, acquisition, rehabilitation, or conservation.

During the first round of data collection, many jurisdictions complained that the lack of a common framework for organizing and counting housing units made data impossible to compare across jurisdictions (Baird+Driskell 1999, 4). The second round was designed to overcome this problem. However, the second round of data collection was also plagued by incomplete and inaccurate data.

Jurisdictions rarely maintain ongoing housing production records and require many staff hours to unearth data from several sources. This combination of a lack of data and of staff resources resulted in 12.5 percent of respondents indicating that they were unable to provide complete data, with many jurisdictions providing incomplete responses. The accuracy of the data collected is questionable since many of the jurisdictions did not respond to all or some of the income categories. Additionally, since jurisdictions used varying definitions for each income category, the data does not conform to a common standard. For example, San Francisco City/County, known for having a high-demand housing market, unexpectedly reported 5,190 very low-, 2,503 low-, 844 moderate-, and no above-moderate-income units built between January 1, 1988, and December 31, 1998. Further, some jurisdictions only reported certain types of housing, such as only assisted units (Antioch, Marin County, Dixon), or only new construction (Danville).

Table 4-6 summarizes the results of the housing production data collection process. The original data contain information on very low-, low-, moderate-, and above-moderate-income categories; however, the above-moderate-income category was omitted from Table 4-6 because it contained the highest number of omissions. It is important to keep in mind that the data are incomplete, are time sensitive, contain errors, and do not conform to a common standard. Sometimes the best data are not very good. Still, they give a general indication of housing production levels over a 10-year period.

A comparison of the figures in Table 4-6 with the 1988–1998 fair-share allocations shows that every county produced fewer affordable housing units than their fair-share allocations, except for one income level in Sonoma County, which produced 692 more moderate-income units than their fair-share allocation of 4,949. The average difference between housing production (from Table 4-6) and the fair-share allocations (from the 1988–1998 RHND process) was: 3,648 very low-, 2,811 low-, and 2,770 moderate-income housing units (ABAG 1989, 45–52). For the very low-income category, the difference ranged from a shortage of 11,440 housing units in Santa Clara County to a shortage of 427 housing units in San Francisco County. For the low-income category, the difference ranged from a shortage of 9,332 housing units in Santa Clara to a shortage of 660 housing units in Sonoma County.

HCD collects information on the status of housing element compliance. Table 4-7 shows the status of Bay Area local governments housing elements as of August 6, 2002.

Table 4-7 indicates that the plurality of housing elements (42 percent) in the Bay Area are out of compliance with the housing element law or governments have not adopted a housing element (regardless if HCD has deemed the element to be in or out of compliance). Some 22 percent of jurisdictions in the Bay area have not submitted housing elements for the current cycle (listed as *due*), 15 percent have submitted housing elements that are in compliance with the law (listed as *in*), and 20 percent have submitted housing elements that are under review at HCD (listed as *in review*) (California HCD 2002b).

Marin County has no local governments that are in compliance with the housing element law. Santa Clara County has the highest percentage of municipalities with housing elements that are in compliance with the law (31 percent); however, it also has the highest percentage of local governments with housing elements out of compliance. Marin County has the second highest percentage of local governments with housing elements due (75 percent), behind the City and County of San Francisco, which itself had a housing element that was due (the city and county of San Francisco contains only one jurisdiction).

Compliance by Bay Area jurisdictions with California's housing element law does not fare well when compared with the entire state of California. There are 37 percent fewer local governments in compliance in the Bay Area than in all of California. Also, there are 13 percent more local governments out of compliance, 16 percent more cities with plans due, and 10 percent more local governments with plans under review in the Bay Area compared to all of California. Housing elements are reviewed by HCD on a staggered cycle and housing

TABLE 4-6
HOUSING PRODUCTION IN BAY AREA COUNTIES, 1988-1998[1]

Housing Production by Income Level, 1988–1998

County	Very Low Income	Low Income	Moderate Income	Total Production (very low, low, and moderate Income)	Remarks
Alameda	5,261	2,641	9,335	17,237	Four governments with no response, one reporting zero in each category
Contra Costa	4,111	3,741	9,028	16,880	Seven governments with no response, one reporting zero in each category, one reporting "beds not counted", one reporting "nd" in one category
Marin	513	635	1,183	2,331	Four governments with no response, one reporting "nd" in one category
Napa	302	312	953	1,567	One government with no response
San Francisco	5,190	2,503	844	8,537	
San Mateo	2,687	1,286	2,402	6,375	Three governments with no response, three reporting "nd" in one category
Santa Clara	2,769	1,817	3,407	7,993	Three governments with no response, one reporting "nd" in two categories
Solano	1,296	1,854	4,473	7,623	Two governments with no response, one reporting "nd" in each category
Sonoma	3,462	3,397	5,641	12,500	Three with no response
Total	**25,591**	**18,186**	**37,266**	**81,043**	

Source: ABAG "Summary of Results: Housing Production Data Collection," http://www.abag.ca.gov/planning/housingneeds/pastproduction.htm (accessed May 31, 2002).

1. The ABAG web site shows the following disclaimer when accessing the housing production data: *The Summary of Results— Housing Production Data Collection* was submitted to ABAG in 2001 by cities and counties in the San Francisco Bay Area. The data is time sensitive, may contain defects or errors and may not conform to a common standard. ABAG does not warrant or represent that the data will meet the user's needs or expectations. Access to this data is conditioned on the user(s) agreement to hold ABAG harmless for any liability allegedly caused by any use of the data. By accessing *Summary Results—Housing Production Data Collection,* user agrees to the terms set forth above. http://www.abag.ca.gov/planning/housingneeds/pastproduction.htm (accessed August 21, 2002).

elements in the ABAG region were recently due in 2002, which is probably a factor for the low rate of compliance in the ABAG region.

An independent study by two nonprofit groups of the housing elements of 40 key cities and counties in the Bay Area (out of 109 total jurisdictions), released in June 2002, found a disappointing local government track record in meeting long-term housing goals. The study, *San Francisco Bay Area Housing Crisis Report Card,* grades the housing elements on a variety of factors.[10] A chief finding is that from 1988 to 1998, only 32 percent of the planned affordable housing contained in these communities' housing elements was actually built. At the same time, these cities and counties produced 117 percent of the above-moderate-income housing needed, affordable only to those families earning more than 120 percent of the median income.

TABLE 4-7
STATUS OF HOUSING ELEMENTS FOR CITIES
AND COUNTIES IN THE BAY AREA AS OF AUGUST 6, 2002

County	In Compliance	Out of Compliance	In Review	Due	Total
Alameda	2 (13%)	7 (47%)	4 (27%)	2 (13%)	15
Contra Costa	2 (10%)	10 (53%)	4 (21%)	3 (16%)	19
Marin	0	2 (17%)	1 (8%)	9 (75%)	12
Napa	1 (17%)	2 (33%)	2 (33%)	1 (17%)	6
San Francisco	0	0	0	1 (100%)	1
San Mateo	3 (14%)	9 (43%)	4 (19%)	5 (23%)	21
Santa Clara	5 (31%)	9 (56%)	2 (13%)	0	16
Solano	2 (25%)	2 (25%)	2 (25%)	2 (25%)	8
Sonoma	2 (20%)	4 (40%)	3 (30%)	1 (10%)	10
Total	**17 (15%)**	**45 (42%)**	**22 (20%)**	**24 (22%)**	**108**

Source: California Department of Housing and Community Development, *Housing Element Compliance Report*, http://www.hcd.ca.gov/hpd/hrc/plan/he/status.pdf (accessed August 12, 2002).

The report evaluates the housing elements and divides the 40 communities into five groups: an "honor roll" (18 percent); good (10 percent); needs improvement (15 percent); incomplete (28 percent, which were communities whose housing element was not available as of April 1, 2002); and fail (29 percent, where the housing element was missing a requirement component).[11] Communities such as Berkeley, East Palo Alto, Palo Alto, Petaluma (which has a longstanding growth management program), San Jose, Santa Clara City, and Sunnyvale all made the honor roll. The report praises their efforts in establishing jobs-housing linkage programs, mandatory set-asides for affordable housing in market-rate housing projects, and use of redevelopment funds to support the construction and rehabilitation of affordable housing.

According to the *Report Card*, many communities fail to zone enough land to encourage apartments and condominiums or have burdensome regulations, such as requiring each apartment to have more parking spaces than are required for a single-family home. The report also criticizes the fact that "[m]any places around the Bay Area have far more available land designated for commercial uses than residential development" (The Non-Profit Housing Association of Northern California and the Greenbelt Alliance 2002, 10).

The report recommends that the fair-share housing law in California "would be far more effective if targeted incentives and consequences were tied to localities actually meeting—not just planning for—their need for a full spectrum of housing" (p. 9). The report also points to the threat of state laws that authorize private lawsuits when a municipality fails to satisfy housing element requirements. It describes a suit brought by a low-income renter against the city of Folsom, where Folsom ultimately settled by entering into an agreement to rezone land for affordable housing (in this case, 128 acres of land at densities feasible for 2,900 low- and very low-income multifamily homes). The city also agreed to increase its set-aside of redevelopment funds from 20 to 25 percent for affordable housing, create a housing trust fund from a $1.10 per square foot charge on commercial and industrial development, and adopt an inclusionary zoning ordinance that required new residential developments to include 10 percent very low-income units plus 5 percent low-income units, or pay in-lieu fees.

An independent study by two nonprofit groups of the housing elements of 40 key cities and counties in the Bay Area (out of 109 total jurisdictions), released in June 2002, found a disappointing local government track record in meeting long-term housing goals.

San Diego Association of Governments (SANDAG), San Diego

The San Diego Association of Governments (SANDAG) region is composed entirely of San Diego County and is 4,260.5 square miles in area. There are 18 cities and an unincorporated area in the region, which was home to 2,813,833 people in 2000. The city of San Diego has the largest population in the region, with 1,223,400 residents in 2000. Del Mar has the smallest population in the region, with 4,389 residents in 2000.

Parkview Terrace affordable rental housing, developed by Bowron Group Limited Partnership, in Poway, California, SANDAG region.

Rebecca Davis

The SANDAG region grew by more than 431,000 people (or 18.1 percent) between January 1990 and January 2000. During that time the largest share of the region's new housing units were constructed in the region's largest jurisdictions: the city of San Diego and the unincorporated area, with 42 percent and 15 percent of all new housing construction, respectively. According to SANDAG, the region's current rate of population growth will require the construction of approximately 17,000 housing units per year (SANDAG 2000b, 2). As of January 2000, 59 percent of the region's housing was single family, 36 percent multiple family, and 5 percent mobile homes. However, SANDAG believes that these ratios may be shifting: "Although multiple family dwelling units have accounted for about 36 percent of the region's housing stock for many years, this may soon change. Only about 23 percent of the units constructed in 1999 were multiple family, which constitutes a trend we have seen for several years now" (SANDAG 2000b, 7).

In 1995 SANDAG sponsored a bill (A.B. 1715) for a pilot program to allow jurisdictions in the SANDAG region to self-certify their housing elements. SANDAG's self-certification process has three purposes: "(1) to give jurisdictions more flexibility in how they meet affordable housing goals, (2) to focus on housing production rather than paper generation, and (3) to eliminate the State Department of Housing and Community Development's (HCD) review and certification of the updated housing elements" (SANDAG 2000a, 135). The regional share numbers, according to SANDAG staff, are a planning goal, where the focus is on providing adequate sites for affordable housing, while the self-certification goals are actual production goals (Baldwin 2002a).

Through the self-certification process, a jurisdiction in the SANDAG region may opt out of the HCD review of its housing element if its affordable housing goals have been met. It is important to note that the methodology used to determine the self-certification goal is different from the methodology used to determine each jurisdiction's fair-share housing need. The following paragraphs describe these goals and methodologies separately.

SANDAG's current Regional Housing Needs Statement (RHNS) covers the 1999–2004 cycle. The RHNS was developed during the summer and fall of 1998 (SANDAG 2001a 9). Technical guidance came from two committees: the Housing Element Advisory Committee, established to review state housing element laws and legislation, and the San Diego Regional Partners in Homeownership Committee, a public/private partnership formed to identify specific strategies, priorities, and actions to help obtain increased homeownership in the SANDAG region (SANDAG 2001a, 11).

FIGURE 4-3
PRICE OF HOME PEOPLE CAN AFFORD AT DIFFERENT INCOME LEVELS IN THE SAN DIEGO REGION

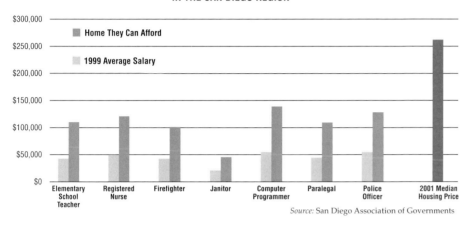

Source: San Diego Association of Governments

The methodology for jurisdictions that elect not to participate in the self-certification process is based on SANDAG's *2020 Cities/County* forecasts for population, employment, and housing in the region. The methodology for assigning each jurisdiction's fair-share allocation by income category is similar to ABAG's method: a jurisdiction's existing share of lower-income households is subtracted from the regional averages (21 percent very low, 17 percent low, 23 percent moderate, 39 percent above-moderate), and that difference is added to the regional average, which is that jurisdiction's need for that income level (SANDAG 2000a, 125).

SANDAG's fair-share housing goal for the 1999–2004 housing element cycle is 95,479. It is allocated among jurisdictions and income categories as shown in Table 4-8.

The first row of Table 4-8 shows the regional share of each income level; for example, 21 percent of the residents in the SANDAG region fall into the very low-income category. The other rows show the regional fair-share allocation for each city in the region in addition to the percentage of that city's total allocation that falls into each category. For example, Carlsbad's total share of the regional fair-share goal is 6,214 housing opportunities. Of that total fair-share allocation, 28 percent (1,770) should be opportunities for very low-income residents, 23 percent (1,417) should be for low-income residents, 23 percent (1,436) should be for moderate-income residents, and 26 percent (1,591) should be for above-moderate-income residents. Every jurisdiction's percentage of moderate-income housing is the same (23 percent). The adjustment for the very low- and low-income categories was taken as a reduction from the above-moderate-income category.

The share of the very low-income goal ranges from 2 percent in National City to 32 percent in Poway. The share of the low-income goal ranges from 8 percent in Imperial Beach to 26 percent in Del Mar. The share of the above-moderate-income goal ranges from 20 percent in Poway to 66 percent in National City.

TABLE 4-8
REGIONAL HOUSING NEEDS IN THE SANDAG REGION, 1999-2004

Jurisdiction	Population in 2000[1]	Very Low Income (21%)	Low Income (17%)	Moderate Income (23%)	Above Moderate Income (39%)	Total Regional Fair-Share Allocation (1999-2004)
Carlsbad	78,247	1,770 (28%)	1,417 (23%)	1,436 (23%)	1,591 (26%)	6,214
Chula Vista	173,556	1,889 (18%)	1,535 (15%)	2,388 (23%)	4,589 (44%)	10,401
Coronado	24,100	24 (30%)	17 (21%)	18 (23%)	21 (26%)	80
Del Mar	4,389	7 (30%)	6 (26%)	5 (22%)	5 (22%)	23
El Cajon	94,869	118 (15%)	97 (12%)	185 (23%)	409 (51%)	809
Encinitas	58,014	441 (28%)	340 (21%)	366 (23%)	437 (28%)	1,584
Escondido	133,559	504 (19%)	391 (15%)	598 (23%)	1,110 (43%)	2,603
Imperial Beach	26,992	12 (13%)	8 (8%)	22 (23%)	53 (56%)	95
La Mesa	54,749	141 (20%)	109 (16%)	159 (23%)	284 (41%)	693
Lemon Grove	24,918	87 (18%)	79 (16%)	113 (23%)	212 (43%)	491
National City	54,260	9 (2%)	34 (9%)	86 (23%)	249 (66%)	378
Ocanside	161,029	1,474 (22%)	962 (14%)	1,561 (23%)	2,784 (41%)	6,781
Poway	48,044	232 (32%)	174 (24%)	166 (23%)	145 (20%)	717
San Diego	1,223,400	7,463 (19%)	6,797 (17%)	9,137 (23%)	16,388 (41%)	39,785
San Marcos	54,977	761 (21%)	478 (13%)	843 (23%)	1,585 (43%)	3,667
Santee	52,975	729 (27%)	478 (18%)	622 (23%)	862 (32%)	2,691
Solana Beach	12,979	27 (26%)	26 (25%)	24 (23%)	28 (27%)	105
Vista	89,857	540 (20%)	395 (14%)	631 (23%)	1,178 (43%)	2,744
Unincorporated	N/A	3,823 (24%)	2,888 (18%)	3,600 (23%)	5,307 (34%)	15,618
Total	**2,813,833**	**20,051 (21%)**	**16,231 (17%)**	**21,960 (23%)**	**37,237 (39%)**	**95,479**

Source: San Diego Association of Governments, "Regional Housing Needs Statement" (San Diego: SANDAG, February 2000), 129.

1. United States Census Bureau, "American Factfinder," http://factfinder.census.gov/servlet/
BasicFactsTable?_lang=en&_vt_name=DEC_2000_PL_U_GCTPL_ST2&_geo_id=04000US06 (accessed September 6, 2002).

A unique aspect of SANDAG's methodology is the credit system that is used to measure and reward performance. The system gives extra credit for difficult-to-accomplish housing opportunities, such as transitional housing and housing for people with AIDS, to encourage jurisdictions to make the extra effort needed to provide these types of housing. The credit system was established, in part, to help ensure that zoning for multiple-family housing actually resulted in the creation of affordable housing instead of higher-income housing such as luxury condominiums. "You need multi-family housing opportunities in conjunction with the programs, " said Senior Regional Planner Susan Baldwin, AICP, (2002a) of SANDAG. The credit system is not applicable for the self-certification process.

The system has five categories of housing programs and projects ranging from the most difficult to accomplish due to political sensitivity and effort (category one) to programs and projects that are generally easier to accomplish politically and administratively (category five). Examples of category one programs are permanent housing for the homeless and alcohol and drug rehabilitation housing (SANDAG 1998, 31). Category two programs include new construction of senior citizen projects, limited equity co-ops, and mixed-income developments. Examples of category three programs are units funded by the State Mobile Home Resident Owner program and other mobile home purchase or ownership programs with no deed restrictions, loan programs for private owners to rehabilitate rental units, and locally funded rental assistance programs (vouchers or certificates). Category four programs include mobile home rental programs and new federally funded rental assistance programs realized through competitive processes. Examples of category five programs are shared housing programs operated by nonprofit agencies funded by the subject jurisdiction, and rehabilitation of owner-occupied homes. Table 4-9 shows the allocation of credits for each type of housing opportunity.

| TABLE 4-9 SANDAG CREDIT SYSTEM FOR 1999-2002 HOUSING ELEMENT CYCLE | | Extra Credit | | | | |
| | | Length of Affordability | | Number of Bedrooms | | |
Category	Base Credit	30-54 Years	55 or More Years	3	4	5
One	1.1	0.05	0.1	0.5	1.0	1.5
Two	1.05	0.05	0.1	0.5	1.0	1.5
Two (construction / rehab)	N/A	N/A	N/A	0.05	0.15	0.2
Three	1.0	0.05	0.1	0.5	1.0	1.5
Four	0.95	0.05	0.1	N/A	N/A	N/A
Five	0.9	0.05	0.1	N/A	N/A	N/A

Source: San Diego Association of Governments, *Housing Element Self-Certification Report: Implementation of a Pilot Program for the San Diego Region* (San Diego: SANDAG, June 1998), 36.

As Table 4-9 indicates, the base credit that a jurisdiction can earn from providing a housing opportunity listed in one of the categories ranges from 1.1 for category one to 0.9 for category five; each credit is worth one housing unit. Additionally, a jurisdiction may earn more credit for certain lengths of affordability and number of bedrooms. For example, a category one program with a length of affordability between 30 and 54 years and with five bedrooms would earn a 1.1 base credit, 0.05 extra credit for length of affordability, and 1.5 extra credit for number of bedrooms, resulting in a total credit of 2.65 that would be counted towards that jurisdictions affordable housing goal. Also, a bonus credit of 0.05 is available for each category one housing opportunity that is created in a census tract with a median income exceeding 120 percent of that jurisdiction's median income because SANDAG recognized the difficulty of building new low-income housing or special needs housing in high-income areas.

The methodology for determining housing goals for the self-certification pilot program is different than the regional fair-share need methodology as described above. The self-certification methodology begins with (step 1) the number of housing units per jurisdiction estimated by the California Department of Finance (DOF) as of January 1, 2004. That number is then increased (step 2) by 10 percent to account for HCD's concern that the DOF methodology did not identify the maximum number of housing opportunities that a jurisdiction could provide and did not account for the full spectrum of available regulatory measures. Next, (step 3) an unencumbered redevelopment funds factor is added to the result of step 2 to account for any housing opportunities that may result from unencumbered redevelopment set-aside funds that were available at the end of the 1991–1999 housing element cycle. This step uses information from the fiscal year ending in 1999, taking the jurisdiction's unencumbered affordable housing fund less 1.5 times its latest annual set aside. A factor of 1.5 assumes that communities will use the funds in approximately 1.5 years, and SANDAG wanted to give jurisdictions a way to account for this lapse (Baldwin 2002b). This number is then divided by 25,000 because the subsidy needed to build an affordable housing unit is assumed to be approximately $25,000 (although Baldwin says that in practice the subsidy is now closer to $50,000). This final step results in the number of additional low-income housing opportunities required of the jurisdiction (SANDAG 1998, 31).

SANDAG then allocates a number of housing units for each income category by determining the proportion of each income category in the region, based on 1990 census data. The census data showed that approximately 41 percent of housing opportunities must be provided for low-income households, 32 percent for very low-income households, and 27 percent for extremely low-income households. Accordingly, SANDAG established the following rule:

"A jurisdiction will be considered to be in compliance with AB 1715's proportionality requirement if excess housing opportunities are created at the extremely low- or very low-income levels as follows: at least 27 percent of the housing opportunities benefit extremely low-income households *and* at least 59 percent of the housing opportunities benefit extremely low- or very low-income households" (SANDAG 1998, 33). The regional averages for each income level are different than the averages used for the self-certification process because different data were used for the two methodologies.

Program Results

The status of HCD's certification of housing elements in the SANDAG region is shown in Table 4-10.

Table 4-10 indicates that the majority of housing elements in the SANDAG region have been found by HCD to be in compliance with California's Housing Element Law (58 percent). Eleven percent have been found to be out-of-compliance, 11 percent are under review at HCD, and 21 percent of jurisdictions have chosen to self-certify their housing elements and not seek HCD certification.

SANDAG's categorization of the status of housing elements is slightly different than HCD's

TABLE 4-10
STATUS OF HOUSING ELEMENTS IN SANDAG REGION AS OF AUGUST 6, 2002

Jurisdiction	Status of Housing Element
Carlsbad	In
Chula Vista	In
Coronado	Out
Del Mar	In
El Cajon	Self-Certified
Encinitas	In Review
Escondido	Self-Certified
Imperial Beach	Self-Certified
La Mesa	In
Lemon Grove	In Review
National City	Self-Certified
Ocanside	In
Poway	In
San Diego City	In
San Diego County	In
San Marcos	In
Santee	Out
Solana Beach	In
Vista	In
Total	**In: 11 (58%)**
	Out: 2 (11%)
	In Review: 2 (11%)
	Self-Certified: 4 (21%)

Source: California Department of Housing and Community Development, *Housing Element Compliance Report*, http://www.hcd.ca.gov/hpd/hrc/plan/he/status.pdf (accessed August 12, 2002).

(Baldwin 2002b). If a jurisdiction chooses to self-certify its housing element and not send it in to HCD for review, it is then ineligible for certain state programs and bonus points for certain programs, including a state infrastructure bank program (bonus points), the Housing Enabled by Local Partnerships (HELP) program that is administered by the California Housing Finance Agency, and a jobs/housing balance improvement program that is currently unfunded. SANDAG reports that there are four jurisdictions (Chula Vista, La Mesa, Oceanside, and San Diego County) that were self-certified but also had their housing elements found in compliance by HCD; these jurisdictions are listed as "in" on the HCD compliance report. Additionally, one jurisdiction (El Cajon) was listed by HCD as being "in review," whereas SANDAG considers it out of compliance. HCD categorizes one jurisdiction (Lemon Grove) as "in review," but SANDAG lists it as in compliance. Also, another jurisdiction (Vista) is listed as self-certified and in review by SANDAG, whereas HCD lists it as in compliance (Baldwin 2002b). These discrepancies might be attributed to each report's publication date, SANDAG's on August 13, 2002, HCD's on August 6, 2002. Legislation has been introduced in the California Senate (SB 167 in 2002), which SANDAG supports, that would allow self-certified jurisdictions to be eligible for all state funds, bond finding, and programs.

Although only four jurisdictions (according to HCD) chose to participate in the self-certification program, performance totals were calculated for each jurisdiction. Table 4-11 shows the calculations for the self-certification program.

The first column in Table 4-11 lists the name of each jurisdiction in the SANDAG region. The second column shows the number of affordable housing units provided between July 1, 1991, and June 30, 1999. The third column shows each jurisdiction's affordable housing goal for the purposes of self-certification. These goals are based on the projected number of low-income households in need of assistance, population, housing, income, and employment characteristics, although the methodology used to calculate these goals is not the same as that discussed above. Because limited resources are available for affordable housing, the annual fair-share goal for each jurisdiction is calculated as 2.5 percent per year, or 12.5 percent over the five-year cycle. Accordingly, the third column shows each jurisdiction's affordable housing goal, which is 12.5 percent of the fifth column. The fourth column shows the percentage of the affordable housing goal that was met (SANDAG 2001, Table 1). The fifth column, as mentioned above, shows the fair-share housing need (for self-certification) for the 1991–1999 cycle, and the sixth column shows the percentage of the fair-share need (for self-certification) that has been met.

Although the five-year housing element cycle was extended to end in 1999 instead of 1996, which made it an eight-year cycle, SANDAG did not revise the fair-share goals because of two factors: "(1) the low level of construction that occurred because of the recession, and (2) the decision to use the fair-share goals for self-certification, a purpose for which they had originally not been intended" (SANDAG 2001, Table 1). Jurisdictions had until June 30, 1999, to meet their self-certification fair-share goal, which would make them eligible for self-certification.

Table 4-11 indicates that there were 12 jurisdictions that had met their self-certification goal for the 1991–1999 cycle as of June 30, 1999: Chula Vista, Coronado, El Cajon, Escondido, Imperial Beach, La Mesa, National City, Oceanside, San Marcos, Santee, Vista, and San Diego County Unincorporated. The percentage of self-certification goals that have been met (as of June 30, 1999) range from 14 percent in Del Mar to 1,500 percent in National City.

TABLE 4-11
SELF-CERTIFICATION PROGRAM PERFORMANCE IN SANDAG REGION
JULY 1, 1991–JUNE 30, 1999

Jurisdiction	Affordable Housing Provided, July 1, 1991– June 30,1999[1]	1999 Fair-Share Goal [Self-Certification Goal]	% of Affordable Housing Goal [Self-Certification Goal] Met	Fair-Share Housing Need[2] [1991-1999 Housing Element Cycle]	% of Fair-Share Need Met [1991-1999 Housing Element Cycle]
Carlsbad	814	1,125	72 %	9,000	9 %
Chula Vista	2,320	1,058	219 %	8,466	27 %
Coronado	387	259	149 %	2,073	19 %
Del Mar	9	65	14 %	521	2 %
El Cajon[3]	1,941	470	413 %	3,761	52 %
Encinitas	240	538	45 %	4,307	6 %
Escondido[4]	2,071	846	245 %	6,765	31 %
Imperial Beach	217	42	517 %	335	65 %
La Mesa	624	452	138 %	3,612	17 %
Lemon Grove	113	174	65 %	1,391	8 %
National City	555	37	1500 %	298	186 %
Oceanside	1,677	967	173 %	7,734	22 %
Poway	160	565	28 %	4,518	4 %
San Diego	3,641	9,319	39 %	74,529	5 %
San Marcos	551	528	104 %	4,221	13 %
Santee[5]	794	655	121 %	5,239	15 %
Solana Beach	99	194	51 %	1,552	6 %
Vista	775	458	169 %	3,662	21%
Unincorporated	4,160	3,979	105 %	31,828	13 %
Total	**21,148**	**21,731**	**97 %**	**173,812**	**12 %**

Source: San Diego Association of Governments, *Draft Affordable Housing Performance Report* (San Diego: SANDAG, October 18, 2001), Table 1. SANDAG has not revised the "draft" report so the figures contained in it are, for all practical purposes, final.

1. The SANDAG *Draft Affordable Housing Performance Report* (San Diego: SANDAG, October 18, 2001), Table 1, states: "This number includes a wide variety of housing programs, including: Acquisition, Rehabilitation, Rent Subsidy Programs, Home Buyer Assistance, Preservation, Second Dwelling Units, Illegal Unit Conversions, and Transitional Housing."

2. The SANDAG *Draft Affordable Housing Performance* Report (San Diego: SANDAG, October 18, 2001), Table 1, states: "Fair Share Need estimates the number of lower income households that need assistance. This term is no longer used by SANDAG."

3. The SANDAG *Draft Affordable Housing Performance Report* (San Diego: SANDAG, October 18, 2001), Table 1, states: "Information for [El Cajon] is incomplete. Actual totals may be higher, and will be provided in the final draft of this document."

4. The SANDAG *Draft Affordable Housing Performance Report* (San Diego: SANDAG, October 18, 2001), Table 1, states: "Information for [Escondido] is incomplete. Actual totals may be higher, and will be provided in the final draft of this document."

5. According to the SANDAG *Draft Affordable Housing Performance Report* (San Diego: SANDAG, October 18, 2001), Table 1, "Information for [Santee] is incomplete. Actual totals may be higher, and will be provided in the final draft of this document."

Table 4-11 also indicates that most jurisdictions have not met much of their total fair-share need. National City, which achieved 186 percent of its fair-share figure for the 1991–1999 cycle, is the only jurisdiction to meet its need. Imperial Beach, which had the second highest percentage, met 65 percent of its fair-share need. Alternatively, Del Mar, Poway, and San Diego ranked the lowest, with 2 percent, 4 percent, and 5 percent, respectively. Overall, the region met 12 percent of its total regional fair-share need for the 1991–1999 housing element cycle.

Poinsetta Station affordable rental units in Carlsbad, California, SANDAG region.

SANDAG has initiated several programs to increase the supply of affordable housing in the region, including making housing part of its *Region 2020* growth management strategy. SANDAG has established a regional housing task force—a coalition of business leaders, housing advocates, developers, realtors, elected officials, and others—who have identified several strategies to increase the supply of affordable housing in the region. The categories of the strategies include: (1) implementing smart growth land use strategies, (2) removing barriers to housing development, (3) creating funding sources and incentives for housing and smart growth, and (4) implementing an educational program (SANDAG 2002a).

Fulton Street affordable rental housing in San Diego, California.

Southern California Association of Governments (SCAG)

The Southern California Association of Governments (SCAG) region is composed of six counties and 154 cities. Between 1990 and 2000 the Southern California region's population grew from 14.6 million people to 16.5 million people, an increase of 12.81 percent. At the same time, however, the number of building permits issued for single-family homes increased only

According to SCAG, the housing affordability problem is worsening in the region, particularly in coastal areas.

2 percent, and multifamily permit issuance decreased by 45 percent (SCAG 2001, 9). Between 1990 and 1999 just under three-quarters of building permits issued in the SCAG region were issued in unincorporated cities, and one-quarter were issued in unincorporated county communities.

According to SCAG, the housing affordability problem is worsening in the region, particularly in coastal areas. While the number of households in the region increased 24 percent between 1980 and 1996, the number of vehicle miles traveled increased at more than three times that rate—82 percent—in the same time period (SCAG 2001, 14). This substantial increase suggests that people are moving farther away from places of employment in search of affordable housing.

Within the context of its Regional Comprehensive Plan and Guide (RCPG), which provides a planning framework for housing issues to Southern California jurisdictions, SCAG developed its most current Regional Housing Needs Assessment (RHNA) in 1999 (SCAG 1999, ii). The RHNA is based on the four main goals of the RCPG, which are: "(1) [d]ecent and affordable housing choices for all people, (2) adequate supply and availability of housing, (3) housing stock maintenance and preservation, and (4) promotion of [a] mixture of housing opportunities regionwide" (SCAG 1999, 2).

As noted above, California's housing element statute, California Government Code Section 65584 (1999), allows councils of governments (COGs) to delegate responsibility for making housing need determinations to subregional agencies. Under the law, a COG provides a subregional agency with its share of the regional housing need and delegates responsibility for providing allocations to jurisdictions in the subregion to that agency, if this responsibility is requested. SCAG was the only COG in the state to delegate housing need determination responsibility to subregional agencies. SCAG developed a delegation agreement and scope of work with its 14 subregional partners, which defines the partners' scope of work, duties, timing, conditions, and processes. For the 1990 RHND process, five subregional agencies representing 90 jurisdictions—San Gabriel Valley COG, Ventura COG, Orange County COG, Western Riverside COG, and Coachella Valley COG—requested delegation authority to make housing need determinations. The remaining nine subregional agencies in the SCAG region participate in the 1998–2005 RHNA process with nondelegation status (SCAG 1999, 3).

SCAG's methodology for determining housing need is similar to the ABAG methodology. It consists of two measures: (1) existing need, which uses census data, and (2) future (construction) need, which is determined by summing the forecasted household growth, vacancy rates, housing replacement need, and a fair-share adjustment.

The fair-share adjustment is applied to the future need determination to distribute each jurisdiction's housing need to each income category, similar to ABAG's method. The difference between SCAG's and ABAG's methods is that SCAG shifts each municipality's distribution towards the regional average according to three levels of deviation from the regional average. For jurisdictions that have 0 to 26.5 percent of households in an income range (low impaction), the income distribution shifts toward the regional average at one-quarter of the difference between the jurisdiction's average and the regional average. For jurisdictions that have between 26.6 and 51.5 percent of households in an income range (average impaction), the income distribution shifts one-half of the way toward the regional average. For jurisdictions with between 51.6 and 100 percent of households in an income range (high impaction), the income distribution shifts three-quarters of the way toward the regional average. For example, 29 percent of the residents of Long Beach were in the very low-income category, according to the RHNA website, and the regional average for this income

California Association of Bay Area Governments and the Nonprofit Housing Association of Northern California.

SCAG uses two criteria to determine housing need: existing need (based on census data) and future need (based on household growth, vacancy rates, housing replacements, and fair-share adjustments).

range was 24 percent, a difference of 5 percent. Therefore, Long Beach's percentage would be adjusted 1.25 percent (one-quarter of the 5 percent difference) toward the regional average. The resulting figure is the distribution of housing construction need for the very low-income category (28 percent, adjusted for rounding) (SCAG and the University of California at Los Angeles Advanced Policy Institute 2002).

Program Results

HCD originally determined that SCAG's fair share of California's housing need was 504,758. However, SCAG adopted a housing need of 437,984, a difference of 66,774 (Lieb 2002). According to correspondence between SCAG and HCD, HCD reviewed and approved SCAG's draft RHNA plan in December 1999 before SCAG lowered the housing need total by 66,774 units. The approval letter stated that any adjustments of housing need as a result of appeals by local jurisdictions are to be reallocated within the region in order to maintain or exceed the regional housing need. As it concluded the RHNA process, SCAG lowered its regional construction need total, submitting a final RHNA of 437,984 for HCD's approval (Hardinson 2000).

However, HCD did not find the final RHNA consistent with state housing needs and thus rejected it. HCD instead approved an RHNA that was a mix of SCAG's approved draft and its later, downward-revised plan. HCD did accept revised allocations for some local governments contained in the final RHNA as a result of the appeals process. But for all other jurisdictions, HCD used the draft allocations previously submitted by SCAG and already approved by HCD for all other jurisdictions (the allocations for most jurisdictions were not changed from the draft figures). It thus rejected allocation reductions for ten local governments, mostly in the Inland Empire jurisdictions, western Riverside county, and San Bernardino county (Shigley 2001, 14). HCD concluded that the total regional share for the planning period 1998–2005 was to be 503,356, which, according to HCD, "constitut[es] a minor reduction yet consistent with the statewide housing need" (Creswell 2000). SCAG and several of its jurisdictions responded with a lawsuit that claims HCD overstepped its authority when it rejected SCAG's proposed reduction (Lieb 2002). On August 1, 2002, a California Superior Court judge turned down SCAG's request for a writ of mandate ordering HCD to accept SCAG's lower number, finding that HCD's rejection of SCAG's revised RHNA set forth "valid and sufficient reasons for such rejection" (HCD 2002a).

The status of housing elements in Southern California, based on SCAG's RHNA allocations that were accepted by HCD, is shown in Table 4-12.

TABLE 4-12
STATUS OF HOUSING ELEMENTS FOR CITIES
AND COUNTIES IN SOUTHERN CALIFORNIA
AS OF AUGUST 6, 2002

County	In Compliance	Out of Compliance	In Review	Due	Total
Imperial	6 (75%)	2 (25%)	0	0	8
Los Angeles	44 (49%)	39 (44%)	6 (7%)	0	89
Orange	23 (68%)	7 (21%)	4 (12%)	0	34
Riverside	12 (48%)	13 (52%)	0	0	25
San Bernardino	11 (44%)	12 (48%)	2 (8%)	0	25
Ventura	7 (64%)	2 (18%)	2 (18%)	0	11
Total	**103 (54%)**	**75 (39%)**	**14 (7%)**	**0**	**192**

Source: California Department of Housing and Community Development, *Housing Element Compliance Report,* http://www.hcd.ca.gov/hpd/hrc/plan/he/status.pdf (accessed August 12, 2002). Note that HCD updates its housing element status table on a regular basis, and the above information is based on August 6, 2002 data. For current data, see the HCD website.

As Table 4-12 indicates, cities and counties in the Southern California region have done a good job of submitting their housing elements to HCD: none of the jurisdictions have housing elements that are due. Two counties, Imperial and Riverside, do not have any jurisdictions with housing elements that were under review at HCD (as of August 12, 2002), and the rest of the counties have small percentages of their housing elements under review. The county with the highest percentage of jurisdictions with housing elements that are in compliance with the housing element law is Imperial (75 percent), and the county with the lowest is San Bernardino (44 percent). The county with the highest percentage of jurisdictions with housing elements that are out of com-

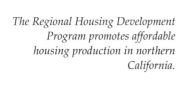

The Regional Housing Development Program promotes affordable housing production in northern California.

California Association of Bay Area Governments and the Nonprofit Housing Association of Northern California.

pliance is Riverside (52 percent), and the county with the lowest is Ventura (18 percent). The higher rate of non-compliance in Riverside and San Bernardino Counties may be due to the lawsuit brought against HCD as described above, which involved seven jurisdictions in those two counties that account for 50,000 of the disputed 66,774 units (Shigley 2001, 14).

According to SCAG, "one of the major challenges in producing RHNA99 [the Regional Housing Needs Assessment] is the lack of recent data and a condensed time frame in which to conduct research. There is also a significant gap between available income, vacancy and other data, largely based [on] census information and current market conditions. Year 2000 Census information will not be available for use in the upcoming housing element" (SCAG 1999, iii). Despite these challenges, SCAG maintains that major improvements were made to the RHNA process in 1999, including "the use of a bottom up growth forecast process, availability of alternative dispute resolution and mediation services, subregional delegation of state housing planning requirements, and the Housing Southern Californians website and the housing need calculator (in conjunction with the UCLA Advanced Policy Institute)" (SCAG 1999, ii).

In November 2000 SCAG adopted the Regional Housing Development Program in an effort to increase affordable housing in Southern California. The program consists of emphasizing programs to promote affordable housing production, expanding the Location Efficient Mortgage program, preparing a midterm report, and increasing its monitoring and technical assistance efforts related to housing (SCAG 2002d). The program also includes plans to augment its monitoring of housing-related activities, assisting communities in designing approaches and incentives for affordable housing, and proposing and supporting legislation that removes obstacles to affordable housing production.

SCAG has not reported housing production data by income level.

SCAG likewise adopted a set of four priorities for housing element reform. According to SCAG, "reform of the State of California's Housing Element and Regional Housing Needs Assessment process is badly needed. The process, as envisioned under current law (California Government Code, Section 65583-4), is complex, needlessly contentious, and lacks credibility among local governments and others" (SCAG 2002, E1). The four reforms that SCAG proposes (in order of priority) are:

1. Base Regional Housing Need Determinations on regional transportation plan (RTP) forecasts only.

2. Require the state to address inconsistent and contradicting mandates linked to housing (i.e., Coastal Commission, transportation planning, and water policy requirements).

3. Allow communities to address the conflicts between housing allocations and extenuating circumstances at the local level (i.e., land limitations, cost of land, agricultural lands, etc.)

4. Create or augment incentives to local governments for building and planning for housing. (SCAG 2002, E1)

SCAG has not reported housing production data by income level. However, using data from the Construction Industry Research Board, SCAG reported in its February 2002 *Housing Element Compliance Report* the total number of building permits issued over a four-year period. This report indicates that 211,482 new housing units were permitted between January 1998 and December 2001, which represents one-half of the period covered by the RHNA. Again, these data do not indicate the number of housing units for each income level and therefore cannot be used to determine progress in complying with the housing element law.

PORTLAND METRO, OREGON

Title: Portland Metro Regional Affordable Housing Strategy

Inception: 2000

Administration: The Portland Metro Council, whose jurisdiction covers three counties that include 24 cities, unveiled in 2000 its first regional fair-share housing plan. Metro's policies are driven by Oregon's statewide land-use planning program, which was established in 1973. In accord with the program, the state reviews and acknowledges or certifies local plans for compliance with state goals and administrative rules. Metro has established a regional housing needs benchmark for the Portland region at 90,479 housing units, which is the total forecasted need for housing units for households at or below 50 percent median household income (MHI) for 2000 to 2017. Of that, 66,245 housing units (75 percent) should be for households with incomes below 30 percent MHI. Because of the difficulty of meeting this goal, Metro developed a five-year housing production goal for affordable housing that was 10 percent of the total goal (9,048 housing units).

Key objectives: Establish voluntary fair-share housing goals for each city and county within the Portland Metro region and encourage use of the implementation program contained in the plan.

Accomplishments: No progress report was available in late 2002, although one will be forthcoming.

Caveats: The strategy is voluntary. A Metro survey disclosed that there is a relatively slim range of tools being used for the creation of affordable housing. The most popular method is permitting accessory dwelling units (listed in the land-use category), with 14 jurisdictions using this method. The most popular cost reduction tool is programs for seniors and the disabled, with seven jurisdictions using this method. The most popular funding tool is CDBG funds dedicated to housing; only three jurisdictions draw on their general funds as a source. In 1999, at the behest of the Oregon Building Industry Association, the state of Oregon adopted a law that bars cities, counties, and the Portland Metro from adopting land development regulations requiring a mandatory set-aside of affordable housing for sale (but not for rent) as part of a market-rate housing project or as a freestanding project, although the law does allow voluntary incentives. It represents a significant limitation on local government's ability to stimulate the production of affordable housing.

Affordable housing in the Portland Metro Region.

The Portland Metro region is composed of 24 cities and three counties (Clackamas, Multnomah, and Washington). The region was home to an estimated 1,467,300 people in 2002 (Metro Council 2002c). The Metro Council is an elected regional government—a metropolitan service district—that provides transportation and land-use planning services, manages regional parks and open spaces, and oversees the Portland region's urban growth boundary, which includes 364 square miles of land.

Affordable housing, according to Metro, is a regional issue because the connection between the location of housing and employment is very important to both employers and employees and because the provision of affordable housing exceeds the powers of any individual local government in the Portland area (Metro Council 2000b, 1-2).

Metro's policies are driven by Oregon's statewide land-use planning program, which was established in 1973. In accord with the program, the state reviews and acknowledges or certifies local plans for compliance with state goals and administrative rules. Goal 10 (of 19 adopted by the state Land Conservation and Development Commission) states that local governments must provide for the housing needs of the citizens of the state.

Buildable lands for residential use shall be inventoried and plans shall encourage the availability of adequate numbers of needed housing units at price ranges and rent levels commensurate with the financial capabilities of housing location, type, and density. (Oregon Administrative Rule, Section 660-015-0000(10), as amended August 30, 1996)

Guidelines for housing elements of local plans interpret this goal as requiring, among other things, that the elements must include a determination of expected housing demand at varying rent ranges and cost levels. Under these guidelines, plans must provide for ongoing review of housing need projections and establish a process for accommodating necessary revisions.

One of the best-known aspects of the Oregon system is the urban growth boundary requirement intended to fulfill Goal 14, whose purpose is "to provide for an orderly and efficient transition from rural to urban land use." Inside the boundary, urban development is permitted and is to be supported by urban services; outside the boundary, rural lands are preserved.

In the Portland area, a special metropolitan housing rule, adopted in 1981, requires minimum housing densities in local zoning ordinances. The rule requires communities within the Portland metropolitan area to allow development at minimum densities of six and eight units per net buildable acre in suburban areas and 10 units per buildable acre in more urbanized communities such as Portland, Beaverton, and Lake Oswego. In addition, the rule requires all jurisdictions except small developed cities to zone land so that one-half of all newly constructed residences are attached single-family housing or multifamily housing (Section 660-07-000).

In December 1997, Metro released its *Regional Framework Plan*, which lists several goals intended to increase the supply of affordable housing in the region. The goals include: adopting a regional fair-share strategy and a regionwide mandatory inclusionary zoning policy and completing an inventory of publicly owned lands and a review of all lands inside the UGB that are designated for residential use (Portland Metro 1997b, Section 1.3).

In June 2000, following the recommendations of a regional affordable housing task force formed in late 1998, Metro unveiled its Regional Affordable Housing Strategy (RAHS). RAHs was accepted by the Metro Council on June 22, 2000. RAHS calls for the local governments within the region to adopt "voluntary affordable housing production goals"— fair-share requirements, in other words—and a series of land-use strategies, including density bonuses, transfer of development rights, no-net-loss policies on affordable housing, and fast-tracking for affordable housing projects, among other approaches (Uba 2002a).

RAHS also calls on local governments to report periodically their progress in meeting voluntary production goals and undertaking recommended actions. It likewise makes a series of recommendations for federal and state action, among them a regional housing fund to help meet targeted regional affordable housing production goals (Metro Council 2000b). Similarly, it recommends that the Oregon legislature enact a real estate transfer tax (RETT) to help capitalize the regional housing fund. Under the task force's proposal, monies from the tax would be allocated to:

(a) provide new and rehabilitated housing units to households earning less than 50 percent;

(b) help lower-income first-time homebuyers purchase homes throughout the region; and

(c) fund local infrastructure improvements for affordable housing development. (Metro Council 2000b, 71)

Plans must provide for ongoing review of housing need projections and establish a process for accommodating necessary revisions.

A RETT would ensure that part of the benefit of increased land and housing values is dedicated to affordable housing. RAHS has proposed exempting the tax on all homes sold for less than $120,000. Potential revenues range from $4.8 to $40.6 million per year. Under the RAHS, Metro would also be responsible for developing a regional best practices handbook containing model ordinances and guidelines that local governments could implement (Portland Metro 2001a, 71). Although the Oregon Legislature has not enacted the RETT, strong support for it remains in place (Harmon 2002).

The strategies addressed in the plan can be divided into three categories: land use, non-land use, and regional funding approaches (Portland Metro 2000b, 28). The strategies that the plan offers for local government consideration are summarized in Table 4-13.

TABLE 4-13
SUMMARY OF LOCAL GOVERNMENT STRATEGIES,
PORTLAND METRO REGIONAL AFFORDABLE HOUSING PROGRAM

Cost Reduction	Land Use and Regulatory	Regional Funding

• System development charges
• Permit fees
• Property tax exemption
• Government coordination
• Land cost and availability
• Off-site improvements
• Local regulatory constraints and discrepancies
• Building codes requirements
• Parking
	• Long-term or permanent affordability
	• Density bonuses
	• Replacement housing
	• Inclusionary zoning and urban growth boundary considerations
	• Transfer of development rights
	• Elderly and disabled housing
	• Regional housing resource / database
		• Maximize existing resources
		  – Training Program
		  – Consistent consolidated plans
		  – Allocation of HOME funds
		  – Changes in federal programs
		  – Regional acquisition fund
		• New funding sources
		  – Employer sponsored housing
		  – Real estate transfer tax
		  – Regional housing fund

Source: Metro, *Regional Affordable Housing Strategy* (Portland, Ore.: Metro, June 2000), http://www.metro-region.org/metro/growth/tfplan/affordstrategy.html (accessed Sept. 18, 2002), 28.

The strategies contained in RAHS are only advisory, however; the Metro Code contains the laws regulating affordable housing that have been enacted by Metro Council (n.d.). The functional plan states that each jurisdiction in the Metro region *should* adopt the voluntary affordable housing production goals recommended by Metro in the RAHS. RAHS proposes that jurisdictions include measures in their comprehensive plans to increase their supply of affordable housing and consider using tools such as density bonuses, inclusionary housing, and transfer of development rights. (See Table 4-13.)

Reporting requirements are part of the plan as well:

1. Within the first year, municipalities must submit a progress report showing the tools and strategies they are using to meet the housing production goals.

2. Within the second year, municipalities must submit a report describing the status of their comprehensive plan amendments and the adoption of land-use tools that increase the supply of affordable housing.

3. Within the third year, municipalities must submit a report updating the status of amendments to their comprehensive plans, the outcomes of affordable housing tools that have been implemented, and any other affordable housing that has been or will be developed. (Section 307.740)

The voluntary affordable housing production goals recommended by the code are calculated by multiplying the number of projected households in each jurisdiction for the year 2017 by the regional growth proportion of

Affordable housing, according to Metro, is a regional issue because the connection between the location of housing and employment is very important to both employers and employees and because the provision of affordable housing exceeds the powers of any individual local government in the Portland area

households in each income group and then subtracting credits for existing supplies of affordable housing units in that income category. Ten percent of the resulting figure (which is the overall benchmark production goal) determines the five-year production goal for each income category. Some data are still based on the 1990 census and need to be updated, according to Rex Burkholder, an elected Metro Council member. "There is some work we need to do which is not funded in this year's [2002] budget," said Burkholder, " including updating our data with 2000 Census information. I hope to have this funded for next spring [2003]" (Burkholder 2002).

The regional housing needs benchmark for the Portland region is 90,479 housing units, which is the total forecasted need for housing units for households at or below 50 percent median household income (MHI) for 2000 to 2017. Of that, 66,245 housing units (75 percent) should be for households

Across the 24 cities and three counties in the region, a relatively slim range of tools is being used for the creation of affordable housing.

with incomes below 30 percent MHI. Because of the difficulty of meeting this goal, Metro developed a five-year housing production goal for affordable housing that was 10 percent of the total goal (9,048 housing units). The five-year *voluntary* affordable housing production goals that were adopted by Metro Council in 2000 are shown in Table 4-14.

As Table 4-14 indicates, Portland and the urban unincorporated areas in Clackamas and Washington counties have the highest affordable housing production goals. There are two cities (Johnson and Maywood Park) that have goals of zero. Most of the affordable housing goals are for households earning less than 30 percent MHI (6,419 housing units). A total of 2,628 housing units are allocated for households earning between 30 and 50 percent MHI. A "county urban, unincorporated area" is the part of each county's unincorporated area that is located within the urban growth boundary (Uba 2002a).

The RAHS includes estimates of the financial resources that will be needed to meet the housing production goals. According to the plan, the total annual cost of meeting the five-year housing production goal is $124,210,944 per year.[12] The total resources currently available annually from state and federal government programs such as Community Development Block Grants (CDBGs), HOME Funds, and the Oregon Housing Trust Fund amount to $27,077,586 per year, assuming all available resources from state and federal governments that could be dedicated to housing are used for that purpose and that resource funding levels remain constant. Therefore, the remaining resources that are needed to achieve the affordable housing goals in the Metro region are $97,133,358 per year.

Program Results

In preparing the RAHS, Metro asked local jurisdictions for information on the tools they use to encourage affordable housing. Metro mailed its survey in September 1999, and responses were accepted until February 2000. Eighteen jurisdictions completed the survey, which was a 67 percent response rate (Metro Council 2000b, 29). The results are presented in Table 4-15.

Table 4-15 shows that, across the 24 cities and three counties in the region, a relatively slim range of tools is being used for the creation of affordable housing. The most popular method is permitting accessory dwelling units (listed in the land-use category), with 14 jurisdictions using this method. The most popular cost reduction tool is programs for seniors and the disabled, with 7 jurisdictions using this method. The most popular funding tool is CDBG funds dedicated to housing. Only three jurisdictions draw on their general fund as a source.

Metro's efforts to provide affordable housing were dealt a setback in 1999 when, at the behest of the Oregon Building Industry Association, the state legislature adopted a law that bars cities, counties, and Metro from adopting land development regulations that require a mandatory set-aside of affordable housing for sale (but not for rent) as part of a market-rate housing project or as a freestanding project, although it does allow voluntary incentives. The law, which represents a significant limitation on local government's ability to stimulate the production of affordable housing, states:

> (1) Except as provided in subsection (2) of this section, a city, county or metropolitan service district may not adopt a land use regulation or functional plan provision, or impose as a condition for approving a permit under ORS 215.428 or 227.178, a requirement that has the effect of establishing the sales price for a housing unit or residential building lot or parcel, or that requires a housing unit or residential building lot or parcel to be designated for sale to any particular class or group of purchasers.

TABLE 4-14
FIVE-YEAR VOLUNTARY AFFORDABLE
HOUSING PRODUCTION GOALS,
PORTLAND METRO REGION

Jurisdiction	Population in 2000[1]	2001–2006 Affordable Housing Production Goals		
		Housing Needed for Households at or below 30% Median Household Income	Housing Needed for Households between 30-50% Median Household Income	Total Affordable Housing Needed
Beaverton	76,129	427	229	656
Cornelius	9,652	40	10	50
Durham	1,382	6	4	10
Fairview	7,651	42	31	73
Forest Grove	17,708	55	10	65
Gladstone	600	43	10	53
Gresham	90,205	454	102	556
Happy Valley	4,519	29	28	57
Hillsboro	70,186	302	211	513
Johnson City	634	0	0	0
King City	1,949	5	0	5
Lake Oswego	35,278	185	154	339
Maywood Park	777	0	0	0
Milwaukie	20,490	102	0	102
Oregon City	25,754	123	35	158
Portland	529,121	1,791	0	1,791
Rivergrove	324	1	1	2
Sherwood	11,791	67	56	123
Tigard	41,223	216	103	319
Troutdale	13,777	75	56	131
Tualatin	22,791	120	69	189
West Linn	22,261	98	71	169
Wilsonville	13,991	100	80	180
Wood Village	2,960	16	1	17
Clakamas County, Urban, Unincorporated	N/A	729	374	1,103
Multnomah County, Urban, Unincorporated	N/A	81	53	134
Washington County, Urban, Unincorporated	N/A	1,312	940	2,252
Total	**1,021,153**	**6,419**	**2,628**	**9,047**

Source: Portland Metro, *Urban Growth Management Functional Plan*, Section 3.07.720, Table 3.07-7.

1. United States Census Bureau, "American Fact Finder," http://factfinder.census.gov/servlet/
BasicFactsTable?_lang=en&_vt_name=DEC_2000_PL_U_GCTPL_ST7&_geo_id=04000US41 (accessed September 24, 2002).

TABLE 4-15
TOOLS USED TO INCREASE THE SUPPLY
OF AFFORDABLE HOUSING IN METRO REGION

Tools	Number of Jurisdictions
Land Use Tools	
Accessory Dwelling Units	14
Density Transfer	4
Density Bonus for Affordable Housing	3
No Net Loss Provisions for Housing	3
Increased Density in Transit Corridors	2
Replacement Housing Ordinance	2
Conversion of Rental to Owner Occupied Unit	2
Requirements for the Relocation of Mobile Home Parks	2
Linkage Programs	1
Incentive Based Inclusionary Zoning	1
Cost Reduction Tools	
Programs for Seniors and Disabled	7
Land Banking	3
Long-Term or Permanent Affordability Requirements	3
Property Tax Abatement for Housing	3
System Development Charges Abatements for Affordable Housing	3
Tax Foreclosed Properties Donated for Affordable Housing	3
Building and Land Use Fee Waivers	2
Funding Tools	
CDBG Funds Dedicated to Housing	7
General Funds Dedicated Specifically to Housing	3
Other Financial Incentives	3

Source: Metro, *Regional Affordable Housing Strategy* (Portland, Ore.: Metro, June 2000), http://www.metro-region.org/metro/growth/tfplan/affordstrategy.html (accessed Sept. 18, 2002), 29.

(2) Nothing in this section is intended to limit the authority of a city, county or metropolitan service district to adopt or enforce a land use regulation, functional plan provision or condition of approval creating or implementing an incentive, contract commitment, density bonus or other voluntary regulation, provision or condition designed to increase the supply of moderate or lower cost housing units. (1999 Oregon House Bill 2658, Chapter 848 Oregon Laws 1999, effective October 23, 1999)

Although jurisdictions in the Metro region were required to report on their affordable housing activities to Metro in January 2002, only eight of them did (Uba 2002a). Metro's only plan to enforce this requirement is to send nonreporting jurisdictions a reminder (Uba 2002a). The second and third reports are due in January 2003 and January 2004, respectively. Metro will then produce a comprehensive report on local government efforts to implement affordable housing strategies. In addition, Metro will use 2000 census information to determine if its initial affordable housing needs estimates were correct. As Metro program manager Gerry Uba (2002a) said, since the first report covers only the progress of affordable housing in ju-

Marya Morris

risdictions and not production numbers or comprehensive plan changes, the first report will not be a good indication of how well the region is meeting its affordable housing goals. Further, since the program is only about one year old, the time frame for reporting does not allow an adequate measure of progress. The absence of comprehensive reporting in the region means there currently is no effective way to know how local governments have progressed in meeting their affordable housing production goals.

The Coalition for a Livable Future (CLF), a group of 50 nonprofit organizations in the Portland region, took a lead role in bringing together affordable housing groups and advocates in the region to push for the affordable housing strategy. According to CLF's assistant coordinator Theresa Huntsinger (2002), CLF is working to "convince Metro that they need to follow up with the strategy and get it implemented." The coalition is also working to "launch a campaign strategy to develop new funding strategies for affordable housing." Huntsinger also noted that there is currently no funding and no staff time dedicated to affordable housing at Metro and that Metro may not be "really as fully committed as they need to be at seeing affordable housing as part of their job. Maybe they don't see it as being a core part of their responsibility," she speculated, or they are "fearful of flexing their political muscle too much."

Metro Councillor Burkholder (2002) acknowledged that the role of Metro in the affordable housing arena has been subject to dispute. "Metro is not a provider, rather a planning agency with some policy oversight of local jurisdictions," Burkholder stated. "There is a lot of dispute over what role Metro should play. The regional affordable housing strategy is a first attempt to assert a regional role and is very limited due to concerns by local jurisdictions of the expansion of Metro's power to a new area." Burkholder lauded CLF for helping to put affordable housing on Metro's agenda. But,

The Coalition for a Livable Future (CLF), a group of 50 nonprofit organizations in the Portland region, took a lead role in bringing together affordable housing groups and advocates in the region to push for the affordable housing strategy.

he said, "what form regional efforts take have yet to be seen. Right now we are in the documentation stage. My personal feeling is that our best approach is to work to increase the supply of housing to reduce market pressure on prices."

Ed Sullivan (2002), a Portland land-use attorney, said that Metro's plan is weak because "it estimated the need on a market-based approach, and what was left out of the equation was the lower end—people who really can't afford housing." Further, Sullivan said, from the start "it didn't set a very high bar. It only looked at 10 percent of the need." Sullivan also noted that the plan's emphasis on voluntary compliance made unclear enforcement and requirements for local governments.

Lack of funding and political will combined with the local governments' fear of Metro's expansion into the affordable housing arena appear, at least partially, to blame for the lack of progress in the region's affordable housing program. Likewise, Burkholder pointed out that, when elected, he replaced the main supporter of Metro's affordable housing efforts. Metro's attention to housing has thus wandered somewhat, he admitted. "Council attention wavered for awhile," he said. "In addition, the current [Metro] executive did not provide funding in our planning budget for this fiscal year."

NEW HAMPSHIRE

Title: Regional Housing Needs Assessments

Inception: 1988

Administration: New Hampshire requires by statute that each regional planning commission in the state compile a regional housing needs assessment to be used to assist municipalities in preparing master plans. By statute a municipal master plan or plan update may include a "[a] housing section which assesses local housing conditions and projects future housing needs of residents of all levels of income and ages in the municipality and the region as identified in the regional housing needs assessment performed by the regional planning commission . . . and which integrates the availability of human services with other planning undertaken by the community." The language concerning "and ages" was added by amendment in May 2002, and it was intended to ensure that local governments address both family and senior housing.

Key objective: Provide a regional framework for local governments that choose to prepare housing elements of local comprehensive plans.

Accomplishments: All regional planning commissions have completed regional housing needs assessments. Some incorporation of regional housing production goals and strategies into local plans has occurred. The three regional housing needs assessments reviewed were of uniformly high quality even though they were produced with low budgets.

Caveats: There are no statewide totals on the number of affordable units produced. Compliance with assessments are voluntary, but a 1991 New Hampshire Supreme Court case, *Britton v. Town of Chester*, requires local governments that zone to take into account the affordable housing needs of the surrounding region.

Davidson Landing affordable housing in Nashua, New Hampshire.

New Hampshire requires by statute that each regional planning commission in the state compile a regional housing needs assessment to be used to assist municipalities in preparing master plans. By statute a municipal master plan or plan update may include a "[a] housing section which assesses local housing conditions and projects future housing needs of residents of all levels of income and ages in the municipality and the region as identified in the regional housing needs assessment performed by the regional planning commission . . . and which integrates the availability of human services with other planning undertaken by the community" (NHRSA, Section 673:2). The language concerning "and ages" was added by amendment, approved in May 2002, and is intended to ensure that local governments address both family and senior housing. However, the housing element is still optional, so the effect of this language change is unclear.

The regional housing assessment must include an assessment of the regional needs for housing "for persons and families of all levels of income," updated every five years and made available to all municipalities in the planning region (Section 36:47II). The regional assessments are advisory documents and thus not binding for cities and towns. Local governments have no obligation to plan for affordable housing.

In 1991, the New Hampshire Supreme Court ruled in *Britton v. Town of Chester* (134 N.H. 434, 595 A.2d 491) that purpose language in the state zoning enabling statute—the language that requires zoning to be enacted for the "general welfare of the community"—bars the enactment of exclusionary zoning (Blaesser et al. 1991). That phrase, the court held, includes the welfare of the larger region surrounding a town that adopts zoning regulations. The court thus did not find it necessary to decide the case on state constitutional grounds. While the court did not propose a *Mount Laurel*-style system, it did make clear that each zoning ordinance should provide a realistic opportunity for affordable housing.

The regional planning commissions in the state have taken different approaches in responding to this statutory requirement, with some actually preparing regional fair-share plans that establish housing goals based on regional need calculations (similar to New Jersey's fair-share plans) and others identifying housing need for each income group present in a local government. A review of a selection of these plans, most of them impressive documents, follows.

New Hampshire requires by statute that each regional planning commission in the state compile a regional housing needs assessment to be used to assist municipalities in preparing master plans.

Central New Hampshire Regional Planning Commission (Concord, N.H.)

The Central New Hampshire Regional Planning Commission's (CNHRPC) Affordable Housing Needs Assessment, adopted in May 2000, applies to 21 towns and cities in the region of which Concord is a part. The plan employs what it calls a "theoretical share" approach (in lieu of a "fair-share" approach). This approach assumes that "if all affordable housing development was to be distributed equally in the Central New Hampshire Region, then each community would contain a certain amount as determined by formulas used in the plan" (Central New Hampshire 2002, 2).

The plan does not project housing need for low- and moderate-income households, defined as households that earn 80 percent of the community median income. Instead, it estimates current (1998) housing need using a formula that assumes that the relationship of low- and moderate-income households to total population is the same in 1998 as it was in 1990:

[1990 Households in community @ 80 percent of Median Household Income] divided by [1990 Community Population]

=

[X] divided by [1998 Estimated Community Population]

Solving for X above would provide the estimated current number of low- and moderate-income households in a community.

A weighting factor, the "averaged result," is then computed. The factor is a composite of a community's share of the region's (1) population, (2) job base, (3) income (measured as wages paid), and (4) total assessed property values.

Averaged result for community =

[(Community share of regional population) + (Community share of regional employment) + (Community share of total regional wages paid) + (Community share of regional assessed valuation)]

divided by 4

To determine the "theoretical share" of low- and moderate-income housing, the averaged result factor is applied to the most recent estimate of low- and moderate-income households in the region, which was 13,770 in 1998.

Theoretical share for community =
(Averaged result for community) x 13,770

The plan then calculates "credits" for the number of affordable units that are assumed to exist in the community. It assumes that all manufactured and multifamily units are affordable.

Affordable housing credit for community =

[(2 X Number of multifamily and manufactured housing in community) + (Estimated number of households @ 80 percent of community median income)]

divided by 3

The affordable housing goal is then calculated for each community in the region. If the figure is a positive one, then the community has less than its theoretical share and needs to develop or provide opportunities for more affordable units. If the figure is negative or a zero, it means that the community is providing more than or is exactly equal to its theoretical share of the regional affordable housing stock.

Affordable housing planning goal for community =

[(Theoretical share for community) - (Affordable housing credits for community)]

A subsidized group home in Nashua, New Hampshire.

Nashua Regional Planning Commission

Based on these formulas, CNHRPC calculated that the total number of low- and moderate-income households increased in the region between 1990 and 1998 from 12,997 to 13,770. As of 1998, the region had 17,307 affordable dwelling units. The total of the individual theoretical shares for all 21 communities was 13,761, and the total number of affordable housing credits was 16,128, resulting in a regional negative total of -2,372. CNHRPC concluded that 10 communities had more than their theoretical share of the region's affordable housing and 11 communities had less; its calculations provided communities with specific planning goals that ranged from 24 to as many as 896 units.

In addition to quantifying these allocations, CNHRPC's assessment identifies a series of techniques that local governments can use to increase the supply of affordable housing. These include the provision of affordable housing and manufactured housing, reduced lot sizes, smaller setbacks and lot frontages, streamlined development review processes (e.g., clear language describing requirements), and waiving impact fees for affordable units. It also suggests a number of strategies that can promote affordable housing, including cluster development, accessory dwelling units, inclusionary housing and linkage programs, use of excess publicly owned land for affordable housing development, and rehabilitation carried out through a variety of federal and state programs.

The CNHRPC assessment does have a number of limitations, most of which have been noted by the commission's staff. One problem was a lack of data. Because the 2000 census data were not available, estimates had to be made of the number of low- and moderate-income households using the technique described above. Another was the definition of "affordable housing." The study assumed all multifamily and manufactured housing was "affordable," but, according to staff, this included luxury condominiums. Further, CNHRPC principal planner Matthew Walsh (2002) noted, the definition may have excluded an "undefined number of detached single-family units." He also said, "If more resources were available for this study, the preferred way to determine the number of 'affordable units' would have been to obtain assessing records of each community and query them for housing with an assessed value which would be considered affordable." This preferred approach was impossible, Walsh explained, because of a lack of time and resources. Finally, Walsh noted that, because the report estimates the theoretical fair share of affordable housing that each community in the region should have, "a handful of communities have been using the study as fodder for attempting to zone out some types of housing. This is not the intent of the study." Walsh cautions that the report is instead intended to be a "broad estimate of the state of affordable housing in the central New Hampshire region. Use of the study alone, without additional research, to create housing policy is not appropriate."

The assessment also fails to monitor community-by-community progress on achieving prior housing planning goals established in a 1995 report. Laura Scott (2002), a principal planner, acknowledges this problem and said that the commission does track building permits, including permits for multifamily housing, and that it may be addressed in the next edition of the study.

Despite CNHRPC warnings, however, figures from the regional housing assessment have, in fact, been incorporated into some local comprehensive plans in the central New Hampshire region. For example, a master plan for the town of Epsom prepared with the regional planning commission's assistance includes the assessment's planning goals for each of the towns in the region. In this particular case, Epsom actually had 34 more affordable units than its theoretical fair share, and the plan indicates the town does not need to develop more affordable housing (Central New Hampshire 2002, VI-17). Nonetheless, the plan does recommend some design guidelines on buffering and landscaping for multifamily housing in order to provide housing that is compatible with the area's "rural character." It is also goes on to encourage multifamily housing connected to the town water system to allow for greater development densities and recommends reviewing setback, frontage, and lot size requirements in the zoning code to ensure that such standards are not unreasonable or serve to discourage development of multifamily housing.

Similarly, a planning board conditionally approved a draft of a housing element prepared by CNHRPC for the town of Henniker that showed the town had met its theoretical fair-share allocation of 557 units. (According to the plan draft, in 2000, 27 percent of Henniker's 1,676 units were multifamily and 5.6 percent were manufactured units.) The draft nonetheless observed that "this does not mean that the supply of affordable housing is adequate to meet the demand. In addition, the number of units counted as affordable within the community assumes that all manufactured housing and multifamily housing units are affordable, which may or may not be accurate." In order for Henniker to have a thriving economic and residential base, there needs to be a "diversity of housing that is adequate to meet the needs of the current and future population" (Henniker Master Plan 2002, 13). The plan also recommends measures that include consideration of inclusionary and elderly zoning ordinances as well as updating regulations affecting manufactured housing.

Nashua Regional Planning Commission (Nashua, N.H.)

The Nashua Regional Planning Commission's (NRPC) Housing Needs Assessment (1999) takes a somewhat different tack for its region, which consists of 12 member communities. The report contains a very thorough review of the housing stock, noting that, in the late 1990s, the region found itself in the midst of steady growth. This resulted in rental vacancy rates at their lowest point in a decade, "as rent levels and home sales prices are the highest" (NRPC 1999, 1). Rental costs were increasing at the greatest rate in Nashua, where the rental vacancy rate was 0.4 percent, in contrast to New Hampshire's overall rate of 2.3 percent. The report also catalogues condominiums and apartments as well as assisted housing in the region.

Clocktower Place apartments in downtown Nashua, New Hampshire, a former industrial building converted to a mix of subsidized and unsubsidized apartments.

In contrast to the CNHRPC's assessment, NRPC's report did not update its earlier (1994) estimates of the number of rental units needed for three income groups in the region, which were based on the 1990 census. The income groups were households of less than 22 percent of the median income, 22 to 44 percent of median, and 44 to 76 percent of median. The study evaluated the number of units needed for each income group by community, a calculation of *existing* housing needs in 1999. It found a deficiency of 1,194 units for the lowest group, and surpluses of 1,018 units and 6,075 units for the middle and highest groups, respectively (NRPC 1999, 31). It also contained a projection of *future* housing needs in 2000 by income group, based on anticipated population growth. These projections predicted need for housing for an additional 184 households in the lowest group, 203 households in the next, and 375 households in the third. It also added a fourth group, those households at greater than 76 percent, for which it calculated need for an additional 3,638 households. Together, these projections for 2000 anticipated housing need for 4,400 households more than in 1999 (NRPC 1999, 33 and A-1–A-7). Especially notable is the study's analysis of total household need for all income groups, not just of affordable units.

The report also discusses strategies for meeting local housing needs, including inclusionary housing programs, cluster housing, elderly housing zones, accessory housing, group homes, manufactured housing, and the establishment of principles for maintaining community character. In a cluster housing development, it notes, the individual house lot or private yard area dedicated to each unit is usually smaller than those found in conventional developments, while the overall density is the same or even lower. While the previous (1994) regional housing needs assessment touted cluster housing as an affordable housing mechanism, this edition declares that it is simply a technique to preserve open space associated with subdivisions. It observes that "[t]here is no evidence to suggest that clustered housing provisions result in the creation of affordable housing. . . . In terms of affordable housing, it is neutral" (NRPC 1999, 36–37).

Across the region, local comprehensive plans often cite the obligation to address affordable housing needs, but these plans are not always specific on where it is to be located and how it is to be provided. According to Steve Heuchert (2002), senior planner and land-use program coordinator with the commission, "Just about every local plan within our 12 communities has some kind of housing needs analysis that incorporates the regional housing needs assessments." But, he observed, "the depth of the analysis will vary."

While the previous (1994) NRPC regional housing needs assessment touted cluster housing as an affordable housing mechanism, this edition declares that it is simply a technique to preserve open space associated with subdivisions.

Anne's Place, Enfield, New Hampshire; part of Twin Pines Housing Trust's effort to provide supportive housing in Vermont and New Hampshire. This project involves Cape House (left), dating from 1840, and West House (center), which will include eight new apartments.

Ray Brewster, Twin Pines Housing Trust

Heuchert also said that, as a consequence of the inclusion of the housing needs assessment in Nashua's 2000 master plan—which was based on and incorporates the regional report—the city's mayor created an affordable housing task force. The Nashua plan itself contains a number of specific recommendations. For example, one suggests an increase in the city's supply of rental housing to meet the needs of all income groups; another proposes a review of the city's zoning ordinance to assess the opportunity for alternative housing design. Indeed, the plan points out that Nashua has already loosened zoning ordinance provisions for accessory housing and allows such units as a special exception. In addition, while observing that Nashua is nearly built out, the plan notes that vacant parcels in the southwest portion of the city offer the potential for 1,000 to 1,400 dwelling units, depending on the zoning applied to them. The plan contains a listing of these large, subdividable parcels in the city and their current zoning (Nashua 2002a).

Similarly, in a comprehensive plan that NRPC prepared for the town of Lyndeborough, a section acknowledges that "the ability of housing affordable to individuals of all income levels has become one of the region's most critical issues" (NRPC 2002, II-8). The plan goes on to note that, to afford any basic rental housing in the region, the renter would have to earn $1.50 more per hour than the statewide average and would have to work longer hours, depending on the rental type. There is no assisted housing in the town, the plan narrative observes (although, it should be noted, Lyndeborough's 2000 population was only 1,585). In order to meet the statewide and regional average of 3.1 percent of the housing stock of assisted housing, the town would need to provide opportunities for 18 units of assisted housing. The plan also recommends that the town develop regulatory measures to facilitate the provision of affordable housing, such as a "Housing for Older Persons Ordinance" or "a refinement of the provisions allowing for accessory dwelling units so that such units can be constructed to a maximum of 800 square feet and contribute towards the provision of assisted housing under Federal or State programs" (p. II-9). The plan does not designate any areas for affordable housing.

A plan for the town of Pelham makes similar findings, citing the 1999 Regional Housing Needs Assessment. Here, the plan notes a shortfall of 64 units of affordable housing (the town already had 48 units of elderly housing). Pelham had approved projects for an additional 64 units of elderly housing, but they had not been constructed at the time the plan was prepared. There is no provision for assisted family housing in the plan. The Pelham plan contains identical implementation recommendations as the Lyndeborough plan (NRPC 2002, II-8–II-10).

North Country Council (Bethlehem, N.H.)

The North Country Council's (NCC) Housing Needs Assessment (1995) updated an earlier report from 1989. It approaches its subject by dividing the 51-municipality North Country region into a series of four small labor market areas around Littleton (20 towns), Berlin (15 towns), Conway (8 towns), and Plymouth (8 towns). Like the other assessments, NCC's identifies the number and rate at which housing units are increasing or decreasing, the types of housing structure, and estimates of future housing growth. Of the four subregions, the assessment projects Conway, along the Maine border, to have the highest housing growth rate for the period 1990 to 2010, growing from 6,428 units to 11,951 units, an increase of 83 percent over the 20-year period (North County Council 1995, ch. 1).

The report also analyzes housing costs by type and finds that for the region's three counties—Carroll, Coos and Grafton counties—purchase prices of housing actually declined by an average of 25 percent between 1988 and 1993 as housing growth slowed. At the same time, median rental unit costs increased by 12 percent over the same period. The report attributes these shifts to "[o]verriding economic conditions related to employment, wages and consumer confidence" (pp. 28–29) during this period.

The NCC assessment establishes fair-share goals for each of the towns in the region using a methodology similar to that used in New Jersey. NCC's allocation process begins with the calculation of indigenous housing need–the total number of households earning 75 percent of the county median household income and paying 30 percent or more of the household's income for rent or owner costs. Thus, in contrast to the New Jersey system, which incorporates present and future need, this approach only analyzes present need.

Spencer Square, Lebanon, New Hampshire; a project by the Twin Pines Housing Trust that includes three buildings with a total of 26 affordable apartments.

Ray Brewster, Twin Pines Housing Trust

NCC's methodology then divides the total household need for all the towns in each of the region's labor markets according to each town's percentage of the total dwelling units. The numbers that result represent the equal distribution of housing need. The indigenous household need less the equal distribution figure is called excess need. Not all towns have excess need; it exists only in those towns where indigenous need proportionally exceeds what could be expected through an equal distribution of the town's percentage of dwelling units. Excess need is then totaled for all towns in a small area labor market and redistributed using a formula that takes into account proportion of area employment, vacant developable land, and equalized assessed valuation. The excess need figure was 770 units for 1995.

The basic fair-share obligation for communities with excess need is their regional housing need given equal distribution. The basic obligation for communities without excess need is their regional housing need given equal distribution plus any excess units allocated to them. These figures are then factored up by a vacancy rate, so if a town had a basic obligation of 100 units, the figure would be adjusted upward by 3 percent (the presumed vacancy rate) for a total of 103 units.

The NCC assessment also provides towns with credits to reflect progress made from 1990 to 1993 in meeting fair-share goals. These include one credit for each manufactured housing unit permit issued, one for each unit in existing structures built or rehabilitated for rental-assisted housing (but excluding Section 8 certificates and vouchers). Finally, one credit is also given for each 10 miles over 20 miles of the distance between the town and the small labor market area growth center defined by NCC, so that the obligation is reduced somewhat by distance from urbanization.

The adjusted fair share for units, prior to credits, was 6,540 dwelling units. Credits of 743 units reduced that number to 5,797, the fair-share total for all towns in the region. The region's housing stock in 1993 totaled 50,435 units, so the fair-share total was about 11.5 percent of that amount.

NCC found that 16 towns had excess housing need, which means that these towns had a sufficient number of housing units but that many families living in these units had incomes below the county median and were spending more than 30 percent of their incomes on rent or owner costs. The assessment proposes several strategies for towns in this situation. These include the enactment of zoning provisions that allow for the conversion of large single-family dwelling units into duplexes and multifamily, elderly or other smaller, affordable dwelling units It also proposes using federal Community Development Block Grant funds and other similar sources to maintain or rehabilitate the existing affordable housing stock (North County Council 1995, 45).

Communities without excess housing needs have an insufficient number of affordable units to provide for the community's regional fair-share obligation. Here, the assessment proposes focusing on new construction. Strategies include using excess public land for the development of affordable housing, awarding density bonuses and incentive bonuses, enacting zoning provisions that would allow substandard lots (lots not meeting current zoning requirements) for affordable housing, and requiring developers to construct a certain percentage of affordable units in any project of 10 dwelling units or more.

Given the lack of a state mandate to ensure that local comprehensive plans contain a housing element, the New Hampshire program is nonetheless effective as far as it goes.

Program Results

Given the lack of a state mandate to ensure that local comprehensive plans contain a housing element, the New Hampshire program is nonetheless effective as far as it goes. Regional planning agencies do prepare housing needs assessments and then work with their member governments to incorporate the assessments into local plans. Still, the regional assessments are strictly advisory, and the regional agencies and the state do not have the authority to compel a city or town to do anything, as William Ray (2002), director of planning and policy for the New Hampshire Housing Finance Authority, has pointed out. Part of what success the regional agencies have had may be the result of the close relationship between the agencies and their member communities: the regional agency is viewed by the local governments as an extension of themselves. Steve Heuchert (2002) of the NRPC commented that, in addition to state statutory requirements, the fact that housing is reflected in local plans at all may have to do with the "very strong sense of volunteerism in New Hampshire—people promote causes and they rely on the regional planning commissions to help them." He added that governments recognize that "it's getting to the point now where middle-income people can't afford housing" and that much of the housing now being built is single-family residences with three to four bedrooms on large lots.

Ray also pointed out that a uniform approach to the regional housing needs assessment is "unlikely," given the distinctive character of the state's regions. The Nashua area, a bedroom community for Boston, is characterized by high demand and high housing prices. The region to the north in central New Hampshire is just beginning to experience some of the same housing pressures that the Nashua area has undergone. The NCC area includes large areas that are made up of national forests, very little rental housing, and a surplus of owner-occupied housing. Ray also said that because the state does not have an income tax, it is difficult to get good current data on per-capita income and household income to help determine affordability. The better and more current data are, he said, "the easier it is to make a convincing argument" that affordable housing is needed in different parts of the state. For Ray, "affordable housing is what you produce when the housing market is balanced." Currently, the New Hampshire market is unbalanced; it simply "doesn't produce housing for the full range of households," he added.

Jeffrey Hayes (2002), AICP, the NCC assistant director, believes that the preferences of local housing agencies work against the full dispersal of new affordable housing. "There seems to be a consensus among housing agencies," he says, "to focus their efforts on larger service center communities where public housing occupants can have easy access to public and non-profit services and food shopping. In addition, it is politically easier to gain support in a larger community where such a housing project may have a larger impact on community services."

Ben Frost (2002), a senior planner with the New Hampshire Office of Planning, agrees. He believes the current approach to assessing regional housing needs will not change until state statutes do. Since there is no mechanism for enforcement, he says, "municipalities have an incentive to shunt housing demand off to adjacent communities. This is exacerbated by our tax structure, which makes communities treat family housing as a pure expense."

Local recognition of affordable housing need may be prompted by the prospect of a challenge to a local zoning ordinance along the lines of the 1991 *Britton v Town of Chester* decision, where regional housing needs enter the picture and local governments are expected to account for them in their zoning. William Ray sees this as less of a factor in 2002 than in 1991 because of the passage of time and the lack of any aggressive *Britton*-style litigation in the early and mid 1990s, when the state housing market went into decline. Nonetheless, said Steve Heuchert, there is still "a political dichotomy between protecting rural character and providing affordable housing" that makes it difficult to persuade towns to change their zoning practices.

Bruce Mayberry (2002), a planning consultant in Yarmouth, Maine, is advising the New Hampshire Housing Finance Authority on needed changes to the regional housing needs assessments. He notes that the original assessments were formulated using guidance from the New Hampshire Office of State Planning. That guidance followed portions of the framework established by the New Jersey *Mount Laurel* anti-exclusionary zoning decisions, discussed above (Applied Economic Research 1987). The key difference, however, was that New Hampshire's assessments tend not to look at total future housing needs (including

"Municipalities have an incentive to shunt housing demand off to adjacent communities. This is exacerbated by our tax structure, which makes communities treat family housing as a pure expense."

—BEN FROST, SENIOR PLANNER, NEW HAMPSHIRE OFFICE OF PLANNING

Affordable Housing, Education, and Development (AHEAD)

To be effective, local housing elements need to affirmatively demonstrate that the municipality enables realistic opportunities for the creation of multifamily, duplex, and attached housing units in developments of varying density, or that there is a vacant land supply appropriately zoned to accommodate such units.

market-rate housing) but instead focus on existing deficiencies for low- and moderate-income housing. "What the regions have done is positive," Mayberry said. "Most of the plans articulate very well the *Britton v. Chester* decision. They are emphasizing the nonexclusion aspect, which is a point that has to be driven home. The fair-share core has raised consciousness of that regionality."

Mayberry said that the regional plans and therefore the local housing elements must be future oriented and examine housing needs for all income groups. In addition, his analysis shows that local housing plans, where they exist, are often not integrated with the economic goals of the local master plan. "While there may be extensive planning for more land to be zoned for industrial and commercial development and a focus on attaining job growth and increased nonresidential assessed value," he says, "there is rarely a commensurate level of analysis on the need to allocate land to housing of various types and densities that will accommodate the regional and local housing needs generated by that economic development."

To be effective, Mayberry believes, local housing elements need to affirmatively demonstrate that the municipality enables realistic opportunities for the creation of multifamily, duplex, and attached housing units in developments of varying density, or that there is a vacant land supply appropriately zoned to accommodate such units. "However, it is rare to see such an analysis in a local or regional needs assessment," he says.

Related to the impact of regional housing plans are efforts to amend local zoning ordinances to provide for affordable housing. In New

Hampshire, out of the 234 communities studied by planning consultant Philip Herr (2000a, 2000b, 2000c), 95 had adopted zoning. Of that number, 44 had adopted some type of "affordability zoning," which constituted 19 percent of all communities in the state and 46 percent of all communities with zoning. According to Herr's analysis, only one New Hampshire town, Portsmouth, had adopted an inclusionary mandate, and it was for a specific development site.[13]

The New Hampshire legislature has recognized the ongoing severity of the state's housing crisis. In November 2002, a specially created legislative commission on "workforce housing" issued a report, *Reducing Regulatory Barriers to Workforce Housing in New Hampshire* (New Hampshire Legislative Commission 2002). The commission concludes that "local land use regulations and the municipal regulatory process have had a significant role in preventing or deterring the private sector from responding to the shortage of workforce housing." The report defines "workforce housing" as "a housing unit that is affordable to a household with income of 80 percent or less of the median income of the region in which it is located, adjusted for household size" (p. 1). The commission urges the legislature to take steps to revamp local zoning and planning procedures as well as state policies and regulations to promote the development of workforce housing, not impede it. Its recommendations include:

- Implement the 1991 ruling of the [New Hampshire] Supreme Court in *Britton v. Chester*, which requires that municipalities provide reasonable opportunities for the creation of workforce housing, and reaffirm that this obligation extends not only to addressing the local need for such housing but to providing for *a share of the regional need as well* [emphasis supplied].

- Create a selective mechanism for expediting relief from municipal actions, under criteria established by the Legislature, which deny, impede or significantly delay qualified proposals for workforce housing. Establishment of an expedited relief process is vital to the effective implementation of both existing law and the recommendations included here—and it is unlikely that any real change will occur without the relief provided by this mechanism.

- Direct technical assistance to assist communities to carry out their responsibilities to offer opportunities for the creation of workforce housing.

- Create a study commission to identify and review state agency rules, and regulatory policies that affect the cost of housing development or limit such development. The goals of the commission should be (1) to identify ways of reducing their adverse impact on housing development or cost and (2) to recommend specific legislation and regulatory changes. The study commission should include legislators, representatives of regulatory agencies, planning interests, home building industry representatives, and representatives from business generally. (Legislative Commission 2002, 2)

Finally, the report proposes that the state legislature should direct the New Hampshire Housing Finance Authority and the New Hampshire Office of State Planning to "establish a uniform methodology for the development of the regional housing needs assessment" (p. 6) required by state law. It also recommends providing direct financial incentives to encourage communities to meet regional workforce housing needs.

AN INCENTIVE PROGRAM

METROPOLITAN COUNCIL, TWIN CITIES REGION, MINNESOTA

Title: Livable Communities Act (LCA)

Inception: 1995

Administration: Administered by the Metropolitan Council for a seven-county area, the LCA is an incentives-based program that provides grants to participating municipalities.

Key objectives: Increase production of affordable housing by the region's municipalities and eliminate regulatory barriers to such housing.

Accomplishments: In 1998, according to the Metropolitan Council, 77 percent of new affordable ownership units were built in the developing suburbs (2,820 of 3,677 units), up slightly from 74 percent in 1997. Some 80 percent of new ownership units were constructed in developing suburbs in 1998. At the same time, 46 percent of new rental units constructed in the region in 1998 met affordability criteria, but the actual number of new affordable apartment units built in 1998 was down from the previous two years. In terms of new planning and zoning efforts to facilitate affordable housing, 12 communities offered density bonuses while 17 communities used land cost write-downs

Caveats: This program has been criticized for rewarding participation rather than results. The voluntary nature of the program makes it possible for municipal governments in the region to do nothing by electing not to participate. Critics of the Metropolitan Council say that focusing on the LCA ignores the state Land Use Planning Act, which they believe requires the council to determine the region's affordable housing needs and each city's fair-share allocation to meet that need.

Minnesota enacted the Livable Communities Act (LCA) in 1995 (Minnesota Statutes Sections 473.25 et seq. (1999)). The act is administered by the Metropolitan Council, the multicounty regional planning authority for the seven-county Twin Cities area. It authorizes the council to levy funds to create affordable housing, promote redevelopment through cleaning up polluted sites, and develop compact high-density neighborhoods that are both pedestrian and transit friendly to residents. Participation by local governments is voluntary. The three requirements of LCA funding are that communities: (1) elect to participate; (2) negotiate affordable and life-cycle housing[14] goals with the council; and (3) agree to make expenditures toward implementing their local housing goals.

Under the LCA, monies for loans and grants come from three distinct funds controlled by the council :

- the Local Housing Incentives Account (LHIA), which provides grants to help participating communities create affordable and life-cycle housing opportunities;

- the Tax Base Revitalization Account (TBRA), which provides grants to help communities clean up polluted land in order to reduce obstacles to economic development; and

- the Livable Communities Demonstration Account (LCDA), which provides both loans and grants to communities pursuing projects that produce compact development at higher densities with a mix of housing types and costs.

In 1999, the Minnesota legislature created an additional fund, the Inclusionary Housing Account (IHA), under which the council provides grants to communities willing to waive restrictions that "otherwise would increase costs of construction" and to include "units affordable to households with incomes at or below 80 percent of area median income" (Section 472.255).

From 1996 through 2001, the council distributed more than $83.3 million to cities with projects designed to meet LCA goals. These grants included:

- 51 LHIA grants totaling $8.1 million to 39 communities;

- 68 LCDA grants totaling $35.3 million to 29 communities; and

- 90 TBRA grants totaling $35.7 million to 23 communities.

In addition, in 2000, the council awarded the first 11 grants from the new IHA. These totaled $4.2 million and went to eight communities in the region (Metropolitan Council 2002, 8-10).

The council publishes an annual report card on affordable units produced in the region under the LCA. In 1999, 143 (76 percent) of the region's municipalities reported. Of the 101 LCA participants in the region, 96 returned surveys. Based on the average number of permits issued between 1996 and 1998, the council estimates that, by 2010, there will be an additional 56,050 affordable owner-occupied housing units in the seven-county area, although this will fall short of goals negotiated in 1997 calling for 68,553. Similarly, by 2010, based on the same three-year average, there will be an additional 9,030 renter-occupied affordable units, less than the 2010 negotiated goals. (Note that the negotiated goals represent goals for only those communities that participate in the LCA.) LCA participants have negotiated the addition of 81,438 affordable units for the region for the year 2010. If the same level of construction continues, the region would experience a shortfall of 16,500 units relative to negotiated goals (Metropolitan Council 1999, 1, 11, 14). Table 4-16 shows the pattern of production over time since LCA reporting began.

TABLE 4-16
REGIONAL GOALS AND PRODUCTION LEVELS OF
AFFORDABLE UNITS, 1996-2000, TWIN CITIES REGION

Affordable housing units	New units reported 1996	New units reported 1997	New units reported 1998	New units reported 1999	New units reported 2000	Projected through 2010	2010 goals (negotiated) in 1999
Owner	4,146*	3,470*	3,724**	2,638**	2,227**	48,615	63,806
Renter	788	523	495	430	1,222	10,374	12,308

*The majority of these units were deemed affordable from building permit valuations. These values do not represent selling costs, because they do not usually include lot prices and finishing costs.

**Affordable owner units reported in 1998, 1999, and 2000 have been adjusted to include an average lot cost where affordability determinations were based on building permit values. These adjustments tend to better represent the selling price of new homes.

It is worth noting that Table 4-16 appears to suggest an ongoing decline in the production of affordable owner-occupied housing in recent years, although the council's footnoted explanation about incorporating calculations of lot costs makes this decline difficult to verify. An ongoing decline in rental housing seems clearer but is disrupted by the aberrational leap in 2000, which may have been due to the completion of several large projects.

Negotiating Housing Goals

Because goals for affordable housing have become an important part of this scheme, the process of negotiating goals is itself important. The LCA does not prescribe how the council is to negotiate affordable housing goals with partici-

The council's procedure is not linked to the actual needs of low-income people in the region. Instead, it is based on the council's division of the region's communities into eight sectors.

pating communities. The council's procedure is not linked to the actual needs of low-income people in the region. Instead, it is based on the council's division of the region's communities into eight sectors; the council then considers each community's stage of development (developing, fully developed, free-standing), and creates benchmark ranges for each sector and type, with the aim of incrementally advancing production of affordable units. Thus, regardless of the percentage of negotiated goals that communities achieve, there is no direct correlation between those numbers and the collective regional needs of households below 80 percent of median income (for owner-occupied housing) or 50 percent (for rental housing). This fact, in turn, is at the core of much of the controversy surrounding the question of the LCA's effectiveness. The divergence between goals, actual production, and needs according to income formulas virtually ensures a prolonged debate about whether the region's affordable housing cup is half full or half empty.

In an effort to strengthen the incentives for developing affordable housing, the council claims it "give priority for regional infrastructure investments or expenditures of public dollars to communities that have implemented plans to provide their share of the region's low- and moderate-income and life-cycle housing opportunities" (Metropolitan Council 1996, 57). The council has adopted guidelines that enshrine this principle in its grant-making activities, providing points on a scale of 0 to 100 for cities and counties seeking funding for community development, transportation, and environmental programs, including TEA-21 (the Transportation Efficiency Act, which is the current federal transportation legislation; the council's review criteria tie TEA-21 funding to land-use and housing performance criteria), Metro Environment Partnership grants, and parks and open space. Every community is given an annual performance score under this rating system. For example, in 2001, Minneapolis topped the list with 98 of 100 possible points, followed by St. Paul with 97, while three communities tied for last with one point each. The median score was 23. Only 39 of 182 rated communities scored 50 or better (Metropolitan Council 2001b). Table 4-17 is a summary of the rating system the council applies to cities; a separate system applies to counties, and scores are averaged where multiple jurisdictions are applying jointly for a grant. The full list of guidelines is somewhat more detailed than what appears here. Where the term "affordable" is used in this summary, it is shorthand for the full guidelines' use of the term according to the council's standard criteria described above.

It is difficult, however, to ascertain how much influence this scoring system will have over time on communities' affordable housing policies and practices because, as the guidelines state, "The amount of emphasis or weight given to the housing performance score or rank . . . will be at the discretion of the Metropolitan Council at the time it solicits applications for any of these discretionary funding activities" (Metropolitan Council 2001a).

Program Results

According to the council, in 1998, 77 percent of new affordable ownership units were built in the developing suburbs (2,820 of 3,677 units), up slightly from 74 percent in 1997. Some 80 percent of new ownership units were constructed in developing suburbs in 1998. At the same time, 46 percent of new rental units constructed in the region in 1998 met affordability criteria, but actual numbers of new affordable apartment units built in 1998 were down from the previous two years (Metropolitan Council 2001a, 12).

In terms of new planning and zoning efforts to facilitate affordable housing, 12 communities offered density bonuses while 17 communities used land cost write-downs. The council also offers the following "quick facts" regarding how well new affordable housing is being distributed throughout the region (all figures since 1996):

**TABLE 4-17
SUMMARY OF METRO COUNCIL "GUIDELINES
FOR PRIORITY FUNDING FOR HOUSING PERFORMANCE"
FOR CITIES IN THE TWIN CITIES REGION**

Affordability and Diversification

0-8 points — Percent of owner-occupied housing with assessed valuation equal to or below affordable levels, plus total number of mobile homes

0-8 points — Percent of total housing stock composed of affordable rental units, including all federally subsidized rental units.

0-6 points — Percent of housing stock that is not conventional single-family detached units

0-10 points — Percent of net units added to housing stock that is affordable since monitoring began in 1996

0-4 points — Housing for special needs (one point for each of the following types of housing):

- Housing for which federal, state, county, local, or nonprofit funds were used to purchase and operated rental units or provide licensed housing for transitional placement of adult offenders or adjudicated delinquents
- Publicly subsidized or nonprofit group home licensed by Health or Human Services department, providing housing for physically handicapped, mentally ill, developmentally disabled, or chemically dependent
- Publicly subsidized or nonprofit-operated shelter for homeless persons and families or battered women
- Housing for homeless, with transitional stay of six to 24 months

Local Initiatives to Facilitate Affordable Workforce Housing Development or Preservation

0-15 points — *Fiscal tools and initiatives*—one of the following is in place in comprehensive plan or local housing plan (3 points per tool used) to assist affordable workforce or life-cycle housing:

- Tax increment financing
- Housing revenue bonds
- General obligation bonds
- Local property tax levy
- Local tax abatement
- Local fee waivers or reductions
- Credit enhancements
- Taxable revenue bonds
- Land write-down or sale
- Collaboration and participation with a community land trust to preserve
- Long-term affordability

0-15 points — *Initiatives regarding local regulation and development requirements*— municipality has allowed the reduction, adjustment, or elimination of one of the following controls in the past two years or made a commitment to do so upon request to facilitate development or preservation of affordable housing (3 points per initiative, no more than 6 points per activity aided):   *(continued)*

- 120 communities have added at least some affordable ownership or rental housing;

- 73 of these have added units that represent more than 20 percent of all their new units;

- 44 cities have or will have federal low-income housing tax credit rental housing development built in their jurisdiction; and

- over 2,974 tax-credit rental units (new or preservation) in these cities have received tax credits. (Peterson 2002)

▌ **TABLE 4-17** *(continued)*
**SUMMARY OF METRO COUNCIL "GUIDELINES
FOR PRIORITY FUNDING FOR HOUSING PERFORMANCE"
FOR CITIES IN THE TWIN CITIES REGION**

Local Initiatives to Facilitate Affordable Workforce Housing Development or Preservation

- Density bonus system, inclusionary housing requirements, or some other innovative zoning approach
- Use of variances, rezoning, special or conditional permits or similar variations from zoning standards
- Revision of local design requirements to reduce costs of public services
- Modifications in public services standards or requirements (streets, sewer and water hookups, etc.)
- Reduction of such standards as the required street right-of-way, surfacing width or depth design for residential streets, or size of sewer or water service lines

0–12 points	*Initiatives regarding housing preservation and rehabilitation*—having in place locally initiated and administered (by city or county) housing preservation, home improvement and/or rehabilitation programs, or other tools (2 points per initiative), not limited to the following examples:

- Housing maintenance code and enforcement program for rental housing
- Same for owner-occupied housing
- Housing rehabilitation loan or grant program for rental housing
- Same for owner-occupied housing
- Home improvement loan or grant program
- Home improvement resource center
- Local tool-sharing center or program

1–5 points	Average net density for attached housing units (per acre)
1–5 points	Average net density for detached housing units (per acre) (Note: Unsewered communities gain higher rank for lower net density)
0 or 6 points	Current zoning ordinance allows densities for residential development consistent with densities set forth in the local comprehensive plan revised pursuant to the 1995 Land Planning Act amendments.
0 or 6 points	In previous two calendar years, has approved development or local financial participation in a proposed development of new affordable housing, or involvement in preservation and reinvestment in existing affordable housing—ownership or rental—that has not as yet been undertaken for reasons beyond municipality's control, as follows:

2 points—less than 20 units

4 points—20 to 39 units

6 points—40 or more units

Source: Metropolitan Council, "Guidelines for Priority Funding for Housing Performance" (St. Paul: Metropolitan Council, 2001).

In addition, during the past three years, three county housing redevelopment agencies and more than 12 cities agreed to accept additional federal low-income public housing units (Peterson 2002).

The 2000 survey revealed some interesting shifts. Overall, reporting by municipalities appeared to be declining slightly, with only 137 responding (Metropolitan Council 2002, 2). Although the numbers are not broken out in the text of the report, the map of response patterns indicates that at least nine participating LCA communities failed to respond, up from five two years

earlier. (It should be noted that, in 2000, the council added three new participating communities.) The report concedes that the lower response rate results
in probable undercounting in the calculations of affordable housing units built.
Still, it reports that production was up 12 percent from 1999, with one-third of
those new units being rental; at the same time, however, new owner-occupied
affordable housing units fell from earlier years to 2,227 (for example, the 1996
total was 4,146). Overall, the 2002 report notes that the total of negotiated additional affordable housing units to be produced by 2010 among participating
communities was 76,114, which would appear to be about 5 percent less than
the goal that was set in 2000. The report also states that at current production
rates, actual production would miss that goal by about 17,000 units (p. 2). How
much of this shortfall is due to an apparent decline in reporting by participating communities is difficult to determine from the data available.

*Heritage Park in Minneapolis, a mixed-
income housing development that
received funding from the Livable
Communities Act through the
Metropolitan Council.*

Criticisms of Metropolitan Council and LCA

The voluntary nature of the LCA, its use of incentives and avoidance of
mandates and sanctions, and its steady retreat from the use of terms like
"low- and moderate-income housing" have drawn criticism from advocates of affordable housing.[15]

A 1998 critique by the University of Minnesota Center for Urban and
Regional Affairs (CURA) of the LCA and its administration concluded
that the implementation of the act "undermines its goal of increasing affordable housing" (Goetz and Mardock 1998, 3). For example, the program's
definitions of affordability, which classify 68 percent of all housing units in
the region as "affordable," should be revised, the CURA study suggests.
The benchmark system used to establish affordability goals "ignores housing need altogether by being based only on previous development and

rewards underperforming communities with lower standards"; CURA proposes that it be revised. CURA's critique also recommends firmly tying affordable housing to the receipt of state aid and to modifications of sewer areas and the urban service area for the region; likewise, it calls for granting the state power to override local zoning when it has unnecessarily restricted affordable housing. In the absence of these changes, the report predicts that a majority of communities in the seven-county region "will not be adding affordable housing in higher portions than currently exist, and there will be an aggregate reduction in the proportion of affordable ownership and rental housing in the Twin Cities region by 2010" (p. 3).

The Metropolitan Council's report acknowledges this shortfall. It notes that "[w]hen all new affordable housing in the region is included, regardless of LCA participation, construction at current rates would result in approximately 12,700 fewer owner units and 3,850 fewer rental units than negotiated by 2010" (Metropolitan Council 1999, 2).

Critics at CURA also argue that the affordable housing goal-setting process of the LCA has overshadowed a longstanding, but neglected, component of Minnesota's Land Use Planning Act (LUPA) of 1976. They note that the statute provides the basis for mandatory land-use planning in the seven-county region, including the preparation of a housing element subject to review by the council for its adequacy in meeting "the local unit's share of the metro area need for low- and moderate-income housing" (Minnesota Statutes, Section 473.859, subdivision 2). They contend that LUPA establishes the groundwork for a fair-share program in the region that goes well beyond the voluntary participation of LCA, noting that the statute requires local comprehensive plans to:

> . . . include a housing element containing standards, plans and programs for providing adequate housing opportunities to meet existing and projected local and regional housing needs, including but not limited to the use of official controls and land use planning to promote the availability of land for the development of low- and moderate-income housing (Section 473.859, subdivision 4).

A key underlying premise of this critique is that, for more than 25 years, the council has had the authority to review local plans to determine whether their housing elements meet the community's fair share of regional low- and moderate-income housing needs. From this perspective, the council's recent adoption of guidelines for rating performance in this area is not innovative but instead "represents merely the reactivation of a policy that the council routinely followed during the 1970s, but had abandoned for most the 80s and all of the 90s" (Goetz, Chapple, and Lukermann 2001).

A new lawsuit, filed August 15, 2002, has challenged the council and the city of Eagan over precisely this point. The suit, initiated by the Metropolitan Interfaith Council on Affordable Housing (MICAH), the Community Stabilization Project, and the Alliance for Metropolitan Stability, argues that the council has failed to follow LUPA requirements that it determine the region's affordable housing needs and each city's fair-share allocation to meet that need (Brandt and Kaszuba 2002). "We believe the law says the council needs to measure the regional need and tell the communities what their share is," said Joy Sorenson Navarre, the executive director of MICAH. "And we believe the sum of the parts should equal the larger number" (Sorenson 2002).

The suit arose from Eagan's decision not to participate in the voluntary LCA program and from what housing advocates have long claimed is the city's unfair discrimination against minorities and welfare recipients, a charge the city denies. Although the city maintains that it has met the council's affordable housing targets, the suit argues that those targets are

Overall, the 2002 Metropolitan Council report notes that the total of negotiated additional affordable housing units to be produced by 2010 among participating communities was 76,114, which would appear to be about 5 percent less than the goal that was set in 2000.

too weak because of the council's failure to follow LUPA (Brandt and Kaszuba 2002). MICAH said that it worked for more than two years to persuade the council to fulfill its duties before filing the lawsuit (Sorenson 2002). The council responded with a motion to dismiss; the suit is currently (as of November 2002) ongoing.

Heritage Park in Minneapolis was one of the projects that gave the city a score of 98 (out of 100) for affordable housing provision in 2001.

The CURA critique can be summarized in a series of points that trace what its researchers—over the years, primarily Edward G. Goetz and Barbara Lukermann—see as a steady deterioration, at least until recently, of the council's commitment to vigilance on the issue of affordable housing. This critique begins with the observation that, under LUPA, the council had created a numerical allocation plan that established regional goals for low- and moderate-income housing. The council then developed an allocation plan with specific numbers for each community within the Municipal Urban Service Area (MUSA) in order to determine compliance with the LUPA requirement of a housing element in the local land-use plan. However, because the council lacked authority to prescribe a specific amount of low- and moderate-income housing, it used the amount of land a community set aside for high-density residential development as a surrogate. A 2002 CURA report added that the council also developed a set of advisory zoning and land-use guidelines with suggestions on issues like lot size and garages that would affect housing prices (Goetz, Chapple, and Lukermann 2002). The report states that this shift from income-based to land-based criteria clearly made a difference. Between 1975 and 1982, the share of the region's subsidized housing units concentrated in the central cities of Minneapolis and St. Paul fell from 82 percent to 59 percent, one of the best performances of any program in the nation (p. 17).

The CURA report examines what it calls three waves of comprehensive plans produced under LUPA. One begins in 1976 with the law's passage and continues until 1982; a second goes from 1983 to 1995; and the third follows the passage of LCA in 1995. The logic of CURA's categorization of the plans is that the council followed its land-based allocation policy until the early 1980s, when a steep decline in federal funding of housing programs reduced the availability of money for affordable housing projects. At that time, the council quietly abandoned both its allocation policy and its guidelines. Passage of LCA triggered, beginning in 1996, the latest wave of plans addressing affordable housing under the negotiated goals that are current today. CURA chose 25 communities, largely on the basis of their high-growth patterns, for closer examination; its study analyzes the plans each community submitted to the council across all three periods and tries to determine the extent to which the earliest plans resulted in the production of affordable housing in those communities (pp. 7-12).

CURA found that the first wave of plans reviewed by the council included explicit references to the allocation formula. With the change in council policy in the early 1980s, however, those references vanished almost completely in the second wave. But, CURA notes, with the council's abandonment of its allocation policy, communities also had no reference point for determining their fair share of regional housing, even presuming a community's desire to comply with such goals, which was not always the case. In the third wave, the LCA-negotiated goals had completely replaced the LUPA fair-share formula to the point where many planners interviewed in the sample communities considered the LUPA requirement to be either irrelevant or superseded by LCA. The CURA report's authors dispute the latter perception vehemently (pp. 23-28).

The CURA report argues that communities' unwillingness in their third-wave plans to detail specific regulatory actions they plan to take to facilitate low- and moderate-income housing contrasts strongly with their willingness to do the same in their first-wave plans. Table 4-18, taken from the 2002 report, documents their contention that such actions had essentially declined by half between 24 first-wave plans and 16 third-wave plans examined.

CURA's study also examines the eventual disposition of the high-density residential land set aside in the first wave of plans. The researchers tracked the use of these parcels to see whether the expectation that they would host affordable housing proved accurate. In fact, there was almost no correlation between density and housing value. Only about 6 percent of the land set aside in 1980 was used 20 years later for low- and moderate-income housing. The study concludes that "high-density set-asides are not a good indicator of future housing affordability" (p. 113).

In 2001, Minnesota's Office of the Legislative Auditor (OLA) undertook a program assessment of the LCA at the request of members of the Legislative Audit Commission. The assessment found that the lack of affordable housing was more severe in the Twin Cities metropolitan area than elsewhere in Minnesota, with 26 percent of households in the metro area spending more than 30 percent of their income on housing (Minnesota Office of the Legislative Auditor 2001, 6–7). More specifically, it states that low-income metro area households face a tough rental market in which average

TABLE 4-18
POTENTIAL REGULATORY RELIEF
MENTIONED IN COMPREHENSIVE PLANS OF
SAMPLE COMMUNITIES IN THE TWIN CITIES REGION

Local regulatory actions to facilitate low- and moderate-income housing listed in comprehensive plans	First-wave plans	Percentage	Third-wave plans	Percentage
Rezoning	4	16%	3	18%
Increased densities	14	58%	3	19%
Planned unit development (PUD)	18	75%	9	56%
Decreased square footage requirements	14	58%	2	12%
Streamlined permit approval	2	8%	0	0%
Reduction in fees	4	16%	1	6%
Reduced setbacks	6	25%	1	6%
Manufactured housing	7	29%	1	6%
Nondiscrimination	4	16%	1	6%
Tax increment financing (TIF)	2	8%	4	25%
Other	10	42%	3	18%
Average	**3.54**		**1.75**	

Source: Edward G. Goetz, Karen Chapple, and Barbara Lukerman, *The Affordable House Legacy of the 1976 Land Use Planning Act* (Minneapolis, Minn.: University of Minnesota Center for Urban and Regional Affairs, 2002), 27.

rents had risen 34 percent in the past decade while their incomes had risen by only 9 percent. The low vacancy rate of 1.5 percent was indicative of the intractable nature of these households' problem.

At the same time, new housing was not necessarily an answer to the problem (except indirectly, of course, as it might relieve the stress of a tight market). The OLA study found that the cost of building new housing often made such housing unaffordable to lower-income households in the absence of subsidies. Those homes that are affordable within the metro area tend to be multi-family construction, such as townhouses, which also provide higher densities. Likewise, the typical Twin Cities cost for building an apartment in 2001 was $75 to $85 per square foot, yielding rents of $950 per month, which far exceeded the rent needed to meet affordability criteria, which is $738 per month for two-bedroom units. In short, without subsidies, high construction costs mean that the market cannot produce new affordable housing (pp. 20-21). When asked what factor most inhibited the production of new affordable housing, builders, developers, and housing organizations ranked the cost of materials, labor, or land as the most important factor (pp. 26-27). They also agreed that governmental assistance was needed in order to facilitate the production of affordable housing, and they ranked financial assistance and regulatory waivers as the most important types of assistance that could be provided (pp. 44-47).

Considering the obstacles to production of affordable housing, the OLA examined state statutes and concludes in its report that: "Minnesota gives local governments considerable discretion in determining how their communities develop, including if and how they accommodate affordable housing" (p. 31).

The OLA report also notes that other states take a more prescriptive approach. But Minnesota's voluntary, incentives-based approach through LCA, the study argues, "rewards *participation*" (emphasis supplied) rather

In short, without subsidies, high construction costs mean that the market cannot produce new affordable housing.

Jason Wittenberg

A study of comprehensive plans in the region found that many communities did not detail specific regulatory actions to facilitate construction of affordable housing.

than demonstrated progress in achieving affordable housing production goals. Overall, the study found only a loose connection between real needs for affordable housing and the goals and achievements of communities under LCA. A municipality, it states, "does not need to increase its supply of affordable housing to receive benefits from the program." In the end, it concludes, LCA "has been only marginally successful in producing more affordable housing" (pp. 75–83). Not surprisingly, the council took exception to the report's findings, noting that the LCA "is not housing production legislation" but nonetheless had encouraged communities to address affordable housing issues (Lindgren 2001).

Program Results

Given these critiques, why did Minnesota adopt the approach it has taken? Myron Orfield, who during the 1990s served in both houses of the Minnesota legislature, has offered what is probably the most thorough diagnosis of the politics that surrounded the passage of the LCA. Orfield was the leading promoter of legislation to expand tax-base sharing among communities within the metropolitan area, as well as other legislation dealing with fair housing and a redistribution of regional infrastructure investments. Over three legislative sessions from 1993 to 1995, Orfield and other legislators concerned about such issues drafted, redrafted, and consolidated various pieces of legislation, many of which were vetoed by Governor Arne Carlson.

Carlson's successive vetoes forced a good deal of renegotiation and compromise between shifting coalitions of suburban, urban, and non-metropolitan representatives and senators. In the end, Senator Ted Mondale, now the president of the council, helped to assemble a successful coalition that won passage of the Livable Communities Act in 1995. The price of this compromise, however, was a significant shift away from mandatory planning and fair-share measures toward a largely voluntary approach built around the incentives that the council now uses. In short, the LCA was a product of extensive compromise forged amid a welter of conflicting political interests. It proved to be as far as the Minnesota legislature and Governor Carlson would go at the time to reach agreement on ways to address regional equity issues surrounding affordable housing and infrastructure investment (Orfield 1997).

There are, however, defenders of the LCA. One who assisted in drafting the legislation was architect William Morrish, now at the University of Virginia School of Architecture and formerly director of the Design Center for the American Urban Landscape at the University of Minnesota. Morrish (2002) said he agreed with Orfield's decision in the early 1990s to cast the debate over housing issues in terms of the housing needs of inner-ring suburbs; he likewise had used the Design Center as the ideal "planning and design forum for this kind of conversation." He notes that the mismatch of jobs and housing locations is "a bigger problem than the actual cost of the housing." He also argued that the nature of the problem has shifted fundamentally since 1978–1979, when "everyone was doing regional planning. Nuclear families then were 76 percent of the population, and now are below 29 percent to 26 percent. It's a very different topic now."

Morrish maintains that there are many economic problems in trying to produce new affordable housing. "Costs are not going to come down for raw timber," he says. "Construction costs are not going to come down as you're going to pay people living wages. We can save some costs here and there, building 1,800 square feet instead of 2,800." Instead, he suggests that one key issue is how to preserve much post-World War II housing instead of tearing it down simply because of the need to "make existing housing more affordable." The problem with council planning in the middle to late 1990s, he says, is that "they focused on the 1 to 2 percent of growth that happens on the edge" instead of on problems in first-ring suburbs. "That is the reason Orfield got so much support," he insists.

Because of demographic changes, Morrish say the situation today demands new means of assessing the problem, such as a focus on life-cycle housing. "Local government in first-ring and maturing second-ring suburbs [supported Orfield] in response to bad numbers," he says, "especially when it came to fair share." These governments also realized that "their population was aging and the price of housing was forcing their elderly to move out." Life-cycle housing, the meeting of the needs of all age groups within the community, he says, "is at the core of that."

In helping to write the new legislation, he recalled, "our agenda was to use the money as a catalyst to realign policies" through experimentation, asking communities how they had changed their rules and getting major developers to "change their building types and change the market.... I think it was very effective that way," he adds.

Morrish notes, however, that some confrontation necessarily followed this strategy once the council became more aggressive in pursuing its goals. He says of the new infrastructure grant guidelines: "There were huge fights with Metro Council transportation people. Road engineers were not willing to see this integration." But, he adds, there is now "a little more trust about the data because local governments are contributing to the database." The LCA grants also "have given local communities freedom to think without council oligarchies breathing down on them.... Now mayors understand why they have the Metro Council."

Morrish's critique of these "oligarchies" echoes the reasoning behind one of the council's newer coalition-building experiments, the Mayors'

Regional Housing Task Force, the focus of which has been broadening life-cycle housing opportunities in Twin Cities communities. Convened in May 2000 by the council, it is composed of mayors from 16 cities representing the different development stages of the metropolitan area. Its aim is to engage mayors, who are the political leadership of the region, in determining what works and what must change for the region to achieve its affordable housing goals, and to produce recommendations for bringing about those changes. In essence, it is another way to direct mayors' attention to specific policy problems connected to affordable housing. It also provides them a forum to offer policy solutions. The task force produces an annual report summarizing its findings; its latest report, *Affordable Housing: Making It a Reality,* was released in October 2002.

Mayor Karen Anderson (2002) of Minnetonka, a member of the Mayors' Regional Housing Task Force, described the task force as "just one thing" that she said is helping "to turn the tide of public and suburban opinion." In the last four years, she said, she has seen "a sea change in terms of suburban acknowledgment of affordable housing, a needed and growing awareness and political commitment." Anderson said the task force reports "have gone along with the Metropolitan Council's philosophy of incentives rather than penalties" and succeed in building political support among mayors precisely because they are seen as "nonthreatening," to the point where at least two fellow mayors told her they want to be on the task force.

Anderson links part of this "sea change" to "a very large marketing effort by the Family Housing Fund" and the advocacy of a three-year-old group, Housing Minnesota, a coalition of various advocacy and housing development groups. The fund has published studies in recent years demonstrating that there was no measurable impact from affordable housing on market values in adjacent neighborhoods.[16] Anderson credited this compilation of well-publicized research and statistics with combating nega-

The Family Housing Fund has published studies in recent years demonstrating that there was no measurable impact from affordable housing on market values in adjacent neighborhoods.

Jason Wittenberg

tive perceptions of affordable housing; she also says that the task force reports have helped to "share ideas and best practices that are doable within your own local authority and give you an advantage when seeking support from the federal or state government." In essence, Anderson and likeminded suburban colleagues believe that, given good information and support for their efforts, including financial support, most suburban communities will address affordable housing needs more enthusiastically than if they are the target of requirements produced by divisive and negative politics.

Moreover, Anderson insists that the quality of the affordable housing being built in Minnetonka today is superior to that of the units built in the 1970s under Metropolitan Council mandates. Then a member of the League of Women Voters, she says she helped to get the earlier housing produced, but it was "of an inferior quality, not placed in a good area geographically, and never had public transit (service) until three years ago." Today, she believes, "I've seen suburban communities accept and adopt affordable housing under the incentive program [in a way] that never happened before."

Metropolitan Council Response

Despite the emphasis on life-cycle housing and its greater political acceptability, the council does not see it as a substitute term for "affordable housing." According to Guy Peterson (2002), a senior planner for the council, "We have used [life-cycle housing] as a term to convince cities that they need a full range of housing options and choices for citizens as they move through the life cycle; that is, apartment and townhouses for young people, houses for families, townhouses, condos for empty nesters and early retirees, and senior citizen housing for older seniors and of course, different facilities for the aged and frail." In other words, at least ideally, the discussion of life-cycle housing is in part a means to an end, but it is also a way of considering affordable housing as part of a larger discussion of how best to achieve an overall balance of housing types to meet all the needs within the community.

Life-cycle housing is also a way of considering affordable housing as part of a larger discussion of how best to achieve an overall balance of housing types to meet all the needs within the community.

That said, Peterson concedes some weaknesses in the current program, even as the council maintains that the LCA's incentive-based approach, combined with a worsening regional housing situation, has "contributed to increased local efforts regarding affordable housing." Given a wish list for amending the LCA, it is clear that the council wants to address what it sees as several shortcomings in the current program.

The largest of these, Peterson said, is "underfunding. Only $1.5 million is available specifically to assist affordable housing to leverage the nearly $20 million available each year from the Minnesota Housing Finance Agency and other philanthropic contributors." In other words, the council is working on a large rock of potential funding with a very short crowbar.

Peterson also cited a "lack of specific statutory authority in the Metropolitan Land Planning Act to make cities plan and guide land for affordable housing." This claimed lack might seem to contradict the CURA authors, who repeatedly in their works criticize the council for failing to use the review powers it already has with regard to housing. But the council argues that, while it does have specific authority under LUPA to mandate planning of "regional systems"—namely, water resources, transportation, aviation, and open space and recreation—housing does not qualify as a regional system, making its controls in this area necessarily looser. Clearly, the council and its critics are looking at the problem of authority through very different lenses. However, Peterson noted, "in the end, without the financial resources to implement the goals and plans, better planning and attention to goals becomes a somewhat moot point."

Finally, the council cited as a major shortcoming the data quality under the LCA reporting system. As noted earlier, not all communities respond to the council's annual LCA survey of housing accomplishments because there is no requirement that they do so. The return rates average roughly between two-thirds and three-fourths of the region's communities from year to year. These nonresponders complicate the council's mandated task under the LCA of producing a comprehensive annual report on regional housing activity. Reporting inconsistency poses a serious problem for the council when it tries to evaluate how both individual communities and the region as a whole are performing over time. Moreover, Peterson points toward what he calls "a more disturbing issue" in data reporting:

> Communities are hard pressed to estimate the numbers of units at various values. In fact, many report the building permit value of a property because it is readily available. Unfortunately, the permit value often excludes the low cost and various finishing costs that would drive the selling price up dramatically. Without a clear directive to communities, first, to report housing construction activity to the council, and, second, to report within defined guidelines, the quality of the reporting on LCA cannot be as complete and as accurate as we'd like.

Without accurate data, it is clear that the Metropolitan Council cannot hope to fulfill the LCA's fundamental purpose. Failing to obtain such data from local governments will only leave the council open to more withering attacks from critics like CURA.

ENDNOTES

1. In 2002, the New Jersey Supreme Court reaffirmed the use of the builder's remedy in a case against the Township of West Windsor, which had not sought substantive certification by the Council on Affordable Housing (*Toll Brothers v. Township of West Windsor*, 173 N.J. 502, 803 A.2d 53 (2002)). Through a 1984 judgment in a builder-initiated *Mount Laurel* lawsuit, West Windsor had, under court supervision, adopted a housing plan and zoned 11 sites for affordable housing. However, by 1994, only 2 of the 11 sites had been developed, and West Windsor had satisfied only 241 units of its 929-unit fair-share obligation. All of the remaining sites were mainly zoned for multi-family housing or zero-lot-line homes. A developer, Toll Brothers, which owned a 293-acre tract in the township, brought suit in 1993 contending that West Windsor had engaged in unconstitutional exclusionary zoning. Toll Brothers argued that there was no market for such housing, and was unsuccessful in persuading West Windsor to change the zoning. Consequently, the developer sought a builder's remedy to rezone its site to permit market-rate single-family detached houses on small lots in addition to affordable rental units that would consist of both single-family zero-lot-line housing and detached homes. The New Jersey Supreme Court ruled unanimously in the Toll Brothers' favor. Merely designating land for multifamily housing and expecting it to develop, despite shifting market demands, said the court, does not provide a realistic opportunity for affordable housing. The court also observed that, while none of the remaining designated sites for affordable housing had been developed, construction of expensive single-family homes on large lots continued unabated.

2. See New Jersey Administrative Code, Chapter 93, Technical Appendices E and I. For a discussion of the technical aspects of ensuring that such units remain affordable, see Mallach (1994). In an e-mail to the authors of this study, Mallach (2002), a professional planner in New Jersey who has been closely involved with *Mount Laurel* litigation, observes: "While *Mount Laurel II* indicated that 20 percent should be the norm,

COAH's regulations have deviated widely from this, and in practice routinely approve inclusionary projects with lower, even substantially lower, percentages of low- and moderate-income housing, on occasion below 5 percent. COAH operates on the basis of a perverse theory that the lower the density, the lower the inclusionary percentage, regardless of other factors."

3. For a critical review of the New Jersey allocation system, see Payne (1997). Payne advocates the use of a "growth-share" formula. Under it, a community's duty is a "simple obligation to allocate a share of whatever growth actually occurs to low- and moderate-income housing. This means all of the growth, residential and non-residential, and it also means new development that occurs on raw land as well as redevelopment of previously used land. This latter qualification is extremely important because it is this redevelopment-based aspect of the growth share/fair share that can move the *Mount Laurel* doctrine to the older suburbs" (p. 6). A proposal drafted by New Jersey Planner Alan Mallach, AICP, that would implement the growth-share formula was submitted to the New Jersey Legislature for consideration in October 2002. Under this proposal, COAH must "adopt a methodology which establishes the municipal fair share obligation, over and above satisfaction of the municipality's indigenous need, as a proportion of projected growth in the municipality, including all residential and non-residential development and redevelopment, and which, as nearly as practicable, establishes the proportion of total growth to be represented by low and moderate income housing at a level which will make realistically possible the provision of the full prospective need for low and moderate income housing across the state. In so doing, [COAH] shall adopt criteria and guidelines for determining the amount of low and moderate income housing to be provided as a result of residential development and redevelopment in a municipality based on at least a 20 percent set-aside of total housing units developed as a result of non-residential development and redevelopment in a municipality based on generally accepted coefficients of job creation to square feet of different categories of non-residential development and redevelopment" (Mallach 2002b, 4).

4. New Jersey Administrative Code, Section 5.93-2.19, "Calculation of indigenous need; selected urban aid cities." COAH itself does not determine which "urban aid cities" are exempt. That determination is made by the state pursuant to New Jersey Statutes Annotated, Sections 52:27-178 et seq.

5. Cordingley (2002). Urban Aid municipalities are municipalities that are eligible for the Municipal Urban Aid Program because their property tax base is insufficient to provide the funds necessary to support all of the services needed for the municipality to function, as determined by the New Jersey Department of Community Affairs.

6. "As a rule," Mallach (2002a, 17) observes, "sending municipalities [to regional contribution agreements] are affluent suburban jurisdictions and receiving municipalities [are] small or large older communities with disproportionately large housing needs and limited resources to address them." RCAs are controversial because they allow affluent municipalities a way of buying out a proportion—up to 50 percent—of their fair-share obligation.

7. California Government Code Section 65584(c). For examples of housing allocations, see ABAG (2001) and SANDAG (2000). Communities in San Diego County have been able to bypass HCD reviews through self-certification of the housing element of their general plans. The self-certification provisions appear at Section 65585.1, and their implementation is described in SANDAG (1998). See also Calavita, Grimes, and Mallach (1997).

8. The reporting requirements were initiated in the 1990s but suspended shortly thereafter, so it has only been since 2000 that local jurisdictions were required to submit their reports. HCD has received these reports from some jurisdictions and for only some years. Moreover, HCD indicates there is no accurate consistent method to obtain the affordability category for market rate housing that is not subject to any man-

datory local reporting of sales prices or rents, sales instruments, or information on buyer or renter income (Wheaton 2002).

9. See, for example, *Camp v. Mendocino County Board of Supervisors* (176 Cal. Rptr. 620 (Ct. App., 1st Dist. 1981)), which found that the county housing element did not substantially comply with statute. See also *Black Property Owners Association v. City of Berkeley* (29 Cal. Reptr.2d 305 (1994)), rejecting plaintiff's claims that city had failed to comply with statute; *Hernandez v. City of Encinitas* (33 Cal. Rptr.2d 875 (Ct. App. 4th Dist. 1995)), finding city had substantially complied with statute; *Buena Vista Garden Apartments Association v. City of San Diego* (220 Cal. Rptr. 732, 737, 740 (Ct. App. 4th Dist. 1985)), finding city substantially complied with statute except for statutory provision that requires city to "[c]onserve and improve the conditions of the existing affordable housing stock" (quoting California Government Code, Section 65583(c)(4)); and *Hoffmaster v. City of San Diego* (65 Cal. Rptr.2d 684, 697 (Ct. App. 4th Dist. 1997)), finding city failed to identify adequate sites for emergency shelters and transitional housing.

10. See Non-Profit Housing Association of Northern California and the Greenbelt Alliance (2002). The study's criteria for judging these factors reflect whether a community: (1) has result-oriented housing production programs which include measurable outcomes, timelines, a responsible agency or official, and source of funds; (2) has enough land to meet all of its housing need as identified by ABAG, zoned appropriately for all income groups; (3) uses smart growth strategies, including infill housing development, compact housing types, mixed-use zoning, zoning for higher densities near transit, and decreased parking requirements; (4) commits local funding, such as redevelopment funds (from tax increment financing), to low- and/or moderate-income housing; (5) has adopted "inclusionary zoning" requiring all new housing development to include homes affordable to low- and/or moderate-income families; (6) has programs to preserve and stabilize existing affordable housing; (7) solicits input from the public in developing its housing element and commits to annual reporting to the public on progress in implementation, as required by law; and (8) has developed unique initiatives to meet local affordable housing requirements (p. 7). The report's criteria are broader than those used by HCD to evaluate housing elements.

11. Alameda County, despite its history of successful partnerships with nonprofit housing developers, received a failing grade because of the housing element's failure to identify sites for affordable housing, as every housing element is required to do (Non-Profit Housing Association of Northern California and the Greenbelt Alliance 2002, 24). Alameda County also had "hundreds of acres zoned at low densities that are feasible for more expensive housing" (p. 11).

12. "The total cost assumes a 50/50 split between new construction and acquisition/ rehabilitation, with the average cost of new construction $105,000 per unit, and the average cost of acquisition/rehabilitation $60,000 per unit. A 100 percent subsidy is needed for households below 30 percent MHI, and a 40 percent subsidy is needed for households at 50 percent MHI. The percentage of units allocated to below 30 percent MHI and to 31–50 percent MHI is based on the affordable housing distribution formula: less than 30 percent MHI = 72 percent and 31–50 percent MHI = 28 percent" (Metro Council 2002, 26).

13. Herr also notes that there were no strong inclusionary mandates in either Rhode Island or Connecticut, but there was a stronger pattern in Massachusetts.

14. For a community to have adequate life-cycle housing, it must have enough variety in its housing stock to support the physical needs and fit the financial resources of residents throughout their lives. Life-cycle housing includes rental units for young people setting up their first household, starter homes for first-time home buyers, move-up units to accommodate households as they earn higher incomes and add

more members, easy-to-maintain units for empty nesters and retirees, and supportive environments for the elderly.

15. In an letter responding to a series of e-mailed questions from APA, Guy Peterson (2002), senior planner on the Metropolitan Council staff, noted, "The term 'affordable' housing was coined in Council policy in the mid-90s as a change from what had become a 'red flag' term 'low- and moderate-income housing.' But, subsequently, 'affordable' has come to have the same negative associations by the NIMBY detractors and it's become somewhat confusing because some people say 'affordable to whom' even though we have always identified it as affordable to households at or below 50 percent of median income for rental and 80 percent for ownership."

16. Probably the most significant of these studies was prepared for Family Housing Fund by Maxfield Research Inc. (2000).

CHAPTER 5

Regional Housing Trust Funds

This chapter evaluates a variety of regional affordable housing trust funds.[1] The chapter includes a discussion of the Vermont Housing and Conservation Board, a statewide trust fund for affordable housing, farmland and open space conservation, and historic preservation; A Regional Coalition for Housing, a multijurisdictional affordable housing trust fund in suburban Seattle; the Sacramento Housing and Redevelopment Agency, which administers two trust funds in the city and county of Sacramento; the Columbus/Franklin County Affordable Housing Trust, a new fund in Columbus, Ohio; and the Montgomery County housing trust fund, a countywide entity in Dayton, Ohio.

THE VERMONT HOUSING AND CONSERVATION BOARD (VHCB)

Inception: 1987

Administration: A nine-member board of directors authorizes grants from the trust fund, which is supported by appropriations from the state legislation and 50 percent of the state's real estate property tax transfers.

Key objectives: Providing affordable housing and conserving natural, agricultural, historic, and recreational areas.

Accomplishments: Since its inception in 1987 through 2002, VHCB has awarded over $155 million to nonprofit housing and conservation organizations and municipalities. Those funds have been used to create 6,675 units of affordable housing (an average of approximately 445 units per year) and conserve more than 338,388 acres of agricultural, recreational, and natural areas. Additionally, from 1987 to 2002, funds awarded by VHCB have helped leverage approximately $515 million from other private and public sources.

Caveats: As originally conceived, it was thought that some of VHCB's awards would fund projects that had both an affordable housing and a conservation component, such as purchasing and preserving a farm that was threatened by development, and funding the construction of affordable housing on a small corner of that farm or converting the farm structures into affordable housing units. In practice, however, VHCB has found that most projects receiving awards are either affordable housing projects or conservation projects, but not both.

This historic building was rehabilitated to provide 10 affordable apartments, six artists studios, and six commercial spaces, including an art gallery, antiques store, and artists storefront.

The State of Vermont has established a trust fund administered by the Vermont Housing and Conservation Board (VHCB) that has the twin goals of providing affordable housing as well as conserving natural, agricultural, historic, and recreational areas. Both the affordable housing and conservation aspects of the program include smart growth provisions such as giving preference to rehabilitation, historic preservation, infill, and projects that are part of a neighborhood or downtown revitalization plan.

According to the 2002 report, *Between a Rock and a Hard Place: Housing and Wages in Vermont* by VHCB, the Vermont Housing Council, and the Vermont Housing Awareness Campaign, there is a growing gap between demand and supply of housing that working families can afford in Vermont (Vermont Housing Council 2002). "Between 1990 and 2000, Vermont added only enough new housing units to accommodate five out of every six new households," the report states (p. 3). Housing prices are also rising in Vermont: the median price of a single-family house in Vermont increased by over 29.8 percent between 1996 and 2000 (p. 4). Like other affordable housing programs in the state, VHCB has been effective at alleviating the housing problem in Vermont, the report concludes; however, "the need for affordable housing far exceeds what the resources can deliver" (p. 17).

VHCB was created by the Vermont Housing and Conservation Trust Fund Act (Vermont Statutes Annotated, Title 10, Chapter 15 [1987]). The state legislature appropriated $3 million for its first year. In 1988 the State of Vermont had a budget surplus, and the legislature directed $20 million to the fund (Vermont Housing and Conservation Board 2002e). In addition, it designated a portion of the property transfer tax revenues for VHCB. Today, that designated portion is 50 percent of the state's property transfer tax revenues and provides $11–12 million to VHCB.

The statute set up a nine-member board of five citizens appointed by the governor, and, ex officio, the commissioner of the Vermont Department of Agriculture, Food, and Markets, the secretary of commerce and community development, the secretary of natural resources, and the executive director of the Vermont Housing Finance Agency. Two of the five citizens on the board must include a farmer and a representative of lower-income citizens of Vermont. The board operates as a quasi-governmental agency, and the housing and conservation components operate under separate administrative divisions (Weinstein 2002).

The Vermont Housing and Conservation Board

The Lamoille Housing Trust developed this eight-unit senior apartment building, with the first floor leased to the U.S. Postal Service, using funds from the Vermont Housing and Conservation Board.

The statute established a set of priorities that VHCB must evaluate when reviewing applications for funding. "In determining the allocation of funds available for the purposes of this chapter," the statute states, "the board shall give priority to projects which combine the dual goals of creating affordable housing and conserving and protecting Vermont's agricultural land, historic properties, important natural areas or recreation lands..." (Section 322(a)). Additionally, the statute directs the board to consider a number of other factors, including the need to maintain balance between these two goals, the appropriateness of a timely response due to circumstances or opportunities, the level of funding and participation by other public and private sources, and the resources that will be needed in the future to sustain the project. The board must also weigh the project's likelihood of displacing lower-income households, what its overall long-term effect will be, and whether it will provide perpetual affordability. Likewise, VHCB is required to prevent the loss of subsidized housing units and determine the geographic distribution of funds.

Although by statue VHCB must give priority to projects by nonprofit organizations and municipalities from areas of the state with high unemployment and low per-capita income, it has funded projects in all 14 counties of the state (Section 312(b)). (See Figure 5–1.)

The board adopted a policy in May 2001 that includes five thresholds and five priorities that any affordable housing project must meet so as to be considered for VHCB funding. The first threshold, perpetual affordability, means that the housing unit must remain affordable forever. This threshold is a unique aspect of the program; the project must include mechanisms that ensure perpetual affordability and a long-term plan for maintenance. The second threshold dictates that the project cannot be located in an area that has a large number of negative features, such as excessive traffic or proximity to noncompatible uses. Third, the project must be ready to proceed should funding be awarded, and predevelopment work must be undertaken prior to the application. Fourth, the project must be financially viable. Fifth, the project must include a plan for addressing major health and safety issues when such issues exist (Vermont Housing and Conservation Board 2002c).

The two mechanisms used to ensure that the housing units funded by VHCB remain affordable forever are *housing subsidy covenants* and *ground leases*—both deed restrictions. A housing subsidy covenant is a document used for multifamily housing (and in some cases single-family homes) that maintains affordability by setting restrictions on the maximum income of the residents and the sale price of the property. A ground lease is generally used for single-family homes: it separates the land from the structure and leases the land to the persons who own the structure. The ground lease restricts both the future sale price of the home and the maximum income of the homebuyer (Nichol 2002b).

FIGURE 5-1
PROJECT AWARDS BY COUNTY, 1987–2001

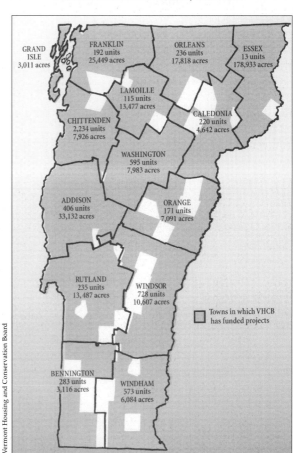

Vermont Housing and Conservation Board

In addition to the above thresholds for funding affordable housing projects, the VHCB policy establishes five priorities for funding projects; the board favors projects that (1) fulfill need, (2) contribute to neighborhood or downtown revitalization, (3) serve very low-income households or households with special needs, (4) have the dual goals of conservation and affordable housing, and (5) correct health or safety threats. According to VHCB's director of federal housing programs, David Weinstein, by giving priority to rehabilitation over new construction, using historical buildings over nonhistorical buildings, and favoring infill housing projects, the board has taken measures to ensure that projects funded by the trust fund will conform to certain standards for smart growth, even projects that do not include an explicit conservation component (Weinstein 2002).

In addition to the thresholds and priorities for funding, VHCB considers other contributing factors such as leverage, proximity to public transportation and services, capacity and track record of the applicant in housing development and management, cost effectiveness of the project, and long-term plan for stewardship. The board also takes into account the level of community involvement in and support for the development and management of the project, its livability, available amenities, and location in a village area or compact growth center where municipal infrastructure already exists or will exist in the near future(Vermont Housing and Conservation Board 2002c). Additionally, VHCB has a policy of causing no displacement, especially of lower-income households, and VHCB-funded projects should create or contribute to mixed-income developments or communities, or they should be located in middle- or upper-income communities.

Program Results

Between its inception in 1987 and 2002, VHCB has awarded more than $155 million to nonprofit housing and conservation organizations and local governments. Those funds have been used to create 6,675 units of affordable housing (an average of approximately 445 units per year) and conserve more than 338,388 acres of agricultural, recreational, and natural areas. Additionally, during that same period, funds awarded by VHCB have helped leverage approximately $515 million from other private and public sources (Vermont Housing and Conservation Board 2002d, 36). (See Figure 5–2.)

This 13-unit apartment building, developed by the Regional Affordable Housing Corporation in Bennington, was converted from a vacant school. The project was funded by the Vermont Housing and Conservation Board.

Vermont Housing and Conservation Board

In fiscal year 2001, VHCB received about 45 percent of its funding from the state property tax transfer revenue, 21 percent from federal grants, 19 percent from state supplemental appropriation, 9 percent from Farms for the Future, and the rest of its funds from other sources, such as loan repayments and interest income. In fiscal year 2001, approximately 77 percent of VHCB expenditures were grants and loans, 9 percent were other project related expenses, 8 percent were for administration, and 6 percent were Farms for the Future interest expense (Vermont Housing and Conservation Board 2002d, 47). Farms for the Future is a farmland conservation funding source (Hannan 2002).

VHCB originally intended that some of its awards would fund projects that had both an affordable housing and a conservation component, such as purchasing a farm threatened by development and then funding the construction of affordable housing on a small corner of that farm or the conversion of farm structures into affordable housing units. In practice, however, VHCB has found that most projects receiving awards are either affordable housing projects or conservation projects, but not both. Approximately 55 percent of the Housing and Conservation Fund monies are directed toward affordable housing projects, and 45 percent are directed toward conservation projects (Weinstein 2002).

That balance is unlikely to change anytime soon. As the 2002 VHCB annual report states, "Recent studies show that Vermont's most acute hous-

Developed by a partnership between three nonprofit organizations, Lake Champlain Housing Development Corporation, Cathedral Square Corporation, and Burlington Community Land Trust, this development includes 10 units in one building for people with developmental disabilities and two affordable single-family homes.

Vermont Housing and Conservation Board

ing need continues to be rental housing for lower income households. A household must earn more than two times that state minimum wage to afford a typical two-bedroom apartment. . . . For this reason, the majority of the Board's awards continue to be directed toward multi-unit rental developments for families, individuals, and households with special needs" (Vermont Housing and Conservation Board 2002d, 47).

VHCB also supports nonprofit housing delivery organizations throughout Vermont: it provides them with operating support, technical assistance, and training, in addition to project implementation funding for affordable housing projects that conform to its priorities. According to the VHCB's director of federal housing programs, David Weinstein, the network of housing organizations that the board assists are primarily countywide housing organizations (Weinstein 2002). In this manner, VHCB has focused on building regional capacity to provide affordable housing through the non-profit housing organizations that it supports (Nichol 2002a).

Because VHCB supports reinvestment in older housing in small town and village centers, the board hopes its contribution to downtown neighborhoods will spur increased private investment in those areas. VHCB sees historic preservation and affordable housing as a way to reinvest in and revitalize downtown areas in Vermont. Twenty-six percent of the trust fund awards have supported affordable housing in buildings that are eligible, nominated for, or listed on the National Register of Historic Places (Weinstein 2002).

Because VHCB concentrates on rehabilitating existing buildings, communities across Vermont have welcomed the board's efforts and see the rehabbed buildings as an asset to neighborhood and downtown revitalization efforts (Nichol 2002a). VHCB has thus helped to steer nonprofit housing organizations in the direction of historic preservation and neighborhood revitalization. As Ed Stretch (2002), executive director of the Gilman Housing Trust in rural northern Vermont—a recipient of VHCB funds—confirms, "If you have two projects competing for the same funds, and one is a historic preservation project and the other is new construction, the historic preservation project will score higher."

Brenda Torpy (2002), executive director of the Burlington Community Land Trust in Chittenden County, which has also received funding from VHCB, maintains the fund has made a difference in the provision of affordable housing. "The match-up works very well," Torpy observes, "because there is never enough money for affordable housing or historic preservation." Additionally, Torpy likes the fact that VHCB allows her organization, located in Vermont's most urban county, to improve the entire community as well as to provide affordable housing. "With VHCB," she says, "we were able to raise conservation funds to pay for a community park and get green back into the city." The dual goals of VHCB have thus helped recipients win community support for their projects. "It has helped communities accept affordable housing," Torpy observes. "When you come into a community with a package—with historic preservation, neighborhood revitalization, affordable housing, and conservation—the community is more receptive to the project."

An important aspect of VHCB is that it is often the first to award funding to a project. Many affordable housing projects use between seven to 10 sources of funding, including community development block grants (CDBGs), home investment partnerships program funds (HOME), historic preservation tax credits, debt financing, low-income housing tax credits, private foundation grants, and other state and federal funding programs. According to Ed Stretch (2002), "the role that the VHCB often plays is to be the first [funder], which is very important and helps build momentum with other [funders]." As the first funder, the board also demands that the project is thoroughly developed. "They do a good job in underwriting projects," Stretch notes. "They ask critical questions, make sure that we have everything ready, and make sure that the market is secure in the area, so that we are ready to go to other [funders]."

Through its funding decisions, VHCB has been successful in attaining several goals simultaneously: it has created affordable housing while it has also conserved and protected agricultural land, natural areas, and historic properties. It has demonstrated that smart growth and the substantial provision of affordable housing are compatible. Despite its success, however, VHCB recognizes that the need for affordable housing still greatly outweighs the organization's ability to provide it.

FIGURE 5-2
VHCB FUNDS

VHCB funds have leveraged
$515 million from other private and public sources

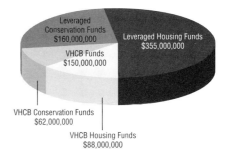

Leveraged Conservation Funds
$160,000,000

Leveraged Housing Funds
$355,000,000

VHCB Funds
$150,000,000

VHCB Conservation Funds
$62,000,000

VHCB Housing Funds
$88,000,000

Vermont Housing and Conservation Board

A six-unit service supported affordable housing development for adults with developmental disabilities funded by the Vermont Housing and Conservation Board.

A REGIONAL COALITION FOR HOUSING (ARCH), KING COUNTY, WASHINGTON

Inception: 1992

Administration: ARCH is a regional housing trust fund that covers 15 cities in Eastern King County (Seattle), Washington. Created through an interlocal agreement, it has two boards: an executive board, made up of the chief administrator of each member city (such as a city manager), and a citizen advisory board, which consists of citizens of the member cities who have interest or expertise in affordable housing issues. King County is a member of the ARCH board but does not contribute to or use funds from ARCH because it has its own affordable housing program. The trust fund is supported by federal Community Development Block Grant monies, municipal general fund contributions, and other local funds such as revenues from linkage fees.

Key Objectives: Established to increase the supply of affordable housing and respond to Washington State Growth Management Act, which requires all affected counties and cities to plan for affordable housing

Accomplishments: A total of 1,709 housing units and 74 beds for group housing have been constructed using funds from ARCH between 1993 and spring 2001—an average of 198 units/beds per year.

Caveats: ARCH funds projects when an opportunity arises. That means participation in the regional housing trust fund does not always translate directly into the creation of affordable housing in each member community. Of the 44 projects approved, 17 were in Bellvue, the oldest and most urbanized community in ARCH.

A Regional Coalition for Housing (ARCH) was created in 1992 by several suburban governments in east King County, Washington, a wealthy fiscally conservative area of suburban Seattle. ARCH was established to respond to rising housing costs in the county and to comply with the state of Washington's Growth Management Act, which requires all cities to plan for affordable housing. Since ARCH is a voluntary program, member cities are free to leave the program whenever they choose (Sullivan 2002a).

In an area where, in 1999, the average price of a single-family home was $270,743, the average rent for a two-bedroom/one-bathroom apartment was $744, the median household income was $53,200 (King County Office of Regional Policy and Planning 2002), and Bill Gates, chairman of Microsoft, would be a typical neighbor in some areas, providing affordable housing has been a challenge (Sullivan 2002a).

Founded through an interlocal agreement to cooperatively address affordable housing, ARCH currently includes 15 communities: Beaux Arts Village, Bellevue, Bothell, Clyde Hill, Hunts Point, Issaquah, Kenmore, Kirkland, Medina, Mercer Island, Newcastle, Redmond, Sammamish, Woodinville, and Yarrow Point. Also, although King County is a member of ARCH, it does not contribute to or use funds from the trust fund because the county has its own countywide affordable housing program. However, the county is a member of ARCH and participates in a variety of its planning, community outreach, and other activities.

ARCH has two boards: an executive board, made up of the chief administrator of each member city (such as a city manager), and a citizen advisory board, which consists of citizens of the member cities who have interest or expertise in affordable housing issues. The city councils of each member city also have a role in the operation and administration of ARCH.

The annual budget and work program are developed by the executive board but must be ratified by all of the member city councils before it can be adopted. ARCH's two boards also make separate recommendations for projects to be funded through the trust fund, but the funding must also be approved by the city council of each member city. Because all of the projects funded by the trust fund must be ratified by every member city council, as well as recommended by the citizen advisory and executive boards, applicants must generate significant community acceptance. According to ARCH, their approval process has worked very well to build support within the member communities.

Projects are approved for funding based on a combination of need and opportunity. Therefore, the development of affordable housing throughout the member cities is based on where opportunities to build projects arise (Shirk 2002). ARCH prefers—but does not require—that the projects using funds from the trust fund be located in the city that provides the funds. If a proposed project is not sited in the city that provides the funds, the applicants must demonstrate how the project meets the communities' targeted needs. Other factors for site selection include proximity to jobs, transportation, and services (ARCH 2002a).

Eligible applicants include nonprofit organizations, private for-profit organizations, public housing authorities, and public development authorities. Eligible uses for funds include acquisition, financing, predevelopment, rehabilitation, new construction, and on-site and off-site costs. Additionally, tenant assistance programs, such as loan programs for security deposits, can be funded by the trust fund. Financing for mixed-income projects is allowed, but the trust fund will only pay for the parts of the project that create low- and moderate-income housing.

Archdiocesan Housing Authority Harrington House, a transitional housing, maternity, and new mother affordabe housing development funded by A Regional Coalition for Housing.

A Regional Coalition for Housing

ARCH bases its funding decisions on the following criteria:

- Duration of affordability

- Soundness of the project

- Relevance of the project to local needs

- The project's ability to meet the needs of low-income (earning 50 percent or less than the Seattle metropolitan statistical area mean income, adjusted for household size) and, in special cases, moderate-income (earning 80 percent or less than the Seattle metropolitan statistical area mean income, adjusted for household size) households

- The project's ability to meet target area needs

In order to avoid overemphasis on one type of affordable housing, ARCH does not set priorities for housing categories (Sullivan 2002a). Instead, it has developed a set of long-term goals for the percentage of funding awarded to cover a wide spectrum of affordable housing needs. The housing goals are:

- housing for families (including single households) should comprise 56 percent of all ARCH funding;

- homeless and transitional housing should comprise 13 percent;

- elderly housing should comprise 19 percent; and

- housing for special needs populations should comprise 12 percent.

Because they are long-term goals, the percentages may not reflect the make-up of housing projects in any given funding cycle. Proposals for funding by the trust fund must include one of the target population priorities (ARCH 2002b). According to ARCH program manager Arthur Sullivan, the goals take into consideration the relative expense of creating each type of housing. Sullivan recognizes, for example, that less than 12 percent of overall housing need consists of special population need. But, he says, "in acknowledgment of the relatively high amount per capita it costs to help persons with special needs, their goal for funding is higher than their relative percentage of need" (Sullivan 2002d).

In a 1997 assessment of the ARCH program, ARCH staff, the executive board, and local city councils expressed concerns about the inequality of contributions to and distributions from the trust fund (Sullivan 2002a, Conrad 1998). A working group of city council representatives, ARCH staff, and the executive board responded with a formula, called the parity program, to address concerns that some cities were contributing more than their fair share to the trust fund. The overall objective of the parity program is to "establish a means for members to attain an equitable distribution of resources being contributed to affordable housing" (Conrad 1998). Assuming that no single formula adequately considers the variety of issues faced by members of ARCH, the working group developed several formulas that establish ranges based on current population, projected housing growth, and projected job growth. According to ARCH, using funding ranges rather than setting minimum funding levels acknowledges that different cities can face different budget constraints from year to year (Sullivan 2002a). Because funding is measured over a five-year period, years with relatively low contributions to the trust fund by certain cities can be offset by years with higher contributions. Additionally, the parity program encourages member cities to use a variety of sources to meet their contribu-

tion goals, including monetary assistance from general funds and Community Development Block Grant funds, indirect monetary assistance such as fee waivers, and donations of city-owned land.

St. Andrews Ellsworth senior housing in Mercer Island, Washington.

Three formulas were developed, therefore, with the understanding that each city had different circumstances and should be able to apply whichever formula was most appropriate. In each of the formulas, ranges establish low-end and high-end contribution levels for local governments. The low-end level is the lowest contribution produced by any of the three formulas, and the high-end level is the highest contribution produced by any of the three formulas. The three formulas are based on (1) current population, (2) projected increase in demand for housing due to job growth, and (3) projected housing growth.

In the first formula, based on the current population, each member city's contribution is based on its population relative to other member cities. For example, in 1998 when the formula was developed, the population of Kirkland (43,720) was approximately 17 percent of the overall population of all of the member cities combined. Thus Kirkland's contribution would be 17 percent of the overall goal.

The second formula for projected housing growth is similar to the formula for current population. Each member's contribution is based on the amount of projected housing growth, in accordance with its local comprehensive plan, relative to the other member cities. For example, in 1998, Bothell was projected to add 85 new housing units annually, which was approximately 5.25 percent of the projected housing growth for all of the member cities combined (1,620 units annually). Thus, under this formula, Bothell's contribution to the trust fund would be 5.25 percent of the overall goal.

The Village at Overlake Station, developed by the King County Housing Authority, is a transit-oriented affordable family rental housing development funded by A Regional Coalition for Housing.

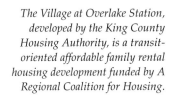

The third formula, based on the projected creation of new jobs, linked each member's contribution to the trust fund to the amount of projected job growth as a percentage of the total projected job growth for all of the member cities. The amount of projected job growth for each city was made in accordance with its comprehensive plan. For example, in 1998, Bellevue was expected to add 1,400 jobs annually, which was approximately 35 percent of all the new jobs projected to be added to all of the member cities. Therefore, Bellevue's contribution under this formula would be 35 percent of the overall goal.

Cambridge Court, a senior affordable rental development located in Bellevue, Washington, funded by A Regional Coalition for Housing.

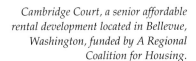

The parity program set an initial baseline goal of $1 million in local government contributions to the trust fund (for the low-end goal) and an initial challenge of up to $2 million annually as an acknowledgment of level of need for affordable housing in the communities (the high-end, or challenge, goal). The baseline of $1 million was derived from the contribution levels of member cities in the years prior to the development of the parity program. Using the overall goal, the low end of the contribution range for each city is calculated using the lowest funding level outcome of the three formulas. The high end of the range is the highest outcome of the three formulas. ARCH has increased the program's baseline as additional cities have joined the program. When a new city joins the program, its contribution is calculated and the corresponding contribution amount is added to the range. Today, with 15 member cities (excluding King County), the overall goal is $1.15 million (low end), with a challenge goal of $2.2 million (high-end) (Sullivan 2002d).

Program Results

The parity system was developed as a five-year trial program, and it is now in its fourth year. According to the city manager of Mercer Island, Richard Conrad (2002), a member of ARCH, "cities feel more comfortable under the parity system because they know that each city is contributing their fair share to the trust fund." Since the parity system was implemented, many cities have actually increased their contributions toward the high-end of the contribution ranges, and two cities, Bellevue and Mercer Island, have exceeded the high end of their averaged contribution ranges between 1999 and 2002 (ARCH 2001). Since the overall $1.15 million goal reflects the low end of each city's contribution range, the goal is exceeded when cities contribute more than the lowest value on their range. The high-end goal of $2.2 million was exceeded in 1999, 2000, and 2001.

The sources of funds contributed to the trust fund between 1999 and 2002 are summarized in Table 5-1. The highest amount of contributions to the trust fund come from cities' general funds, although there are not considerably large differences between each of the funding sources. The funds allocated have been made available as both grants and low-interest contingent loans; approximately 60 percent of the funding has been in the form of loans.

A total of 1,709 units and 74 beds have been constructed using funds from ARCH between 1993 and spring 2001—an average of 198 units/beds per year.[2] A total of $14,117,002 in ARCH funds was used to fund these units/beds. Special needs housing, which is often for unrelated individuals living in group quarters, is expressed as the number of beds produced; while family, senior, and homeless and transitional housing is expressed as the number of units produced, which may house numerous people in one unit. Special needs housing funded by ARCH between 1993 and spring 2001 included 74 beds and 14 units.

The affordable housing funded by the trust fund is not dispersed throughout all of the participating cities. Most of the projects are concentrated in Bellevue, with 17 of a total of 44 projects. Bellevue is the largest, oldest, and most urbanized member city, with a population of 109,827 in 2000. Table 5-2 shows a breakdown of projects that have been funded by ARCH from 1993 to 2001.

As Table 5-2 indicates, most of the projects that ARCH has funded have been concentrated in Bellevue, Redmond, and areas identified as "other" that include unincorporated King County, Bellevue/Redmond, Bellevue/Kirkland, and other locations. Several cities that contribute to the trust fund have not yet had any affordable housing projects built, including Yarrow Point, Hunts Point, Medina, Clyde Hill, and Sammamish.

The trust fund has done well at funding family housing and senior housing, with 1,216 family units and 437 units/beds of senior housing built between 1993 and spring 2001. However, it has had less success at funding special needs housing (88 units/beds) and homeless/transitional housing (42 units/beds). The target population goals have fallen short for certain populations. Housing for special needs populations reached only 8.3 percent of the housing funded by ARCH—4 percent short of the target goal, based on the number of units/

TABLE 5-1
ARCH, SOURCE OF FUNDS, 1999-2002

Source of Funds	Amount
CDBG	$2,369,745 (28.3%)
General Fund	$3,501,105 (41.7%)
Other[1]	$2,514,978 (30.0%)
Total	$8,383,828 (100%)

Source: ARCH: "ARCH Affordable Housing Assistance Program," (January 2002).

[1]Other includes: payments from developers in lieu of building affordable housing units, fee waivers, and transfers of property.

TABLE 5-2
ARCH, PROJECTS FUNDED, 1993–2001

Municipality	Population in 2000[1]	Number of Units/Beds[4]	funding($)	Number of Projects
Bellevue	109,569	730	6,631,209	16
Redmond	45,256	513	3,538,595	8
Other[2]	N/A	171	1,201,281	8
Woodinville	9,194	100	300,000	2
Bothell	30,150[3]	64	445,000	3
Mercer Island	22,036	59	900,000	1
Kenmore	18,678	50	65,000	1
Kirkland	45,054	28	645,000	2
Newcastle	7,737	12	190,708	1
Issaquah	11,212	56	325,209	2
Total	**298,886**	**1,783**	**14,242,002**	**44**

Source: ARCH, "List of Projects Funded," http://www.archhousing.org (Spring 2001).

1. U.S. Census Bureau, "American FactFinder," http://factfinder.census.gov/(accessed May 8, 2002).

2. Other includes: King County, Bellevue/Redmond, Bellevue/Kirkland, and locations to be announced.

3. Both King County and Snohomish County include parts of Bothell. In 2000, the population of Bothell residing in King County was 16,185, and the population of Bothell who resides in Snohomish was 13,965.

4. A total of 74 beds and 1,709 units were funded using ARCH funds. Beds were funded in unincorporated King County (6), Redmond (19), Kirkland (4), Bellevue/Redmond (9), Bellevue (18), Issayuah (6), Bothell (4), and locations to be announced (8).

beds funded between 1993 and spring 2001. Six percent of the units funded by ARCH were for homeless/transitional populations—7 percent short of the target goal. ARCH notes that in the last year, after the range of these figures, it has funded several transitional developments and has now met its goal for homeless/transitional populations (Sullivan 2002e). Alternatively, the trust fund has met target population priorities for families, and it has exceeded

Habitat of East King County for-sale affordable housing in Newcastle, Washington.

A Regional Coalition for Housing

priorities for elderly by 12 percent. Sullivan comments that ARCH is in the process of reviewing the housing goals: "we are now just beginning a process to look at our goals to see if they need to be refined/updated based on current conditions in the community" (Sullivan 2002d).

While King County does not contribute to ARCH, it is a member and works closely to synchronize its affordable housing program with ARCH's. Using 1990 census data, the King County Consolidated Housing and Community Development Plan, which covers all of King County except Seattle, states that there are 70,000 households in the county who are in need of housing assistance (over 18 percent of all households). This figure does not account for the estimated 4,000 homeless people in the area. The plan also considers 14,300 elderly households (20.6 percent), and 54,828 other households (79.3 percent) to be in need of housing assistance (King County Consortium 1999, 38).

Hopelink transitional, affordable rental housing in Bellevue, Washington.

A Regional Coalition for Housing

According to the plan, the eastern region of King County (which includes Beaux Arts, Bellevue, Bothell, Carnation, Clyde Hill, Duvall, Hunts Point, Issaquah, part of Kenmore, Kirkland, Medina, Mercer Island, Newcastle, North Bend, Redmond, Snoqualmie, Woodinville, Sammamish, Yarrow Point, and parts of unincorporated King County) has the most expensive rents in the region. The median rent there in 1998 was $810, which was $141 more than the region's overall median rent of $669. The plan proposes several goals to meet the demand of affordable housing in King County outside of Seattle, including the development or preservation of an annual average of 700 units,[3] and the provision of rental assistance to an average of 1,600 low- and moderate-income households (King County Consortium 2002, 143).

Although King County is a noncontributing member, ARCH-funded housing helps the county meet its affordable housing goals. By constructing an average of 198 units/beds per year, ARCH fulfills 28.2 percent of the overall goal for King County outside of Seattle of developing or preserving an annual average of 700 units per year of affordable housing, but none of the goal of providing rental assistance to an annual average of 1,600 households per year.

A Regional Coalition for Housing

Archiocesan Housing Authority Harrington House, a transitional housing, maternity, and new mother affordable housing development funded by A Regional Coalition for Housing.

Overall, ARCH has succeeded at obtaining higher-than-expected contribution levels from most of the member cities, with approximately 42 percent of the total contribution coming from member cities' general funds. However, like many other affordable housing programs, that funding does not seem to go very far, given the high overall need for affordable housing in King County. Constructing an average of 198 units per year is unlikely to meet all of the demand for affordable housing in the area, especially since the ARCH program area has the most expensive rents in King County.

Although one of ARCH's evaluation criteria is duration of affordability, there is no requirement that the housing units funded by ARCH remain affordable for a certain number of years or in perpetuity. However, ARCH program manager Arthur Sullivan (2002c) notes that the typical duration of affordability is 50 years or more.

ARCH gains community acceptance for affordable housing projects by promising good design that fits with the community, refusing to fund something that is not well-conceived, and assuring community input through the citizens advisory board. According to the chairperson of the Citizens Advisory Board Paul Carson (2002), "The reason we have had so much success is because we have assured good design that fits in well with the neighborhoods...so the communities trust that we are not going to underwrite something bad. The design details have been crucial, an issue as big as money."

ARCH has succeeded at obtaining a high level of community acceptance for its projects and has taken steps to ensure good design that fits in well with the community, something not always easily accomplished in affordable housing projects, especially in very affluent areas like eastern King County. By requiring that all of the projects that are funded by ARCH be ratified by every city council, the program also guarantees that all of the projects have local approval.

SACRAMENTO, CALIFORNIA, HOUSING AND REDEVELOPMENT AGENCY

Inception: 1989 (city trust fund) and 1990 (county trust fund)

Administration: The redevelopment agency, created in 1973 to serve the city and county, administers two housing trust funds.

Key Objectives: Raise local funds to finance the development of affordable housing near employment centers

Accomplishments: Housing trust fund collections totaled $26,967,152 as of September 2001. Between 1993 and 2001, 1,053 units have been constructed with funds from the city trust fund and 1,244 units have been constructed with funds from the county trust fund, with a total of 2,298 units at an average of 230 units per year. City trust fund monies leveraged a total capital investment of $153 million. County trust fund monies leveraged a total capital investment of $114.4 million.

Caveats: County and city housing trust funds raise revenue for affordable housing through fees for nonresidential development based on a nexus analysis of new very low- and low-income workers who will be attracted to the area as a result of the new development. No general fund monies are involved. Because of the jobs/housing nexus requirement, elderly housing is not eligible for funding. Housing units produced with money from the trust fund must be located within a reasonable commuting distance of the employment-generating uses that pay housing trust fund fees. The funds operate separately, although discussions are ongoing on how to allow for their joint operation and how to establish a regional fund that would involve several counties.

Sacramento County, California, covers approximately 994 square miles in the Central Valley in California. The county population in 2000 was 1,268,770 while the city's was 407,018.

The Sacramento Housing and Redevelopment Agency (SHRA) is a joint powers public authority created by the city and county of Sacramento in 1973. It is the lead public agency and public developer for both the city and county of Sacramento for affordable housing, public housing, and redevelopment projects. As one of the largest housing authorities and redevelopment agencies in California, SHRA was originally created by merging the public housing authorities and redevelopment agencies from both the city and county of Sacramento (SHRA 2002b).

With a 2002 budget of some $159 million, SHRA has several departments that manage housing and redevelopment, including community development departments for the city and county, development services, housing authority, and financing. SHRA provides a wide range of housing and redevelopment services and programs for the city and county of Sacramento as well as for other cities in the county.

SHRA states that its vision for the Sacramento region is one "where all neighborhoods are excellent places to live, work, and do business; where all people have access to decent, safe and affordable housing; and where everyone can obtain a job and attain financial sufficiency" (SHRA 2002b). SHRA also issues tax-exempt mortgage revenue bonds, administers jointly the city's inclusionary housing program with the city of Sacramento planning department, and oversees home repair programs, multifamily housing financing, and direct development of large projects. SHRA owns and maintains 3,600 public housing units and administers approximately 10,000 housing choice vouchers (formerly Section 8) (SHRA 2002c).

Sacramento Housing and Redevelopment Agency

Village Crossing affordable apartments in Sacramento, California.

SHRA currently administers 16 housing loan and grant programs, which are funded by redevelopment housing 20 percent set-aside funds, Community Development Block Grants, HOME Investment Partnership Program Funds, local housing trust funds, and other sources (SHRA 2002a, 86). Its housing programs can be grouped into two categories: homeownership programs and multifamily financing programs.

The primary programs for homeownership include down payment assistance, which assists about 600 families per year who have an average family income at 60 percent of the median. This program operates through more than 100 local mortgage brokers and provides $3,500 to $5,000 in down-payment and closing-cost assistance and forgivable, no-payment second loans. The next primary homeownership program is a property improvement loan program for low-income homebuyers and homeowners, with special provisions for senior citizens. This program offers loans of up to $35,000 for property improvement in addition to $2,500 beautification grants. SHRA's boarded/vacant property program provides incentives to small contractors to purchase and rehabilitate boarded and vacant single- family homes and sell them to low- and moderate-income homebuyers. More than 100 of these properties have been put back into productive use. Finally, mortgage credit certificates offer individual tax credits to low-income home purchasers with special incentives in redevelopment target areas.

Primary programs for multifamily financing include acquisition/rehabilitation and rehabilitation loans, new construction loans for rental properties and for-sale properties, and mortgage revenue bonds. In 2002, SHRA received private activity bond allocations for seven multifamily developments totaling

1,294 units (567 very low- and low-income units); the total project costs were $157.4 million, with bond issuances covering $117.2 million.

Sacramento city and county housing trust fund ordinances were adopted in 1989 and 1990, respectively (SHRA 2001c, 3), with the mission of raising local funds to finance the development of affordable housing near employment centers. The North Natomas Housing Trust, a separate fund for the North Natomas area, was also available to fund infill projects in the North Sacramento Community Plan area. In February 2001, however, this fund was eliminated and its revenues were moved to the city housing trust fund.

County and city housing trust funds raise revenue for affordable housing through fees for nonresidential development based on a nexus analysis of

Auberry Park Apartments, funded by the Sacramento Housing and Redevelopment Agency

Sacramento Housing and Redevelopment Agency

new very low- and low-income workers who will be attracted to the area as a result of the new development (SHRA 2001a, 9). The nexus analysis determines the extent to which the construction of new commercial projects—such as offices, business parks, hotels, and shopping centers—will attract new very low- and low-income residents to Sacramento (SHRA 2001c). The fees are then used to increase the supply of affordable housing near places of employment. Funds from the trusts are generally used for new construction or substantial rehabilitation.

Because of the jobs/housing nexus, however, elderly housing is not a use eligible for funding. Also, the housing units produced with trust monies must be "located within a reasonable commuting distance of the employment-generating uses that pay housing trust fund fees" (SHRA 2001c, 3). A reasonable commuting distance is defined as being within a seven-mile radius.

The city of Sacramento trust fund is available to households with incomes up to 80 percent of the area median income, with a preference for very low-income households. The Sacramento County trust fund is available to households earning up to 50 percent of the area median income. For both trust funds, at least 20 percent of the units in a development must be affordable to households earning less than 50 percent of the area median income. Likewise, there must be "a reasonable expectation that the prospective residents will be in the labor force in the area" (SHRA 2001a, 9). Housing funded by the trust fund may be rental or owner-occupied housing. The funds may be used for a wide range of purposes, including loans, grants, and equity participation. Preference is given to locations within one-quarter mile of existing or planned transit services (SHRA 2001c, 19).

Pensione K mixed-use development with affordable housing on the upper floors, funded by the Sacramento Housing and Redevelopment Agency.

Under SHRA's homeownership policies, the agency has a shared equity recapture program that is triggered when the initial household sells the home at market rate or to a purchaser who is not low-income. Under this policy, SHRA shares in the home's appreciated value (the difference between the original subsidized sales price and the new market value) in proportion to its investment. The funds are then returned to the housing trust fund (Fretz-Brown 2002).

In addition to the housing trust fund, Sacramento city and county have 11 redevelopment areas that generate funds from tax increment financing (TIF). Twenty percent of the funds generated by the TIF districts must be used for very low-, low-, and moderate-income housing (set aside funds) under California's Community Redevelopment Law (California Government Code, Section 33334). Affordable housing funded with TIF funds must be located in the same redevelopment area from which the funds came unless a housing development outside of the redevelopment area can be proven to benefit the redevelopment area (SHRA 2001a, 9).

18th and L Building affordable housing development, funded by the Sacramento Housing and Redevelopment Agency.

SHRA also administers a multifamily mortgage revenue bond program for financing multifamily rental housing. Under the name of the housing authority of the city and county of Sacramento, SHRA issues tax-exempt mortgage revenue bonds and lends the proceeds of the bonds to developers of multifamily rental housing at rates below commercial loan rates.

Program Results

Housing trust fund collections have totaled $26,967,152, with $10,688,532 for the city trust, $15,159,468 for the county trust, and $1,119,152 for the North Natomas trust. Table 5-3 shows the city housing trust fund expenditures for 1993-2001.

Table 5-3 indicates that between 1993 and 2001, $11.4 million in city housing trust funds were used to develop 1,053 units of very low- and low-income housing. According to SHRA, 51 percent of these units are projected to be affordable to very low-income households, and 40 percent will be affordable to low-income households. The city trust fund leveraged a total capital investment of $153 million. The average housing subsidy for the city trust fund was 7.4 percent of the total cost (SHRA 2001c, 10). For the county trust fund, $10.25 million had been used to finance the development of 1,245 very low- and low-income housing units. The county trust fund leveraged a total capital investment of $114.4 million in the unincorporated county, and the average housing trust fund subsidy was 8.96 percent of the total project cost. The total number of housing units that were funded (in part) by the trust fund was 2,298 between 1993 and 2001, an average of approximately 255 units per year.

TABLE 5-3
SHRA HOUSING TRUST FUND EXPENDITURES, 1993-2001

Fund Name	Total Number of Units	Number of Assisted Units	Housing Trust Funds	Total Development Cost
City/North Natomas Fund	1385	1053	$11,401,431	$153,112,807
North Natomas Fund[1]	17	17	$298,000	$1,835,305
County Fund	1312	1245	$10,252,805	$114,446,125
Total	**2714**	**2315**	**$21,952,236**	**$269,394,237**

Source: Sacramento Housing and Redevelopment Agency, *Performance Report for the Housing Trust Funds of the City and County of Sacramento*, (Sacramento, CA: Sacramento Housing and Redevelopment Agency, November 2001), 8-10.

1. The North Natomas housing trust fund has been merged with the city housing trust fund in February 2001. These developments predate the merger. Information for this row is for 1993-2000.

Table 5-4 shows the status of the combined housing trust funds for the years 1993-2001.

Table 5-4 demonstrates that SHRA has successfully leveraged funds from other sources for affordable housing development. The highest concentration of projects funded by the trust fund have been located in the central city, according to SHRA; this "reflect[s] a purposeful redevelopment effort to increase residential life downtown" (SHRA 2001c, 10). SHRA also notes that the higher per-unit cost for central city developments reflects the higher cost of land, parking, infrastructure, and environmental issues in the central city.

SHRA's funding is grounded on its assumption that "economic growth, especially in California, is tied to the production of housing. Economic growth also stimulates the need for affordable housing, the production of which contributes back to the economy. Housing production can be de-

TABLE 5-4
SACRAMENTO CITY AND COUNTY HOUSING TRUST FUNDS
COMBINED PRODUCTION STATUS, 1993-2001

Status	Total Number of Units	Total Number of Assisted Units	Amount of Trust Funds Used	Total Project Cost	Cost Per Unit[1]	Percentage Housing Trust Funds	Housing Trust Funds per Assisted Unit
Application	254	117	$1,800,000	$38,672,067	$152,252	4.7%	$10,169.49
Funded	497	333	$4,904,752	$62,857,635	$126,474	7.8%	$14,728.98
Under Construction	557	411	$3,511,446	$58,927,425	$105,794	6.0%	$8,543.66
Complete	1,389	1,377	$11,438,038	$107,101,805	$77,107	10.7%	$8,306.49
Total	**2,697**	**2,298**	**$21,654,236**	**$267,558,932**	**$99,206**	**8.1%**	**$9,423.08**

Source: Sacramento Housing and Redevelopment Agency, *Performance Report for the Housing Trust Funds of the City and County of Sacramento,* (Sacramento, CA: Sacramento Housing and Redevelopment Agency, November 2001), 11.

1. Cost per unit is the total project cost divided by the total number of units.

Sacramento Veteran's Resource Center, funded by trust funds from the Sacramento Housing and Redevelopment Agency.

scribed as a one-time infusion of development capital that creates jobs, generates wages, and ultimately produces tax revenues derived from a stimulated economy" (SHRA 2001c, 16). To that end, SHRA completed an analysis of the economic impact expected from trust fund projects, summarized in Table 5-5.

Table 5-5 describes an economic analysis that predicts the ripple effect on economic growth of new housing construction using trust funds between 1993 and 2001. The second column, "direct," shows the impacts from the construction of any given housing unit on money spent on labor, building materials, and related construction expenses. The third column, "indirect," shows the economic impacts from the purchase of items by new homeowners, such as lawnmowers and shower curtains. The fourth column, "induced impacts," includes the effects of retailers

TABLE 5-5
ECONOMIC IMPACTS EXPECTED FROM SACRAMENTO CITY
AND COUNTY HOUSING TRUST FUND PROJECTS

Economic Impacts	Direct	Indirect	Induced	Total
Total Industry Output[1]	$267,569,000	$117,490,000	$196,797,000	$581,856,000
Personal Income	$51,748,000	$42,249,00	$63,039,000	$157,036,000
Total Income	$68,049,000	$66,009,000	$115,804,000	$249,862,000
Value Added	$68,979,000	$73,849,000	$131,430,000	$274,258,000
Employment	2,726	2,111	3,068	7,905
Per Employee	$18,982	$20,019	$20,546	$59,547
Multipliers:				
Total Industry Output	1	0.44	0.74	2.17
Personal Income	1	0.82	1.22	3.03
Total Income	1	0.97	1.70	3.67
Value Added	1	1.07	1.91	3.98
Employment	1	0.77	1.13	2.90

Source: Sacramento Housing and Redevelopment Agency, *Performance Report for the Housing Trust Funds of the City and County of Sacramento*, (Sacramento, CA: Sacramento Housing and Redevelopment Agency, November 2001), 16, citing Real Estate Analytics and Sacramento Housing and Redevelopment Agency.

1. Direct reduced for imports

and providers of services. The bottom six rows of the table show the multipliers used for the estimates. The second row, " total industry output," is the total economic impact for the construction project. "Personal income" is the economic impact that people such as construction workers actually earn, and "total income" is the total income for those people, including expenses such as taxes. "Value added" is the market value of the housing minus construction costs, such as materials and labor. "Employment" is the number of worker hours produced as result of the housing, and "per employee" is the average wage per employee as a result of the housing projects (Krohn 2002).

Table 5-5 also shows that trust fund projects leveraged approximately $267 million in direct expenditures and approximately $582 million in direct, indirect, and induced impacts from housing construction (SHRA 2001c, 16). The total personal income that resulted from the housing projects was approximately $157 million, and the total income was approximately $250 million.

County housing trust funds can only be used in the unincorporated areas of the county. However, according to Beverly Fretz-Brown (2002), SHRA director of development services, SHRA is "currently discussing a new collaboration with recently incorporated cities which have maintained the [housing trust fund] ordinances. The discussions are very preliminary; but we see cost savings in administering the fund for the new cities—with their approving the projects, of course. Down the line, we are also considering pooled expenditures of trust funds, but this would require a change in the ordinances and probably state legislation under California's housing element law. Still further, "the city and county are now working with the six counties in our regional planning area on how to raise additional funds for affordable housing. This may lead to the adoption of a regional housing trust fund or countywide trust funds."

COLUMBUS/FRANKLIN COUNTY, OHIO, AFFORDABLE HOUSING TRUST FUND

Inception: 2000

Administration: An 11-member board of trustees and a president are responsible for oversight of the trust fund. It covers the city of Columbus and Franklin County. It was funded initially through a $1 million contribution from Franklin County's general fund revenues, a $1 million Urban Development Action Grant, and $2 million from a hotel/motel bed tax in the city of Columbus. The city's hotel/motel tax provides continued funding. Annual funding from Franklin County is derived from its general fund and is not a dedicated source of funding.

Key objectives: Funding is directed to projects that benefit low-income and very low-income households. Half of its funds are available to households earning 60 percent the area median income (AMI) or less, and the remainder are for households earning between 60 and 120 percent AMI.

Accomplishments: Through its various programs from October 2001 to September 2002, the trust has agreed to partially finance 784 homes. The majority of the current projects are for-sale single-family homes, townhomes, and condominums; 350 are rental apartments, and 150 senior housing rental units. As of September 2002, construction had begun on 468 units.

Caveats: A request for proposals for projects was initially sent out to 170 nonprofit and for-profit developers, but only 17 project proposals for some 200 units resulted, which the trust staff viewed as disappointing.

Covering 540 square miles in central Ohio, Franklin County had a population of 1,068,978 in 2000. Columbus is the largest city in the state, with a population of 702,132 in 2000. Fueled by recent growth in Columbus, Franklin County had the highest percentage increase in population (3.3 percent) of any Ohio county between 1990 and 1998 (Garber Consulting 2000, 1-4).

According to the Columbus and Franklin County Consolidated Plan, there has been a significant decrease in the number of new homes priced under $130,000 in Franklin County (Garber Consulting 2000, 3-1). In 1996, there were an estimated 60,000 low-income renter households paying more than 30 percent of their household income for housing, with 85 percent of those households living in the city of Columbus and 15 percent living elsewhere in the county. That same year, one affordable rental unit was available for every two extremely low-income renter households, which produced a deficit of about 22,000 affordable rental units for households with incomes at or below 30 percent of the median income. Further, a disconnect between the location of jobs and the location of affordable housing has generated longer commuting times and increased traffic congestion (Merritt 2002b). The Columbus housing market has also been scarely affected by the recent recession, and home builders continue to construct homes above the $150,000 price range that remain far out of reach for low-income households.

The Columbus/Franklin County Affordable Housing Trust was created in September 2000 by the city of Columbus and Franklin County. The timely alignment of a number of factors produced the trust: a new mayor, pressure from a faith-based organization, a pressing need for affordable housing near employment centers, and an urban center that was losing population and housing units. Furthermore, the trust was conceived so as to further the revitalization of the urban center and community building thought to be crucial to the health of the region.

With an 11-member board of directors and a president, the housing trust was established as a nonprofit organization in October 2001. It was funded through a $1 million contribution from Franklin County's general fund revenues, a $1 million Urban Development Action Grant, and $2 million from a hotel/motel bed tax in Columbus. The city's hotel/motel tax provides continued funding. Annual funding from Franklin County is derived from its general fund and is not a dedicated source of funding.

Affordable housing is a regional issue in Franklin County, according to Nan Merritt (2002c), principal planner and project manager for the trust. "Affordable housing is everyone's issue," she explains. "Franklin County, which contains the city of Columbus and its 22 suburbs, all share the same economic engine. Adequate housing for all its citizens is just infrastructure, like roads, water, and sewers." From the trust fund's inception, the city, county, developers, and neighborhood organizations had conflicting ideas about how it should be structured and what it should provide. Allocation of funding to low-income and very low-income households caused the most disagreement. The trust eventually decided that half of its funds should be dedicated to households earning 60 percent or less of the area median income (AMI), with the remainder for households earning between 60 to 120 percent AMI. This goal will be spread over a four-year period. The trust is currently focusing on homeownership because community building and increased homeownership are believed necessary in the central city.

FIGURE 5-3
LOCATION OF ENTRY-LEVEL JOBS
IN THE COLUMBUS, OHIO, REGION IN RELATIONSHIP
TO LOCATION OF LOW-INCOME HOUSEHOLDS

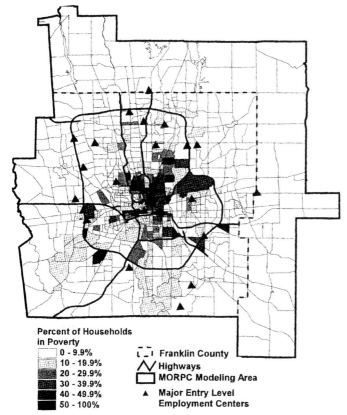

Percent of Households in Poverty

- 0 - 9.9%
- 10 - 19.9%
- 20 - 29.9%
- 30 - 39.9%
- 40 - 49.9%
- 50 - 100%

- Franklin County
- Highways
- MORPC Modeling Area
- ▲ Major Entry Level Employment Centers

Source: Roberta F. Garber Consulting (2002).

The trust initially believed that, if it offered funding for affordable housing, developers would flock to the trust with ideas and projects. That didn't happen.

The trust underwrites loans in conjunction with other lending institutions, and it structures the loans so that they mitigate risk for the various stakeholders. According to Steve Torsell (2002), president of Homes on the Hill Community Development Corporation, which has received trust funds, the trust's willingness to mitigate risk to the banks is especially important. He also applauds the trust's funding work: "it really helps us increase our capacity to have these funding sources. It has helped us double our production [of affordable housing]." All of the trust's projects are located in the city's five tax abatement districts, where homeowners receive a 15-year tax abatement for building or rehabilitating a home in the district. Other areas in the county have tax abatement programs, where the trust also plans to support housing development in the future (Merritt 2002c).

The trust uses a variety of tools to increase the supply of affordable housing in the county, including a request for proposals (RFP) that was sent to 170 non-profit housing agencies and for-profit developers. Merritt (2002a) explains that the trust's goal "was to get nonprofit community development corporations and the for-profit developers through various incentives to produce housing together. Each group has distinct abilities to bring to the table." Through this process, the trust fund offered to provide about $1.6 million in several kinds of loans and lines of credit. Also, the trust depends on Columbus and Franklin County for downpayment assistance financing through federal HOME funds and the residential 15-year tax abatements in certain areas. Although the trust was disappointed with the low response rate to the RFP—only 17 proposals were returned—it did match developers with builders who, the trust hopes, will produce up to 200 units of affordable housing (Merritt 2002a).

In addition to the RFP and loans, the trust has also optioned and purchased property to do predevelopment work and rezoning for larger projects. After the predevelopment work is completed, the property will be sold to a developer to build affordable housing at 60 to 120 percent AMI.

Future plans include purchasing central city parcels within a narrow geographic radius and developing them (with another developer) into a scattered-site infill subdivision, with the goal of maximum neighborhood impact. Also, the trust hopes to assist in the rehabilitation of abandoned buildings in the central city. Planning for these initiatives has already begun, and the trust is currently coordinating its infill project with its rehabilitation program (Merritt 2002a).

In the short time since its inception, the housing trust has experienced a good deal of success. Through its various programs between October 2001 to September 2002, the trust has agreed to partially finance 784 homes. Although the trust tries to simplify the process of building affordable housing, it remains complex, and therefore the trust expects that only about half of the current projects will be built. The majority of the current projects are for-sale single-family homes, townhomes, and condominiums; another 350 are rental apartments, and 150 are senior housing rental units. As of September 2002, construction had begun on 468 units.

Program Results

The trust initially believed that, if it offered funding for affordable housing, developers would flock to the trust with ideas and projects. That didn't happen, Merritt (2002a) admits. "So we went out and talked to everyone—meeting with bank presidents, home developers, community groups, faith based organizations, etc." This approach has proved successful. As Torsell (2002) attests, "They [the trust fund] help us make things happen that would otherwise not happen."

The trust is working on more projects that have not yet been finalized, and their goal is 500 homes by January 2004. Merritt attributes the early success of the program to knowledgeable, dynamic, and dedicated leadership and staff. She also credits the trust's small size and quick reaction time, which, she says, gives it far more flexibility than city and county government.

A lesson the trust learned very early was that its limited accomplishments were not due to a lack of money. Merritt (2002a) argues that, in fact, it is a lack of public awareness that has limited the program's success. "There is money available in the community to revitalize the central city and build affordable housing," she explains. "It's more a question of public education, of finding the developer and companies of good will that realize that they 'have a dog in the fight.' We need to do a better job of educating the public and private sectors about what affordable housing is and is not, who needs affordable housing, and why."

MONTGOMERY COUNTY, OHIO, HOUSING TRUST FUND

Inception: 1990

Administration: Montgomery County's housing trust fund is administered by County Corp, the county's quasi-governmental affordable housing and economic development organization. The trust fund has, since 1990, received an annual appropriation of $1 million from a one-half-cent sales tax increase collected for affordable housing, economic development, and arts and cultural programs. The funding commitment was extended for 10 years in 1999 by the Montgomery County Commission. County Corp is responsible for allocating funds from the housing trust fund, leveraging private and public funds to increase the total amount of funding available for affordable housing in the county, assisting with the identification of affordable housing needs, and finding new and innovative ways to address long-term needs throughout the county. Additionally, to ensure that countywide affordable housing needs are met, County Corp may proactively solicit the development of affordable housing, improve housing conditions, or expand housing services by issuing requests for proposals.

Key objectives: The trust fund has five priorities: (1) rehabilitation of owner-occupied housing stock; (2) rehabilitation of rental units; (3) construction of new housing for households with an income up to 80 percent of the median area income; (4) homebuyer counseling and other housing-related services; and (5) transitional housing for the homeless.

Accomplishments: The trust fund has funded, in part, the development of 2,784 housing units between 1990 and May 2002, an average of 232 units per year.

Caveats: The largest portion of trust fund monies goes to projects in Dayton, where there are the largest number of low-income households. There is less emphasis on building new affordable units in suburban areas in Montgomery County, including the city of Kettering, the county's second largest municipality.

Located in southwestern Ohio, Montgomery County has a population of 559,062 centered in the two urban centers of Dayton and Kettering. The Montgomery County Housing Trust was created in 1990 by the county's board of commissioners. For the fund's first 10 years, the program was administered by a nonprofit organization, the Affordable Housing Commission. In 1999, County

Mercy Manor, a neighborhood revitalization project in Dayton, Ohio, consisting of 24 newly constructed and 11 rehabilitated affordable for-sale homes.

Corp, Montgomery County's quasi-governmental affordable housing and economic development organization, assumed its administration. County Corp was created in 1980 to do the development work that an Ohio county was unable to under the Ohio Revised Code (County Corp 2002a). County Corp was the first housing and economic development nonprofit organization in any Ohio county (County Corp 2001b).

The Montgomery County Commission created the housing trust fund to provide a flexible source of financial resources to address the housing needs of low- and moderate-income households in the county. Since its inception, the trust has received an annual appropriation of $1 million from a one-half-cent sales tax increase collected for affordable housing, economic development, and arts and cultural programs. In 1999, the Montgomery County Commission extended its funding commitment for 10 years.

County Corp is responsible for allocating funds from the housing trust fund, leveraging private and public funds to increase the total amount of funding available for affordable housing in the county, assisting with the

Genesis Project, CityWide Development Corporation, an affordable housing and neighborhood revitalization project that consists of 24 newly constructed homes and 11 rehabilitated homes.

identification of affordable housing needs, and finding new and innovative ways to address long-term needs throughout the county. Additionally, to ensure that countywide affordable housing needs are met, County Corp may proactively solicit the development of affordable housing, improve housing conditions, or expand housing services by issuing requests for proposals (County Corp 2001b).

Although the housing trust fund disperses monies as both grants and loans, it is primarily a source of loans. Loaned funds include deferred payments, forgivable payments with terms, and loan guarantees. Grants are considered in cases where the project cannot support a loan on the best terms that can be made available. Projects requesting forgivable loans and combinations of loans and grants are given preference over requests for 100 percent grant financing. Since County Corp began administering the program, approximately $729,000 in loans and $569,000 in grants have been awarded (Longfellow 2002).

Municipalities, for-profit developers, public housing authorities, community housing development organizations, nonprofit developers, and affordable housing service providers are eligible to apply for funds. The trust's financial support may constitute no more than 50 percent of the total cost of a project (County Corp 2002c). Of those projects that benefit households with incomes over 80 percent of the area median, financial support from the housing trust may constitute no more than 25 percent of the total cost of the project or program (County Corp 2001b).

The trust evaluates applications for funding on the basis of four sets of separate priority areas: (1) housing need, (2) neighborhood need, (3) income priorities, and (4) the provision or retention of affordable housing units. The first priority area, housing need, has five subpriorities, which, after the first two, are in no particular order. The first priority for housing need is the rehabilitation of owner-occupied housing stock. The second is the rehabilitation of rental units. The remaining priorities are: construction of new housing for households with an income up to 80 percent of the median area income (80 percent the median area income for a family of four in 2001 was $45,500); homebuyer counseling and other housing-related services; and transitional housing for the homeless.

The second broad priority area includes two subpriorities for neighborhood need. The first subpriority is transitional neighborhoods where property values are depressed, rental housing is increasing, abandoned housing is increasing, and maintenance is declining. The second favors unstable neighborhoods where absentee owners and renters outnumber owner-occupied housing units, and vacant and abandoned structures are prevalent (County Corp 2002c).

The third priority area holds that the majority of the funds available from the housing trust fund shall directly benefit households with incomes below 80 percent the median area income. Additionally, no more than 10 percent of the funds in any given fiscal year shall be allocated to directly benefit households with incomes greater than 80 percent of the area median income. The benefit of such projects, however, must be part of a larger project that meets other community development objectives.

The last priority area requires that affordable housing projects and programs be directly related to the provision or retention of affordable housing units. Emergency housing repair programs are not eligible for funding (County Corp 2001b).

Eighty percent of the funds available from the trust are allocated for broad-based projects and programs that address the highest-need priorities. The remaining 20 percent is allocated for proposals that are evaluated on a project-by-project basis (County Corp 2002c).

Warder Place, Oikis Community Development Corporation, a rehabilitated single-family, affordable home in Dayton, Ohio, funded by County Corp.

Apart from the goals for neighborhood need, such as funding projects in transitional and unstable neighborhoods, the fund is generally targeted for use by county jurisdictions. While it does not specifically target particular neighborhoods or communities, which may have the potential for leaving some area's housing needs unmet, the housing trust has the latitude to issue requests for proposals to address gaps in service areas (Wenig 2002).

The *Report on the Countywide Housing Strategy*, prepared for County Corp by Diana T. Myers and Associates, surveyed government agencies, developers, neighborhood organizations, service providers, and other interested parties in 2000. The survey found that 47.5 percent of the respondents answered yes to the question "Should affordable housing be distributed to jurisdictions throughout the region based on population?" Additionally, 59 percent of the respondents felt that special needs housing should be distributed to jurisdictions throughout the region based on population. Of those people who answered no to either of these two questions, nearly 50 percent responded that the distribution should be based on need.

Program Results

In 2000, a year after County Corp took over administration of the housing trust, a total of $946,407 was awarded and $692,445 was disbursed for affordable housing projects and programs. Of the total amount awarded, $912,607 was for actual housing units and $33,800 for supportive housing programs, such as a homebuyer fair and a contribution to the Miami Valley Fair Housing Center. The housing trust fund assisted in the development of a total of 315 housing units. Most of the funds directed to Dayton. Projects and programs in Dayton were awarded $729,635 in funds, while the rest of the funding ($216,772) was for countywide programs and projects (County Corp 2000).

In 2001, a total of $1,183,700 was awarded and $1,329,879 disbursed. Of the total amount awarded, $155,000 was for affordable housing programs and $1,028,700 for affordable housing units, which produced 138 housing units.

The allocation of funds for projects since the trust fund was established in 1990 to May 2002 is shown in Table 5-6.

TABLE 5-6
MONTGOMERY COUNTY, OHIO,
HOUSING TRUST FUND,
PROJECTS FUNDED BY TYPE
1990–MAY 2002

Type of Project	Number of Projects	Amount Funded
New construction or rehabilitation activities	77	$9,527,284.11 (83%)
Housing services	43	$1,675,708.63 (14%)
Activities such as studies, assessments, etc.	13	$323,703.46 (3%)
Total	**133**	**$11,526,696.20 (100%)**

Source: Gloria Smith, Housing Trust Manager, County Corp, e-mail interview with Rebecca Retzlaff, April 26, 2002.

As Table 5-6 indicates, the funding for the majority of the projects (83 percent) has been directly for the construction or rehabilitation of affordable housing. This distribution is consistent with the trust fund's priorities.

Between 1990 and May 2002, 133 projects and programs had been funded, at a total investment of $11,526,696.20. The breakdown of projects by location is shown in Table 5-7.

TABLE 5-7
MONTGOMERY COUNTY, OHIO,
HOUSING TRUST FUND,
PROJECTS FUNDED BY LOCATION
1990–MAY 2002

Municipality	2000 Population	Number of Projects	Total Amount Funded
City of Dayton	166,179	73	$6,017,974
City of Kettering	57,502	2	$75,162
Balance of Montgomery County	335,381	25	$3,554,818
Countywide Benefit awards	N/A	33	$1,878,741
Total	**559,062**	**133**	**$11,526,696**

Source: Gloria Smith, Housing Trust Manager, County Corp, e-mail interview with Rebecca Retzlaff, April 26, 2002.

As indicated in Table 5-7, the majority of funds from the housing trust have been allocated in Dayton (approximately 52 percent), the county's largest and most urbanized city. According to the 2000 census, Dayton

Wolf Creek Homes, Improved Solutions for Urban Systems (ISUS), a neighborhood redevelopment project in Dayton consisting of about 70 new homes, improvements to existing homes, and neighborhood improvements such as parks and green space. As part of the project, about 250–300 high-risk youth will receive high school diplomas and college prep credits though ISUS.

County Corp

is home to approximately 30 percent of the population in Montgomery County. In contrast, Kettering is home to approximately 10 percent, but the housing trust allocated less than 1 percent of the total funding available to it. The rest of Montgomery County is home to approximately 60 percent of the county's population; it receives approximately 31 percent of the funds available from the housing trust. However, as County Corp points out, according to 2000 census data, 18 percent of the families in Dayton are below poverty level. In contrast, 5 percent of the families in Kettering and 5 percent in the balance of the county are below poverty level (Wenig 2002).

Since 1990, the total investment of $11,526,696 has leveraged an additional $321 million from other sources. The housing trust has assisted the development of 2,784 affordable housing units from 1990 until May 2002, which is an average of about 232 units per year (Smith 2002). It is important to note that this number does not reflect the housing programs that do not produce any housing units, such as homebuyer counseling programs and homebuyer fairs.

Overall, the Montgomery County Housing Trust has supported a substantial number of projects and leveraged additional affordable housing dollars. However, like many other programs analyzed in this report, it is unclear if the demand for affordable housing in the county is being met. As in many other areas, the need for affordable housing may far outweigh the capacity of local agencies to provide it.

The housing trust has succeeded in being flexible enough to allow funding for programs such as homebuyer fairs and homebuyer counseling as well as for nontraditional housing types, such as single room occupancy units, transitional housing for the homeless, and cooperatives. Also, by targeting unstable and transitional neighborhoods, the housing trust's activities may have the dual benefit of providing affordable housing and revitalizing distressed neighborhoods. Further, the dedicated $1 million derived from the county's sales tax has added to the stability of the program, allowing the trust fund to be a permanent option for funding affordable housing projects in Montgomery County.

ENDNOTES

1. For a general discussion of housing trust funds, see Brooks (2002).

2. The "units/beds" notation refers to a typical convention of measurement when referring to housing: "units" refers to one family living in the same unit, and "beds" refers to any number of unrelated individuals living in group quarters. Family units are measured in number of units, which may have many beds in it. Group living arrangements are measured in the number of beds.

3. According to the Consolidated Annual Performance and Evaluation Report for the Year 2001 (King County Housing and Community Development Program 2001), King County outside Seattle exceeded this goal, using federal and county funds to create, improve, or repair a total of 1,960 housing units.

4. According to SHRA's Beverly Fretz-Brown, the implementation of trust fund ordinances, adopted in 1989, were delayed until 1993 by litigation over their constitutionality. (Fretz-Brown 2002).

CHAPTER 6

State Affordable Housing
Appeals Systems

Massachusetts, Rhode Island, and Connecticut have state-level housing appeals laws. These laws are intended to streamline permit approvals for affordable housing projects by centralizing decision-making authority in one local agency. They also are intended to streamline appeals by assigning responsibility to a state board (in Massachusetts and Rhode Island) or court (in Connecticut), which is given the responsibility to decide the appeal quickly based on criteria contained in a statute.

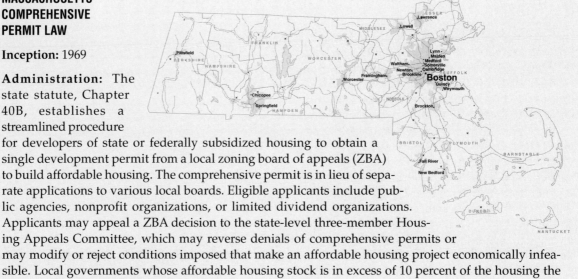

MASSACHUSETTS COMPREHENSIVE PERMIT LAW

Inception: 1969

Administration: The state statute, Chapter 40B, establishes a streamlined procedure for developers of state or federally subsidized housing to obtain a single development permit from a local zoning board of appeals (ZBA) to build affordable housing. The comprehensive permit is in lieu of separate applications to various local boards. Eligible applicants include public agencies, nonprofit organizations, or limited dividend organizations. Applicants may appeal a ZBA decision to the state-level three-member Housing Appeals Committee, which may reverse denials of comprehensive permits or may modify or reject conditions imposed that make an affordable housing project economically infeasible. Local governments whose affordable housing stock is in excess of 10 percent of the housing the city or town are immune from appeals.

Key objectives: Accelerate the granting of development permit approvals for affordable housing and provide clear routes for appeals of denials and onerous conditions.

Accomplishments: As of October 1999, 18,000 affordable housing units had been built with 373 comprehensive permits in 173 jurisdictions. As of April 2002, 27 of 351 communities had achieved the 10 percent housing goal. On a statewide basis, 213,459 units (8.45 percent) counted as state or federally subsidized housing units. The Housing Appeals Committee has tended to support applicants over local governments in its decisions, but it has also pressed the two parties to negotiate compromises. Such negotiations are encouraged because they reduce subsequent litigation and ensure that affordable housing is actually built.

Caveats: The law has been in effect for 33 years, but only 7.7 percent of local governments have met their 10 percent housing goal. There is some indication that the law has been the impetus for the enactment of "affordability zoning" provisions of various kinds, but the impact of these tools on housing production has been modest at best.

Massachusetts was the first of three New England states to adopt a housing appeals statute. Adopted in 1969, the Comprehensive Permit (CP) Law (Massachusetts General Laws Chapter 40B, Sections 20-23) establishes a streamlined procedure for developers of state or federally subsidized housing to obtain a single development permit from a local zoning board of appeals (ZBA) to build affordable housing.[1] The comprehensive permit is in lieu of separate applications to various local boards. Eligible applicants include public agencies, nonprofit organizations, or limited dividend organizations.

An applicant cannot apply for a CP without first obtaining preliminary approval from applicable state or federal subsidy programs. The applicant then submits that approval, typically in the form of an eligibility letter, with preliminary development plans to the local ZBA. The ZBA then notifies all other local boards of the application, holds a hearing within 30 days of the receipt of the application, and makes a decision on the permit. It has the same authority as all other boards or officials who would otherwise act on the application, and it can attach conditions to its approval. The ZBA is required to take into consideration the views of other local boards and may use consultants to assist it. The statute requires a decision on the permit within 40 days of the termination of the public hearing, although the ZBA and the applicant may mutually agree to extend the decision period. If the ZBA fails to act within that time period, the application is deemed approved. The CP statute also provides that any person aggrieved by the issuance of a permit may appeal it to court (but that court appeal is distinct from one to the housing appeals committee, which is described below).

If a ZBA denies an application for a CP or grants the CP with conditions that make the building or operation of such housing "uneconomic,"[2] the applicant can appeal to the Housing Appeals Committee (HAC) located in the state Department of Housing and Community Development (DHCD) within 20 days of the notice of the ZBA's decision. The HAC then notifies the ZBA of the appeal request, sets a hearing date, requests a copy of the ZBA's decision as well as its reasons, and holds a hearing on the appeal petition. It must then decide the appeal within 30 days after the hearing's termination, although in practice the HAC typically extends the decision-making period to allow the parties to negotiate a resolution (Lohe 2002). The HAC's decision may be challenged in superior court.

The statute limits the HAC's review to determining whether, in the case of denial of a comprehensive permit, the ZBA's decision was "reasonable and consistent with local needs" and, in the case of conditional approval, whether the conditions were uneconomic. An application is consistent with local needs if it meets one of two criteria: (1) if existing low- or moderate-income housing exceeds 10 percent of the housing in a local government as reported in the last census or on sites comprising 1.5 percent or more of the government's total land area zoned for residential, commercial, or industrial use (excluding land owned by public agencies, including the U.S. government); or (2) if construction of low- and moderate-income housing on sites comprising more than 0.3 percent of the jurisdiction's land area or 10 acres, whichever is larger, would begin as a result of the proposed project in any one calendar year.

The practical effect of the first criterion is to set a statewide housing goal of 10 percent state or federally assisted housing. If a city or town's housing stock includes more than 10 percent assisted housing, the municipality is immune from virtually all appeals under the act. However, these percentages can become a matter of dispute in a hearing before the HAC (see discussion of burdens below). The Massachusetts DHCD maintains an inventory of the total number of subsidized housing units in a community that is presumed to be accurate for the purposes of the hearing, but the DHCD's count can be challenged (Code of Massachusetts Regulations, Section 31.04(1)).

The second criterion allows the local ZBA to turn down comprehensive permit applications if the municipality has made "recent progress" toward achieving the local housing unit minimum. The HAC judges "recent progress" by the number of housing units created during the 12 months prior to the date of the comprehensive permit application; to count as "progress," that number must be at or more than 2 percent of the municipality's total housing units (Code of Massachusetts Regulations, Section 31.04(d)).

Under HAC rules, the applicant has the burden of proving certain jurisdictional requirements, including that the project is fundable by a subsidizing agency under a low- and moderate-income housing program and that the applicant has control of the site. In the case of a denial, the applicant may establish a prima facie case by proving that those aspects of the proposal that are in dispute comply with federal or state statutes or regulations or with generally recognized standards as to matters of health, safety, the environment, design, open space, or other matters of local concern. In

If a city or town's housing stock includes more than 10 percent assisted housing, the municipality is immune from virtually all appeals under the act.

The HAC must render its decision in writing, and it cannot issue any order that would permit the building or operation of such housing with standards "less safe" than the Federal Housing Administration or the Massachusetts Housing Finance Agency.

the case of an approval with conditions, the applicant has the burden of proving that the conditions imposed make the building or operation of the housing uneconomic. Finally, in the case of either a denial or an approval with conditions, the applicant may also argue that local requirements or regulations have not been applied as equally as possible to subsidized and unsubsidized housing. Again, the applicant carries the burden of proof (Code of Massachusetts Regulations, Section 31.06(1) to 31.06(4)).

The local ZBA has similar burdens to counter the applicant's assertions. In any case before the HAC, the ZBA must show "conclusively" that its decision was "consistent with local needs" by proving that one of the statutory minima described in the administrative rules has been satisfied (see Code of Massachusetts Regulations, Section 31.06(5), which includes statutory minima for the housing unit minimum, the general land area minimum, and the annual land area minimum). For example, if the applicant contends that an imposed condition rendered the project uneconomic, the local ZBA has the burden of first establishing that there is a valid health, safety, environmental, design, open space, or other local concern that supports such conditions; it must then prove that such concern *"outweighs the regional housing need"* (Code of Massachusetts Regulations, Section 31.06(7); emphasis added).

During its review process, a ZBA can consider the size of the project when judging whether an application is consistent with local needs. A large-scale project is defined as equal to either a fixed percentage of all housing units in a municipality or a certain number of dwelling units, depending on the size of the jurisdiction. For example, a municipality with 5,000 to 7,500 housing units can deny an application for a comprehensive permit if an application proposes the construction of a large-scale project, defined as more than 250 housing units (Code of Massachusetts Regulations, Section 31.07(1)(g)(2)). The HAC's administrative rules also allow a ZBA to deny a comprehensive permit if, in the previous 12 months, an applicant filed an application for a variance, special permit, subdivision, or other approval related to construction on the same land and that application included no low- and moderate-income housing (Code of Massachusetts Regulations, Section 31.07(1)(h)). This provision is intended to bar applicants "from using Chapter 40B as a threat to get conventional housing built," according to Sharon Perlman Krefetz (2002), a professor of government at Clark University in Massachusetts who has studied the law's impact.

The HAC must render its decision in writing, and it cannot issue any order that would permit the building or operation of such housing with standards "less safe" than the Federal Housing Administration or the Massachusetts Housing Finance Agency. The act also gives the HAC and the petitioner the power to enforce the HAC's order in court (Chapter 40B, Section 23).

Program Results

The most comprehensive and masterful review of the law's impact was completed by Krefetz (2001) for a special symposium issue of the *Western New England Law Review* published to coincide with the law's 30th anniversary. Krefetz surveyed the law's impact since its inception to 1999. Here is what she found:

(1) Since Chapter 40B went into effect, at least 655 applications for CPs to build over 50,000 units of housing have been submitted to zoning boards in at least 221 cities and towns throughout the state. As of October 1999, more than 21,000 units of housing, approximately 18,000 of which are affordable units, have been built with 373 CPs.

(2) Low- and moderate-income housing has been built in at least 173 cities and towns. Most of these CP housing developments are located in the suburbs of Boston, Worcester, Springfield, and Fall River, and on Cape Cod. The number of local governments that exceed the 10 percent goal is still modest, from three in 1972 to 23 in 1997, out of a total of 351 cities and towns. The number of communities with no affordable housing at all dropped from 173 to 55. About half of Massachusetts' communities now have affordable housing because of the act. "Most of the communities that continue to have no subsidized housing units are very small, rural towns in the western part of the state, where housing costs and demand are relatively low, and only one suburb of Boston (Boxborough) had no affordable housing as of 1997" (pp. 392—94).

Krefetz concludes:

> While relatively few communities have reached the 10 percent goal that chapter 40B set for affordable housing, it is important to recognize that this target was actually an arbitrary number intended to stimulate a "reasonable supply" of affordable housing. Progress toward that goal in a good number of communities is noteworthy: whereas in 1972 only 4 communities had between 7 and 10 percent low- and moderate-income housing, and all of these were cities (Cambridge, Lawrence, Malden, and Quincy), 44 communities had this amount in 1997. A sizeable number of these communities are suburbs, including several middle- and upper-middle-class suburbs, such as Framingham, Burlington, Littleton, Andover, and Westwood, in which multiple CP projects have been built. While "only" about 20 percent of all the subsidized housing built since the early 1970s was built directly through chapter 40B, and the number of units built overall still falls far short of the need for such housing, it seems clear that without the Act the amount of affordable housing that does exist would be much lower, and the locations of this housing would be far more limited (i.e., much more heavily concentrated in the cities and inner-ring "suburbs"). (p. 395)

Krefetz also analyzed the pattern of appeals to the HAC. Table 6-1 shows the results of all of the HAC appeal decisions in Krefetz's study. The largest percentage of HAC decisions overrule ZBAs (28 percent or 94 cases) while only 5 percent (18 cases) of the ZBA determinations were upheld. Nonetheless, over the last three decades the number of cases that were overruled has decreased from 45 percent in the 1970s to 47 percent in the 1980s and to 25 percent in the 1990s. The proportion of cases decided by "stipulation," which is a negotiated compromise between the parties, increased from 13 percent to 38 percent over the same period.

Krefetz theorizes that the decline in HAC decisions overruling ZBAs and the increase in stipulations are linked to efforts by the HAC to encourage negotiation between local governments and CP applicants to ensure that housing would actually be built instead of being blocked by subsequent litigation. Most of the time, the parties reached a settlement after the appeal was heard but before a decision was rendered. HAC encouraged these negotiations, Krefetz says, so as to preclude the possibility of cities and towns "dragging out the proceedings through lengthy court appeals, which often resulted in developers not being able to sustain the carrying costs over time or losing their land options or financing" (p. 404). As a result, more than half of all cases appealed to the HAC have resulted in affordable housing being built.

Krefetz also found that, at the local level, outright denials of CPs declined from more than 40 percent in the 1970s to 20 percent in the 1990s. She speculates that, after an initial period of "almost unvarying and intense opposition," many communities began to accept proposals for affordable housing.

Low- and moderate-income housing has been built in at least 173 cities and towns.

Rather than flat denials or unreasonable conditions, "most communities have been granting CPs with conditions that are intended to make the projects more acceptable to local sensibilities, for example, by specifying landscaping features, types of lighting, and parking locations" (p. 402).

The majority (55 percent) of housing projects built under the Act to 1999 have been family housing. Another 30 percent were elderly, 12 percent were mixed, and the remaining 3 percent provided special needs housing. In terms of project size, 37 percent of the built (in contrast to proposed) projects had 1–24 units, 20 percent had 25–49 units, 26 percent had 50–99 units, 14 percent had 100–199 units, and 4 percent had 200 or more units. Project size dropped over the analysis period. Nearly half the projects built in the first analysis period, 1970–79, had 100 or more units, but in the period from 1990 to 1999, more than half of the projects had less than 25 units. This drop, Krefetz contends, indicates that fewer low- and moderate-income households are being served. She calls this trend "worrisome" because the need for affordable housing has become more acute (p. 402).

This downward trend in project size may also be explained by the loss of available resources. In 1990, Massachusetts created a Local Initiative Program

One other consequence of Chapter 40B appears to have been the enactment of local inclusionary zoning provisions, even though they are not required by the act.

TABLE 6-1
HOUSING APPEALS COMMITTEE DISPOSITION OF CASES IN FOUR TIME PERIODS

HAC Appeal Decision	1970-79	1980-84	1985-89	1990-99	Total
ZBA Upheld	6%	9%	2%	13%	5%
ZBA Overruled	45%	24%	23%	25%	28%
Case Withdrawn	12%	2%	15%	11%	12%
Dismissed	4%	0%	7%	9%	6%
Decision / Stipulation	13%	24%	25%	38%	25%
Other	20%	40%	28%	5%	24%
Number	**69**	**45**	**165**	**56**	**335**

Source: Sharon Krefetz, "The Impact and Evolution of the Massachusetts Comprehensive Zoning Appeals Act: Thirty Years of Experience with a State Legislative Effort to Overcome Exclusionary Zoning," 22 *W. New Eng. L. Rev.* 381.

(LIP), which allowed developers who do not have a government subsidy to use the CP process if, among other things, at least 25 percent of the units they propose are affordable and they receive the approval of the chief elected official of the town. The units are made affordable by an internal subsidy from the market-rate units. The program requirements for LIPs allow a local preference for 70 percent of the units—that is, housing built goes to "deserving" local families. The LIPs have been responsible for a significant decrease in the size of Chapter 40B projects proposed and built in the 1990s. Nearly half of all the CPs proposed in the 1990s (82 out of 175) were LIPs. The majority of LIPs have had fewer than 25 units, and the largest LIP has been for 100 units. On the average, reports Krefetz, their small size means these projects are producing only about six to eight units of affordable housing per project (pp. 410-411).

Since Krefetz's review, the Massachusetts DHCD has updated statewide figures on the subsidized housing inventory under Chapter 40B. As of April 24, 2002, 27 of the state's 351 communities had achieved the 10 percent housing goal, and 8.45 percent of the total housing stock, or 213,459 units, counted as state or federally subsidized housing units.[4]

According to Werner Lohe (2002), chair of the HAC, there has recently been a major upsurge of appeals: 32 have been filed with the HAC in 2001–2002. Lohe attributes this increase to the availability of a new subsidy program from the Federal Home Loan Bank's (FHLB) New England Fund that, while "very shallow," did provide money that was "readily available to private developers throughout the FHLB system." The *Boston Globe* on August 14, 2002, estimated that the amount of money from the New England Fund program had reached 60 percent of the affordable housing projects proposed in that same year under Chapter 40B by the time the fund program was suspended by FHLB in August 2002.[5]

One other consequence of Chapter 40B appears to have been the enactment of local inclusionary zoning provisions, even though they are not required by the act. In a study sponsored by the Massachusetts Housing Partnership to examine the use and effectiveness of such provisions for the period 1990–1997, planning consultant Phillip Herr (2002) found that 118 of the 351 communities in the state (33.6 percent) had enacted them. The provisions included mandates (a fixed percentage of new developments as affordable housing) and incentives (density bonuses), as well as exemptions from growth rate provisions and lesser devices (e.g., fee waivers, fast tracking of permits). Herr found that the adopting communities are chiefly in the eastern region of the state where the disparity between market and affordable housing prices is the widest, with only 21 of the 118 adopting communities located west of Worcester. He estimates that "perhaps 200 affordable units per year have been permitted under such provisions over the 1990–97 period studied, or 1 percent of total statewide housing production. Chapter 40B, the state-adopted 'Anti-Snob Zoning Act,' has clearly been relied upon much more commonly" (p. 1).

Herr concludes that "local zoning incentives, even powerful ones, can do little that Chapter 40B can't do even more powerfully to support developers seeking to develop affordable housing." Chapter 40B, he observes, "obliges communities to accept affordable developments, but it doesn't oblige land owners and developers to propose them, and neither do more than a handful of locally adopted zoning rules" (p. 1).

Herr's analysis looked at several other New England states, including Connecticut and Rhode Island, both of which have housing appeals procedures. His findings are discussed below.

Herr concludes that "local zoning incentives, even powerful ones, can do little that Chapter 40B can't do even more powerfully to support developers seeking to develop affordable housing."

THE RHODE ISLAND LOW- AND MODERATE-INCOME HOUSING ACT

Inception: 1991

Administration: The Rhode Island statute, like its Massachusetts counterpart, authorizes a local board of zoning review to issue a single comprehensive permit for low- and moderate-income housing in lieu of all other permits and on behalf of all other local boards. An applicant has the right to appeal to the state housing appeals board if the application is denied or granted with conditions and requirements make the building or operation of the housing "infeasible." Local governments whose affordable housing stock is in excess of 10 percent of the housing in the city or town are immune from appeals. In addition, local governments with 5,000 occupied rental units that comprise at least 25 percent of its housing stock and of which in excess of 15 percent are affordable are also immune from appeals.

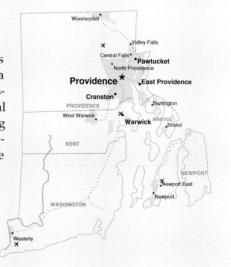

THE RHODE ISLAND LOW- AND MODERATE-INCOME HOUSING ACT *(continued)*

Key objectives: Accelerate the granting of development permit approvals for affordable housing and provide clear routes of appeals for denials and onerous conditions.

Accomplishments: In January 1992, when Rhode Island began tracking achievement under the housing appeals act, 7.09 percent (29,324 units) of the state's housing stock qualified as low– and moderate-income housing under the law. Five towns—Central Falls, East Providence, Newport, Providence, and Woonsocket—had more than 10 percent of their housing qualify as low– and moderate-income housing. By August 2001, 7.96 percent (34,913 units) of the state's housing stock qualified as affordable housing. The supply of affordable housing increased by 19 percent from 1992–2001. Since the law's inception, 12 local decisions have gone to the housing appeals board. Eight were overturned, one upheld, one deemed not properly before the board, one remanded to the town, and one appellant was ineligible to bring to the claim before the board. Together these cases represent 298 units for families, 44 single-family units/ limited equity co-ops, and 195 rental units for the elderly or disabled. Forty-one percent of Rhode Island cities or towns have enacted "affordability zoning" of varying degrees of effectiveness and applicability.

Caveats: There has been no change since the law's enactment in the number of cities or towns whose affordable housing amounts to at least 10 percent of their housing stock.

Enacted in 1991, the Rhode Island Low and Moderate Income Housing Act is nearly identical in structure and procedure to the Massachusetts law discussed above (Rhode Island General Laws, Chapter 45-53).[6] The act authorizes a local board of zoning review to issue a single comprehensive permit—also called a special exception[7]—for low– and moderate-income housing in lieu of all other permits and on behalf of all other local boards. In reviewing a permit request, the zoning board may deny it for any of the following reasons:

> [I]f the proposal is inconsistent with local needs, including, but not limited to, the needs identified in an approved comprehensive plan, and local zoning ordinances and procedures promulgated in conformance with the comprehensive plan

> [I]f the proposal is not in conformance with the comprehensive plan;

> [I]f the community has met or has plans to meet the standard of 10 percent of the units or, in the case of an urban town or cities, 15 percent of occupied rental units as defined in Section 45-53-3(2)(1) being low and moderate income housing

> [I]f concerns for the environment and the health and safety of current residents have not been addressed. (Rhode Island General Laws, Sec. 45-53-4)

The act defines "consistent with local needs" differently based on the number of occupied rental units in a community. In an urban city or town with at least 5,000 occupied rental units, the local zoning and land-use ordinances are "consistent with local needs" (1) if the total number of occupied rental units, as reported in the latest decennial census, comprises 25 percent or more of the community's total housing units, and (2) if in excess of 15 percent of the total rental units are affordable. If both of these criteria are met, the community has sufficient low- or moderate-income housing. In all other cities of towns, their ordinances are "consistent with local needs" if in excess of 10 percent of the housing units reported in the census are affordable (Section 45-53-3(i)). "Consistent with local needs" also applies where a city or town has promulgated zoning or land-use ordinances so as to implement a comprehensive plan (1) which has been adopted and approved pursuant to state law and (2) which includes a required housing element the comprehensive plan that provides for low- and moderate-income housing is in excess of either 10 percent of total housing units or 15 percent of total occupied rental housing units (Section 45-53-3(ii)).

As in the Massachusetts statute, an applicant has the right to appeal to the state housing appeals board if an application is denied or if it is granted with conditions and requirements that make the building or operation of the housing "infeasible" (Section 45-53-35; "infeasible" is defined similarly to "uneconomic" in the Massachusetts statute). The nine-member housing appeals board uses a set of five standards when it reviews the appeal.[8] If it finds, in the case of a denial, the zoning board's decision was unreasonable, the board must vacate the decision and then issue a decision and order approving the application. If it finds, in the case of an approval with conditions, that the zoning board's decision makes the building or operation of the housing infeasible and that the decision is not consistent with local needs, the board must issue a decision and order modification or removal of any condition or requirement so as to make the proposal no longer infeasible. Again, like the Massachusetts statute, the Rhode Island law prohibits the board from imposing building and site plan standards that are less safe than those of HUD or the Rhode Island Housing and Mortgage Finance Corporation, whichever agency is financially assisting the housing.

Table 6-2 shows the change in the supply of low and moderate income housing from 1992 to 2001 in all 39 Rhode Island towns. In January 1992, when Rhode Island began tracking achievement under the housing appeals act, 7.09 percent (29,324 units) of the state's housing stock qualified as low- and moderate-income housing under the law. Five towns—Central Falls, East Providence, Newport, Providence, and Woonsocket—had more than 10 percent of their housing qualify as low- and moderate-income housing. By August 2001, 7.96 percent (34,913 units) of the state's housing stock qualified as affordable housing. Rhode Island's supply of affordable housing increased by 19 percent from 1992 to 2001. However, there was no change in the number of towns with more than 10 percent of their housing as affordable housing (they are shown in bold-faced type in the table); these municipalities are exempt from the jurisdiction of the State Housing Appeals Board.

As noted above, the act also contains another method of determining which urban cities and towns are exempt from the act. The alternative calculation results in an exemption when a town has 5,000 occupied rental units that comprise at least 25 percent of its housing stock and when more than 15 percent of these units are affordable. Under this calculation, the following towns are also exempt from appeals: Cranston, North Providence, Pawtucket, Warwick, and West Warwick (they are shown in bold-face, italic type in the table).

Since the law's inception, 12 local zoning board of review decisions have gone to the housing appeals board, with one appeal withdrawn. Overall, eight local decisions were overturned, one decision upheld, one decision was deemed not properly before the board, one decision was remanded to the town, and in one situation the appellant was deemed ineligible to bring an appeal before the board. Of these decisions, four were appealed to the Rhode Island Supreme Court, which upheld the decision of the state housing appeals board in one case, remanded the case to the board in another case (where it was settled by the parties at the local level), and had not made a decision on two appeals as of September 2002 (State Housing Appeals Board 2002). Together these cases represent 298 homes for families, 44 single-family homes/limited equity co-ops, and 195 rental homes for persons with disabilities or the elderly.

Rhode Island's supply of affordable housing increased by 19 percent from 1992 to 2001.

TABLE 6-2
CHANGE IN LOW- AND MODERATE-INCOME HOUSING SUPPLY
BY RHODE ISLAND TOWN OR CITY 1992-2001

Town	Total Units 1990	Total Low/Moderate 1992	% Low/Moderate 1992	Total Units 2000	Total Low/Moderate 2001	% Low/Moderate 2001
Barrington	5,822	6	0.10%	6,199	91	1.47%
Bristol	7,959	234	2.94%	8,705	543	6.24%
Burrillville	5,751	390	6.78%	5,821	417	7.16%
Central Falls[1]	7,337	898	12.24%	7,270	1,046	**14.39%**
Charlestown	4,256	2	0.05%	4,797	44	0.92%
Coventry	11,788	475	4.03%	13,059	525	4.02%
Cranston[2]	30,516	1,542	5.05%	32,068	1,753	***5.47%***
Cumberland	11,217	570	5.08%	12,572	719	5.72%
East Greenwich	4,663	174	3.73%	5,226	213	4.08%
East Providence	20,808	2,198	10.56%	21,309	2,313	**10.85%**
Exeter	1,919	3	0.16%	2,196	37	1.68%
Foster	1,525	31	2.03%	1,578	36	2.28%
Gloster	3,460	42	1.12%	3,786	72	1.90%
Hopkinton	2,662	115	4.32%	3,112	151	4.85%
Jamestown	2,517	69	2.74%	2,769	103	3.72%
Johnston	10,384	706	6.80%	11,574	879	7.59%
Lincoln	7,281	481	6.61%	8,508	581	6.83%
Little Compton	1,850	0	0.00%	2,103	1	0.05%
Middletown	5,846	479	8.19%	6,345	630	9.93%
Narragansett	8,206	178	2.17%	9,159	331	3.61%

(continued)

The law, said Derry Riding (2002), a principal planner with the Rhode Island Department of Administration, has not produced many appeals "because there hasn't been real money for subsidies." Nonetheless, she added, "It really has served to get people to think in other ways about how to address the question of affordable housing outside of subsidies. I think we need some real incentives to get people to start to look at their regulations and zoning ordinances to address affordable housing." While planners realize the need for affordable housing, she said, "opposition to it and to the perception of the added school children that it brings are strong. The question is how to get the local boards and commissions to understand the need."

TABLE 6-2 *(continued)*
CHANGE IN LOW- AND MODERATE-INCOME HOUSING SUPPLY
BY RHODE ISLAND TOWN OR CITY 1992-2001

Town	Total Units 1990	Total Low/Moderate 1992	% Low/Moderate 1992	Total Units 2000	Total Low/Moderate 2001	% Low/Moderate 2001
Newport	13,094	1,965	15.01%	13,226	2,098	**16.86%**
New Shoreham	1,264	16	1.27%	1,606	27	1.68%
North Kingston	9,348	694	7.42%	10,743	830	7.73%
North Providence	14,134	953	6.74%	14,867	1,216	***8.18%***
North Smithfield	3,835	140	3.65%	4,070	327	8.03%
Pawtucket	31,615	2,434	7.70%	31,819	2,614	***8.22%***
Portsmouth	7,235	113	1.56%	7,386	181	2.45%
Providence	66,794	7,646	11.45%	67,915	9,212	**13.56%**
Richmond	1,874	4	0.21%	2,620	53	2.02%
Scituate	3,520	27	0.77%	3,904	41	1.05%
Smithfield	6,308	246	3.90%	7,396	322	4.35%
South Kingston	9,808	412	4.20%	11,291	582	5.15%
Tiverton	5,675	50	0.88%	6,474	115	1.78%
Warren	4,786	174	3.64%	4,977	209	4.20%
Warwick	35,141	1,658	4.72%	37,085	1,795	***4.84%***
Westerly	10,521	412	3.92%	11,292	517	4.58%
West Greenwich	1,370	0	0.00%	1,809	20	1.11%
West Warwick	12,485	822	6.58%	13,186	997	***7.56%***
Woonsocket	18,739	2,965	15.82%	18,757	3,272	**17.44%**
Total	**413,313**	**29,324**	**7.09%**	**438,579**	**34,913**	**7.96%**

Source: Data provide by Rhode Island Housing and Mortgage Insurance Corporation for 1992 and 2001; calculations by authors.

1. Cities and towns that have in excess of 10 percent of their housing as affordable housing are shown in bold-face type.

2. Cities and towns that satisfy the alternate housing goal in Rhode Island are shown in bold-face italic type; such a city or town has at least 5,000 occupied rential units that comprise at least 25 percent of its housing stock and more than 15 percent of those units are affordable.

A possible consequence of the act, as documented in the study by planning consultant Phillip Herr described above, is the enactment of pro-affordability zoning. According to the Herr study, as of 1999, 16 of Rhode Island's 39 municipalities (41 percent) were identified as having adopted provisions for affordable housing of varying degrees of effectiveness and applicability, a slightly higher proportion than had done so in Massachusetts, although no Rhode Island communities required set-asides for affordable housing. Six of 16 jurisdictions provided density bonuses (Herr 2000, 7).

THE CONNECTICUT AFFORDABLE HOUSING APPEALS PROCEDURE

Inception: 1989

Administration: Under this law, Section 8-30g of the Connecticut General Statutes, a town bears the burden of proving certain facts in court if an applicant appeals the decision of any municipal commission, board, or agency exercising zoning or planning authority on an affordable housing project. An applicant may be a nonprofit or for-profit entity. If at least 10 percent of the town's dwelling unit stock is "affordable" as defined in the act, the town is subsequently exempt from the appeal provisions. The applicant may appeal the decision if the affordable housing application is denied or is approved with restrictions that have a substantial adverse impact on the viability of the development itself or on the degree of affordability of the affordable dwelling units. The law is different from the Massachusetts and Rhode Island statutes in that the appeal is to a court rather than to a housing appeals committee at the state level.

Key objectives: Provide for court review of denials or conditional approvals of development permits for affordable housing.

Accomplishments: When the state compiled the initial list of which communities were exempt from the program in 1990, 25 cities and towns were exempt from its provisions. A state analysis showed that between 1990 and 1998 a total of 10,084 affordable units were added to the housing stock base of the 144 towns subject to the act. This represented about 1.3 percent of their total housing for a base year of 1991. Total housing stock increased by about 6.1 percent during the same period. As of October 2001, 32 Connecticut cities and towns exceeded the minimum requirements of the law. The municipality with the highest percentage is Waterbury with 23.86 percent while the lowest is Danbury with 10.53 percent. Appeals to state courts under the law have tended to support applicants.

Caveats: A consultant-prepared analysis of Connecticut zoning codes showed that, of the 169 towns in Connecticut, only 11 seem to have amended their zoning regulations in direct response to Section 8-30g, although 74 communities do have some form of "affordable zoning." Despite the recommendations of study commissions and subsequent amendments to the law, a number of unresolved issues remain. These include applicants' inability to appeal decisions of local water and sewer commissions, which affect access to public infrastructure, the right of neighbors to intervene in appeals, and the abuse of eminent domain to condemn a site that is the subject of an affordable housing application.

Connecticut's affordable housing land-use appeals procedure legislation, Section 8-30g of the Connecticut General Statutes, was enacted in 1989 as a consequence of recommendations made by a legislatively created Blue Ribbon Commission. The legislation was slightly amended in 1995, more extensively amended in 2000 following recommendations of a second Blue Ribbon Commission, and amended once again in 2002.

Under this law, a municipality bears the burden of proving certain facts in court if an applicant appeals the decision of any municipal commission, board, or agency—referred to generically by the act as "the commission"— exercising zoning or planning authority on an affordable housing project. An applicant may be a nonprofit or for-profit entity. If at least 10 percent of a municipality's dwelling unit stock is "affordable" as defined in the act, it is subsequently exempt from the appeal provisions. The act also requires that Connecticut's commissioner of economic and community development compile annually a list of these municipalities. The applicant, which the act defines as "any person," may appeal the decision if the affordable housing application is denied or is approved with restrictions that have a substantial adverse impact on the viability of the development itself or the degree of affordability of the affordable dwelling units.[10] If the court finds that the municipality does not satisfy its burden of proof, it must wholly or partly revise, modify, remand, or reverse the decision from which the appeal was taken in a manner consistent with the evidence in the record before it. The statute requires the chief court administrator to assign a small number of judges, sitting in geographically diverse parts of the state, to hear appeals, "so that a consistent body of expertise can be developed" (Section 8-30g(f)).

Four categories of units are considered affordable:

(1) housing built or substantially rehabilitated under governmental program; construction or substantial rehabilitation of low and moderate income housing; and any housing occupied by persons receiving federal rental assistance;

(2) housing currently financed by Connecticut Housing Finance Agency mortgages;

(3) set-aside units, in which not less that 30 percent of the dwelling units will be conveyed by deeds that require the units to remain affordable for 40 years after the initial occupation of the proposed development; and

(4) as of October 1, 2002, mobile manufactured homes located in mobile manufactured home parks or legally approved accessory apartments that are subject to deed restrictions or covenants preserving the homes or apartments as affordable for a period of 10 years. (Connecticut General Statutes Secs. 8-30g(a)(3) and (k)

The Connecticut appeals law applies only to approvals from agencies exercising zoning and planning powers.

Any commission may, by regulation, require that an affordable housing application seeking a change of zone shall include the submission of a conceptual site plan. Section 8-30g(g) requires that the local commission demonstrate the "reasons cited for such decisions," which must be "supported by sufficient evidence in the record." Under the law, where a commission has rejected an application or imposed onerous conditions on it, the applicant may (but need not), within the period for filing an appeal of such decision, submit to the commission a proposed modification that responds to some or all of the objections or restrictions that the commission has made. These are treated as an amendment to the original proposal. If the commission held a public hearing on the original proposal, it must hold a public hearing on the proposed modification; it may also hold a public hearing if it did not hold one previously. Failure of the commission to render a decision within a certain time established by the statute constitutes a rejection of the appeal.

The Connecticut appeals law applies only to approvals from agencies exercising zoning and planning powers. Hence the appeals procedure does not apply to decisions on wetlands permit applications sought from the Connecticut Inland Wetlands Agency even though the wetlands permit would be issued in conjunction with zoning and planning approvals necessary for the affordable housing project (Sections 8-26, 22a-32, 22a-33, and 22a-34).

The law also provides for a moratorium on appeals arising from decisions by municipalities subject to it. The moratorium provisions were en-

Between 1990 and 1998, a total of 10,084 affordable units were added to the housing stock base of the 144 towns subject to the act.

acted in 2000 at the recommendation of the second Blue Ribbon Study Commission established by the state legislature (Blue Ribbon Commission to Study Affordable Housing 2000). Under these provisions, a municipality is exempted from the affordable housing appeals procedure for a period of four years after the commissioner of economic and community development has certified completion of an affordable housing project or after notice of a commission's provisional approval of the project. The moratorium procedure applies only when one or more affordable housing developments that create housing-unit-equivalent points have been completed within the municipality. These developments' points, which are computed by the commissioner under a formula in the statute, must be equal to 2 percent of all dwelling units in the municipality as of the last census or to 75 total points, whichever is greater, for the municipality to be granted a moratorium. However, this moratorium provision does not apply to affordable housing applications for assisted housing in which 95 percent of the dwelling units are restricted to persons or families whose income is less than or equal to 60 percent of the state or area median income. It also does not apply to other affordable housing applications for assisted housing containing 40 or fewer dwelling units or to applications that were filed with the local commission prior to the date when the moratorium took effect.

The act, it should be noted, differs from the Massachusetts and Rhode Island statutes in that the appeal is to a court rather than to a housing appeals committee at the state level. Terry J. Tondro (1999, 1,123), a professor of law at the University of Connecticut and a co-chair of the first Blue Ribbon Commission in the state, said that the commission believed that creating a state-level appeals board with the power to override local zoning decisions would be politically and administratively difficult, in part because the governor would be responsible for appointing the board's members. Such appointments, he wrote, would create the negative "symbolism of a state take-over of local government." Instead, said Tondro, the first Blue Ribbon Commission "chose to leave affordable housing appeals to the courts to decide, believing that this was the most neutral available venue" (p. 1,139).

Program Results

When the state compiled its initial list of communities that were exempt from the program in 1990, it included 25 cities and towns, all with more than 10 percent of their housing stock in affordable units (Bergin 1990). A report prepared by the Connecticut General Assembly's Office of Legislative Research at the end of 1999 analyzed the number of affordable units—as defined above—built between 1990 and 1998 for the 144 towns that were initially subject to the act. (There are a total of 169 cities and towns in Connecticut.) These units included state and federally subsidized housing, single-family homes financed with Connecticut Housing Finance authority mortgages, and, as of 1992, units subject to deeds restricting their sale or rental to low- and moderate-income persons. As noted, in 2002, manufactured homes in parks and accessory dwelling units, both subject to affordability restrictions, were added to the list of units deemed to be "affordable."

Between 1990 and 1998, a total of 10,084 affordable units were added to the housing stock base of the 144 towns subject to the act. This represented about 1.3 percent increase to their total housing for the base year of 1991 (the base year includes all units that existed in 1990). Total housing stock increased by about 6.1 percent during the same period.[11] Over this same period, seven additional towns (Colechester, Danbury, Groton, Killingly, Norwalk, Plainville, and West Haven) were exempted from the act after the number of affordable units exceeded 10 percent of their total housing stock (Rappa 1999). No information is available on the number of affordable housing units lost during this period through demolition, gentrification, or other causes.

As of October 2001, 32 Connecticut cities and towns exceeded the minimum requirements of the act. The municipality with the highest percentage is Waterbury with 23.86 percent; the lowest is Danbury with 10.53 percent.[12]

In a 2000 analysis of all Connecticut communities, Massachusetts planning consultant Philip B. Herr found that 74 (44 percent) had some type of "affordability zoning," of various stripes including those that simply provide a "policy, intent, or exhortation," without any real effect. Such zoning is most common along the Atlantic coast, he reported, and least common in the low-development northeast corner of Connecticut (Herr 2000). Of these 74 communities, 11 seemed to have amended their zoning codes in direct response to Section 8-30g, he found (see also Tondro 2001).

By comparison, a survey conducted by a student at the University of Connecticut under Tondro's direction found that of 139 towns surveyed, 45 had amended their zoning regulations to achieve affordability objectives. The most common change, the survey found, was the creation of an affordable housing district or overlay zoning in which a bonus was provided if affordable housing units were included in the development. Fifteen of the towns adopted a new multifamily zone with the affordable housing bonus. Another nine of the 45 towns allowed accessory apartments. Other towns authorized waivers of certain zoning regulations if the proposed development included affordable housing, such as the waiver of a zoning requirement that nonconforming lots be merged. One town created a trust fund to make affordable housing grants to eligible persons and to build affordable housing projects while another town approved owner-occupied duplexes if one of the units was affordable (Tondro 2001, 134).

Tondro, citing a study by Connecticut attorney Timothy Hollister, speculates that an objective of the law, to get municipalities to more fairly appraise proposals for affordable housing and to negotiate the specifics of the affordable housing proposal, was being satisfied. Hollister's data, which Tondro cites and considers "soft," suggests that about two-thirds of the affordable housing built in the 1990–1996 study period resulted from negotiations rather than litigation (p. 133).

A 1999 analysis by the Connecticut General Assembly's Office of Legislative Research examined the case law for the first decade of the statute's operation. It summarizes 10 decisions where the town's denial of an application for affordable housing was sustained by a court. Next, it looks at the five cases where the local commission's approval was sustained against the abutter's appeal, and then it discusses the 20 cases where the commission's denial was overturned by a court. Finally, it summarizes two procedural cases that discuss the appeals process and who is entitled to appeal (Rappa, McCarthy, and Leonard 1999). Tondro (2001, 137–52) updates that analysis in his 2001 article. In general, applicants win in appeals of local commission's adverse decisions more often than towns. It is, however, beyond the scope of this report to discuss fully the case law surrounding Section 8-30g and its perceived impacts (including whether the law allows developers to intimidate local governments with threats of litigation).[13]

Tondro's review of the first decade of Section 8-30g highlights a number of problem areas that remain unresolved by the recommendations of the second Blue Ribbon Commission. One is how to limit a town's ability to block affordable housing proposals by refusing to supply the necessary infrastructure for an affordable housing development. Tondro points out that Section 8-30g does not apply to appeals of local water and sewer com-

As of October 2001, 32 Connecticut cities and towns exceeded the minimum requirements of the act.

Another problem is a local government's use of eminent domain to condemn a site that is the subject of an affordable housing application.

mission decisions and that it is well established in the state that such decisions are virtually unappealable (p. 159).

A second problem is the ability of neighbors to intervene in court cases. In a least one case, a town, Farmington, and a developer had already agreed to a much-negotiated project only to have the neighbors object. "Neighbors can often win simply by delaying a project," Tondro observes (p. 159, fn. 79).

A third problem is a local government's use of eminent domain to condemn a site that is the subject of an affordable housing application. "This is a costly defense of a town's 'right to' exclude the poor, but it does work and until recently has been judicially approved," Tondro notes (p.159).[14]

Tondro also comments that, in appeal proceedings, towns should have used better defenses and might have prevailed had expert testimony on their behalf—such as testimony that a particular development would contaminate groundwater—been introduced at hearings before local commissions. Doing so would have provided the primary means to prove that the town's rejection of the affordable housing application was not pretextual. "It is quite surprising, therefore, to see how casually towns have defended their decisions on points they probably could have carried if they had brought in an expert on their side," he writes (p. 159). Of course, an applicant faced with a local government's adverse testimony could challenge the testimony's validity and the motivations of the government's expert. It could also introduce expert testimony to dispute that of the local government.

Finally, the Federal Housing Administration's refusal to insure any mortgage for a property that is subject to resale restrictions—such as a cap on a unit's resale price—is problematic, Tondro argues: "HUD has, in effect, given towns a very simple means of stopping affordable housing proposals; the town simply requires a resale restriction, and the developer cannot get any insurance from HUD" (p. 159, fn. 182).[15] But some developers, he adds, have persuaded banks to forego HUD insurance by telling them that funding for affordable housing will "look good on [federally mandated] Community Reinvestment Act reports" (p. 159, fn. 183).[16]

Connecticut's statute was also amended in 2000 to require 15 percent of the residents of a set-aside affordable housing development built with governmental assistance to have incomes not exceeding 60 percent of the area's median income (Section 8-30g(a)(6)). This change, observes Tondro, "encourages development of housing that is more like that built under the nearly defunct public housing program, rather than a mechanism for reducing housing costs at the lower (not lowest) end of the income spectrum" (pp. 161-62). One consequence, he argues, is that the cross-subsidies from the market rate units will probably not be sufficient to provide housing for the very poor. Builders seeking to use the appeals act, he remarks, will be much more dependent on securing governmental subsidies to make up the difference between what the tenants can pay and what the housing actually costs.

ENDNOTES

1. See *Bd. of Appeals of Hanover v. Housing Appeals Comm.*, 363 Mass. 339, 294 N.E.2d 393 (1973), which upholds the constitutionality of the statute. The administrative rules for the Housing Appeals Committee appear at 760 Code of Massachusetts Regulations, Sections 30.00 to 31.00.

2. "Uneconomic" means "any condition brought about by any single factor or combination of factors to the extent that it makes it impossible for a public agency or nonprofit organization to proceed in building or operating low or moderate income housing without financial loss, or for a limited dividend organization to proceed and still

realize a reasonable return in building or operating such housing within the limitations set by the subsidizing agency or government on the size or character of the development or on the amount or nature of the subsidy or on the tenants, rentals and income permissible, and without substantially changing the rent levels and unit sizes proposed by the public, nonprofit or limited dividend organizations" (Massachusetts General Laws Chapter 40B, Section 20).

3. Krefetz conducted a survey of all 351 cities and towns in March 1997. The response rate was 83 percent, representing a total of 290 cities and towns, which constitutes 83 percent of all Massachusetts communities. Krefetz also interviewed over 20 state and local officials who have had direct experience with Chapter 40B over the past two decades. Notes Krefetz:

   > The communities in this study include the vast majority of all suburbs in the Boston, Worcester, and Springfield areas, as well as most Cape Cod towns. Those that did not reply to the survey were, for the most part, small, rural towns in the western part of the state, although Boston and a small number of Boston area suburbs were also among the non-respondents. Overall, the localities likely to have had the most growth and housing development activity are well-represented. Therefore, the non-response bias does not pose a major threat to the reliability of the data. However, it is important to note that since it is possible, and even likely, that CPs were applied for in some of the 61 cities and towns not included in this study, the data probably undercounts the number of communities directly affected by chapter 40B. Consequently, the numbers reported for total CP applications, total housing units proposed, and total housing projects and units built are conservative figures and thus should be viewed as minimums. (p. 389)

4. This total reflects only 27 of 28 communities. The 27 communities include the following: Amherst (10.54 percent); Aquinnah (21.94 percent); Beverly (10.33 percent); Boston (19.63 percent); Brockton (12.24 percent); Cambridge (15.60 percent); Chelsea (17.03 percent); Chester (10.61 percent); Fall River (10.56 percent); Framingham (10.17 percent); Gardner (15 percent); Greenfield (13.86 percent); Holyoke (20.58 percent); Lawrence (14.96 percent); Lowell (13.49 percent); Lynn (12.73 percent); Malden (12.20 percent); Middlefield (14.85 percent); New Bedford (11.33 percent); North Adams (12.83 percent); Northampton (11.34 percent); Orange (13.44 percent); Revere (10.07 percent); Salem (12.50 percent); Springfield (17.83 percent); Wendell (19.01 percent); and Worcester (12.29 percent) (Massachusetts DHCD 2002).

   According to Krefetz (2002), the Town of Georgetown also has gone over the 10 percent limit with 13.46 percent as of September 23, 2002, but the town has not been reflected in the official tally of units by the Massachusetts DHCD.

   The percentage of low- and moderate-income units on a statewide basis only applies to the 27 towns contained in the official April 24, 2002, inventory.

5. The *Globe* article describes the enactment of emergency rules by Massachusetts Acting Governor Jane Swift that allow, for example, towns to deny Chapter 40B projects for one year if they have increased the number of affordable units in the previous year by 2 percent (Flint 2002a). Swift adopted the rules after vetoing a bill that would have weakened Chapter 40B.

6. The Rhode Island Supreme Court upheld the statute's constitutionality in *Curran v. Church Community Housing Corporation*, 672 A.2d 453 (R.I. 1996).

7. The statute uses the term "special exception," but the administrative rules for the act define a "comprehensive permit" to mean "a single application for a special exception to build low and moderate income housing in lieu of separate applications to applicable boards" (Rhode Island General Laws Section 45-53-4 and Rules Implementing the Rhode Island Low and Moderate Income Housing Act pursuant to R.I.G.L. 45-53, Section 2.04).

8. The Rhode Island housing appeals board standards for reviewing the appeal include but are not limited to:

· the consistency of the decision to deny or condition the permit with the approved comprehensive plan;

· the extent to which the community meets or plans to meet the 10 percent standard for existing low- and moderate-income housing units;

· the consideration of the health and safety of the existing residents;

· the consideration of environmental protection; and

· the extent to which the community applies local zoning ordinances and special exception procedures evenly on subsidized and unsubsidized housing applications alike. (Rhode Island General Laws, Section 45-53-6(b))

Note that these standards seem to imply a belief that low- and moderate-income housing deserves a higher level of review for "consideration of environmental protection" than conventional housing.

9. For several years in the late 1990s, Middletown's affordable housing percentage was as high as 12.04 percent; however, the status of some units changed, bringing its affordable housing percentage down to 9.93 percent in 2001.

10. In an appeal, the burden is on the municipal commission to prove, based on the evidence in the record of the decision compiled before the commission, that "(A) the decision is necessary to protect substantial public interests in health, safety or other matters which the commission may legally consider; (B) such public interests clearly outweigh the need for affordable housing; and (C) such public interests cannot be protect by reasonable changes to the affordable housing development, or . . .(A) the application which was the subject from which such appeal was taken would locate affordable housing in an area which is zoned for industrial use, and (B) the development is not assisted housing [as defined in the act]" (Section 8-30g(g)).

11. These figures, which are approximations, were calculated by APA based on reports by Rappa (1999) and Bergin (2002).

12. Ciccalone (2002) notes that the data come from different federal, state, and local sources and programs, which makes it difficult for the state to ensure complete accuracy: "Of particular importance to data accuracy is local administrative review and input on the street addresses of units and projects, and information on deed restricted units" (p. 1).

13. For a thorough review of various opinions on whether Section 8-30g allows developers to bully—or, as some allege, blackmail—towns into accepting affordable housing projects while relaxing good planning principles, see Vodola (1997) and Tondro (2001). Tondro comments that Vodola "is more sympathetic to the problems of public officials attempting to implement the act than I am, and he does not share my concern that the zoning system in Connecticut is tilted against the developer. Yet while he quotes many officials' and planners' complaints about developer's 'blackmail,' we do agree that there is little actual evidence of developer abuse of the act" (pp. 128-128 and fn. 57).

14. One solution would be simply amending state statutes that authorize eminent domain so that they bar its use by local governments to block an affordable housing project during the pendancy of an application before a local commission.

15. Tondro here refers to 24 Code of Federal Regulations, Section 203.41(b)(2000), which is the U.S. Department of Housing and Urban Development policy against restrictions on the use of properties that the federal government insures through the Federal Housing Administration.

16. Tondro here refers to United States Code, Title 12, Section 2906(a) (1994), which requires banks to file reports on the loans they have made to the communities in which their branches are located.

CHAPTER 7

Private-Sector and Other Initiatives

This chapter highlights private-sector affordable housing initiatives in the San Francisco Bay Area and Chicago. Case studies from Maryland, Iowa, Vermont, and New Hampshire that do not easily fit into the categories discussed elsewhere in this report are included in this chapter as well.

PRIVATE-SECTOR INITIATIVES

BAY AREA COUNCIL, SAN FRANCISCO REGION, CALIFORNIA

Inception: 1945

Administration: The Bay Area Council is a membership business organization that consists of approximately 275 large businesses in the Bay Area. The council works in the areas of transportation, housing, land use, energy policy, environmental quality, sustainable economic development, education and workforce preparation, telecommunications and information technology, and water policy. The council is not directly involved in the construction of affordable housing; however, it has developed a set of strategies for achieving an adequate supply of housing in the Bay Area.

Key objectives: The council's housing and land-use project has three goals for housing in the Bay Area: (1) work toward regional strategies for housing in the Bay Area, (2) work at the state level to change the incentive and financial structure of housing development, and (3) change the investment and development patterns in the Bay Area to include more mixed-use projects.

Accomplishments: The council's Job-Housing Footprint project has produced maps that detail the projected acreage needed for housing between 1995 and 2020 based on household growth and the number of new jobs per county. Working with the Job-Center Housing Coalition, the council has had success in having one of the seven housing-related bills that they support enacted by the California legislature. In a 1999 fair-share housing evaluation report, the council assessed whether local governments in the Bay Area were meeting their housing needs as determined in the Regional Housing Needs Assessment (RHNA) by the Association of Bay Area Governments (ABAG). The council tallied results for the 50 reporting municipalities across the four income categories (very low-, low-, moderate-, and above-moderate-income) required by the state housing element law. It found that the fair-share housing goals were not fulfilled for any of the income categories. Of the 50 reporting municipalities, the very low-income category fared the worst: out of a projected need for 36,672 housing units, approximately 9,759 (27 percent) were provided. Because the council's new $60 million Smart Growth Fund can be used for a broad array of projects (retail, offices, mixed-use, and affordable housing), the potential for the program to produce a large number of affordable housing units is uncertain.

Caveats: The council's approach to the housing problem in the Bay Area emphasizes study and analysis with some legislative advocacy rather than the actual production of affordable housing. Although it is too soon to determine the effectiveness of the Smart Growth Fund, it is important to note that the first two projects likely to draw funding are retail projects with no affordable housing component.

The Bay Area Council is a membership business organization that consists of approximately 275 large businesses in the Bay Area. Founded in 1945, the mission of the Bay Area Council is to promote economic prosperity and quality of life in the region. The council works in the areas of transportation, housing, land use, energy policy, environmental quality, sustainable economic development, education and workforce preparation, telecommunications and information technology, and water policy. The council is not directly involved in the construction of affordable housing; however, it has developed a set of strategies for achieving an adequate supply of housing in the Bay Area (Michael 2002). Its overall housing strat-

Affordable housing in the Bay Area, California.

Association of Bay Area Governments and the Nonprofit Housing Association of Northern California

egy is to achieve an adequate supply of housing that is sufficiently afford-able to the entire population, particularly to the workforce, in order to sus-tain long-term economic prosperity (Bay Area Council 2000).

That the Bay Area Council has taken an active role in affordable hous-ing issues reinforces the fact that affordable workforce housing is a major concern to many employers as well as to housing advocates, planners, and others. "Because of the unavailability of affordable housing in the vicinity of job centers," a Bay Area Council report states, "the region's workforce has increasingly moved to the outer fringes of the Bay Area in [its] quest for homes. The expanded commute for the workforce is exacerbating traffic congestion and air pollution and reducing quality of life in the Bay Area." The report calls "sobering" the potential impact not only on the environment but also on "the economic prosperity of the region. Leading executives representing a wide range of industries in the region are now reporting their immense difficulties in finding and retaining workers who find it difficult or impossible to live in the area" (Bay Area Council 2002c).

The council's housing and land-use project has three broad goals for housing the Bay Area:

(1) Work toward regional strategies for housing in the Bay Area

(2) Work at the state level to change the incentive and financial structure of housing development

(3) Change the investment and development patterns in the Bay Area to include more mixed-use projects

For the housing policy itself, the Bay Area Council employs three ap-proaches:

(1) Increase public official awareness of the housing crisis through research, analysis, and publications

(2) Advocate for state, regional, and local policies and legislation that meet their housing goals

(3) Collaborate with other stakeholders to foster actions that support hous-ing at the regional and local levels and to create a positive policy con-text for major systematic change

The council has also developed a number of housing policy priorities:

(1) Increase supply and planning to accommodate a sufficient supply of housing, to achieve a jobs-housing balance, and to discourage voter initiatives that constrain supply of housing

(2) Reform construction tort liability and reduce defect litigation

(3) Promote housing as the linchpin of smart growth

(4) Streamline the California Environmental Quality Act (CEQA) for affordable housing

(5) Provide a variety of fiscal incentives for local governments to approve and provide affordable housing, including linking local government infrastructure funding to progress in housing

(6) Promote brownfield redevelopment to accommodate housing (Bay Area Council 2000)

To implement these priorities, the council has pressed ahead on its Jobs-Housing Footprint project, a fair-share housing evaluation report, a specialized portfolio of investment funds to meet smart growth objectives, and advocacy of legislation to increase the supply of housing or remove barriers to it. The council's Jobs-Housing Footprint project seeks to develop data and maps that compare where housing could be developed with areas where natural ecosystems must either be protected or restored (Bay Area Council 2002c). The council has also taken a leadership role in the Job-Center Housing Coalition, a organization of housing and labor advocates, consumer and ethnic advocacy groups, businesses, and taxpayer associations to promote statewide legislative reforms that increase housing supply and affordability (Job-Center Housing 2002c). The organization has supported seven bills that address housing issues in the Bay Area:

(1) A.B. 1086, which would streamline the review process for CEQA and reduce delays in the construction of new affordable housing

(2) A.B. 1170, which would provide down payment funding from the state to low- and moderate-income households as one of several fiscal incentives offered to local governments so as to encourage the reduction or removal of regulatory barriers to housing, including the costs of permits, impact fees, design requirements, and environmental mitigation

(3) A.B. 1284, which would provide fiscal incentives to local governments to plan for and approve new housing development; it would also give property tax rewards to specified job centers of the state that approve and build housing that is affordable to the workforce

(4) A.B. 2418, which contains findings related to the statewide housing crisis in California

(5) A.B. 2757, which declares the intent of the California Legislature to protect the interests of homeowners against construction defects

(6) S.B. 910, which would provide that, for a council of governments whose members have a combined population of more than 10 million, a resolution to adopt the allocation of regional housing need be approved by a majority of voting members from each county on the governing board (whereas existing law requires every city or county to prepare and adopt a general plan for its jurisdiction that contains certain mandatory elements, including a housing element)

(7) S.B. 1963, which would provide liability protection to innocent land-owners and prospective purchasers of brownfields and would autho-rize local governments to require landowners to conduct Phase I Envi-ronmental Investigations

Of these bills, only A.B. 1170 was enacted, in 2002. This legislation cre-ated the Building Equity and Growth in Neighborhoods (BEGIN) Program and BEGIN Fund. Monies in the fund will be made available, upon appro-priation, to the state's Department of Housing and Community Develop-ment (HCD) for grants to cities and counties that have taken prescribed actions to remove barriers to affordable housing. The grants will provide assistance in the form of second mortgage loans for down-payment pur-poses to qualifying new homebuyers in those cities and counties. Enact-ment of A.B. 1170 was dependent on voter approval of the Housing and Emergency Shelter Trust Fund Act, which was passed as Proposition 46 in the November 5, 2002, general statewide election.

The council completed in 1999 a fair-share housing evaluation report to assess how well local governments in the Bay Area were meeting their hous-ing needs (see sidebar).

The Bay Area Council began a new investment fund portfolio in October 2001, the Bay Area Family of Funds. The investment funds are generally limited to initial investors and certain later investors and will only operate for 10 years (Zoger 2002). The portfolio's goal is to produce "double bottom line results—to promote economic prosperity, social equity, and environ-mental quality while generating favorable rates of return for the Fund in-vestors" (Bay Area Council 2002a). The portfolio includes: the Bay Area Smart Growth Fund, scaled at $75 million to $100 million to invest in mixed-use, mixed-income real estate developments; the California Environmental Re-development Fund, scaled at $50 million to $75 million to invest in the resto-ration of environmentally contaminated sites; and the Community Equity Fund, scaled at $75 million to $100 million to make equity investments in businesses that are capable of generating substantial job and wealth creation in target neighborhoods. A study, *A Guide to the Bay Area's Most Impoverished Neighborhoods*, by the Bay Area Partnership, a regional partnership of fed-eral, state, and local governments as well as nonprofit and business groups, identified the 46 most impoverished neighborhoods in the Bay Area, which will be the target communities for the portfolio (Bay Area Alliance 2002).

The Bay Area Smart Growth Fund had raised $60 million as of April 2002 (Zoger 2002). The fund seeks to invest in projects that will make a positive impact on its targeted neighborhoods, and benefit, rather than dis-place, local residents (Bay Area Council 2002a). According to the fund's principal manager, Adam Zoger of Pacific Coast Capital Partners, the fund will invest market-rate capital to benefit underserved communities, includ-ing affordable housing, retail, and commercial uses in low- to moderate-income census tracts. For affordable housing investment, the fund will in-vest in mostly mixed-use and mixed-income housing because, Zoger said, investing in housing projects that are entirely affordable will not return a profit for investors. The Smart Growth Fund had not yet invested in any projects as of April 2002; however, Zoger reported it was considering two retail projects in a Latino neighborhood that lacks retail space.

Program Results

The Council's Job-Housing Footprint project has produced maps that de-tail the projected acreage needed for housing between 1995 and 2020 based on household growth and the number of new jobs per county.

FAIR-SHARE HOUSING INVENTORY

Released in 1999, the Bay Area Council's fair-share housing inven-tory reported the progress of local cities toward meeting the fair-share housing goals established by the Association of Bay Area Govern-ments (ABAG). The inventory tallied results from 50 of the 109 Bay Area local governments, including four counties and 46 cities. The reporting local governments accounted for 101,490 housing units built during the years 1988–1995, which fell far short of their cumulative projected need of 182,542 by 81,052 units (Bay Area Council 2002c).

The council totaled results for the 50 local governments across the four income categories (very low, low, moderate, and above-moderate) re-quired by the state housing element law. It found that the fair-share hous-ing allocations were not being met for any of the income categories. Of the 50 reporting governments, the very low-income category fared the worst: out of a projected need for 36,672 housing units, only 9,759 (27 percent) were provided. The report-ing local governments provided 35 percent of the fair-share housing need for the low-income category, 53 percent for the moderate-income cat-egory, and 78 percent for the above-moderate-income category.

For its policy initiatives project, the Bay Area Council, working with the Job-Center Housing Coalition, has had legislative success with one of seven bills they support enacted by the California legislature. As described above, the bill aims to provide fiscal incentives to local governments so as to lessen and remove regulatory barriers to housing.

To some degree, the fair-share housing report places the Bay Area Council in a watchdog position over ABAG and local governments, and it may have the potential to influence certain local governments who are not meeting their individual housing needs. Because the council's new $60 million Smart Growth Fund can be used for a broad array of projects—retail, offices, mixed-use, and affordable housing—the potential for the program to produce a large number of affordable housing units is uncertain; the retail projects currently being considered by the Smart Growth Fund, for example, include no affordable housing component.

METROPOLIS 2020, CHICAGO

Inception: 1999

Administration: The Chicago Metropolis 2020 organization grew out of the efforts of the Commercial Club, whose Chicago Metropolis 2020 plan, a new private regional plan for the six-county area, was released in 1999. The organization, which has a small professional staff, is governed by an executive board made up of business, civic, labor, governmental, and religious organizations.

Key objectives: Detail and implement the recommendations of the Chicago Metropolis 2020 plan.

Accomplishments: While it does not undertake a comprehensive analysis of specific affordable housing issues, the Chicago Metropolis 2020 plan does offer approaches that address home ownership, sustainability, mobility, segregation, fair housing, and strengthening nonprofit housing organizations. Since its publication, parts of the plan have been translated into a detailed agenda aimed at improving the availability of workforce housing in the Chicago region. Among its recommendations is the creation of regional housing plan. A high priority of Metropolis 2020 is the establishment of a state cabinet-level authority that would be responsible for the formalization of housing policies and an agenda for state action.

Caveats: For Metropolis 2020, its emphasis thus far has been analyzing and studying affordable housing in the Chicago region. Because the initiative is still in its early stages, it is unclear how the Metropolis 2020 plan will translate into the actual provision of affordable housing.

The Chicago Metropolis 2020 plan was created by the Commercial Club of Chicago, a membership organization consisting of the Chicago region's leading business and civic leaders. The Chicago Metropolis 2020 organization itself grew from the efforts of the Commercial Club, with the goal of implementing the ideas contained in the Chicago Metropolis 2020 plan, which was released in 1999 and published in 2001. The organization, which has a small professional staff, is governed by an executive board made up of business, civic, labor, governmental, and religious organizations. Half

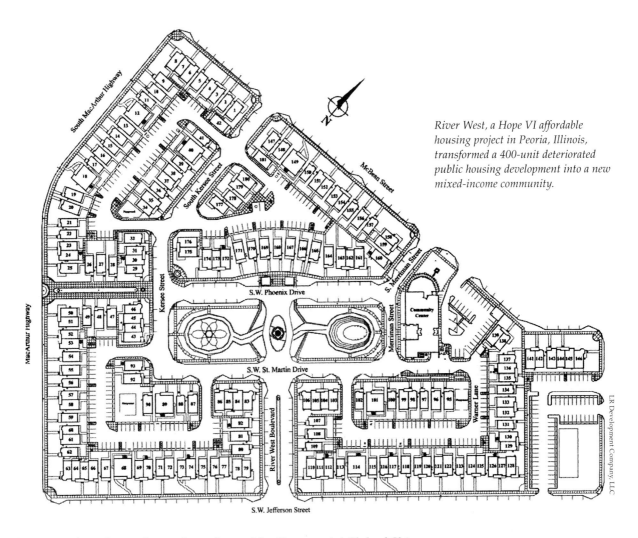

River West, a Hope VI affordable housing project in Peoria, Illinois, transformed a 400-unit deteriorated public housing development into a new mixed-income community.

of executive board is made up of members of the Commercial Club of Chicago (Chicago Metropolis 2002a).

Additionally, the organization includes a team of senior executives who have agreed to volunteer at least 50 percent of their time to various projects that contribute to the goals of the plan. The team of senior executives consists of lawyers, business leaders, CEOs, and doctors.

One of the Commercial Club's early efforts to engage in planning for the Chicago region came in 1909, when the club worked with Daniel H. Burnham and Edward H. Bennett to develop the *Plan of Chicago* (the "Burnham Plan"), which has become one of the most famous and influential city plans in history.

The goals of the Chicago Metropolis 2020 plan are to "enhance the economic vibrancy of the Chicago region and provide the best possible conditions of living for all its residents" (Johnson 2001, 1). The plan was developed privately, with no formal community involvement process and thus "has no official status and is not binding on anyone. Rather, it constitutes an open invitation to the residents of the region to engage in a public dialogue and to help develop solutions that refine and build on the present document's analyses and recommendations" (p. 1)

The Chicago Metropolis 2020 plan focuses principally on the six-county metropolitan Chicago area, which includes Cook, DuPage, Kane, Lake, McHenry, and Will counties. The plan is divided into six sections: economic development, education, governance, land use and housing, taxation, and transportation, each of which was developed by a committee.

One of the most important recommendations in the plan calls for the creation of a regional coordinating council to deal with policies and practices concerning transportation, land use, housing, and the environment (Johnson 2001, 111). The plan's proposed approach to regional planning is incentive rather than requirement based. The regional coordinating council would offer incentives to reward localities for land-use regulations that are regionally coordinated and oriented toward common goals. The chief incentive would be bonds: the regional coordinating council would issue bonds to cities and municipalities that meet certain criteria that, in turn, advance the mission of the council.

The plan also recommends improving housing conditions for poor minorities. Its strategies are twofold: they aim (1) to "create greater opportunities for low-income households to live in mixed-income developments" and (2) to give low-income households "much greater freedom to choose to live in communities outside the poverty-concentrated areas in which so many of them now seem destined to exist" (p. 119). The first strategy addresses the supply side of affordable housing by recommending the demolition of the existing stock of high-rise affordable housing projects and the building of a new stock of mixed-income land-use developments intended to end the isolation of poor minority households. The second strategy addresses the demand side: it wants to improve household mobility by empowering residents of affordable housing units to make housing choices

FIGURE 7-1
HOURLY WAGES FOR CHICAGO REGION WORKERS

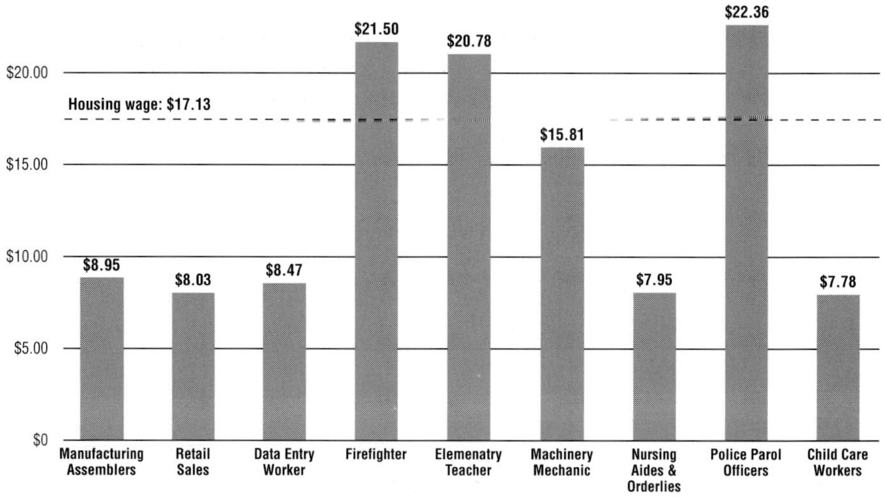

Source: Chicago Metropolis 2020 (2002d)

that will better their specific circumstances. To do this, the plan proposes that the federal government expand existing HUD Section 8 certificate and voucher programs in the region. It also recommends that counseling, training, and technical assistance be provided to affordable housing residents; and that every locality in the region comply with uniform building and zoning requirements that open the way for the construction of substantially more rental housing (p. 121).

Building strong neighborhoods is another of the plan's goals, for which it suggests four strategies. The first recommends that the federal government affirm and expand the low-income housing tax credit by raising the per capita from $1.25 to $1.75 per resident per year. The tax credit increases private investment in affordable housing development by offering an absolute income tax credit.

Humboldt Ridge affordable housing in Chicago, which includes 30 three-bedroom, 52 two-bedroom, and 18 one-bedroom apartments.

The second strategy focuses on community development corporations (CDCs) and suggests that corporations and foundations with headquarters in the Chicago region work to facilitate the creation of networks among the CDCs in the city and suburbs. The plan recognizes that CDCs have a substantial effect on transforming depressed areas into vibrant and successful neighborhoods because the CDCs have proven records of delivering results in low-income, segregated neighborhoods.

The third strategy is aimed at building creditworthiness. The plan urges employers to take advantage of individual investment accounts, part of a new national pilot project established by the federal government to help low-income people accumulate wealth. Through the program, deposits to restricted savings accounts at the two participating institutions in Chicago—South Shore Bank and the Women's Self-Employment Project—are matched on a two-to-one basis by those institutions. The goal of the program is to enable a low-income resident to jump-start a savings account that will then allow the purchase or leveraging of an asset within two years. The matching funds are provided by the federal government, private foundation grants, and private employers. The latter are entitled to a federal income tax deduction for matching contributions to employees' accounts. This strategy seeks to lower delinquency and foreclosure rates among homeowners who have secured mortgages from banks that have adjusted their screening processes so as to allow low-income households to qualify for loans.

The plan's fourth strategy for building strong neighborhoods urges private-sector groups to continue to press for vigorous enforcement of fair housing laws. This strategy seeks to establish a mechanism for testing throughout all parts of the housing market; it also would impose stronger monitoring of banking, real estate, appraisal, and insurance industry practices.

While it does not undertake a comprehensive analysis of specific affordable housing issues, the Chicago Metropolis 2020 plan does offer approaches that address home ownership, sustainability, mobility, segregation, fair

FIGURE 7-2
HOUSING AFFORDABILITY IN THE CHICAGO REGION, 2000

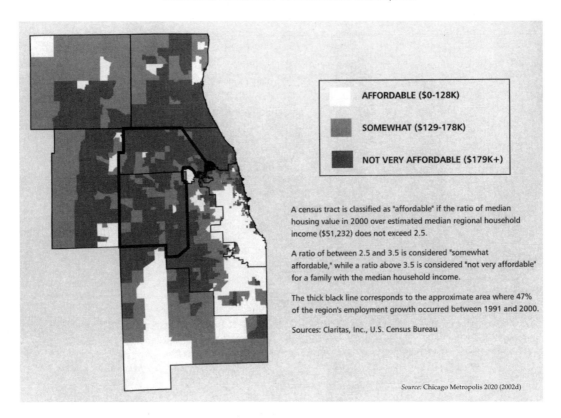

AFFORDABLE ($0-128K)

SOMEWHAT ($129-178K)

NOT VERY AFFORDABLE ($179K+)

A census tract is classified as "affordable" if the ratio of median
housing value in 2000 over estimated median regional household
income ($51,232) does not exceed 2.5.

A ratio of between 2.5 and 3.5 is considered "somewhat
affordable," while a ratio above 3.5 is considered "not very affordable"
for a family with the median household income.

The thick black line corresponds to the approximate area where 47%
of the region's employment growth occurred between 1991 and 2000.

Sources: Claritas, Inc., U.S. Census Bureau

Source: Chicago Metropolis 2020 (2002d)

housing, and strengthening nonprofit housing organizations. In 2002, the
Metropolis 2020 group drafted an agenda and guide for workforce housing with the purpose of taking a in-depth look at workforce housing problems in the Chicago region. The policy agenda, entitled *Recommendations
for Developing Attainable Workforce Housing in the Chicago Region*, makes specific proposals that address the workforce housing problems in the Chicago region (Chicago Metropolis 2002d).

The agenda advocates regional planning for affordable housing. It states:
"What our region clearly needs is a well thought out, comprehensive housing plan which identifies what can be done by government, civic, business
and housing industry leaders, locally, regionally, statewide and nationally
to address our growing attainable workforce housing problem" (p. 13).
The agenda includes specific recommendations to address workforce housing under five categories:

(1) Local government actions

(2) Regional actions

(3) State actions

(4) Federal government actions

(5) Private sector actions

Recommendations for local governments focus on changing zoning and
development regulations, building codes, code enforcement, and development processes to encourage the construction of affordable housing, improve review procedures, and accelerate the development review processes.
The agenda also recommends expanding housing rehabilitation programs

and increasing the amount of land available from local governments for affordable housing. The city of Chicago should acquire land to complete a transformation of the Chicago Housing Authority (CHA), it suggests. Additionally, the plan recommends using tax-reverted vacant lots to build affordable modular housing in Chicago, establishing community development guidelines, decreasing the amount of unincorporated land in Cook County, reducing tax assessment disparities, and forming subregional housing rehabilitation programs.

For the region, Chicago Metropolis 2020 encourages the expansion of regional affordable housing workshops and the creation of a regional housing database. Also, the report recommends that business, nonprofit organizations, and governments in the region consider forming a nonprofit organization to promote the development of affordable housing and the revitalization of neighborhoods.

The recommendations for state actions include new legislation that would adopt a uniform state building code, provide tax incentives for people who participate in the federal housing voucher program, increase Illinois' real estate transfer tax on property sales over $200,000 to support affordable housing, and require local governments to address affordable housing. The agenda includes recommendations for funding, such as investing in rehabilitation programs, giving priority infrastructure and public works funding to communities that develop housing for all income levels, subsidizing the construction of new multifamily housing, and reforming the tax system so that the majority of school funding comes from the state. Additionally, the report includes a recommendation to modify the structure of the Illinois state government so that housing matters have higher priority.

River West mixed-income housing development in Peoria, Illinois.

LR Development Company, LLC

Federal government recommendations focus on HUD programs. Recommendations for the private sector include promoting business support of affordable housing and encouraging businesses to locate new facilities in communities that support affordable housing, business, nonprofit organizations, and government partnerships.

Program Results

"We are beginning to talk about a strategy to start implementation," said Nancy Firfer (2002a), senior advisor for Metropolis 2020. Because of the state's budget crisis in 2002, she said, "we are going to start with the things that cost less money, such as rehabilitation of existing buildings and encouraging local communities to do comprehensive planning as it was defined in recent planning legislation."[1] Firfer added: "The first thing that we are going to work on is the creation of a state position with cabinet-level authority that would create housing policies and an agenda for state action."

The Metropolitan Mayors Caucus, a partnership between the city of Chicago and nine suburban municipal associations, has been working with Metropolis 2020 "on various issues, including their housing recommendations," according to Dave Bennett (2002), executive director of the caucus. "The region has come a long way over the past four to five years on these issues," Bennett added. "Mayors and business leaders have realized that to maintain and improve quality of life, they need to address affordable housing, smart growth, public transportation, and make sure people have a place to live and are able to get to their jobs." Metropolis 2020 has joined with the Mayors Caucus, which also has a separate housing agenda, to write and refine the Metropolis 2020 housing agenda, but agenda implementation has not begun.

Like the Bay Area Council program, the emphasis to date for Metropolis 2020 has been analyzing and studying the issue of affordable housing in the Chicago region, which has not yet resulted in the construction of any affordable housing units. Because the initiative is still in its early stages, it is unclear as to how the Metropolis 2020 plan will translate into the actual provision of affordable housing.

OTHER APPROACHES

MARYLAND'S LIVE NEAR YOUR WORK PROGRAM

Inception: 1997

Administration: Maryland's Live-Near-Your-Work (LNYW) program is administered by the state's Department of Housing and Community Development. It has private-sector and state employee components. The LNYW private-sector employee program, established in 1997, offers homeowners a minimum of $3,000 toward the costs associated with purchasing a home in targeted neighborhoods near worksites with local jurisdiction, state of Maryland, and the private employer each contributing $1,000. The LNYW state-employee program, established in November 2001, also offers a total of $3,000 toward the purchase of a new home, with $1,000 contributed from the local jurisdiction and $2,000 from the state of Maryland. Both components have similar locational restrictions in order to link homes to worksites.

Key objectives: Strengthen neighborhoods through increased homeownership, promote links between employers and local communities, reduce commuting costs, and support compliance with the federal Clean Air Act.

Accomplishments: Since the program began in 1997, the LNYW program has helped 807 households purchase homes throughout Maryland.

Caveats: Because part of the funding for the program comes from the local or county government, local participation is crucial to the success of the program. There are currently only eight (for the private employee program) and seven (for the state employee program) participating local or county governments, which appears to have limited the program. Participating local governments are mostly in the Baltimore/Washington, D.C., region.

Affordable housing units (left) next to market-rate housing (right) in Maryland.

Montgomery County Department of Housing and Community Affairs

Maryland has developed a program to encourage people to live near their place of employment in certain targeted neighborhoods. The Live Near Your Work (LNYW) program is a partnership between the Maryland Department of Housing and Community Development (DHCD), local governments, and Maryland employers. Administered by DHCD, the program has separate components for private-sector employees and state employees.

Affordable townhouses in the Potomac Regency subdivision in North Bethesda, Maryland.

Montgomery County Department of Housing and Community Affairs

The goals of the LNYW program are to strengthen neighborhoods through increased homeownership, promote links between employers and local communities, reduce commuting costs, and support compliance with the federal Clean Air Act. The program offers workers the opportunity to own their own homes and seeks to reduce employee turnover, training, and recruitment costs. Additionally, the program wants to make Maryland a more attractive place for businesses.

An eligible neighborhood is one designated by the local government (with DCHD approval) as being in need of revitalization (Basu 2002a). Additionally, employers may choose to designate a smaller target area for their employees within the local government's designated neighborhoods (Maryland DHCD 2002).

The LNYW private-sector employee program, established in 1997, offers home purchasers a minimum of $3,000 toward the costs associated with purchasing a home. The employees are required to contribute at least $1,000 toward the home purchase, while the employer, local government, and DHCD each contribute $1,000. The $1,000 that DHCD contributes is allocated as a grant to the local government. Additionally, DHCD provides technical assistance to local governments' LNYW programs. There are eight jurisdictions participating in the LNYW private employee program: Baltimore City, College Park, Hagerstown, Montgomery County, Prince George's County, Salisbury, Westminister, and Wicomico County.

The LNYW state employee program, established in November 2001, also offers a total of $3,000 toward the purchase of a new home, with $1,000 contributed by the local jurisdiction, and $2,000 by the state of Maryland. Home purchasers are required to contribute at least $1,000.

While all Maryland state employees are eligible for the program, at least 51 percent of the participating homebuyers in each jurisdiction must be families of limited income; namely, family income must be 100 percent of the statewide or area median income, whichever is higher. There are seven jurisdictions participating in the state employees program: the cities of Baltimore, College Park, Hagerstown, and Salisbury; and Anne Arundel, Montgomery, and Prince George's counties.

For both the private-sector employee and state employee programs, the housing unit must be located within five miles of the employee's place of work, within a priority funding area, and within a participating jurisdiction. The home can be a single-family dwelling or a multifamily dwelling no larger than four units. The employee must remain in residence in the dwelling for a minimum of three years.

Since the program began in 1997, the LNYW program has helped 807 households purchase homes throughout Maryland.

Program Results

Since the program began in 1997, the LNYW program has helped 807 households purchase homes throughout Maryland (Basu 2002b). Because part of the funding for the program comes from local or county government, local participation is crucial to the success of the program. There are currently only eight (for the private employee program) and seven (for the state employee program) participating governments, which appears to have limited the program. According to Papagni (2002), the program is looking to expand: "we would like to bring other local governments on board," he said, "but it is up to them." LNYW staff is currently working to include other local governments in the program, particularly Baltimore County and Howard County, which have recently agreed to join the program.

While not specifically regional in nature, the LNYW program has been implemented on a de facto regional basis because the participating municipalities are mostly concentrated in the Washington D.C./Baltimore region. The exceptions are Hagerstown, Salisbury, and Westminister. The two municipalities that are working to be included in the program, Baltimore County and Howard County, are also located in the Washington D.C./Baltimore region.

One important aspect of the program is that it has reduced the miles traveled to work for the participating homebuyers, observed John Papagini (2002), a special projects officer for the DHCD. "The results have been encouraging," he said. "We have seen a dramatic reduction in miles traveled to work and increased usage of public transit. Although we are a housing agency, a related benefit is the reduction in environmental and social costs of travel to work." A LNYW survey of 427 homebuyer participants in the program, adjusted for multiple modes of travel, found that 15 percent of the homebuyers switched from driving to walking, car pooling, or taking public transportation to work. This decreased their average commute from 13.5 miles to 1.5 miles. Conversely, 33 percent of the homebuyers continued to drive to work, and 23 percent continued to walk, car pool, or take public transportation to work. Overall, average miles traveled to work fell from 10 miles to 3.4 miles, and the average commute time fell from 25 minutes to 14 minutes (Maryland DHCD LNYW 2001).

Although the LNYW program does not specifically target low- and moderate-income persons, the program has helped many low-income households purchase homes that they otherwise would not have been able to afford. The homebuyer survey indicated that approximately 56 percent of the homebuyers have an annual household income of $50,000 or less, and 25 percent have a household income of $30,000 or less. Approximately one-third of the program's participants indicated that they would not have been able to purchase their homes without the LNYW incentive, and 75 percent of all participants are first-time homebuyers (Maryland DHCD LNYW 2001). The LNYW program also has the added benefit of investing in distressed neighborhoods. The homebuyer survey indicated that 43 percent of the buyers needed to renovate their homes. Since the eligible neighborhoods have been designated by the local community as being in need of revitalization, the program helps the revitalization effort by increasing homeowner investments in the neighborhood.

Overall, the LNYW program has proven successful by providing small incentives to homebuyers in the Washington D.C./Baltimore region, as well as in other areas. The program fills a void in affordable housing programs because it gives potential homebuyers a little extra aid in purchasing their home. The LNYW program has been effective at increasing housing opportunities for families who may not need or be eligible for many other affordable housing programs but who do need assistance with down-payment and other housing costs. Although the LNYW program is small, such a program might be used to fill a gap in a more extensive regional or statewide affordable housing strategy. Additionally, the LNYW program has many added social and environmental benefits, such as reducing commuting times, increasing pedestrian activity, and revitalizing certain targeted neighborhoods.

On the other hand, the LNYW program does not provide the kinds of affordable housing benefits that will solve the affordable housing problem, although it is not specifically intended to do so. The program provides minuscule benefits when viewed in terms of the overall need for affordable housing, and it does nothing to help people who need more than the $3,000 incentive to purchase a home. The program does, however, provide an incentive for homebuyers to consider purchasing a home in neighborhoods they might not otherwise consider, and it helps to get people thinking about homeownership.

The LNYW program does not provide the kinds of affordable housing benefits that will solve the affordable housing problem, although it is not specifically intended to do so.

CITY OF AMES AND STORY COUNTY, IOWA, PARTNERSHIP

Inception: 1997

Administration: The program is staffed by the Ames Department of Planning. Preceding its establishment were the creation of a task force and the preparation of a formal housing needs analysis for the county, which contained a series of detailed recommendations. Because of the nature of the housing market in the county, the program was designed to have a regional dimension. As currently administered, the program mainly involves down-payment and closing-cost assistance in addition to construction financing for new and infill construction.

CITY OF AMES AND STORY COUNTY, IOWA PARTNERSHIP *(continued)*

Key objectives: Encourage owner-occupied affordable housing on a multijurisdictional basis.

Accomplishments: Eight cities participate in the voluntary program, including Ames, Collins, Colo, Huxley, McCallsburg, Maxwell, Nevada, and Zearing. In 2001, 63 persons from 15 cities submitted applications for the down-payment and closing-cost assistance program, and 50 of those applicants completed the program's homebuyer educational seminar. From July 1999 to December 2001, the program assisted 19 homebuyers with the purchase of a home; 18 were first-time homebuyers. The infill lot development program provides developers with financing for the construction of new infill development. The price of a home purchased through the program may not exceed $120,000. Only one loan was granted through the infill lot development program in 2001, which resulted in the development of one affordable single-family home in Colo.

Caveats: A change in the housing market in Story County made it less costly to provide down-payment and closing-cost assistance in municipalities outside of Ames than to construct new homes and apartments in Ames. This shift resulted in a less ambitious program than contemplated in the initial housing needs assessment. Also, local budgetary constraints make it difficult for small municipalities to contribute to the program's maintenance, planners have said.

The Ames/Story County Partnership-Affordable Housing Program was created in 1997. It is now administered by the Ames Department of Planning and Housing and governed by a board composed of representatives from each participating city. Prior to 1997, according to Brian P. O'Connell (2002a), director of the Ames Department of Planning and Housing, Ames had operated a housing program limited to the city itself that provided subsidies in the form of second mortgages at favorable rates to qualified low- and moderate-income homebuyers. The homebuyer was required to stay in the home for a certain period of time and, when the home was sold, the city took a percentage of the sales price to recover the subsidy. The city did not try to limit appreciation by linking housing prices to a consumer price index or some other device to offset speculative gains.

Ames has always had a very strong housing market, O'Connell said, and as a result it was very expensive to capitalize a fund to provide low-interest mortgages. The idea for a countywide program, in which loans could be made outside Ames in towns with much lower housing prices.

Affordable housing ribbon cutting in Ames, Iowa.

Ames Department of Planning and Housing

The first step toward the program was a housing needs assessment study in 1998, which was funded by a grant from the state of Iowa through its Local Housing Assistance Program (LHAP). Ames and Story County were the applicants and put up the matching share. A task force consisting of representatives from various cities in Story County oversaw the preparation of the consultant-prepared plan (RDG Crose Gardner Schukert 1998, 8).

"Ames was spilling over," said Vanessa Baker-Latimer (2002), the Ames housing coordinator. "Rather than 14 communities [in Story County] trying to do things separately, it made more sense to do things together. Otherwise, the communities would be competing for the same money from the state."

The needs assessment is composed of three parts: (1) a definition of key issues, (2) an assessment of housing demand, affordability, conditions, and a survey of rents, and (3) a review of countywide housing needs and an action plan to address those needs.

To define the key issues surrounding affordable housing, the task force completed two surveys and questioned 19 focus groups throughout Story County. One of the surveys measured the housing perceptions of 107 people with special knowledge of housing issues while the second gauged the housing preferences of 530 employees of the county's major job centers.

Next, the task force conducted a needs assessment to determine the individual needs of all 14 municipalities in Story County. Later integrated with a regional assessment of housing priorities and targets, the needs assessment analyzed housing production targets for owner-occupied and rental housing, and regional rehabilitation needs. The housing production targets for Story County are as follows:

> Analysis indicates a ten-year demand of 4,574 units, or about 457 units for the next ten years. Between 1998 and 2002, the communities in the county should produce a combined total of 2,610 units, or 522 units annually. Of these units, about 52 percent should be owner occupied, 48 percent should be renter occupied. (RDG Crose Gardner Schukert 1998, 6)

O'Connell (2002a) explained that the rate of growth over 10 years would not keep pace with that of the next five: "There appears to be a slightly higher near-term demand," he said

The methodology used in the assessment, explained O'Connell, "was based on 1990 Census data projected forward to 1998. From that projected number, a model was created for each community in Story County using migration variables, future growth projections, existing and projected housing vacancy rates, housing replacement estimates, and existing and future housin- density characteristics." The methodology then applied income variables to future populations, and housing price points were established for various income levels. "The results of this analysis," O'Connell said, "yielded a projected affordable housing demand for each community that was aggregated to create a Story County affordable housing needs total."

The analysis looked for common themes in housing needs throughout the county to determine the both regional and local strategic housing issues. The issues that were identified as primarily regional concerns included:

- a lack of rental housing;

- a lack of affordable housing;

- preservation of existing housing stock; and

- development capacity and lot availability (RDG Crose Gardner Schukert 1998, 8).

The issues that were identified as primarily local concerns included:

- senior housing;

- economic constraints;

- community development and marketing; and

- economic development policy (RDG Crose Gardner Schukert 1998, 8).

These regional issues became the core of the regional action plan for the participating communities. The plan justifies this regional focus by arguing that the relationship between all of the communities and job centers in Story County and the large amount of cross-travel and commuting make Story County a regional housing market.

The plan identifies three main housing markets in the county:

(1) A high-demand urban market, characterized by the high cost of improved lots, appreciating home values, and a low vacancy rate

(2) A prosperous small town market, characterized by home values that are lower than the urban market but appreciating, lively housing development, and shortages in supply and capacity

(3) A rural housing market, characterized by house values below the other two markets and discouraged and risky development (RDG Crose Gardner Schukert 1998, 10)

These problems faced by all of these markets are addressed through the housing program's four components, each of which draws on regional mechanisms that pool available financial and staff resources.

The first component is production capacity. The ability of the region's communities to produce housing types that are critically needed and are not being produced by the current housing market must be increased, according to the plan. It suggests several policies that should be enacted to meet this goal, including formation of a regional consortium of financial institutions, builders, employers, city and county governments, and non-profit organizations. The consortium would include a housing finance corporation that would be involved in construction lending, mortgage financing, long-term financing, and community assistance, an infrastructure bank to provide communities and developers with front-end financing to develop land, and a development entity. This component of the plan also calls for the formation of an equity fund, a community housing development organization, community partnerships, and for consideration of a regional transportation system.

The second component encourages the development of affordable single-family owner-occupied homes priced within $60,000 to $110,000. This component includes policies that focus on mechanisms designed to reduce public improvement costs for affordable subdivisions and developments, such as standards that allow affordable housing development to occur only in areas that require minimal incremental utility extensions and public improvements and require narrower street widths in subdivisions; the use of public improvement financing such as tax increment financing; increased infill development; and the use of manufactured housing and other alternative forms of housing. The plan calls for the establishment of a mortgage financing program to replace or compliment rural development mortgages. This new mortgage financing corporation should include private mortgage financing through lending institutions or the proposed housing finance corporation, soft second mortgages, down-payment assistance pro-

These regional issues became the core of the regional action plan for the participating communities. The plan justifies this regional focus by arguing that the relationship between all of the communities and job centers in Story County and the large amount of cross-travel and commuting make Story County a regional housing market.

grams in partnership with the Iowa Finance Authority, and continued support for nonprofit housing organizations such as Habitat for Humanity, according to the plan.

The third component is a mechanism intended to develop a range of rental housing choices. This part of the plan suggests the formation of equity partnerships that take advantage of the federal Low Income Housing Tax Credit, public support for development through the use of tax increment financing, Community Development Block Grants (CDBG), historic preservation tax credits, and Home Investment Partnerships Program (HOME) monies. The plan also includes provisions for special siting of certain types of rental housing, such as in historic town centers, and for the development of senior housing.

Affordable housing ribbon cutting in Maxwell, Iowa.

Ames Department of Planning and Housing

The last component is housing conservation and rehabilitation. "[W]hile policies developed for a tight housing market often concentrate on new production," the plan states "the conservation and rehabilitation of the existing housing stock is the most cost-effective method for meeting housing needs" (RDG Crose Gardner Schukert 1998, 9). The plan calls for a regional rehabilitation initiative that makes direct loans and grants from CDBG funds, a leveraged loan program that leverages private loan funding by combining private loans with CDBG or other public funds to produce a below-market interest rate for affordable housing owners, and a special program that combines home ownership with rehabilitation. Also, the plan calls for a program that rehabilitates rental housing.

Program Results

According to O'Connell (2002b), the Ames planning director, the current implementation of the plan mainly involves a down-payment and closing-cost assistance program, and construction financing for infill construction. The down-payment and closing-cost assistance program is for first-time homebuyers with incomes at or below 110 percent of the Story County median income. The program also provides help with funding minor repairs that are needed to meet housing quality standards (Ames Department of Planning and Housing 2002b).

The Ames/Story County partnership has been largely successful in attracting participants: eight of the county's 15 municipalities are now part of the voluntary program.

Ames Housing Coordinator Baker-Latimer (2002) said that the program has emphasized down-payment and closing-cost money for new homebuyers because the housing market in Ames and Story County changed after the housing assessment was completed. "Interest rates dropped and there were more homes on the market," she said. "People realized that they could extend their incomes by buying existing homes rather than building new homes." In Ames, the opportunities to buy existing homes expanded because the occupants of those homes were buying more expensive dwelling units, and housing filtering occurred. At the same time, the rental market in Ames loosened up, and building new rental units was not necessary. The smaller communities in Story County "did not have a huge rental market," she said.

A consortium of representatives from city and county governments, financial institutions, and employers was formed to implement a variety of affordable housing programs, including a local housing assistance program, a consortium of banks and financial resources, and a countywide housing bank. According to O'Connell, local banks have benefited from participating in the consortium because it helps them to fulfill requirements of the federal Community Reinvestment Act.

In 2001, 63 persons from 15 cities submitted applications for the down-payment and closing-cost assistance program, and 50 of those applicants completed the homebuyer educational seminar. From July 1999 to December 2001, the program helped 19 homebuyers to purchase a home; 18 of those people were first-time homebuyers.

The infill lot development program provides developers with financing for the construction of new infill development throughout existing communities. The price of a home purchased through the program may not exceed $120,000. Only one loan was granted through the program in 2001, which resulted in the development of one affordable single-family home in Colo.

An infrastructure development program under the plan provides financing to landowners to develop land for the construction of low- and moderate-income housing, with a price not to exceed $120,000. No projects used this program in 2001 so the funds were transferred into a housing rehabilitation program.

The Ames/Story County partnership has been largely successful in attracting participants: eight of the county's 15 municipalities are now part of the voluntary program, including Ames, Collins, Colo, Huxley, McCallsburg, Maxwell, Nevada, and Zearing. Ames is the largest in terms of population, with 50,731 people, according to the 2000 census; Nevada is the second largest, with a population of 6,659, and McCallsburg is the smallest, with a population of 318. Almost 80 percent—62,814—of Story County's total 2000 population of 79,981 lives in cities that participate in the program.

But, O'Connell (2002b) said, "cities are increasingly reluctant to contribute money to the fund because of budget constraints." Since it is entirely voluntarily, budget cuts and funding constraints in participating cities may severely limit the success of the program. Baker-Latimer (2002) reflected that, if she were to restructure the program, she would reduce the 12-year payback on down-payment assistance and increase the interest rate, which is set at 2 percent. Similarly, she would increase the interest rate on short-term construction loans to builders from 3 to 5 percent. These changes would return money to the revolving loan fund more quickly; it could then be loaned out again and used for program administration.

AFFORDABLE HOUSING, EDUCATION AND DEVELOPMENT INC. (AHEAD), NORTHERN GRAFTON AND COOS COUNTIES, NEW HAMPSHIRE

Inception: 1991

Administration: AHEAD is a small nonprofit housing organization that provides affordable housing services in a two-county rural area of northwestern New Hampshire.

Key objectives: Encourage home ownership and provide affordable rental housing.

Accomplishments: AHEAD provides housing at 250 units that the organization owns, which includes 187 Section 8 elderly units and 63 housing units for low- and moderate-income families. AHEAD's Working Families program gives support to the people who live in its rental units, with a focus on community outreach and family support. Most support is provided on a one-on-one basis in areas such as employment skills, resume writing, and transportation problems. AHEAD also assists homebuyers who are purchasing a home: it helps with such tasks as applying for a mortgage, selecting a home, negotiating a purchase price, and closing. It offers a single-family home repair loan program funded by a HUD Rural Housing and Economic Development grant. AHEAD has worked with approximately 250 to 300 households through the Working Families program. The homeownership program helped 19 families in 2000, its first year, 38 in 2001, and 15 in 2002. Some 350 people have participated in AHEAD's homeownership seminars. Four home repair loans have been authorized in the year-old loan program.

Caveats: None.

Affordable Housing, Education and Development Inc. (AHEAD) is a small nonprofit housing organization based in Littleton, New Hampshire, that provides services throughout northern Grafton and Coos counties, a rural area of northwestern New Hampshire. The largest city in the area is Berlin, with a population of 10,331 in 2000.

Pine Manor affordable rental unit in Bethlehem, New Hampshire.

Affordable Housing, Education, and Development (AHEAD)

The organization was conceived in 1991 by a group of citizens who were concerned about affordable housing. By 1992, the organization had hired its first staff person, and by 1993 it had purchased its first rental housing units.

AHEAD has four main programs. First, it owns 250 rental units for low- and moderate-income families and the elderly. Its second program is the Working Families program, which provides services to those who live in the organization's housing units. Its third program is a homeownership program, which helps people navigate the process of purchasing a home. The fourth program is a single-family home repair loan program funded by HUD.

According to David Wood (2002a), the executive director of AHEAD, the organization's primary focus is providing rental housing through the 250 units that the organization owns, which include 187 Section 8 elderly units and 63 units for low- and moderate-income families. The units, which consist mostly of buildings with two to six apartments, have been funded by CDBGs, tax credits, USDA Rural Development funds, bank financing, New Hampshire Affordable Housing Fund funding, and a variety of other sources. Since its inception, AHEAD has acquired housing mainly by purchasing built units; however, it is venturing into new housing development in its latest project.

The average family living in an AHEAD unit consists of a single parent with two children, earning $16,000 a year. The average income for an elderly tenant is $6,000.

The average family living in an AHEAD unit consists of a single parent with two children, earning $16,000 a year. The average income for an elderly tenant is $6,000, with most of that provided by Social Security benefits. The occupancy rate in units owned by AHEAD is 95 percent (Wood 2002a).

In addition to the rental units, AHEAD has developed an education program called the Working Families program, which provides support to the people who live in AHEAD's rental units, with a focus on community outreach and family support. Most of the support is provided on a one-on-one basis in areas such as employment skills, resume writing, and transportation problems. According to Wood, AHEAD also occasionally offers group programs, such as a self-defense class offered several years ago after requests from single mothers.

AHEAD's homeownership program assists homebuyers who are purchasing a home: it helps with such tasks as applying for a mortgage, selecting a home, negotiating a purchase price, and closing. Through this program, AHEAD provides credit and budget counseling, financial assistance for down payment and closing costs, and special lender programs to help homebuyers apply for mortgages. It also offers home maintenance and lawn and garden repair workshops, home rehabilitation planning and loans, and delinquency intervention to help homeowners overcome financial difficulties.

The homebuyer workshops, held almost every month at different locations throughout the region, are a key aspect of the homeownership program. The workshops offer advice to people aimed at helping them to determine how much of their income they can afford to spend on a house, rebuild a negative credit history, work with real estate agents, negotiate a purchase price and sales agreement, and find money for down payment and closing costs. Also, people who have attended a workshop are eligible to receive a credit on their mortgage of $100 to $500 at the time of closing from participating local banks.

The homebuyer workshop is the first step in AHEAD's program. One-on-one consultations come next, which help homebuyers set up a buying plan, improve their credit histories, and get credit repair assistance. The third step is selecting a mortgage that meets the budget and financial goals of the homebuyer. Here AHEAD helps homebuyers to prepare documents and choose a lender. After approval of the loan, the fourth step in the program is to home finding. AHEAD assists homebuyers by providing infor-

Participants of an AHEAD homeownership class learn the basics of purchasing a home.

Affordable Housing, Education, and Development (AHEAD)

mation on local houses and real estate professionals and on how to negotiate a price. The last step is post-purchase training. As described above, AHEAD offers programs that address home maintenance, budgeting, delinquency intervention, and health and well-being.

A fourth program that AHEAD offers is a single-family home repair loan program funded by a HUD Rural Housing and Economic Development grant. This program provides grants to owners of single-family homes who want to do basic home repair projects. The repair project must be necessary for health, safety, or energy conservation. According to Wood, "The interpretation of this is pretty broad...allowing kitchen and bathroom modernizations but not additions or amenities unless necessitated for overcrowding or therapeutic reasons." The program began in 2001 and is still being developed: "it was off to a slow start," Wood said, "but we have done four [loans] so far."

Program Results

AHEAD's home ownership program is available to all residents of the service area, regardless of income. AHEAD plans to assist over 100 low- and moderate-income families achieve home ownership over the next five years through the homeownership workshop and other programs.

AHEAD continues to work on building and acquiring new housing units to rent to low- and moderate-income families. "We are currently applying for a 20-unit rehabilitation/new construction project—with seven buildings, scattered-site—for large families earning under 60 percent of the county median income in the town of Lisbon," said Wood. Five of the buildings will have their exteriors rehabilitated to meet historic preservation guidelines, he added.

The home ownership program helped 19 families in 2000, 38 in 2001, and 15 families in 2002 . However, the number of individuals educated through the homeownership program is much higher. "We have educated about

AHEAD's Working Families program participants building a playground in their neighborhood.

Affordable Housing, Education, and Development (AHEAD)

350 individuals through our eight-hour seminar," Wood said, "and they all get at least one hour of individual counseling." The number of people who have been educated is higher because many individuals who have attended a seminar have not yet purchased a home.

Since its inception 10 years ago, AHEAD has worked with approximately 250 to 300 households through its Working Families program. Most of the people served are those who have lived in an AHEAD rental unit. "While other households are theoretically eligible," said Wood, "we have never attempted to serve those not living in our housing due to lack of capacity."

TWIN PINES HOUSING TRUST, UPPER VALLEY REGION, NEW HAMPSHIRE AND VERMONT

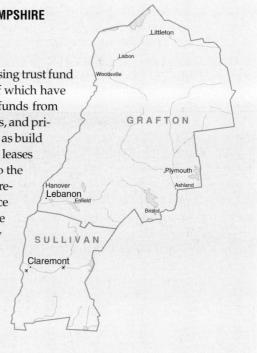

Inception: 1990

Administration: The Twins Pine Housing Trust (TPHT) is a housing trust fund that covers portions of New Hampshire and Vermont, some of which have rapidly rising land costs. Its home ownership program uses funds from both states—state grants, mortgages, rental income, partnerships, and private contributions—to buy existing single-family homes as well as build new ones. To keep the housing affordable, the program uses land leases in which TPHT owns the land under each home and leases it to the homeowner at a reduced price for 99 years. Homeowners can re-sell their homes to lower-income purchasers for the original price plus a portion—usually 25 percent—of the amount that the home has increased in value since purchase. However, TPHT usually has the right of first refusal to purchase the home.

Key objectives: Build family and community stability by providing affordable housing.

Accomplishments: As of 2001, TPHT owned 24 land leases and 108 rental properties.

Caveats: The program receives uneven support from the multiple jurisdictions it covers.

The Twin Pines Housing Trust (TPHT) is a small housing program that was established in 1990 with the mission of building family and community stability by providing affordable housing in the Upper Valley area. With a service area in New Hampshire and Vermont, TPHT is involved in the development of affordable housing grant funding to help low- and moderate-income families purchase single-family homes, and homeownership education programs. According to Ray Brewster (2002), assistant director of TPHT, the dual-state service area "developed around the Connecticut River as farmland, and then became industrial…[and] it evolved as an economy along the Connecticut River" with little regard for state boundaries.

The Upper Valley is a rural area along the borders of eastern Vermont and western New Hampshire that is bisected by the Connecticut River. The largest city in the area that TPHT serves is Lebanon, New Hampshire, which had a population of 12,568 in 2000. According to TPHT (2002a), between the years 1980 and 2000 average rent in the area increased by 175 percent, the average wage increased by 135 percent, the number of households increased by 30 percent, and the number of rental housing units increased by 1 percent. TPHT reported that 2,400 families in the area are in need of affordable housing.

This single-family home in White River Junction, Vermont, is part of a land-lease program. The families own the home; the Twin Pines Housing Trust leases the land to them.

Roy Brewster, Twin Pines Housing Trust

(Above) Overlook House, Hartford Village, Vermont. The large building is a 10-unit apartment building with coordinated social services. The small building in the background is a nine-unit apartment building, both projects of the Twin Pines Housing Trust. (Right) Starlake Village, Norwich, Vermont, a project of the Twin Pines Housing trust and managed under a homeownership program by the Vermont Housing and Conservation board. This development includes nine homes owned by the residents on leased land. An adjacent dairy farm was preserved in the development of the area.

TPHT's home ownership program uses funds from both Vermont and New Hampshire to buy existing single-family homes as well as build new ones. To keep the housing affordable, the program uses land leases in which TPHT owns the land under each home and leases the it to the homeowner at a reduced price for 99 years. Homeowners can resell their homes to lower-income purchasers for the original price plus a portion—usually 25 percent—of the amount that the home has increased in value since purchase. However, TPHT usually has the right of first refusal to purchase the home. This limited equity structure allows low- and moderate-income homeowners to build equity while it preserves long-term housing affordability.

Properties come to the TPHT in three ways. First, owners of properties offer to sell their homes or land to TPHT: "occasionally we get calls from owners of properties who want to sell them," said Brewster. These properties often "are distressed in some way," he added, referring to physically distressed properties in need of rehabilitation, as well as financially distressed properties in danger of foreclosure or repossession. Second, TPHT buys vacant land, homes, or other properties for sale. Third, TPHT has been involved in partnerships with other independent statewide housing organizations that are looking for partners to develop affordable housing.

Program Results

Funded by state public agency grants, mortgages, partnerships, and private contributions, TPHT received $489,000 from rental income, $150,000 in grants, and $27,000 in contributions in 2001 (TPHT 2002b).

As of 2001, TPHT owned 24 land leases and 108 rental properties, although, according to Brewster, it will own up to 60 more by mid-2003. The number of properties is higher in Vermont than in New Hampshire because, Brewster said, "the system is a little more organized on the Vermont side."

One example of a project that TPHT has developed in Vermont is Starlake Village in Norwich, where a neighborhood of 13 homes was built in 1991 on a 10-acre corner of a farmland conservation project. The project was partially funded by the Vermont Housing and Conservation Board (VHCB), a statewide organization discussed in Chapter 6 of this report. The farmland preservation and affordable housing project was a dual-goal project of VHCB, in which farmland was preserved and affordable housing units created. According to Polly Nichol (2002c, 2002d), housing programs director for the Vermont Housing and Conservation Board, TPHT was the grantee of $182,056 for the affordable housing portion of the project, which resulted in the construction of single-family, owner-occupied, limited-equity homes, built on the land trust model in which TPHT holds land leases for all of the homes. For the conservation part of the project, VHCB awarded the Upper Valley Land Trust $235,000 to purchase a conservation easement for 140 acres of farmland, and a one-year $210,000 loan to support the affordable housing property until the trust sold it. According to Nichol, "The farm is located in one of the hottest real estate markets in the state. The town in which it is located, Norwich, is a very wealthy community where home values are far above the state median. The Upper Valley region has experienced rapid and sustained economic growth during the past 20 years."

ENDNOTES

1. Illinois passed the Local Government Technical Assistance Act in August 2002 (Public Act 92-0768). The act, among other things, defines a comprehensive plan and its elements. A comprehensive plan must include a housing element, whose "purpose...is to document the present and future needs for housing within the jurisdiction of the local government, including affordable housing and special needs housing; *take into account the housing needs of a larger region*; identify barriers to the production of housing, including affordable housing; access [sic] the condition of the local housing stock; and develop strategies, programs, and other actions to address the needs for a range of housing options" (emphasis added).

CHAPTER 8

Concluding Thoughts on a Model Program for Regional Approaches to Affordable Housing

T hat there is no one best way to address the provision of affordable housing in the United States on a regional or multijurisdictional basis should be evident from the analyses of programs in the previous chapters. When the programs are viewed together, it is easy to see how diverse the approaches are, given the varying political structures and institutional capacities of states, regions, and local government as well as the interests of the nonprofit and private sectors.

As this report has demonstrated, evaluating *quantitatively* the success of these programs in determining and meeting affordable housing production needs is extremely difficult. The exceptions are those states or regions where there exist: (a) an agreed-upon mechanism for establishing present and future need and (b) a system for monitoring the production and retention of affordable units. Only in states like Connecticut, Massachusetts, New Jersey, and Rhode Island is evaluation clearly possible: each relies on uniform methodologies or a fixed percentage for gauging need, and each has a state-level agency charged with tracking affordable units. In the Twin Cities region, by contrast, the regional affordable housing goals are negotiated between the Metropolitan Council and the local governments. Housing need is what participating local governments agree to in the administration of the Livable Communities Act. And in California there is no effective mechanism for identifying on a statewide or regional basis how much affordable housing is being produced to fulfill statewide and regional needs, as the state's Little Hoover commission has observed.

Finally, this report also shows that the gap between need and production is especially dramatic in high-cost or high-growth areas. For example, while the Massachusetts housing appeals program appears successful at getting affordable housing built, only a small number of local governments have reached the state-established goal of making at least 10 percent of all units in each community affordable, growing from three in 1972 to 23 in 1997, out of a total of 351 cities and towns (see Chapter 6). *These results are for a program that has existed for 33 years.* Although affordable housing has been built in many Massachusetts communities where none existed before, not enough production is occurring because of a lack of either adequate subsidy programs or private developer interest, even with a relatively supportive statewide system in place.

Despite the diversity of approaches, the problem of quantitative evaluation, and the gap between need and production this PAS Report describes, the authors optimistically propose a series of elements that should be taken into consideration when developing a model program for regional approaches to affordable housing. These elements are grouped into two types: second-best alternatives and best alternatives. The former are better at expressing good intentions than producing positive results; the latter are action-oriented solutions more likely to result in actual housing. Nonetheless, both sets of approaches offer a starting point for regions that are contemplating the problem of affordable housing for the first time.

SOME SECOND-BEST APPROACHES

Several approaches described or suggested by this study offer solutions that are not likely to lead to much change, here described as second-best approaches. These include the following:

(1) *Aspirational regional planning for affordable housing that has no express required linkage to local comprehensive planning and land development regulation.*

New Hampshire's statutory structure provides an example of this approach. Despite the high quality of the regional housing plans , meticulous in their attention to detail, and the conscientious efforts of regional planning commissions to set measurable goals, local governments in the state are not required by statute to adopt housing elements or to do anything at all with respect to affordable housing. This nonregulatory approach is more remarkable because of the landmark New Hampshire Supreme Court antiexclusionary zoning ruling, the 1991 *Britton v. Town of Chester* decision, which would suggest that local governments should be bound by statute (see discussion of New Hampshire below). It falls to regional planning agencies, lacking any genuine state authority, to persuade local governments to address regional housing needs in their local plans. Regional housing plans are simply hortatory. As the research shows, the approach that a number of New Hampshire regional agencies have taken is simply to prepare the comprehensive plans with the housing elements for the local governments themselves, which ensures that at least the regional perspective is incorporated into local plans. Nonetheless, the selection of implementation measures and the good will with which they are implemented are fundamentally local decisions and attitudes.

(2) Emphasis in regional and related local planning on study and analysis but with no commitment to production.

This approach is a subset of (1) above. A number of regional and local plans reviewed in this study contain exhaustive documentation of housing conditions and statements of the need for affordable units. Some acknowledge the need but fail to quantify its dimensions in measurable terms. Moreover, when it comes to proposing actions that would actually result in the production of new affordable units or the rehabilitation of existing housing stock and to making certain that the units produced or rehabilitated would remain affordable, these plans fall short. The implementation measures proposed in the plans are mere tinkering, such as suggestions for minor changes to development regulations like optional overlay districts. They fail to create institutional mechanisms and permanent funding sources to ensure affordable housing. They also fail to make substantive changes to local development regulations: they make no efforts, for example, to change densities to make affordable housing feasible, to require set-asides of affordable housing in market-rate developments, to accelerate approval procedures, or to zone adequate vacant land for affordable housing. All of these changes are components of the more successful New Jersey and California programs wherein local governments must also identify sites for affordable housing projects as part of their local housing plans.

(3) Modest grants to study the problem of affordable housing at the regional or local level or modest penalties for failing to do so.

A number of states provide local governments with modest grants to prepare comprehensive plans with housing elements; this approach is typical when planning laws are substantially amended to require the preparation of completely new plans. It is certainly desirable to plan for affordable housing, but mandating that it be done while failing to provide sufficient resources is a good way to generate resentment at the local and regional levels and to ensure inadequate plans.[1] Certain approaches seem to be exercises in futility. These include state programs that (a) penalize local governments for failing to complete acceptable housing plans by cutting off money for grant programs for affordable housing, or (b) authorize private parties (more often than not, nonprofit advocacy groups) to assume the time and expense of enforcing planning requirements for housing with little compensating benefit, as is the case in California.[2]

A PROGRAM OF BEST PRACTICES AND STRATEGIES

This section describes a set of best practices and strategies for affordable housing. Some of the elements were suggested by participants in APA's symposium on regional approaches to affordable housing in Chicago, October 29–30, 2000 (see Appendix C).

(1) The most important element in ensuring the provision of affordable housing on a regional basis is political will and leadership.

Political will and leadership are necessary to raise the issue and keep it before citizens and, at the same time, respond to efforts to oppose affordable housing. This political will and leadership can come from elected officials, as it did in Connecticut when it enacted its housing appeals act, or from the business community, as in the case of the San Francisco Bay Area and the Chicago region. Major employers, especially those who depend on low- and moderate-income workers or who are finding it hard to recruit out-of-the-region employees because of high housing costs, and economic development groups like chambers of commerce must be enlisted in the cause. Alliances must be formed as well with affordable housing advocacy

The most important element in ensuring the provision of affordable housing on a regional basis is political will and leadership.

groups. In any case, political will and leadership are absolutely essential to initiate and maintain a regional strategy.

(2) *Advocates for regional change must reframe the question of the need for affordable housing as a market inefficiency to be corrected rather than as charity or welfare for the poor or less deserving.*

The affordable housing issue must consequently be recast as an issue of jobs and housing or of housing for workers; it must be described as crucial to keep the region economically competitive with other regions that already provide such housing. Bruce Katz, director of the Brookings Institution Center on Urban and Metropolitan Policy, put it this way:

> Affordable housing has been demonized in the public mind. It is largely associated with and saddled with a series of negatives—crime, distressed neighborhoods and declining property values. These public images persist even though many empirical studies have refuted these negative claims and even after the federal government has taken major efforts to demolish the most troubled public housing developments and stimulate the development of economically integrated communities. Affordable housing is associated exclusively with the very poor. That means most Americans assume, wrongly, that the issue has nothing to do with them. It also means that the issue has a weak base from which to build majoritarian coalitions that can spur political and policy action. (Katz 2002)

Provision of affordable housing must become part of a region's political and economic culture.

Without affordable housing, it may be argued, enormous stress is placed on a region's employers (including local government employees, such as firefighters, police officers, sanitation workers, and school teachers) by limiting the available pool of workers within commuting distance. Under this strategy, opinion leaders and elected officials must tie the need for affordable housing to quality-of-life issues like traffic congestion, equal access to educational and employment opportunities, and patterns of development. These connections can be made through the media and by conducting regional forums to give the issue ongoing visibility. Provision of affordable housing must become part of a region's political and economic culture.

A study commission of the New Hampshire legislature on workforce housing (see Chapter 4) has recommended just such an approach. In its November 2002 report, it states, "We must dispel the myths surrounding workforce housing, to change the perception that multifamily housing negatively impacts local budgets, property values, and the quality of life more than other forms of residential development" (New Hampshire Legislative Commission 2002, 2).[3] The report suggests that the state legislature direct the New Hampshire Finance Authority and Office of State Planning to "analyze the impact of residential development, especially of workforce housing, and actively disseminate this information to local decision makers and the general public with the goal of establishing the broadest possible common understanding of the true costs and benefits to individual communities " (p. 6).

(3) *A regional institution must be charged with identifying and understanding the scope of the affordability problem on a regional basis and creating a forum for action.*

Housing markets are regional, not statewide or local. But because the federal government withdrew support for regional housing planning, for more than two decades regional planning agencies have failed to undertake such planning. Consequently, in the areas of the United States where regional housing planning does occur, it is carried out only by private advocacy groups or by regional planning agencies that are charged with the responsibility by state law (as in California and New Hampshire). Many regional planning agencies today focus solely on transportation planning and, to a lesser extent, noncontroversial areas like open space and farmland preservation and thus fail to address the full spectrum of regional interests.

A regional planning agency needs to view affordable housing as part of its regular scope of responsibilities; it cannot be dismissed as someone else's problem. An agency needs to ask such questions as: Where is affordable housing located in the region?; Who lives in or needs it?; To what extent is market activity meeting the needs of low- and moderate-income families?; and To what extent is there an imbalance between jobs and housing? (See also Appendix D.) A regional planning agency needs to be held responsible for setting measurable affordability goals for the region and its local governments and for working with local governments and the private sector as well as the state to see that these goals are achieved. Outside of the programs identified in this report, this goal-setting and cooperation are simply not happening.

(4) *Advocates for affordable housing production must understand the role of the market.*

Those undertaking state, regional, and local plans must grasp the functioning of the housing market in their respective regions. Factors such as commuting times; consumer preferences; labor, land, and materials costs; the capacity of home builders and developers for innovation; and interest rates will all affect regional markets. Sometimes changes in the market can compel changes in strategy. For example, in Ames/Story County, Iowa, discussed in Chapter 7, the market for housing shifted between the initiation of the countywide planning study and the creation of a multijurisdictional housing program. As noted above, in Ames, opportunities to buy existing homes expanded as occupants of those homes purchased more expensive dwelling units. Housing filtering occurred, freeing up owner-occupied dwellings at the moderate-income end of the housing market. At the same time, the rental market in Ames loosened up, and building new rental units was not necessary. However, smaller communities in Story County did not have a sizable rental market. There, it made more economic sense to provide assistance to a program offering down-payment and closing-cost assistance to low- and moderate-income homeowners than to initiate a subsidized program of new construction for owner-occupied housing and rental units. By contrast, in California—and especially in the San Francisco Bay Area—an absolute shortage of housing exists, especially affordable housing. The solution to the housing problem there—both for rent and for sale—is to build more of it, for *all* segments. The approach taken in Story County would not work in San Francisco; planners must therefore fully understand their housing market and be prepared to make rapid shifts to accommodate changing market conditions.

This approach would suggest that housing planning efforts must be revisited constantly, no less than every five years, and in some cases more often. The planning system that identifies housing needs for all levels of income must be a dynamic one. Constant monitoring of production levels, income groups affected, and availability of buildable land are absolutely essential in order to give the planning system credibility. Housing plans that have a 10- to 20-year horizon are clearly unrealistic.

(5) *The state's role is critical, especially in high-cost, high-growth regions of the United States.*

While regional planning agencies have a role to play, the state itself is the strongest actor. It is not surprising that the two most aggressive pro-

The planning system that identifies housing needs for all levels of income must be a dynamic one.

gram types—the fair-share programs in New Jersey (initiated first through lawsuits and later by the legislature under pressure from the state supreme court's *Mount Laurel* decisions) and (to a much lesser extent) California, and the state-level housing appeals acts in Massachusetts, Rhode Island, and Connecticut—grew out of a recognition in these high-cost or high-growth areas that the state needed to intervene aggressively in order to ensure that local governments were providing opportunities for affordable housing. While these programs have met with varying degrees of success, as this report has shown, they nonetheless demonstrate that the state must intervene when voluntary local efforts prove ineffective.

Despite its attractive and rational planning qualities (at least to planners), a fair-share process similar to New Jersey's was rejected by the Blue Ribbon Commission in Connecticut, which in 1989 recommended instead the creation of a state-level housing appeals procedure (discussed in Chapter 6). Terry Tondro, a University of Connecticut law professor who co-chaired the commission, recalled that the group considered a *Mount Laurel*-style approach but rejected it for two reasons. First, it depended on a judiciary "that was active enough to compensate for the lack of initiative in the other two branches of the state government" (Tondro 1999, 1,138). Second, the approach hinged on finding a plaintiff to participate in a lawsuit, and that "would have resulted in a delay of several years before [a fair-share] Act would have had an impact while awaiting a decision on the all but certain appeal to the Connecticut Supreme Court." Added to these potential problems was the necessary, considerable commitment to an independent state bureaucracy that would oversee the administration of a fair-share system by calculating housing need figures, establishing affordable housing goals, and monitoring compliance, which was unlikely in Connecticut.

The state role is critical for other reasons. State government can act independently and use its resources, bureaucratic and fiscal, to reward or punish those who fail to provide affordable housing opportunities. It is interesting to speculate whether the affordable housing problem in certain regions of the United States would have been mitigated by the kinds of aggressive state intervention found in the environmental area, where litigation and the prospect of withholding of federal transportation funds are sticks that can be used to compel compliance. In addition, state government can establish such entities as state-level housing trust funds, through state housing finance agencies, or authorize local governments to establish them. Through them, states can ensure that housing development occurs in areas where public services are or will be available. Similarly, state financing programs can achieve multiple objectives, with affordable housing as one of them. A good example of just such a state program is the Vermont Housing and Conservation Board, which operates a trust fund with the twin goals of providing affordable housing as well as conserving natural areas, agricultural land, historic properties, and recreational lands (see Chapter 5). The affordable housing aspect of the program includes significant measures to prevent urban sprawl by giving preference to rehabilitation, historic preservation, infill, and projects that are part of a neighborhood or downtown revitalization plan. By combining the two objectives under one institutional structure, the state ensures political support for the continuation of the program because its elements are so closely linked.

Finally, the state can establish uniform reporting requirements for regional planning agencies, local governments, and other actors in the provision of affordable housing so that a clear statewide and regional picture can show the extent of the affordable housing problem and the progress

States need to be aggressive in persuading local governments to remove regulatory barriers to affordable housing.

being made to address it. As noted above in Chapter 4, reporting failures are a problem that has beset the California fair-share program; uneven requirements for monitoring the actual provision of bona fide affordable housing among local governments make it difficult to conduct an accurate assessment of the 22-year-old program's effectiveness on a statewide or even regional basis.

(6) *States need to be aggressive in persuading local governments to remove regulatory barriers to affordable housing.*

Lifting regulatory barriers to affordable housing is a theme that has run through federal reports and studies dating from 1968 onward to the Kemp Commission report in 1991 and the Millennial Housing Commission report in 2002. Yet as this study has shown, little significant progress has been made on the matter in any state, except possibly in New Jersey where the removal of regulatory barriers is part of the *Mount Laurel* antiexclusionary zoning doctrine. Indeed, this study was able to unearth only one state-administered program, in Florida: it persuades local governments to systematically analyze local development regulations and their administration so as to make it possible to build housing at lower cost and in less time. California has only recently enacted similar legislation, although the program created has yet to be funded.[4] To the state's credit, a New Hampshire legislative commission on workforce housing has recognized the need to create such a mechanism and has proposed that the state do so. Nonetheless, because land-use regulation is seen as a local issue, state legislatures are reluctant to intervene. Yet it is clear that *overregulation (or merely misdirected regulation) is a significant factor in the availability of sites for affordable housing, the development standards to which such housing must be built, and the procedures by which development permits are approved.*[5]

State intervention can take the form of barrier removal grants, as suggested by the Kemp Commission in 1991, technical assistance, or the development of model codes and development standards. State action to eliminate regulatory barriers may also be linked to state-level procedures to review and certify local housing elements; states can also implement laws to ensure that a local government's own zoning and related codes do not stand in the way of providing the affordable housing opportunities that the housing elements call for.[6] Finally, the failure by local governments to review their development regulations on a periodic basis can provide a legal mechanism for questioning their continuing validity in relation to measurable affordable housing goals contained in local comprehensive plans, with the burden shifting to the local government to justify the lack of congruence between what a plan says and what land development regulations allow or permit.

(7) *Reliable sources of funding for subsidies and for supporting infrastructure for affordable housing are essential.*

If the housing market required no subsidies to build affordable units, such units would (assuming that builders were behaving rationally) be provided in varying degrees as a matter of course. It may, of course, be the path of least resistance for home builders to focus on market-rate or upscale housing because development approval for it will be easy to secure, it involves little governmental entanglement, it is more prestigious, and it generates higher profits. As this report has noted, a large number of housing trust funds, whose purpose is to subsidize the construction and rehabilitation of affordable housing, have been created recently at the state, regional, and local levels.[7] The more visible and interventionist the trust fund, like the regional ARCH fund in Seattle, the more effective it seems to

Yet it is clear that overregulation (or merely misdirected regulation) is a significant factor in the availability of sites for affordable housing, the development standards to which such housing must be built, and the procedures by which development permits are approved.

be.[8] Indeed, in the case of ARCH, the monies can be spent in *any* part of the region that ARCH covers to take advantage of affordable housing opportunities wherever they occur, a desirable objective especially in the high-cost Seattle area.[9] Similarly, affordable units may need to be built in places with limited infrastructure or in places where the infrastructure needs to be revamped (as in central cities), so that grants to provide such infrastructure thus eliminate excuses not to approve affordable housing projects on inadequately served sites as well as provide quality living environments.

One issue that is still unclear to the authors of this PAS Report is the impact of incentives to local governments and to private developers to get them to provide opportunities for affordable housing—specifically how powerful or fiscally sizable must incentives be to change or redirect behavior? As Chapter 4 indicates, one of the best-known incentive programs, the Livable Communities Act (LCA) in the Twin Cities region, has had mixed results in providing affordable opportunities in the seven-county region. In large part, these mixed results may reflect the mixed feelings that metropolitan communities and their political leaders have had with regard to affordable housing opportunities. Those mixed emotions were reflected in the legislative battle that produced the LCA, a struggle chronicled by Myron Orfield (1997, 104-54), a state representative at the time who labored to construct a coalition of mutual interests among urban and inner-ring suburban legislators, mayors, and council members. Unfortunately, the same ambivalence continues to affect participation in the program, the level of effort exerted by municipalities toward the achievement of negotiated goals, and even toward reporting their results. It is undoubtedly also true, as the Metropolitan Council asserts, that the program is underfunded (Peterson 2002), but that clearly is not the only issue—simply one that makes production of affordable housing that much more difficult. It remains to be seen how much progress the Council can make over time in overcoming these challenges.

There is also the question of the degree to which private home builders themselves actually want to build affordable housing, even when faced with a regulatory system that encourages them to do so.[10] One newspaper account of a local government in the Boston, Massachusetts, metropolitan area attempting to providing opportunities for affordable housing in order to comply with the state housing appeals act, Chapter 40B, is indicative of the uncertain lure of certain types of development incentives to the private sector and how well it responds (or wants to respond) to them. According to Anthony Flint in the September 9, 2002, edition of the *Boston Globe*, the town, Grafton, "changed its zoning to encourage multifamily housing close to the center of town, to contain sprawl and offer more affordable choices besides the large-lot single-family home." Despite this effort, "[n]o developer was interested in anything but single-family home subdivisions, however, and today some 400 large, high-end homes are set to be built among the woods and streets." In addition, the town has been subject, nonetheless, to a spate of appeals under Chapter 40B. Town officials believe that "[T]hese developers don't give a hoot about affordable housing." In response, a developer's representative contended that the measures the town took were "economically impractical" and the "town planning was defective."

Similarly, there have been no national efforts (although see the Metropolitan Council effort described in Chapter 4) to clearly tie federal funding for transportation to the provision of affordable housing, which would be one of the most powerful incentives to get states, regions, and local governments to modify transportation priorities by rewarding areas that perform with respect to affordable housing. (At the same time, the reluctance to do so may also be linked by the diversity of the affordable housing prob-

The more visible and interventionist the trust fund, like the regional ARCH fund in Seattle, the more effective it seems to be.

lem in the U.S. and the conceptual difficulty of devising a single or even multiple linkage approaches that would work consistently.) Linking the provision of affordable housing to transportation funding is an approach that was considered by the Millennial Housing Commission, the federal group that was charged by Congress in 2000 with formulating a new direction for the nation's housing program, but the Commission ultimately failed to act on the matter (Eisenberg 2002).

(8) *Local governments must have a full toolbox of techniques to provide affordable housing opportunities. Often this toolbox requires state authorizing legislation or hands-on assistance.*

The toolbox includes:

- authorization or requirements for development incentives for affordable housing such as density bonuses, including mandatory set asides for such housing as part of market-rate development;

- procedures for land-market monitoring in order to ensure that there is always an adequate supply of properly zoned land for affordable housing;

- authorization, as noted above, to establish local and regional housing trust funds and to use general fund monies and linkage fees for affordable housing purposes;

- authorization to waive development permit and impact fees for affordable housing projects;

- authorization or requirements for accessory dwelling units;

- planning enabling legislation that describes in clear terms requirements for a housing element in a local comprehensive plan and that ensures that communities provide a range of housing types beyond upscale single-family homes. Such legislation should ensure that present and future housing needs are analyzed in a regional context and that the analysis is reflected in the housing element itself, with clear, measurable production goals—new production and rehabilitation—for the community. The legislation should require an implementation program that includes concrete public action, including a program of regulatory barrier removal; and

- ongoing technical assistance from the state or regional planning agencies to assist in the development of affordable housing programs, including analysis of housing supply and demand, assistance in establishing mechanisms for establishing subsidy programs, rehabilitation programs to retain low-income housing stock, and regulatory barrier removal (see above).

This study has documented an extraordinary array of regional approaches from around the nation to address the need for affordable housing and a long history of concern about the problem. The diversity of approaches and the fact that such experimentation is taking place at the state, local, and regional levels are clear indications that the issue has gained a far broader constituency that it had more than 34 years ago, in 1968, when the National Commission on Urban Problems made its report to Congress and the president. While these programs vary in effectiveness due to resources, inherent flaws in program design, and aggressiveness in their administration, that they exist at all confirms, as the Millennial Housing Commission stated in its report to Congress (2002, 14), that "Affordability is the single greatest housing challenge facing the nation." It is an understatement to say that the programs described in this study are barely adequate to respond to this immense need. We hope APA's research can help states, regions, local governments, nonprofit organizations, employers, and the private housing sector better address that challenge, and continue to innovate and, in particular, actually produce affordable housing.

"Affordability is the single greatest housing challenge facing the nation."

—Millenial Housing Commission

ENDNOTES

1. Readers should be aware that the authors of this report understand that planners, of course, almost always favor more money for planning. However, during the course of the study, many of those interviewed by APA researchers frequently mentioned the cost of undertaking planning and the substantial impact it has on local governments, particularly on smaller ones with limited resources. This lack of funding is a very real problem, and designers of new housing programs cannot ignore it.

2. In 2002, California amended its planning statutes to prohibit a city or county from reducing, requiring, or permitting the reduction of the residential density—whether by administrative, quasi-judicial, or legislation action—to a level below that used by the state Department of Housing and Community Development to determine compliance with the housing element law, unless the city or county makes written findings supported by substantial evidence that the reduction is consistent with the adopted general plan, including the housing element, and that the jurisdiction's share of the regional housing need as specified. The local government would have to show, among other things, that the remaining residential sites identified in the housing element were adequate to accommodate the jurisdiction's share of the regional housing need. The new law also requires a court, until a sunset date of January 1, 2007, to award attorneys fees and costs of a suit to plaintiffs or petitioners who propose a housing development if the court finds that an action of a city or county violates these provisions, unless the court determines that awarding fees and costs would not further the purposes of the new law or that the action was frivolous (A.B. 2292, approved September 19, 2002, and adding California Government Code Section 64863).

3. The New Hampshire commission concludes, "Local land-use regulations and the municipal regulatory process have had a significant role in preventing or deterring the private sector from responding to the shortage of workforce housing. It is imperative that the Legislature take immediate steps to ensure that zoning and planning procedures at the local level as well as state policy and regulations that influence them change to promote the development of workforce housing, not impede it" (New Hampshire Legislative Commission 2002, 2). The commission report calls for a selective mechanism to expedite relief from municipal actions—as defined by criteria established by the New Hampshire legislature—which deny, impede, or significantly delay qualified proposals for workforce housing. The commission also recommends the provision of direct technical assistance for communities to carry out their responsibilities and to offer opportunities for the creation of workforce housing (referring to the mandate of the 1991 state supreme court decision, *Britton v. Chester,* 134 N.H. 434, 595 A.2d 491), a study commission to identify and review state agency rules, and regulatory policies that affect the cost of housing development or limit such development (p. 2).

4. For a statute providing financial incentives to local governments for removing barriers to low- and moderate-income housing as well as middle-income housing, see Florida Statutes, Sections 420.907 et seq. (2001) concerning the state housing incentives partnership, especially Section 420.9076 about the adoption of affordable housing incentive plans and committees. It should be noted that California has enacted incentive-based legislation, discussed in Chapter 7, that provides monies for assistance in the form of second mortgage loans for down-payment purposes to qualify-

ing cities and counties that have taken prescribed actions to remove regulatory barriers to affordable housing (California Assembly Bill 1170, approved September 20, 2002). The operation of the legislation was conditioned on the enactment of a state bond issue for affordable housing, Proposition 46, which passed in November 2002. Monies must still be appropriated for the program's purposes.

5. See, for example, Luger and Tempkin (2000). This excellent book is based on case studies in New Jersey and North Carolina and quantifies the differential effects of regulation, including land-use controls, on housing costs. It distinguishes "normal" from "excessive" costs.

6. For an example of a model statute that would require periodic review of local development regulations, see Meck (2002, Section 7-406), which requires a systematic review of the local comprehensive plan and development regulations every five years, focusing in particular on affordable housing issues.

7. As of 2002, there were more than 275 housing trust funds in cities, counties, and states. As part of that total, 38 states have established housing trust funds. Of these, 17 were created before 1990; another 15 were created before 1995. The remaining six have been put in place since then (Brooks 2002, 1, 7).

8. It was noteworthy to the authors of this report that local governments participating in ARCH actually contributed monies from their general funds as well as dedicated monies from locally levied linkage fees paid by developers. These contributions represent an important level of commitment (see Chapter 5, Table 5-1).

9. By contrast, the trust funds in Sacramento, California, described in Chapter 5, are separate, and each jurisdiction (the City of Sacramento and Sacramento County) allows homes to be built with the trust funds only in their respective jurisdictions.

10. David Godschalk (1992, 423), a professor of city and regional planning at the University of North Carolina at Chapel Hill has observed: "Attacking state and local regulations has also been popular within the homebuilding industry. This conveniently overlooks the predilection of private builders to orient their production to the up-scale end of the housing market, often ignoring less profitable opportunities to serve lower income consumers. How many times have we seen big, expensive houses crammed onto small lots that had been zoned for moderate-priced units?"

Partially Annotated List of References
and Staff Research Contact List

Adams, Thomas, and Wayne D. Heydecker. 1932. *Regional Survey of New York and Its Environs: Housing Conditions in the New York Region.* New York: Committee on Regional Plan of New York and Environs.

This report, on the New York Region's housing conditions, was prepared as a follow up to the seminal Regional Plan of New York and its environs.

Advisory Commission on Regulatory Barriers to Affordable Housing. 1991. *"Not in My Backyard:" Removing Barriers to Affordable Housing; Report to President Bush and Secretary Kemp by the Advisory Commission on Regulatory Barriers to Affordable Housing.* Washington, D.C.: U. S. Department of Housing and Urban Development.

This report looked at the impact of regulatory barriers to affordable housing at the federal, state, and local levels, and made 31 recommendations for action by federal and state government.

Advisory Committee on City Planning and Zoning, U.S. Department of Commerce. 1928. *A Standard City Planning Enabling Act.* Washington, D.C.: U.S. GPO.

This model statute, along with its companion, the Standard State Zoning Enabling Act, formed the basis for most of the planning legislation in the U.S. It did not, however, expressly address housing conditions as part of the "master plan."

Affordable Housing, Education & Development, Inc. 2002a. "AHEAD Services." Web page [accessed 1 July]. Available at http://www.homesahead.com/services.html.

This web page contains information about the services that AHEAD offers, including credit and budget counseling, financial assistance, special lender programs, home maintenance education, home rehabilitation planning and loans, and delinquency intervention.

_____. 2002b. "One-on-One Consultations." Web page [accessed 8 July]. Available at http://www.homesahead.com/sessions.html.

This web page includes information on the one-on-one homebuyer consultations that AHEAD offers.

_____. 2002c. "Secrets of Homebuying Workshops." Web page [accessed 8 July]. Available at http://www.homesahead.com/secrets.html.

This web page includes information about AHEAD's homebuying workshops.

_____. 2002d. "Affordable Housing, Education & Development, Inc." Web page [accessed 1 June]. Available at http://www.homesahead.com/about/html.

This web page contains general information about AHEAD, including the mission statement, affordable housing program information, education program information, and the development program information.

Allaire, Jerrold R. 1960. *Expressway Interchanges.* Planning Advisory Service Report No. 137. Chicago: American Society of Planning Officials.

This early Planning Advisory Service report by the American Society of Planning Officials, a predecessor organization to APA, looked at the impact of expressway interchanges on local governments and addressed which governmental levels should exercise regulatory control over nearby land uses.

American Society of Planning Officials. 1955. *The Urbanizing Influence of the Expressway and the Need for Planning and Zoning.* Planning Advisory Service Report No. 71. Chicago: American Society of Planning Officials.

An early work on the impact of expressways on undeveloped land in the rural and semi-rural fringes of urban areas.

Ames Department of Planning and Housing. 2002a. "2000 Rental Survey A: Yellow Survey." Web page [accessed 10 June]. Available at http://www.city.ames.is.us/housingweb/Rental_Housing_Survey_a-2000.htm.

This web page contains a survey that was sent out to all registered rental property owners in Ames and Story County, Iowa, regarding housing issues in the region.

_____. 2002b. *2001 Annual Report: Department of Planning and Housing.* Ames Department of Planning and Housing.

This annual report details the work of the Ames Planning and Housing Department in 2001. It includes a summary of housing activities, including information regarding the total number of homebuyers assisted through the Ames/Story County affordable housing program.

_____. 2002c. "Ames/Story County Partnership Affordable Housing Program." Web page [accessed 7 May]. Available at http://www.city.ames.ia.us/housingwebAffordableHousing/housing.htm.

This web page contains information about the Ames/Story County affordable housing program.

Applied Economics Research, Inc. 1987. *New Hampshire Housing Analysis Technical Report.* New Hampshire Office of State Planning, Concord.

A report setting forth a methodology for completing regional housing needs assessments in New Hampshire.

Association of Bay Area Governments. 2002a. "ABAG Regional Housing Distribution Model." Web page [accessed 22 July]. Available at http://www.abag.ca.gov/cgi-bin-rhnd_meth.pl.

This web page contains information about the methodology for distributing housing need allocations to local governments in the Bay Area.

_____. 2002b. "Adopted Platform on Growth Management." Web page [accessed 20 August]. Available at http://www.abag.ca.gov/planning/rgp/platofrm.

This web page contains information about the platform on growth management that has been adopted in the Bay Area by the Association of Bay Area Governments.

_____. 2002c. "Bay Area Census." Web page [accessed 24 July]. Available at http://census.abag.ca.gov/.

This web site provides a variety of information about the demographics of the Bay Area.

_____. 2002d. "Menu of Subregional Land Use Policies." Web page [accessed 22 July]. Available at http://www.abag.gov/planning/rgp/menu/index.html.

This web page contains information about sub-regional land use policies in the Bay Area, including location and intensity of urban development, mobility, natural resource protection and management, housing supply and affordability, and economic development.

_____. 2002e. "Regional Housing Needs 1999-2006." Web page [accessed 31 May]. Available at http://www.abag.ca.gov/cgi-bin/rhnd_allocation.pl.

This web page contains the fair-share housing need allocation for all local governments in the Bay Area.

_____. 2002f. "Regional Housing Needs: Frequently Asked Questions." Web page [accessed 22 July]. Available at http://www.abag.gov/planning/housingneeds.faq.htm.

This web page contains questions and answers about the Regional Housing Needs process.

_____. 2002g. "Regional Housing Needs Methodology." Web page [accessed 22 July]. Available at http://www.abag.ca.gov/planning/housingneeds/meth.htm.

This web page discusses the methodology that was used by ABAG for the 1999-2006 Regional Housing Needs Assessment, which was used to determine each jurisdiction's fair-share housing need. It includes links to sphere of influence numbers, the regional housing needs assessment schedule, and the final 1999-2006 allocation.

_____. 2001a. *Regional Housing Needs Determination for the San Francisco Bay Area: 2001-2006 Housing Element Cycle.* Oakland, Calif.: Association of Bay Area Governments.

This is the regional housing needs determination for the San Francisco Bay Area for the period 2001-2006. It includes a background and overview of housing needs in the Bay Area, a housing needs assessment, explanation of the methodology, local government review and appeals process, specific statutory requirements, a review of changes in California's housing element law since 1989, and related technical information.

_____. 2001b. *Table of Jurisdiction Comments and Proposed Revisions*. Oakland, Calif.: Association of Bay Area Governments.

This table summarizes the comments that were received by the Association of Bay Area Governments from local governments during the comment period for the Regional Housing Needs Analysis.

———. 2000. *Theory In Action: Smart Growth Case Studies in the San Francisco Bay Area and around the Nation*, Oakland, Calif.: Association of Bay Area Governments.

This report includes many case studies of smart growth strategies in the United States. It includes examples of housing supply, compact communities, comprehensive planning, land conservation, and urban revitalization.

_____. 1989. *Housing Needs Determinations.* Oakland, Calif.: Association of Bay Area Governments.

This report is the Association of Bay Area Governments housing needs analysis for 1988-1998 housing element cycle. It contains information about the determination of housing needs, housing needs for each jurisdiction in the Bay Area, and the local government review process.

Baer, William C. 1986. "The Evolution of Local and Regional Housing Studies." *Journal of the American Planning Association* 51, no. 2: 172-84.

Housing studies have evolved over 80 years from a set of disparate techniques into comprehensive fair-share housing allocation plans. During this evolution the individual studies also have served a variety of political purposes, although planners have not always admitted to them. A few states have sought to implement these plans by explicitly bringing them squarely into the political arena. They have done so by using analysis and plan as an agenda for improved vertical and horizontal intergovernmental sharing of control over land use decisions. This article provides a historic review of the evolution of these studies and their political uses as of 1986. The article formed the basis for the initial research in Chapter 2 of this Planning Advisory Service Report.

Baird+Driskell Community Planning. 1999. *Final Report: Housing Production Data Collection Process.* Oakland, Calif.: Association of Bay Area Governments.

This is a report of the effort to collect housing production data in the Bay Area.

Baird+Driskell Community Planning and Robert Odland Consulting. 2001. *Blueprint 2001: Housing Element Ideas and Solutions for a Sustainable and Affordable Future.* Oakland, Calif.: Association of Bay Area Governments.

This document outlines the requirements of California's housing element law, sets forth a process for addressing those requirements, and describes programs and strategies that can be used to address housing needs. It includes information on how to prepare an effective housing element, strategies for community participation, a directory of housing strategies and programs, and a directory of financial resources for housing.

Bay Area Alliance. 2002. "The Community Capital Investment Initiative and the Bay Area Family of Funds." Web page [accessed 24 April]. Available at http://www.bayareaalliance.org/brochure401.html.

This web page includes information about the Community Capital Investment Initiative, an effort to invest in poor neighborhoods in the Bay Area, and promote smart growth. It includes information regarding the objectives and strategies of the Community Capital Investment Initiative, and the role of the Bay Area Smart Growth Fund.

Bay Area Council. 2002a. "Bay Area Family of Funds Overview." Web page [accessed 19 April]. Available at http://www.basgf.com/.

This web page contains information about the Bay Area family of funds and the Bay Area smart growth fund.

_____. 2002b. "Organizational Profile." Web page [accessed 8 April]. Available at http://www.bayareacouncil.org/orgprofl/org_top.html.

This web page contains an overview of the Bay Area Council. It includes a discussion of each of its program areas: transportation, housing and land use, energy policy, environmental quality, sustainable economic development, education and workforce development, telecommunications and information technology, and water policy..

_____. 2002c. "Programs and Policy Initiatives: Housing and Land Use." Web page [accessed 8 April]. Available at http://www.bayareacouncil.org/ppi/hlu/hlu_pe1.html.

This web page includes information about the housing and land-use initiatives that the Bay Area Council is involved in, including the jobs-housing footprint project, legislation to increase the supply of housing, fair-share housing report, framework for sustainable development, and financing initiative for environmental restoration.

_____. 2000. *Housing Policy Strategic Framework.* San Francisco, Calif.: Bay Area Council.

This document contains information about the housing policy initiative of the Bay Area Council.

Bay Area Smart Growth Fund I, LLC. 2002. "Bay Area Smart Growth Fund I, LLC." Web page [accessed 19 April]. Available at http://www.basgf.com/.

This web page provides information about the Bay Area Smart Growth Fund. It includes information about the targeted areas, the goals of the fund, and the fund's management team .

Bergon, Sandy. 1990. Unpublished Memorandum. 9 July.

This memorandum, prepared for the Research Unit in the Connecticut Department of Housing, contains a list of which communities were exempt from the Connecticut housing appeals procedure in 1990. 26 cities were exempt from its provisions, having more than 10 percent of their housing stock in affordable units.

Blaesser, Brian et al. 1991. "Advocating Affordable Housing in New Hampshire: The Amicus Curiae Brief of the American Planning Association in *Wayne Britton v. Town of Chester*." *Journal of Urban and Contemporary Law* 40, no. 3: 3.

This brief was submitted to the New Hampshire Supreme Court by the American Planning Association in *Wayne Britton v. Town of Chester.*

Blue Ribbon Commission. 1989. *Housing Report*, Blue Ribbon Commission, Hartford, CT.

This is an early Blue Ribbon Commission report that resulted in the creation of Connecticut's affordable housing land use appeals procedure legislation, Section 8-30G of the Connecticut General Statutes.

Blue Ribbon Commission to Study Affordable Housing. 2000. *Report of the Blue Ribbon Commission to Study Affordable Housing.* Hartford, Conn.:Blue Ribbon Commission to Study Affordable Housing.

This is the final report of the Blue Ribbon Commission to Study Affordable Housing, established by special act 99-16 during the 1999 Connecticut legislative session. It includes recommendations and findings related to the Connecticut affordable housing land use appeals procedure.

Brandit, and Mike Kaszuba. 2002. "Egan Mayor and a Church Often Go Toe to Toe. *Minneapolis Star-Tribune*, sec. 1B, 14 May.

The City of Eagan, Minnesota, is criticized by a local clergyman for not doing enough about affordable housing.

Brooks, Mary. 2002. *Housing Trust Fund Progress Report 2002: Local Responses to America's Housing Needs.* Frazier Park, Calif.: Center for Community Change.

This report includes the results of a survey of housing trust funds in cities, counties, regions, and states in the U.S.

Buki, Charles. 2001. *Affordable Housing and Growth Management and Sprawl: Equity for Some Versus Affordability for Others*. Washington D.C.: Millennial Housing Commission.

This paper prepared for the Millennial Housing Commission established by Congress includes information about the connection between affordable housing and urban sprawl.

Burchell, Robert W., and *et al.* 1983. *Mount Laurel II: Challenge & Delivery of Low-Cost Housing.* New Brunswick, New Jersey: Center for Urban Policy Research, Rutgers University.

This is a compilation of articles about the Mount Laurel antiexclusionary zoning cases in New Jersey and issues raised by them, including those addressing housing allocation methodology.

Burchell, Robert W., David Listokin, and Arlene Pashman. 1994. *Regional Housing Opportunities for Lower-Income Households: An Analysis of Affordable Housing and Regional Mobility Strategies*. Washington, D.C.: U.S. Department of Housing and Urban Development.

This report, prepared by researchers at the Rutgers University Center for Urban Policy Research, is an extensive analysis of some 30 historic or current (as of 1994) programs intended to promote regional mobility and housing affordability. The programs are group into seven categories: (1) required local housing plans; (2) local housing allocation; (3) specialized access to appeals or rewards; (4) inclusionary zoning; (5) "regional public superbuilders"; (6) affordable housing finance strategies; and (7) portable certificates and vouchers .

Burnham, Daniel H., and Edward H. Bennett. 1970. *Plan of Chicago*. 2 ed. New York: Da Capo Press.

This is an unabridged republication of the first edition of the 1909 plan for the City of Chicago, (the "Burnham Plan"), which is one of the most famous and influential city plans in American city planning history.

Calavita, Nico, and Kenneth Grimes. 1998. "Inclusionary Housing in California: The Experience of Two Decades." *Journal of the American Planning Association* 64, no. 2: 150-69.

This article presents a case study of inclusionary housing in California. The article presents findings from a survey that shows that the 75 inclusionary housing programs that were surveyed produced more than 24,000 units of housing, provided flexibility to developers in meeting requirements, and have generally favored moderate-income homebuyers. Interviews with planners reveal that inclusionary housing programs in California have usually been established as a response to an actual or perceived threat of litigation due to noncompliance with California's housing element law.

California Department of Housing and Community Development. 2002a. *Court Rules in Favor of State in Housing Dispute.* Sacramento, Calif.: California Department of Housing and Community Development.

This is a press release for a Riverside, California, Superior Court decision in favor of the California Department of Housing and Community Development, in their lawsuit with the Southern California Association of Governments over fair-share housing need allocation.

_____. 2002b. "Housing Element Compliance Report." Web page [accessed 12 August]. Available at http://www.hcd.ca.gov/.

This web page is a listing of the status of housing elements in California jurisdictions, listed by county. It includes information about whether each housing element is in compliance, out of compliance, due, in review at HCD, or self certified; and the date that the housing element was reviewed. It should be noted that the figures on this web page are periodically revised.

_____. 2002c. "Housing Element Update Schedule." Web page [accessed 20 August]. Available at http://www.hcd.ca.gov/plainHTML.cgi.

This web page contains information on housing element update schedules for California jurisdictions.

California Department of Housing and Community Development, Division of Housing Policy Development. 2000. *Housing Element Status Report: A Report to the Legislature.* Sacramento, Calif.: California Department of Housing and Community Development.

This is a report to the California Legislature on the status of housing elements in California. It describes the status of local compliance with California's housing element law and highlights significant progress that has been achieved in increasing statewide compliance rates.

Central New Hampshire Regional Planning Commission. 2000. *Affordable Housing Needs Assessment for the Central New Hampshire Region: Year 2000 Update.* Concord, N.H.: The Commission.

This plan is the regional affordable housing needs assessment for the Central New Hampshire region.

_____. 2002. *Epson Master Plan.* Concord, N.H.: The Commission.

Chicago Metropolis 2020. 2002a. "About Chicago Metropolis 2020." Web page [accessed 5 April]. Available at http://www.chicagometropolis2020.org/description.htm.

This web page includes information about the structure, history, and organization of Metropolis 2020, a private organization that represents some of Chicago's business leaders.

_____. 2002b. "Chicago Metropolis 2020: One Region. One Future. Executive Summary of the Chicago Metropolis 2020 Report." Web page [accessed 5 April]. Available at http://www.chicagometropolis2020.org/summary.htm.

This web page is an executive summary of the Chicago Metropolis 2020 report.

_____. 2002c. "Make No Little Plans" What do you think the Chicago region should be like in 2020?" Web page [accessed 5 April]. Available at http://www.chicagometropolis2020.org/workbook.htm.

This web page includes information about the regional forums that were held by the Metropolis 2020 organization to identify issues of concern for the Chicago region.

_____. 2002d. *Recommendations for Developing Attainable Workforce Housing in the Chicago Region.* Chicago: Chicago Metropolis 2020.

This report contains recommendations and an agenda for affordable workforce housing in the Chicago Region, building on the recommendations of the Chicago Metropolis 2020 plan.

_____. 2002e. "Senior Executive Biographical Information." Web page [accessed 5 April]. Available at http://www.mhicagometropolis2020.org/seniorleaders.htm.

This web page includes information about the senior leaders of Metropolis 2020, a group of executives who dedicate their time to the goals and mission of Metropolis 2020.

_____. 2000a. *Getting to Work on Regional Issues.* Chicago: Chicago Metropolis 2020.

This report details the issues that were identified in the Metropolis 2020 plan, and includes information on the work that us being taken on by the organization to implement the plan.

_____. 2000b. "'One Region-One Future'." A Comprehensive Strategy of Regional Outreach and Collaboration: Community Forums." Web page [accessed 5 April]. Available at http://www.chicagometropolis2020.org/sld1.htm.

This web page contains the results of some of the community forums that the Chicago Metropolis 2020 organization held throughout the Chicago region in 1999 and 2000. It includes the top ten goals for the Chicago region that were created by each regional forum.

Ciccalone, Thomas J. 2002. "Affordable Housing Appeals Procedure, Percentages of Assisted Housing Units." Web page [accessed 23 September]. Available at http:www.state.ct.us/ecd/Housing/appeals.htm.

This memorandum identifies the status of Connecticut cities and towns in meeting their obligation under the state's affordable housing appeals procedure.

Committee on Regional Plan of New York and Environs. 1931. *The Building of the City, Regional Plan.* New York: The Committee.

Conrad, Richard. 1998. Memo to City Councils of ARCH Member Cities, July 9.

Council on Affordable Housing. 2002a. "COAH." Web page [accessed 11 October]. Available at http://www.state.nj.us/coah/#aboutcoah.

This website provides detailed information about the New Jersey Council on Affordable Housing.

_____. 2002b. "Council on Affordable Housing." Web page [accessed 11 November]. Available at http://www.state.nj.us/dca/coah.

This web page includes a variety of information about the New Jersey Council on Affordable Housing (COAH), including COAH newsletters, 2002 regional income limits, the New Jersey guide to affordable housing, COAH substantive and procedural rules, the New Jersey Fair Housing Act, a listing of proposed regulations, and other information.

_____. 2001a. *COAH Handbook 2001.* Trenton, N.J.: Council on Affordable Housing.

This handbook includes information on how to determine a jurisdiction's housing obligation, how to prepare a housing element, how to achieve a jurisdiction's fair-share housing obligation, entering the COAH process, sources of funding and assistance, and performance monitoring.

_____. 2001b. *COAH Options: COAHs 2001 Annual Report.* Trenton, N.J.: Council on Affordable Housing.

This annual report contains information about the activities of the Council on Affordable Housing from its inception through 2001.

_____. 2001c. *New Jersey Council on Affordable Housing 2001 Annual Report.* Trenton, N.J.: Council on Affordable Housing.

This annual report includes information on the number of affordable housing units that were completed, zoned, approved, or transferred via regional contribution agreements as of June 30, 2001. It also includes a listing of development fees collected by New Jersey jurisdictions as of June 30, 2001.

_____. 2000. *COAH 2000 Annual Report: Making NJ a Better Place to Live.* Trenton, N.J.: Council on Affordable Housing.

This annual report includes information on the number of affordable housing units that were completed, zoned, approves, or transferred via regional contribution agreements between 1987 and 1999. It also includes a listing of development fees collected by New Jersey jurisdictions as of 2000.

_____. 1999. *The New Jersey Council on Affordable Housing Presents Questions and Answers.* Trenton, N.J.: Council on Affordable Housing.

This report includes many questions and answers concerning the New Jersey Council on Affordable Housing and the New Jersey Fair Housing Act.

County Corp. 2002a. *County Corp: Developing the Dayton Region.* Dayton, Ohio: County Corp.

This PowerPoint presentation describes the history and accomplishments of the Montgomery County (Dayton), Ohio, Housing Trust Fund. It also described how the trust fund works, and includes photographs of housing that was developed using finds from the trust fund.

_____. 2002b. "Housing." Web page [accessed 1 April]. Available at http://www.mrecommerce.net/countycorp/housing.asp.

This web page includes general information about County Corp housing programs, including home improvement loans, homebuyer programs, and the housing trust fund.

_____. 2002c. "Montgomery County Housing Trust." Web page [accessed 1 April]. Available at http://www.mrecommerce.net/countycorp/HousingTrust.asp.

This web page features detailed information about County Corp and the Montgomery County (Dayton) affordable housing trust fund.

_____. 2002d. "Montgomery County Housing Trust Proposal Evaluation Criteria." Web page [accessed 1 April]. Available at http://www.mrecommerce.net/countycorp/HTEvaluation.asp.

This web page provides information about the purposes, administration, and project eligibility of the housing trust fund. It includes a listing of the point system used to evaluate score potential trust fund projects.

_____. 2001a. *County Corp: Developing the Dayton Region: 2001 Annual Report.* Dayton, Ohio: County Corp.

This annual report covers the Montgomery County, Ohio, Housing Trust Fund activities for the fiscal year 2001. It includes a listing of the projects that were funded by the trust find, a listing of expenditures, and demographics information about the recipients of the funds .

_____. 2001b. *Housing Trust Program Guidelines*. Dayton, Ohio: County Corp.

This report describes County Corp in Montgomery County (Dayton), Ohio, and its housing trust fund. It explains County Corp's role in the housing trust fund, who is eligible for funding, the priorities for the use of housing trust fund financing, general underwriting guidelines for trust fund financing, the application and review process, the how potential projects are reviews. Includes an application for funding from the trust fund .

_____. 2000. Projects/Programs funded in year 2000.

This unpublished document is a listing and description of all of the projects and programs that County Corp funded in 2000.

County of Sacramento, California. 2002. "Sacramento Area Facts." Web page [accessed 11 September]. Available at http://www.saccounty.net/portal.about/areafacts.htm.

This web page contains general demographic information about the city and county of Sacramento, California.

Croswell, Cathy E. 2002. Letter to Mayor Ronald Bartes, dated December 13, 2000, available from http://api.ucla.edu/rhna/RegionalHousingNeedsassessment/Correspondence/todayLetter5.pdf [accessed August 14].

Danielson, Michael N. 1976. *The Politics of Exclusion*. New York: Columbia University Press.

This book discusses a variety of affordable housing issues, including fair share approaches to affordable housing, zoning, and subsidized housing. It contains a case study of the adoption and implementation of the Miami Valley Regional Planning Commission's fair-share housing allocation plan for the five-county Dayton, Ohio, region in the early 1970s.

DeForest, Robert, and Lawrence Veiller. eds. 1900. *The Tenement House Problem including the Report of the New York Tenement House Commission of 1900*.

Eisenberg, Robert. 2002. *The Housing Transportation Connection: Building Better Communities through Better Housing and Transportation*. Paper prepared for the Millennial Housing Commission.

Fairbanks, Robert B. 2000. "From Better Dwellings to Better Neighborhoods: The Rise and Fall of the First National Housing Movement." In *From Tenements to the Taylor Homes: In Search of an Urban Housing Policy in Twentieth Century America*, edited by Roger F. Bauman, Roger Biles, and Kristin Szylvian. University Park, Pa.: Pennsylvania State University Press, pp. 21-42.

An excellent review of housing policy in the U.S. from 1895 to 1917.

Feiss, Carl. 1985. "The Foundations of Federal Planning Assistance: A Personal Account of the 701 Program." *Journal of the American Planning Association* 51, no. 2: 175-84.

This article describes the events leading to the Section 701 (of the Housing Act of 1954) federal planning assistance program. It outlines the accomplishments of the program and its importance to professional planning and education.

Field, Ben. 1993. "Why Our Fair Share Housing Laws Fail." *Santa Clara Law Review* 34, no. 1.

A discussion of the problems in obtaining judicial enforcement under the "substantially complies" standard of compliance in the California housing element law.

Fishman, Richard, ed. *Housing for All Under Law: New Directions in Housing, Land Use and Planning Law*. Cambridge, Mass.: Ballinger.

This is the report of the American Bar Association's Advisory Commission on Housing and Urban Growth. The report contains extensive recommendations on housing planning and regulatory barrier removal.

Flint, Anthony. 2002a. "Grafton Fights Loosing Battle on Development." *Boston Globe*. 9 September.

Account of the efforts of the town of Grafton, Massachusetts, to retain historic character, provide affordable housing, and fight mansionization.

_____. 2002b. "Towns Get Greater Housing Control." *Boston Globe*. 14 September.

This article discusses the new rules giving towns in Massachusetts more control over the construction of affordable housing projects built under the state's Chapter 40B affordable housing law.

Godschalk, David R. 1992. "In Defense of Growth Management." *Journal of the American Planning Association* 58, no. 4: 422-24.

Goetz, Edward G., Karen Chapple, and Barbara Lukermann. 2002. *The Affordable Housing Legacy of the 1976 Land Use Planning Act*. Minneapolis, Minn.: Center for Urban and Regional Affairs, University of Minnesota.

This report analyzes the Minnesota Land Use Planning Act of 1976. It focuses on how the Metropolitan Council has interpreted and administered the act and how 25 high-growth suburban communities have implemented it. The authors examine the degree to which land that was set aside for high-density housing twenty or more years ago actually resulted in the creation of affordable housing .2001.

_____. 2001. "Enabling Exclusion: The Retreat from Fair Share Housing in the Implementation of the Minnesota Land Use Planning Act." Paper presented at Annual Meeting of the Association of Collegiate Schools of Planning—November 7-11.

Goetz, Edward, and Lori Mardock. 1998. *Losing Ground: The Twin Cities Livable Communities Act and Affordable Housing*. Minneapolis, Minn.: Center for Urban and Regional Affairs, University of Minnesota.

This report is an analysis of the Minnesota Livable Communities Act. It finds that many communities have goals that will actually reduce their percentage of affordable housing, and that these reductions will have a region-wide impact. The authors argue that the standard by which a regional housing program such as the Livable Communities Act should be judges is the degree to which it increases the relative availability of affordable housing. By this standard, the authors find the program to be ineffective because it not only will fail to increase the availability, but will actually reduce it, for both ownership and rental units.

Hammer, Greene, Siler Associates. 1972. *Regional Housing Planning*. Washington, D.C.: American Institute of Planners.

This report provides a methodology on the analysis and forecasting of requirements for new housing production on a regional basis. Chapter 1 is an introduction. Chapter 2 describes the housing delivery process. Chapter 3 is the housing model intended to describe the supply and production requirements for housing, including the forecasted occupancy characteristics. Chapter 4 describes how to develop local housing policies and programs. A detailed technical appendix addresses sources of housing information, methods and approaches to be used by the planner in evaluating and understanding the local housing delivery system, the sequential procedures and approaches the planner might employ in development of a housing model, and a case example of use of the housing model for a hypothetical planning area. The forecasting methodology draws heavily on the 1970 publication *FHA Techniques of Housing Market Analysis*.

Hardinson, Dee. 2002. Letter to Julie Bornstein, dated August 30, 2000. Available from http://api.ucla.edu/rhna/RegionalHousingNeedsassessment/Correspondence/today2b.pdf [accessed August 14].

Tasha Harmon. n.d. "Tools Proposed or Used in Portland Region to Maintain/Increase Affordable Housing Stock for Low-Income Residents." Handout at *American Planning Association Conference, 2000*.

This conference handout document, written for the 2000 American Planning Association conference, includes a listing of all of the affordable housing tools that are available or used in the Portland region.

Harr, Charles M. 1996. *Suburbs Under Siege*. Princeton, New Jersey: Princeton University Press.

This book examines the activist role that the New Jersey courts took in the *Mount Laurel* anti-exclusionary housing rulings.

Herold, Roberta. 2002. *Between a Rock and a Hard Place: Housing and Wages in Vermont*. Montpelier, Vt.: The Vermont Housing Awareness Campaign and The Housing Council.

This report analyzes the causes and consequences of the gap between housing costs and wages in Vermont, as well as the gap between the demand for and supply of housing that working families can afford.

Herr, Philip B., and Associates. 2000a. *Affordability Zoning: Connecticut*. Newton, Mass.: Philip B. Herr and Associates.

_____. 2000b. *Affordability Zoning Data: Massachusetts*. Newton, Mass.: Philip B. Herr and Associates.

_____. 2000c. *Affordability Zoning Data: Rhode Island*. Newton, Mass.: Philip B. Herr and Associates.

_____. 2000d. *Zoning for Housing Affordability, A Study Prepared for the Massachusetts Housing Partnership Fund*. Newton, Mass.: Philip B. Herr and Associates.

This study was sponsored by the Massachusetts Housing Partnership Fund to examine the use and effectiveness of local exclusionary zoning provisions in providing affordable housing in Massachusetts. The Massachusetts experience with affordable housing was similar to that found in Connecticut, Rhode Island, and New Hampshire, which were also studied for comparison. The report is accompanied by four technical monographs analyzing affordability zoning provisions in each of the states.

Hodge, Gerald. 1963. "Use and Mis-Use of Measurement Scales in City Planning." *Journal of the American Institute of Planners* 29, no. 2: 112-21.

In discussing criteria by the American Public Health Association, Hodge noted studies in Boston and New York where "shabby physical conditions mask a viable social structure," and suggested that "social factors also have to be considered in order to define completely the dimension of sub-standardness".

Job-Center Housing. 2002a. "The Housing Crisis: Creating Housing Opportunities for California's Workforce." Web page [accessed 8 April]. Available at http://www.jobcenterhousing.com/problem.html.

This web page discusses the housing shortage in the Bay Area, California. It includes information on the housing shortage, the jobs/housing imbalance, and the condominium shortage .

_____. 2002b. "The Solution to California's Housing Crunch." Web page [accessed 8 April]. Available at http://www.jobcenterhousing.com/solution.html.

This web page outlines Job-Center Housing's strategy to solve California's housing crisis.

_____. 2002c. "Who We Are." Web page [accessed 8 April]. Available at http://www.jobcenterhousing.com/who.html.

This web page contains information about the Job-Center Housing Coalition, including a listing of housing, consumer, ethnic, labor, and taxpayer organizations that are members of the coalition.

Johnson, Elmer J. 2001. *Chicago Metropolis 2020: The Chicago Plan for the Twenty-First Century*. Chicago: The University of Chicago Press.

This plan for the Chicago region, produced by a private organization, includes goals and principles in five areas: public education and childcare, transportation, land use and housing, governance and taxation, and economic well-being. It includes recommendations in five areas: investing in children, enhancing the region's competitiveness, governing the region, race and poverty, and quality of life.

Joint Center for Housing Studies of Harvard University. 2002. *The State of the Nation's Housing*. Cambridge Mass.: Joint Center for Housing Studies at Harvard University.

This report is a general overview of the state of the nation's housing. It includes information regarding housing and the economy, demographics, homeownership, rental housing, and low-income housing needs.

Kantor, Harvey M. 1973. "Charles Dyer Norton and the Origins of the Regional Plan of New York." *Journal of the American Institute of Planners* 39, no. 1: 35-41.

Profile of Charles Dyer Norton, a banker and civic activist who launched the Regional Plan of New York and its Environs in the 1920s.

Katz, Bruce. 2002. "Increasing Housing Opportunities in Metro Kansas City." Web page [accessed 19 December]. Available at http://www.brookings.org/dybdocroot/es/urban/speeches/kcaffordable.pdf.

Text of a speech given before the Kansas City Forum in Kansas City, MO, by Bruce Katz, director of the Brookings Institution Center on Urban and Metropolitan Policy.

King County Consortium. 1999. *Consolidated Housing and Community Development Plan for 2000-2003*. Seattle, Wash.: King County Consortium.

This plan addresses the housing and community development needs of communities in King County outside Seattle.

King County Housing and Community Development Program. 2001. *Consolidated Annual Performance and Evaluation Report for the year 2001, Draft*. Seattle, Wash.: King County Housing and Community Development Program.

This report is a summary and evaluation of how the King County Consortium used its federal housing and community development funds in 2001 to help carry out the goals and objectives identified in its consolidated plan.

_____. 1998. *King County Market Rate Housing Affordability Study*. Seattle, Wash.: King County Housing and Community Development Program.

This study analyzes housing affordability both rental and ownership in the real estate market in King County, Washington. Includes information about housing affordability for King County as a whole, by region, and by jurisdiction.

King County Office of Regional Policy and Planning. 2002. "Annual Growth Report 2000." Web page [accessed 29 March]. Available at http://www.metrokc.gov/exec/orpp/agr/agr00/.

This is the annual report of growth in the King County (Seattle) region. It includes information about housing units, rental prices, and income.

Kirp, David L., John P. Dwyer, and Larry A. Rosenthal. 1995. *Our Town: Race, Housing, and the Soul of Suburbia*. New Brunswick, N.J.: Rutgers University Press.

This book is a chronicle of and the stories behind the *Mount Laurel* affordable housing litigation in New Jersey .

Koebel, Theodore C. 1987. "Estimating Housing Demand and Supply for Local Areas." *Journal of Planning Education and Research* 7, no. 1: 5-14.

This article presents a relatively simple approach for estimating housing demand and supply by county, based on methodology employed by the State of Kentucky in its

Annual Housing Report. Under it, household forecasts were derived by multiplying projected household population by the percentage of householders (heads of households) for each age, sex, and race category. Data on production (permits, starts, completion) can be obtained through national housing statutes, such as census reports. However, the article notes that reliance on building permits to measure housing production would result in a serious underestimate in Kentucky counties, where they may not be issued. Instead, the article notes that other permits, especially plumbing permits, are useful for supplying the more traditional data on housing production. A special regression methodology was used for estimating the number of mobile home placements by county.

Krefetz, Sharon Perlman. 2001. "The Impact and Evolution of the Massachusetts Comprehensive Permit and Zoning Appeals Act: Thirty Years of Experience with a State Legislative Effort to Overcome Exclusionary Zoning." *Western New England Law Review* 22, no. 381-430.

This study analyzes the Massachusetts Comprehensive Permit and Zoning Appeals Act (chapter 40B). The article includes a discussion of the law's origins, enactment, and provisions, an assessment of the law's impact, a discussion of the evolution of the law's administration by the state-level Housing Appeals Committee, and suggestions for future research. This is the most thorough assessment of the law published to date and is highly recommended as an example of program analysis.

Lieder, Constance. 1988. "Planning for Housing." In *The Practice of Local Government Planning*. 2d ed., edited by Frank S So, and Judith Getzels. Washington D.C.: International City Management Association, 388-91.

This section of *The Practice of Local Government Planning* addresses housing planning, housing forecasting and housing market analysis.

Lindgren, Jay R. 2001. Letter to James Nobles, January 18.

Listokin, David. 1976. *Fair Share Housing Allocation*. New Brunswick, N. J.: Center for Urban Policy Research.

This book analyzes fair-share housing allocation plans for low- and moderate-income housing as they existed in the mid 1970s. A technical appendix discusses housing allocation formulas used in the plan adopted by the Miami Valley Regional Planning Commission in Dayton, Ohio.

Live Baltimore Marketing Center. 2002. "Live Near Your Work Program." Web page [accessed 8 April]. Available at http://www.livebaltimore.com/homebuy/lnyw.html.

This web page offers information regarding the Maryland Live Near Your Work Program, including a list of participating employers, frequently asked questions, and grant instructions.

Luger, Michael I., and Kenneth Temkin. 2000. *Red Tape and Housing Costs: How Regulation Affects New Residential Development*. New Brunswick, N.J.: Rutgers University Center for Urban Policy Research.

Using case studies from New Jersey and North Carolina, this book examines the effects of regulation on housing costs. It begins by distinguishing normal from excessive regulatory costs. Normal regulations are those, it is commonly agreed, that protect health, safety and environmental quality and costs incurred to comply with the regulations in a reasonable period. The excessive costs are those that require developers to incur more hard costs than they would in some baseline case, as well as costs incurred due to unnecessary delays. The book quantifies these costs, and finds that the New Jersey per-unit costs and fees, as compared to North Carolina's, are too high by $9,500.

Mallach, Alan. 2002a. *Creating More Affordable Housing Under the New Jersey Fair Housing Act: Changing COAH Regulations to Increase Housing Production.* Trenton, N.J.: Housing and Community Development Network of New Jersey.

This is a white paper of the Housing and Community Development Network of New Jersey. It discusses New Jersey Council on Affordable Housing (COAH) regulations that govern three areas: inclusionary zoning (set-asides), developer fees, and regional contribution agreements. The report includes recommendations on how to improve the operation of these three components of the state's fair-share housing program.

_____. 2002b. "Draft Amendments to Fair Housing Act." October 31, 2002. Unpublished manuscript supplied to APA research staff.

Mandelker, Daniel R., et al. 1981. *Housing and Community Development: Cases and Materials.* Indianapolis, Indiana: Bobbs-Merrill Co.

Maryland Department of Housing and Community Development. 2002. "Live Near Your Work (LNYW) Fact Sheet." Web page [accessed 4 April]. Available at http://www.dhcd.state.md.us/lnyw/lnyw.cfm.

This web page includes general information on the Maryland Live Near Your Work program, such as eligiblity, application process, funding, and related links.

Maryland Department of Housing and Community Development, Live Near Your Work Program. 2001. *Live Near Your Work Survey Results.* Annapolis, Md.: Maryland Department of Housing and Community Development.

This report details the results of a survey of participants in Maryland's Live Near Your Work Program. It includes information about miles traveled to work, income, the Live Near Your Work incentive, and demographics of the participants.

Massachusetts Department of Housing and Community Development. 2002a. *Ch. 40B Subsidized Housing Inventory Through October 1, 2002, Revised April 24, 2002.* Boston, Mass.: Massachusetts Department of Housing and Community Development.

This report includes a listing of Chapter 40B subsidized housing for every community in Massachusetts. It includes the percent subsidized, the number of Chapter 40B units, and the total development units in 2001.

_____. 2002b. "Chapter 40B." Web page [accessed 18 June]. Available at http://www.state.ma.us/dhcd/Ch40B/Data.htm.

This web page contains information about the Massachusetts Chapter 40B affordable housing law.

_____. 2002c. "Overview of the Massachusetts Comprehensive Permit Law." Web page [accessed 18 June]. Available at http://www.state.ma.us.decd/components/hac/4summ-mc.htm.

This Web page contains general information about the Massachusetts Comprehensive Permit Law (Chapter 40B).

_____. 2001. *Guidance for Interpreting the Most Recent Changes to the Housing Appeals Committee Regulations.* Boston, Mass.: Massachusetts Department of Housing and Community Development.

This report includes information on recent changes to the Massachusetts housing appeals law regulations.

_____. 1999. "Guidelines for Local Review of Comprehensive Permits." Web page [accessed 18 June 2002]. Available at http://www.state.ma.us/dhcd/components/hac/guide.htm.

This web page is an overview of the Massachusetts Chapter 40B comprehensive permit law, which encourages the construction of affordable housing using locally granted permits.

Maxfield Research, Inc. 2000. *A Study of the Relationship Between Affordable Family Rental Housing and Home Values in the Twin Cities*. Minneapolis, Minn.: Family Housing Fund.

This report analyzes the relationship between affordable tax-credit, family rental developments and the values of owner occupied homes that are located near them. The report documented little or no evidence to support the claim that tax-credit rental housing for families has a negative impact on the market for owner-occupied housing in the surrounding area.

Mayberry, Bruce C. 2002. "Regional Housing Need Assessments in New Hampshire: Current Practice and Options for Change." Unpublished draft.

Unpublished draft of recommendations to State of New Hampshire on revamping the Regional Housing Needs Assessments that are required of regional planning commissions by statute.

Mayors' Regional Housing Task Force. 2000. *Affordable Housing for the Region: Strategies for Building Strong Communities*. St. Paul, Minn.: Metropolitan Council.

This report analyzes the need for affordable housing in the seven-county Twin Cities region. Among its conclusions: affordable housing can and must be synomous with quality housing; mixed income developments offer a preferred alternative for providing affordable housing, and higher densities are necessary to increase the supply of affordable housing. Among its recommendations: local officials must be "ambassadors" for affordable housing; and local governments should ensure that their planning and zoning systems enable affordable housing.

McFall, Trudy. 1977. *Housing Planning: How to Meet HUD's 701 Requirements*. Planning Advisory Service Report No. 330. Chicago: American Planning Association.

This report explains how planners can satisfy the housing planning requirements of the U.S. Department of Housing and Urban Development's now-defunct Section 701 (of the federal Housing Act of 1954). Those requirements provided the basis for most housing planning in the U.S. They included, among others, goals, objectives, and evaluation criteria; policies; use of available data; housing needs analyses and plans for the distribution of housing resources; and implementation and coordination programs.

Mckay, Sara. 1998. *Fair Share Allocation Strategies: A Review of Methods and Approaches*, Coalition for a Livable Future and the Community Development Network, Portland, Oregon.

This report surveys fair share policies across the country and summarizes methods used to determine a jurisdiction's share of affordable housing.

Meck, Stuart. ed. 2002. *Growing Smart Legislative Guidebook: Model Statutes for Planning and the Management of Change*. Chicago: American Planning Association.

Model enabling statutes for planning and land-use control in the U.S. in two-volume set. Chapters 4 and 7 contain model legislation for housing planning at the state, regional, and local levels. Model statutes and accompanying User Guide may also be downloaded at: http://www.planning.org/growingsmart/.

Meck, Stuart, and Kenneth Pearlman. 2002. *Ohio Planning and Zoning Law, 2002 Edition*. Eagan, Minn.: West Group.

Chapter 1 of this land-use treatise for Ohio, which is about the evolution of planning in the state, discusses the Miami Valley Regional Planning Commission's fair-share housing allocation plan of the 1970s for the Dayton region.

Metro Council. 2002a. "2040 Framework." Web page [accessed 3 May]. Available at http://www.metro-region.org/metro/growth/tfplan/2040.html.

This web page includes information about the Portland Metro 2040 growth concept, the urban growth management functional plan, the regional affordable housing strategy, and the livable communities workbook.

_____. 2002b. "Metro Code." Web page [accessed 24 September 2002b]. Available at http://www.metro-region.org/article.cfm?articleID=987.

This web page contains the text of the Metro Code, as adopted by Metro Council, the regional council for the Portland region.

_____. 2002c. *Metro Regional Data Book*, Metro Council, Portland, Oregon.

This report includes demographic information about the Portland region, including population, employment, and income data.

_____. 2000a. "Regional Affordable Housing Strategy Plan." Web page. Available at http://www.multnomah.lib.or.us/metro/growth/tfplan/affordable.html.

This is the regional plan for affordable housing for the three-county Portland region. The plan contains a regional housing goals and objectives, and implementation processes and an proposed assessment methodology. The plan sets forth affordable housing production goals extended to 2017 for each city and county (unincorporated area only) for the region. The individual goals total 90,479 units for household at less than 50 percent of the regional median household income. The goals are intended to be guidelines only, and compliance is voluntary. In addition, the plan recommends a series of policy amendments to the overall plan for the region. Extensive appendices document the process of plan preparation.

_____. 2000b. *Regional Affordable Housing Strategy: Recommendations of the Affordable Housing Technical Advisory Committee accepted by the Metro Council*. Portland, Ore.: Metro Council.

This report contains the recommendations of the affordable housing technical advisory committee, and the regional affordable housing strategy. It contains an assessment of affordable housing needs, goals, strategies for increasing and preserving affordable housing, and recommendations for implementation of the strategy.

_____. 1997a. *Housing Needs Analysis*. Portland, Ore.: Metro Council, Growth Management Services Department.

This report is a housing needs analysis for the Portland region. It includes background information, regional housing needs data, cost and attributes of single-family housing production, factors and barriers to affordable housing, an assessment of affordable housing needs and tools, and legal requirements and conclusions.

_____. 1997b. *Regional Framework Plan*. Portland, Ore.: Metro Council.

This plan is the regional framework plan for the Portland region. It includes chapters on land use, transportation, parks and open space, water, regional natural hazards, management, and implementation.

_____. n.d. *Urban Growth Management Functional Plan*. Portland, Ore.: Metro Council.

This is the functional plan for the Portland region. It includes affordable housing provisions.

Metropolitan Council. 2002. *Regional Report: Report to the Minnesota Legislature on Affordable and Life-Cycle Housing*. St. Paul, Minn.: Metropolitan Council.

This report to the Minnesota Legislature reviews the production of affordable and life-cycle housing in the Twin Cities, Minnesota, region in 2000. Summary data for 1996-2000 is also included.

_____. 2001a. "Guidelines for Priority Funding for Housing Performance." Web page. Available at http://www.metrocouncil.org/planning/funding_guidelines.htm.

This web page contains criteria and their relative weight that will used by the Twin Cities Metropolitan Council to determine a score - 0 to 100 points - and rank for cities and counties in the region to be used in the evaluation and prioritization of applications for funding by the Council. Examples of current funding decisions that will be affected include those for   community development - the Livable Communities Account (LCA) Fund and Smart Growth initiatives, transportation - TEA-21, the environment, Metro Environment Partnership grants, and other investments and programs such as those for parks and open space.   Application of these criteria carries out a Metropolitan Council recommendation in its Regional Blueprint.

_____. 2001b. *Housing Performance Scores – 2001.* St. Paul, Minn.: Metropolitan Council.

This report includes housing performance scores, rating sheet, and guidelines under the Metropolitan Livable Communities Act, which applies to the Twin Cities region.

_____. 2000a. *Regional Report: Metropolitan Livable Communities Fund*. St. Paul, Minn.: Metropolitan Council.

This report is the fourth annual report to the Minnesota Legislature on the Metropolitan Livable Communities Fund, established in 1995 by the Livable Communities Act. The report details the activities of the Metropolitan Council's administration of the fund in 1999, and summarizes the fund commitments throughout its operational history from 1996 to 1999.

_____. 2000b. *Regional Report: Participation in the Livable Communities Act Local Housing Incentives Account – 2000*. St. Paul, Minn.: Metropolitan Council.

This report to the Minnesota Legislature is a list of all of the municipalities that participated in the local housing incentive account program in 2000.

_____. 1999. *Regional Report: Report to the Minnesota Legislature on Affordable and Life-Cycle Housing*. St. Paul, Minn.: Metropolitan Council.

This report to the Minnesota Legislature includes three-year summaries of affordable housing construction in respondent communities, an analysis of housing production trends for the 1990s, and appendices of housing indicators. It also includes the results from a local attitudinal survey that addresses affordable housing issues.

_____. 1996. *Regional Blueprint*. St. Paul, Minn.: Metropolitan Council.

This report outlines the policies and steps that are needed in the Twin Cities, Minnesota, region, for the long-term and short-term health of the region. The critical policy issues that the report cites include: encouraging regional economic growth, fostering reinvestment in distresses areas, building strong communities, preserving the natural environment, setting directions for guided growth, expanding life-cycle and affordable housing opportunities, and providing financially sound regional public facilities.

_____. 1994. Housing policy for the 1990s: a Metropolitan Council position paper. St. Paul, Minn.: Metropolitan Council.

Metropolitan Mayors Caucus. 2002. *Housing Task Force: 2002 Housing Agenda*. Chicago: Metropolitan Mayors Caucus.

This report details the action agenda for housing in the Chicago region by the Metropolitan Mayors Caucus, a coalition of mayors in the Chicago region.

Millennial Housing Commission. 2002. *Meeting Our Nation's Housing Challenges: Report of the Bipartisan Millennial Housing Commission appointed by the Congress of the United States*. Washington, D.C.: Bipartisan Millennial Housing Commission.

This report is an overview of the nation's housing challenges. The report examines the importance of affordable housing to the nation's infrastructure, whether the nation is getting the housing outcomes it desires, how the nation can increase private-sector involvement, whether existing housing programs are living up to their potential and what reform measure should be taken, and what are the critical unmet housing needs. It includes recommendations to Congress relating to housing to modify existing federal programs or establish new ones. The report may be downloaded at: http://www.mhc.gov.

Minnesota Office of the Legislative Auditor. 2001. *Program Evaluation Report: Affordable Housing*. St. Paul, Minn.: Office of the Legislative Auditor.

This evaluation of the Livable Communities Act affordable housing program includes background information about affordable housing in Minnesota, information on costs and production of affordable housing, that factors that limit the production of affordable housing, and the resources that are needed to produce affordable housing. The evaluation found that the Livable Communities Act has been only marginally successful in producing affordable housing in the Twin Cities region.

Montgomery County Planning and Development Department and Maryland National Capital Park and Planning Commission. 1989. *Comprehensive Growth Policy Study, Vol. 2*. Silver Spring, Md.: The Commission.

Myers, Diana, and Barbara Hodas. 2000. *Report on the Countywide Housing Strategy*. Dayton, Ohio: County Corp.

This report is a countywide housing strategy for Montgomery County, Ohio. It identifies a vision for affordable housing and major unmet needs for the use of housing trust fund monies. The report includes the results of a survey of government agencies, developers, neighborhood organizations, and housing service providers on affordable housing in Montgomery County (Dayton), Ohio.

Nashua Regional Planning Commission. 2002a. "2000 Master Plan." Web page [accessed 16 August]. Available at http://www.gonashua.com/planning/planningboard/masterplan/housing.htm.

This master plan contains an affordable housing element.

_____. 2002b. *Town of Lyndeborough Master Plan Update*, The Commission, Nashua, New Hampshire.

This master plan contains an affordable housing element.

_____. 2002c. *Town of Pelham Master Plan Update 2002*, The Commission, Nashua, New Hampshire.

This master plan contains an affordable housing element.

_____. 1999. "Regional Housing Needs Assessment." Web page [accessed March 2002]. Available at http://www.nashurpc.org.

This regional housing needs assessment analyzes regional housing trends for people and families of all income levels. The report contains a compilation of relevant demographic and housing data for each of the region's twelve municipalities .

National Commission on Urban Problems. 1968. *Building the American City: Report of the National Commission on Urban Problems to the Congress and to the President of the United States*. Washington, D.C.: U.S. GPO.

Also known as the "Douglas Commission," after its chairman, Sen. Paul Douglas of Illinois, this commission produced the most comprehensive set of recommendations from a federal study group to date on the issues affecting urban areas in the U.S. The report is notable for its emphasis on regional housing planning, the importance of linking jobs to housing, and removal of regulatory and statutory barriers to affordable housing.

Nelson, Arthur C., et al. 2002. "A Discussion Paper Prepared for the Brookings Institution Center on Urban and Metropolitan Policy." In *The Link Between Growth Management and Affordable Housing: The Academic Evidence*. Washington, D.C.: Brookings Institution.

This is a discussion of the link between growth management and affordable housing.

New Hampshire Legislative Commission. 2002. *Reducing Regulatory Barriers to Workforce Housing in New Hampshire, Executive Summary, Report of the Legislative Commission established by Chapter 252 of the Laws of 2001*. Concord, N.H.: The Commission.

Non-Profit Housing Association of Northern California and Greenbelt Alliance. 2002. *San Francisco Bay Area Housing Crisis Report Card*. San Francisco, Calif.: Non-Profit Housing Association of Northern California and Greenbelt Alliance.

This report is about why the Bay Area continues to have a housing crisis, and what local governments can do to help end it. It details three actions that could double the creation of affordable homes in the Bay Area, which include: creating housing choices, dedicating local funds to housing, and adopting inclusionary zoning. The report says that because the California housing element law has no teeth, many city leaders shirk their responsibility of providing affordable housing.

North Country Council, Inc. 1995. *North Country 1995 Housing Needs Assessment*. Littleton, N.H.: The Council.

This affordable housing needs assessment, required by New Hampshire statutes, is for the North Country region surrounding Littleton, New Hampshire.

Ohio Department of Development. 2001. *Ohio County Profiles*. Columbus, Ohio: Ohio Department of Development Strategic Planning Office.

This report provides a variety of information about Ohio cities and counties, including population figures and county size.

Orfield, Myron. 1997. *Metropolitics: A Regional Agenda for Community and Stability*. Washington, D.C.: Brookings Institution Press.

This book discusses how demographic research, mapping, and politics led to the creation of a regional government in Twin Cities, Minnesota, and the passage of land use, fair housing, and tax-equity reform legislation.

Ottensmann, John R. 1992. "Central City Dominance in Metropolitan Areas and the Availability of Affordable Housing." *Journal of Planning Education and Research* 11, no. 2: 96-104.

This article describes how fragmented suburban jurisdictions that dominate metropolitan areas may limit the availability of affordable housing because of their restrictive land-use regulations. The article presents findings from a study of 46 of the largest 100 metropolitan areas. The study found that those areas where over half the population or land was constrained in central cities had fewer land use restrictions, and those areas with fewer land use restrictions had more affordable housing.

Payne, John M. 2001. "Fairly Sharing Affordable Housing Obligations: The *Mount Laurel* Matrix." *Western New England Law Review* 22, no. 365: 365-80.

This article contains background information on the *Mount Laurel antiexclusionary zoning* doctrine from New Jersey, an asssessment of what has been accomplished as a result of the New Jersey fair-share housing program, the "Mount Laurel matrix", and a proposed new approach to *Mount Laurel* compliance that establishes a two-tier system of constitutional fair-share obligations: one a "private share," recognizing the capacity of private markets to meet low- and moderate-income housing needs if regulated in the general interest, and the other a "public share," recognizing the resource capacities that are uniquely governmental.

_____. 1997. "Remedies for Affordable Housing: From Fair Share to Growth Share." *Land Use Law & Zoning Digest* 49, no. 6: 3-9.

Professor Payne argues that the allocation approach used in the New Jersey *Mount Laurel* system is complex and burdensome. A better way, he contends, is to use an allocation technique called "growth share." Under this approach, a community's fair-share obligation of the region's affordable housing would be a simple obligation to allocate a share of whatever growth actually occurs to low- and moderate-income housing. The approach would apply to both residential and nonresidential growth as well as new development on raw land and redevelopment of previously used land.

Pendall, Rolf. 2000. "Local Land Use Regulation and the Chain of Exclusion." *Journal of the American Planning Association* 66, no. 2: 125-42.

The study reported in this article tested connections between five land use controls and the racial composition of the communities that use them. A survey of localities in the 25 largest U.S. metropolitan areas showed that low-density-only zoning, which restricts residential densities to fewer than eight dwelling units per acre, consistently reduced rental housing; this, in turn, limited the number of Black and Hispanic residents. Building permit caps were also associated with lowered proportions of Hispanic residents. Other controls tested-urban growth boundaries, adequate public facilities ordinances, and moratoria-had limited effects on either housing types or racial distribution.

_____. 1999. "Opposition to Housing: NIMBY and Beyond." *Urban Affairs Review* 35, no. 1: 112-36.

A statistical analysis of NIMBY-based opposition to affordable housing projects in the San Francisco Bay Area. Pendall found that projects opposed by neighbors tended to be next to single-family housing and not to be next to multifamily housing. Projects with affordable housing also generated more NIMBY protests, although few citizen complaints explicitly mentioned affordable housing. Antigrowth and NIMBY protests were both more common in jurisdictions with lower median incomes. Institutional structure, Pendall observed, shapes protest with respect to affordable housing. He found that affordable housing projects with streamlined approval processes generated less controversy than the average project, even though one might expect affordable projects to draw more opposition. Pendall also observed that nonprofit groups who built affordable projects in the Bay Area were more professional and sophisticated, doing substantial background research and sometimes meeting with neighborhood residents and elected officials. They also avoid jurisdictions in which a project might die because of delay or denial by elected officials responding to irate constituents. Both of these factors, he wrote, can limit protest against affordable housing projects.

Pioneer Valley Planning Commission. 1989. *Regional Homes Project: Final Report*. Northampton, Mass.: Pioneer Valley Planning Commission.

Polikoff, Alexander. 1978. *Housing for the Poor: The Case of Heroism*. Cambridge, Mass.: Ballinger.

This book, by the attorney who litigated the *Gautreaux* case involving segregated public housing in Chicago, examines how public policies have contributed to metropolitan economic and racial segregation in two mutually reinforcing ways: first, by fostering the confine of impoverished blacks within central cities; and second, by facilitating the exodus of middle class whites from them. The author contends that the city will not lose its monopoly on black poverty unless and until a housing policy is developed that enables and encourages the dispersal of a significant portion of the black ghetto population into suburban white middle class communities. He argues that this will only come about through federal, and not local initiative.

Rappa, John. 1999. "Affordable Units Added between 1990 and 1998." Web page [accessed 19 July 2002]. Available at http://prdbasis.cga.state.ct.us.

This report includes information about towns that are exempt from the Connecticut housing appeals procedure.

Rappa, John, Kevin McCarthy, and Shonda Anne Leonard. 1999. *Affordable Housing Decisions*. Hartford, Conn.: Connecticut General Assembly Office of Legislative Research.

This report examines the case law for the first decade of the Connecticut housing appeals procedure. It summarizes ten decisions where the town's denial of an application for affordable housing was sustained by the court. Next it looked at the five cases where the local commission's approval was sustained against the abutter's appeal, and then discusses the 20 cases where the commission's denial was overturned by a court. It also summarizes two procedural cases that discuss the appeals process and who is entitled to appeal.

RDG Crose Gardner Shukert. 1998. *The Ames/Story County Housing Needs Assessment Study*. Ames, Iowa: Department of Planning and Housing.

This is an affordable housing needs assessment and action plan for Ames and Story County, Iowa. The report prompted a cooperative affordable housing program for municipalities in the county.

A Regional Coalition for Housing. 2002a. "Eastside Housing Trust Funds." Web page [accessed 25 March]. Available at http://www.archhousing.org/HTF/guidelines.html.

This web page includes guidelines and instructions for applying for funding from A Regional Coalition for Housing. It includes information on program funding and priorities.

_____. 2002b. "Eastside Housing Trust Fund Guidelines - 2001: First Round of Applicants." Web page [accessed 25 March]. Available at http://www.archhousing.org/HTF/guidelines.html.

This web page includes information about applying for funding from the ARCH trust fund, the first round of applicants in 2001, and the ARCH organization.

_____. 2001. *ARCH: East King County Trust Fund, List of Projects Funded, 1993-Spring 2001*. Redmond, Wash.: A Regional Coalition for Housing.

This report lists all of the projects that ARCH has funded since 1993, including funding, type of project, and number of units/beds.

Rhode Island State Housing Appeals Board. 2002. State Housing Appeal Board. unpublished document summarizing status of appeals in 2002.

This unpublished document, provided by the Rhode Island Housing and Mortgage Insurance Corporation, summarizes the status of housing appeals in 2002, under the Rhode Island housing appeals board.

Riis, Jacob. 1970. *How the Other Half Lives*. Reprint edition of 1890 edition. Cambridge, Mass.: Belknap Press.

Famed account of deplorable tenement housing conditions in New York City at the turn of the 19th century.

Roberta F. Garber Consulting. 2000. *Columbus and Franklin County Consolidated Plan 2000-2003*. Columbus, Ohio: Department of Trade and the Franklin County Mid-Ohio Regional Planning Commission.

This is the consolidated plan for the City of Columbus and Franklin County, Ohio, prepared to meet requirements of the federal Community Development Block Grant program.

Roberta F. Garber Consulting for the Columbus Urban League. 2001. *Fair Housing Plan: 2001-2003*. Columbus, Ohio: Urban League.

This plan is an analysis and action plan of impediments to fair housing choice in Columbus and Franklin County, Ohio.

Rockingham Planning Commission. 1994. *Regional Housing Needs Assessment 1994*. Exeter, N.H.: Rockingham Planning Commission.

This report was prepared by the commission pursuant to N.H.R.S.A. 36:47 to assist local planning boards in the preparation of local housing needs assessments. It provides a methodology for estimating need for affordable housing on a regional basis and allocating that need to towns within the region. Two allocation approaches are described. One distributes need based on employment, equalized assessed valuation, and vacant developable land. The other distributes need based on equalized assessment, in-town employment, vacant developable land, median family income, and total housing units. The actual allocations are presented in tabular form.

Roudebush, Janice, and Leslie J. Wells. 1980. *Low- and Moderate-Income Housing: Part I. Increasing the Supply and Availability.* Planning Advisory Service Report No. 350. Chicago: American Planning Association.

This report contains a collection of case studies on techniques to increase the supply and availability of affordable housing. These include: land assembly and write-down techniques; development corporations; recycling existing facilities; reducing the costs of home ownership; financing techniques (chiefly tax increment financing); increasing the accessibility of rental housing to low- and moderate-income households; and planning and management techniques, including inclusionary zoning.

_____. 1980. *Low-and Moderate-Income Housing: Part II. Conserving What We Have.* Planning Advisory Service Report No. 351. Chicago: American Planning Association. This monograph discusses techniques for conserving housing stock such as training, rehabilitation grants and loans, and a variety of code enforcement approaches, among others. While the examples are dated, the explanation of techniques is very clear and still relevant.

Sacramento Housing and Redevelopment Agency. 2002a. "Community Redevelopment Implementation Plan." Web page [accessed 30 August]. Available at http://www.shra.org/Content/CommunityDevelopment/ImplPlanTOC.htm. This is a redevelopment plan for communities in the Sacramento region. It includes a housing component and information about housing statutory requirements.

_____. 2002b. "About SHRA." Web page [accessed 30 August]. Available at http://www.shra.org/Content/AboutSHRA/About.htm.

This web page includes general information about the Sacramento Housing and Redevelopment Agency.

_____. 2002c. "Affordable Housing and Homeownership." Web page [accessed 11 September]. Available at http://www.shra.org/Content/Housing/Housing.htm.

This web page includes a lot of information about SHRA's affordable housing and homeownership programs.

_____. 2001a. *Multi-Family Housing Development Assistance Program (Draft).* Sacramento, Calif.: Housing and Redevelopment Agency.

This manual contains detailed information about the multi-family housing development assistance program, by the Sacramento Housing and Redevelopment Agency .

_____. 2001b. *Multi-Family Housing Lending Program.* Sacramento, Calif.: Housing and Redevelopment Agency.

This manual describes the multi-family housing lending program of the Sacramento Housing and Redevelopment Agency, including a program description, funding source requirements, program requirements, application process, and other terms and requirements.

_____. 2001c. *Performance Report for the Housing Trust Funds of the City and County of Sacramento.* Sacramento, Calif.: Housing and Redevelopment Agency.

This report contains information about the revenues and production of housing generated by the housing trust funds of the city and county of Sacramento and recommendations for the housing trust funds.

Sagalyn, Lynne B., and George Sternlieb. 1973. *Zoning and Housing Costs: The Impact of Land-Use Controls on Housing Price.* New Brunswick, N.J.: Rutgers University Center for Urban Policy Research.

A detailed study on land-use controls and their relationship to housing costs for single-family houses in New Jersey, this report found that the size the the house—directly affected by the minimum size regulation and indirectly affected by minimum lot size requirements, is the single most important factor explaining selling price variation. Lot size and large frontage specifications, the study found, are highly significant and highly intercorrelated.

Salkin, Patricia E. 1993. "Barriers to Affordable Housing: Are Land-Use Controls the Scapegoat?" *Land Use Law & Zoning Digest* 45, no. 4: 3-7.

Salkin responds to the 1991 U.S. Advisory Commission on Regulatory Barriers to Affordable Housing (the Kemp Commission) report on the housing cost impacts of local land-use control system in the U.S. Salkin advocates openly discussing the report's recommendations and launching an empirical study to refute or substantiate the document.

San Diego Association of Governments. 2002a. *Solving the Region's Housing Crisis*, San Diego Association of Governments, San Diego, California.

This fact sheet contains information about San Diego's regional approach to affordable housing.

_____. 2002b. "Demographics and Other Data." Web page [accessed 20 August]. Available at http://www.sandag.org.resources/demograohics_and_other_data/demographics/fastfacts/regi.htm.

This web page contains a variety of demographic information about the San Diego region.

_____. 2001. *Draft Affordable Housing Performance Report*. San Diego, Calif.: San Diego Association of Governments, San Diego, California.

This report details the San Diego region's progress toward meeting its affordable housing goals, based on information provided by the jurisdictions.

_____. 2000a. *Draft Regional Housing Needs Statement: San Diego Region*. San Diego, Calif.: San Diego Association of Governments, San Diego, California.

This regional affordable housing needs assessment includes the data and methodology on forecasting housing demand and allocating fair share housing to jurisdictions in the San Diego region.

_____. 2000b. *SANDAG Info: San Diego Region Population and Housing Estimates*. San Diego, Calif.: San Diego Association of Governments, San Diego, California.

This report contains demographic information about the San Diego Region, including housing estimates.

_____. 1998. *Housing Element Self-Certification Report: Implementation of a Pilot Program for the San Diego Region*. San Diego, Calif.: San Diego Association of Governments, San Diego, California.

This report sets forth the procedures developed by the San Diego Association of Governments housing element advisory committee for implementing the housing element self-certification option under California law.

_____. n.d. *San Diego Regional Growth Management Strategy: Solving the San Diego Region's Housing Crisis*, San Diego Association of Governments, San Diego, California.

This is a report on the affordable housing crisis in the San Diego Region and what SANDAG and its local governments should be doing about it as part of a set of regional strategies. The report may be downloaded at: http://www.sandag.org/uploads/publicationid/publicationid_37_732.pdf.

Scott, Mellier. 1969. *American City Planning Since 1890*. Berkeley, California: University of California Press.

A history of urban planning in the U.S. since 1890.

Second Mayor's Regional Housing Task Force. 2002. *Affordable Housing: Making It a Reality*. Minneapolis, Minn.: Metropolitan Council.

This report includes information on new methods to reduce construction costs, new means for improving sustainability, funding recommendations, and a series of case studies of affordable housing.

Seidel, Stephen R. 1978. *Housing Costs & Governmental Regulations: Confronting the Regulatory Maze.* New Brunswick, N.J: Rutgers University Center for Urban Policy Research.

This book analyzes the extent to which government regulations are responsible for the inflation in the price of new housing. Seven areas of regulation are examined in detail: building codes, energy conservation codes, subdivision requirements, zoning controls, growth controls, environmental controls, and financing regulations. It contains recommendations on how to reduce or eliminate unnecessary costs arising from such regulations.

Shafor, Ann M., and Roberta E. Longfellow. 1980. "Fair Share Housing: A Bibliography." *Council of Planning Librarians* 38.

This is a bibliography of reports and monographs on fair-share housing as of 1980. The authors are planners who developed the Miami Valley Regional Planning Commission's regional fair-share housing allocation plan for the Dayton, Ohio, region, the first plan of its type in the nation.

Shigley, Paul. 2001. "SCAG, HCD Fight Over Housing Target." *California Planning and Development Report* (February), p. 14.

This article provides information about the conflict in the San Diego region over fair-share housing needs.

Southern California Association of Governments. 2002a. "Housing Strategies and Plans." Web page [accessed 3 May]. Available at http://api.ucla.edu/rhnaHousingStrategiesPlans/HousingElement/Frams.htm.

This web page contains information about housing elements in California.

_____. 2002b. "Cities in Our Region." Web page [accessed 7 August]. Available at http://www.scag.ca.gov/counties/counties.htm.

This web page contains a variety of information about the local governments in the Southern California region.

_____. 2002c. *Housing Element Compliance Report*, Southern California Association of Governments, Los Angeles, California.

This report includes information about the Southern California's progress toward meeting the planning requirements of the State of California housing element law. If contains two parts: an update on jurisdictions' housing element compliance, and a listing of the building permits issued from January 1998 to December 2001.

_____. 2002d. "Regional Housing Development Program." Web page [accessed 14 August]. Available at http://api.ucla.edu/rhna/RegionalHousingNeedsAssessment/RHNABackground/PDF8aRHDP.pdf.

This web page includes background information about Southern California's regional housing needs assessment.

_____. 2002e. "Southern California Association of Governments Region Question and Answers." Web page [accessed 7 August]. Available at http://www.scag.ca.gov/census/.

This web page contains demographic information about Southern California.

_____. 2001. *Housing in Southern California: A Decade in Review*. Los Angeles, Calif.: Southern California Association of Governments.

This report is an overview of housing affordability, market trends, housing production, population growth, and the job/housing imbalance in Southern California.

_____. 1999. *Draft Regional Housing Needs Assessment*. Los Angeles, Calif.: Southern California Association of Governments.

This is the regional housing needs assessment for the Southern California region for the housing element cycle 1998 to 2005.

_____. n.d. *Regional Housing Need Assessment: Appeals Process for Requesting Revisions of Local Housing Need*. Los Angeles, Calif.: Southern California Association of Governments.

This report includes information about the process for requesting revisions of local housing need in the Southern California region.

Southern California Association of Governments and the University of California, Los Angeles Advanced Policy Institute. 2002. "RHNA Calculator." Web page [accessed 14 August]. Available at http://api.ucla.edu/rhna/.

This web page includes a calculator that allows users to determine the housing need for each local government in the Southern California region.

Southern California Association of Governments, Department of Planning and Policy, Community Development Section. 2002. *Housing Element Compliance Report*. Los Angeles, Calif.: Southern California Association of Governments.

This report contains information about local government's compliance with the California housing element law in Southern California. It also includes recommendations to improve the housing element process. It does not include housing production data by income level.

Southern New Hampshire Planning Commission. 2000. *Regional Housing Needs Assessment*. Manchester, N.H.: Southern New Hampshire Planning Commission.

This report analyzes the regional need for housing in the region surrounding Manchester, N.H. It is required by N.H. RSA 36:47, III. The assessment contains, among other things, housing unit projections for 2000 and 2015, and a fair-share housing apportionment for the 12 municipalities in the region. The allocation is a modification of the New Jersey "fair share" allocation formula. The estimate produced by meeting the formula is intended to be a "guideline" for each town.

Steffens, Lincoln. 1957. *The Shame of the Cities*. New York: Hill and Wang.

This book describes the corruption in city government and the conditions of urban slums in the U.S. at the beginning of the 20th century.

Strafford Regional Planning Commission. 1999. *Housing Needs Assessment for the Strafford Region*. Dover, N.H.: Strafford Regional Planning Commission.

This report is a housing needs assessment for seventeen eastern New Hampshire communities. It focuses on the region's housing growth and examines the status of affordable housing in the region.

Strategic Economics. 1999. *Building Sustainable Communities: Housing Solutions for Silicon Valley*. San Jose, Calif.: Silicon Valley Manufacturing Group.

This report presents an inventory of vacant and underutilized land available for housing development in the Silicon Valley, and calculates the total number of housing units that could be built on this land based on current local land use policy and market constraints. It includes background and demographic information, recommendations for future actions, and a number of land supply maps showing vacant parcels and general reuse areas in 21 Silicon Valley cities.

Tondro, Terry J. 2001. "Connecticut's Affordable Housing Appeals Statute: After Ten Years of Hope, Why Only Middling Results?" *Western New England Law Review* 23: 115-164.

This article explores the design of Connecticut's housing appeals statute, reviews the evidence of the effect of the law on the creation of affordable housing during its initial ten years, Connecticut Supreme Court decisions interpreting the act, and some thoughts on the failure of the "free market" approach to break down barriers to affordable housing.

_____. 1999. "Fragments of Regionalism: State and Regional Planning in Connecticut at Century's End." *St. John's Law Review* 73: 1123-57.

Tondro, a professor of law at the University of Connecticut and co-chair of the first Blue Ribbon Commission in Connecticut, discusses state and regional planning in Connecticut, including the state-level Affordable Housing Land Use Appeals Act.

Town of Henniker, New Hampshire. 2002. "Master Plan. Planning Board Conditionally Approved Chapter on Housing." Web page [accessed 5 September]. Available at http://www.cnhrpc.org/henniker/.

Twin Pines Housing Trust. 2002a. "Twin Pines Housing Trust Mission Statement." Web page [accessed 1 July]. Available at http://www.twinpineshousingtrust.com/summary.html.

This web page contains general information about Twin Pines Housing Trust, including its mission, organizational facts and history, listing of programs and properties, financing, and demographic information.

Twin Pines Housing Trust. 2002b. "Twin Pines News." Web page [accessed 1 July]. Available at http://www.trinpineshousingtust.com/2002june.html.

This web page contains an article about the work of the Twin Pines Housing Trust, a description of the homeownership program, and an update of projects underway.

U.S. Advisory Service on Intergovernmental Relations. 1973. *Regional Decision Making: New Strategies for Substate Districts.* Washington, D.C.: U.S. GPO.

This report discusses strategies for regional decision making.

U.S. Department of Housing and Urban Development. 2001. *Affordable Housing Design Advisor (and project book).* Washington, D.C.: U.S. Department of Housing and Urban Development.

This CD-ROM and accompanying workbook include information about the issues of design of affordable housing, including (1) what is good design, (2) why design is important, and (3) a gallery of affordable housing developments. It includes a design considerations checklist and lectures about various design and affordable housing issues.

_____. 1970. *FHA Techniques of Housing Market Analysis.* Washington, D.C.: U.S. GPO. This is a workbook of techniques developed by the Federal Housing Administration for analyzing regional housing markets.

United States Census Bureau. 2002. "American Fact Finder." Web page available at http://www.factfinder.census.gov/.

This web site provides census data for the United States, including 2000 census data.

Upper Valley Lake Sunapee Regional Planning Commission. 1995. *1995 Fair Share Housing Analysis.* Lebanon, N.H.: Upper Valley Lake Sunapee Regional Planning Commission.

This report is a fair-share housing analysis for a rural New Hampshire region; includes recommendations and conclusions.

Vermont Housing and Conservation Board. 2002a. *Annual Report to the General Assembly.* Montpelier, Vt.: Vermont Housing and Conservation Board.

This annual report details the activities of the Vermont Housing and Conservation Board from its inception through 2002.

_____. 2002b. *The Economic Benefits of Investments by the Vermont Housing and Conservation Board.* Montpelier, Vt.: Vermont Housing and Conservation Board.

This report provides information about the economic impact of investments made by the Vermont Housing and Conservation Board. It finds that investment by the board have leveraged $515 million from other private and public sources.

_____. 2002c. "Policy Position for Affordable Housing Projects." Web page [accessed 25 March]. Available at http://www.vhcb.orh/housingpolicy.html.

This web page includes the policy position for affordable housing projects funded by the Vermont Housing and Conservation Board. It includes five thresholds for using VHCB funds, including (1) perpetual affordability, (2) location in an area without a large number of negative features, (3) ready to proceed should funding be awarded, (4) financially viable, and (5) include a plan for addressing major health and safety issues.

_____. 2002d. *Vermont Housing and Conservation Board: 2002 Annual Report to the General Assembly*, Vermont Housing and Conservation Board, Montpelier, Vermont.

This annual report provides an overview of the community conservation and affordable housing that have been development throughout Vermont with assistance from the Vermont Housing and Conservation Trust Fund up to 2002.

_____. 2002e. "Vermont Housing and Conservation Board: Mission and History." Web page [accessed 25]. Available at http://www.vhcb.org/Mission.html.

This web page discusses the mission, history, and impact of the Vermont Housing and Conservation Board.

_____. 2002f. "Vermont Housing and Conservation Board Policies." Web page [accessed 25 March]. Available at http://www.vhcb.org/vhcbpolicies.html.

This web page includes Vermont Housing and Conservation Board policies, legislation, and adopted rules for housing and conservation.

_____. 1999. *Vermont Housing and Conservation Board: 1999 Report to the General Assembly*. Montpelier, Vt.: Vermont Housing and Conservation Board.

This annual report provides an overview of the community conservation and affordable housing that have been development throughout Vermont with assistance from the Vermont Housing and Conservation Trust Fund. The report states that in 1999 the Vermont Housing and Conservation Board resulted in the conservation of 29 farms, 4,700 acres of open space, and the development or rehabilitation of 408 units of affordable housing.

Vermont Housing Council and the Vermont Housing Awareness Campaign. 2002. "Between a Rock and a Hard Place: Housing and Wages in Vermont." Web page [accessed 25 March]. Available at http://www.vhcb.og/housingandwages.html.

This article discusses the disconnect between housing and wages in Vermont.

Vodola, Peter J. 1997. "A Survey of Case Law, Selected Land Use Board Decisions, and Opinions of Municipal Officials and Developers Concerning the Affordable Housing Appeals Procedure Act, 1990-1996." *Connecticut Law Review* 29: 1,235-91.

This article focuses on the results, in practical terms, of the Connecticut Affordable Housing Appeals Procedure Act. Vodola interviews local planners and others who have been involved with appeals under the act.

Wannon, Urlan A. 1995. *The Regional Imperative: Regional Planning and Governance in Britain, Europe, and the United States.* Bristol, Pa.: Jessica Kingsley.

A comparative analysis of regional planning in Britain, Europe, and the U.S.

Weinstein, Dorothy S. 1995. *North Country 1995 Housing Needs Assessment.* Littleton, N.H.: North Country Council, Inc., Regional Planning Commission.

The purpose of this report is to provide basic information to planning boards in the North Country, New Hampshire, region, for assessing their local housing supply. It includes data on housing characteristics, housing costs, types of housing, and socioeconomic analysis of the region. The report is intended to comply with the New Hampshire statute requiring regional housing need assessment.

Wheaton, Linda, John D. Landis, et al. 2000. *Raising the Roof: California Department of Housing and Community Development Projections and Constraints: 1997-2020, Statewide Housing Plan Update*. Sacramento, Calif.: California Housing and Community Development Department.

This is the statewide housing plan for California. It contains detailed projections of housing need for the state. It is used in the administration of the state's fair-share housing program.

Wheeler, Michael. 1993. "Regional Consensus on Affordable Housing: Yes in My Backyard?" *Journal of Planning Education and Research* 12, no. 2: 139-49.

This article states that the traditional response to exclusionary zoning has been state preemption through judicial intervention or special zoning appeals laws. An analysis of two Connecticut cases suggests another alternative: explicit intermunicipal negotiation over fair-share compacts. The article notes that despite economic downturn, participating communities are ahead of schedule in producing promised affordable housing units. However, the author cautions that difficult questions remain about the political accountability of private mediators, inclusion of stakeholders, and the potentially diminished role of existing regional planning agencies.

White, Mark S. 1992. *Affordable Housing: Proactive & Reactive Planning Strategies*. Planning Advisory Service Report No. 441. Chicago: American Planning Association.

This report describes how local governments are using land-use controls to provide low- and moderate-income housing without jeopardizing the public policies that lead to their implement. It describes proactive, supply-side approaches that employ regulatory controls such as inclusionary zoning, linkage fees, housing trust funds, and tax increment financing. It also discusses reactive, demand-side measures, including reforms in zoning and subdivision standards, the integration of factory-built housing or accessory apartments into a community, adjustment to growth management or environmental regulations, and procedural reforms intended to increase certainty in the approval process.

Staff Research Contact List

Amoroso, Alex. 2002a. Telephone interviews with Rebecca Retzlaff, July 22.

_____. 2002b. Telephone interviews with Rebecca Retzlaff, August 12.

Anderson, Karen. 2002. Telephone interview with James Schwab, November 7.

Baker-Latimer, Vanessa. 2002. Telephone interview with Stuart Meck, July 17.

Baldwin, Susan. 2002a. Telephone and e-mail interviews with Rebecca Retzlaff, August 21.

_____. 2002b. Telephone and e-mail interviews with Rebecca Retzlaff, August 30.

_____. 2002c. Telephone and e-mail interviews with Rebecca Retzlaff, September 3.

Basu, Mitra. 2002a. Telephone interviews with Rebecca Retzlaff, April 8.

_____. 2002b. Telephone interviews with Rebecca Retzlaff, April 15.

Bennett, Dave. 2002. Telephone interview with Rebecca Retzlaff, April 26.

Brewster, Ray. 2002. Telephone interview with Rebecca Retzlaff, July 8.

Burkholder, Rex. 2002. E-mail interview with Rebecca Retzlaff, October 8.

Carlson, Paul. 2002. Telephone interview with Rebecca Retzlaff, March 27.

Conrad, Richard. 2002. Telephone interview with Rebecca Retzlaff, March 27.

Cordingley, James. 2002. E-mail interview with Rebecca Retzlaff, June 25.

Firfer, Nancy. 2002a. Telephone interviews with Rebecca Retzlaff, April 19.

_____. 2002b. Telephone interviews with Rebecca Retzlaff, September 13.

_____. 2002c. Telephone interviews with Rebecca Retzlaff, November 4.

Fretz-Brown, Beverly. 2002. E-mail interview with Rebecca Retzlaff, September 30.

Friedman, Joan. 2002. E-mail interview with Rebecca Retzlaff, August 5.

Frost, Ben. 2002. Telephone interview with Stuart Meck, August 21.

Hannan, Paul. 2002. Telephone interview with Rebecca Retzlaff, June 19.

Harmon, Tasha. 2002. Telephone interview with Rebecca Retzlaff, September 20.

Hayes, Jeffrey R. 2002. E-mail interview with Stuart Meck, September 4.

Heuchert, Steve. 2002. Telephone interview with Stuart Meck, August 12.

Huntsinger, Theresa. 2002. Telephone interview with Rebecca Retzlaff, October 4.

Krefetz, Sharon Perlman. 2002. Telephone interview with Stuart Meck, November 8.

Krohn, Steve. 2002. Telephone interview with Rebecca Retzlaff, October 1.

Lieb, Jacob. 2002. Telephone interview with Rebecca Retzlaff, August 14.

Lohe, Werner. 2002. Memorandum to Stuart Meck, November 11.

Longfellow, Roberta. 2002. Telephone interview with Rebecca Retzlaff, April 1.

Mallach, Allan. 2002. E-mail to Stuart Meck, November 2.

Maus, Robert. 2000. Telephone interview with Stuart Meck, October 12.

Mayberry, Bruce C. 2002. Telephone interview with Stuart Meck, August 15.

Merritt, Nan. 2002a. E-mail interviews with Rebecca Retzlaff, September 6.

_____. 2002b. E-mail interviews with Rebecca Retzlaff, September 9.

_____. 2002c. E-mail interviews with Rebecca Retzlaff, September 18.

_____. 2002d. E-mail interviews with Rebecca Retzlaff, September 30.

Michael, Andrew. 2002. Telephone interview with Rebecca Retzlaff, April 15.

Morrish, William. 2002. Telephone interview with James Schwab, July 2.

Navarre, Joy Sorenson. 2002. Telephone and e-mail interviews with James Schwab.

Nichol, Polly. 2002a. Telephone and e-mail interviews with Rebecca Retzlaff, March 27.

_____. 2002b. Telephone and e-mail interviews with Rebecca Retzlaff, May 16, 2002b, July 8, 2002c, July 11, 2002d.

_____. 2002c. Telephone and e-mail interviews with Rebecca Retzlaff, July 8.

_____. 2002d. Telephone and e-mail interviews with Rebecca Retzlaff, July 11.

O'Connell, Brian. 2002a. Telephone interview with Stuart Meck, June 12.

_____. 2002b. E-mail interview with Rebecca Retzlaff, July 10.

Papagni, John. 2002. Telephone interview with Rebecca Retzlaff, April 19.

Peterson, Guy. 2002a. Letter to James Schwab, July 25.

_____. 2002b. Letter to James Schwab, July 29.

Ray, William. 2002. Telephone interview with Stuart Meck, August 21.

Riding, Derry. 2002. Telephone interview with Stuart Meck, September 18.

Scott, Laura. 2002. Telephone interview with Stuart Meck, July 25.

Shirk, Terry. 2002. Telephone interview with Rebecca Retzlaff, March 27.

Stretch, Ed. 2002. Telephone interview with Rebecca Retzlaff, April 12.

Sullivan, Arthur. 2002a. Telephone and e-mail interviews with Rebecca Retzlaff, March 25, 2002a, April 1, 2002b, May 8, 2002c, October 25, 2002d.

_____. 2002b. Telephone and e-mail interviews with Rebecca Retzlaff, April 1.

_____. 2002c. Telephone and e-mail interviews with Rebecca Retzlaff, May 8.

_____. 2002d. Telephone and e-mail interviews with Rebecca Retzlaff, October 25.

_____. 2002e. \h \r 1Fax to Rebecca Retzlaff, November 12.

Sullivan, Ed. 2002. Telephone interview with Rebecca Retzlaff, October 24.

Thompson, Sean. 2002. Telephone interview with Rebecca Retzlaff, July 17.

Tondro, Terry. 2000. E-mail to Stuart Meck, November 5.

Torpy, Brenda. 2002. Telephone interview with Rebecca Retzlaff, April12.

Torsell, Steve. 2002. Telephone interview with Rebecca Retzlaff, October 1.

Uba, Gerry. 2002a. Telephone and e-mail interviews with Rebecca Retzlaff, September 27.

_____. 2002a. Telephone and e-mail interviews with Rebecca Retzlaff,October 31.

Walsh, Matthew. 2001. Letter to Stuart Meck, May 2.

Weinstein, David. 2002. Telephone interview with Rebecca Retzlaff, March 27.

Westmont, Karen. 2002. E-mail interview with Rebecca Retzlaff, August 20.

Wenig, Deb. 2002a. E-mail interviews with Rebecca Retzlaff, November 20

_____. 2002b. E-mail interviews with Rebecca Retzlaff, November 22.

Wood, David. 2002a. Telephone interviews with Rebecca Retzlaff, July 8

_____. 2002b. Telephone interviews with Rebecca Retzlaff, July 10.

Zoger, Adam. 2002a. Telephone interviews with Rebecca Retzlaff, April 19

_____. 2002b. Telephone interviews with Rebecca Retzlaff, May 8.

List of State Statutes on Local Housing Planning

This digest of state statutes on local housing planning was prepared by John Bredin, Esq., a former Research Fellow with APA for its Growing Smart^{SM} planning statute reform project, and a Chicago area attorney specializing in planning and land-use controls.

Arizona: Housing element required for cities over 50,000 and authorized for all other cities. Must be based on analysis of existing and projected housing needs. (Section 9-461.05) No provision for a housing element for counties, only housing as one land use to be apportioned out in a land-use plan (Arizona Revised Statutes, Section 11-821).

California: Detailed multi-section provision on housing element, with specific reference to regional aspects (California Government Code, Sections 65580 et seq.). Detailed analysis of housing needs of region as well as locality; requirement that zoning provide sufficient land for housing of varied size (houses, multifamily) and type of occupancy (owner-occupied and rental); provision of assistance to affordable housing, and other provisions. Incorporates requirement for review by regional agencies and state department of housing and community development.

Connecticut: State housing plan and coordination with regions and municipalities to implement it (Connecticut General Statutes, Sections 8-37t, 8-37u). Regional plan authorizing section (Connecticut General Statutes, Section 8-35a) does not specifically mention housing. Municipal plans have to make specific provision for housing that considers regional needs, and are specifically required to be coordinated with the aforementioned state housing plan (Connecticut General Statutes, Section 8-23).

Delaware: County comprehensive plans must include a housing element that requires the county to consider "housing for existing residents and the anticipated growth of the area." The plan as a whole is to be coordinated with municipal plans and the plans of adjacent counties (Delaware Code Annotated, Title 9, Section 2656).

Florida: Strategic regional policy plans must address affordable housing—no detailed provided in Section (Florida Statutes, Section 186.507). Local comprehensive plans must include a housing element, described in some detail, under which the state land planning agency performs an "affordable housing needs assessment" for the local government and the local government must employ that assessment (Florida Statutes, Section 163.3177).

Illinois: Local comprehensive plan funded under Local Planning Technical Assistance Act of 2002 must include a housing element. The purpose of this element is to "document the present and future needs for housing within the jurisdiction of the local government, including affordable housing and special needs housing; take into account the housing needs of a larger region; identify barriers to the production of housing, including affordable housing; access [sic] the condition of the local housing stock; and develop strategies, programs, and other actions to address the needs for a range of housing options" (Illinois Public Act 92-0768, enacted 2002).

Idaho: Comprehensive plan must include a housing element, described in some detail, "unless the plan specifies reasons why a particular component is unneeded" (Idaho Code, Section 67-6508).

Kansas: No specific reference to housing, except that municipal comprehensive plans must address the "extent and relationship of the use of land" for, among other uses, residence" (Kansas Statutes Annotated, Section 12-747).

Kentucky: Comprehensive plans may include a housing element. No detail provided (Kentucky Revised Statutes, Section 100.187).

Maine: Local comprehensive plans must include an inventory and analysis of "residential housing stock, including affordable housing" and "ensure that its land use policies and ordinances encourage the siting and construction of affordable housing within the community," among other detailed provisions. Regional coordination with other municipalities is required for "shared resources and facilities" (Maine Revised Statues, Title 30A, Section 4326).

Massachusetts: Master plans must include a housing element that analyzes housing needs and provides objectives and programs to preserve and develop housing with a goal of providing "a balance of local housing opportunities for all citizens" (Massachusetts General Laws, Chapter 41, Section 81D).

Minnesota: The metropolitan government must adopt a development guide—a comprehensive plan—that has as one of its express goals the provision of adequate housing (Minnesota Statutes, Sections 4A.08, 473.145, 473.1455) Within the metropolitan area, local comprehensive plans must be consistent with the development guide (Minnesota Statutes, Section 473.175) and must include housing elements in their land-use plan that provide for "existing and projected local and regional housing needs" (Minnesota Statutes, Section 473.859) All municipalities are authorized and encouraged to adopt "community-based" comprehensive municipal plans that include an express goal of providing adequate housing (Minnesota Statutes, Sections 4A.08, 462.3535).

Mississippi: No specific reference to housing in the comprehensive plan (Missississippi Code Annotated, Sections 17-1-1, 17-1-11) or regional planning, though regional planning commissions are required to advise local governments on the planning of land use among other matters (Mississississippi Code Annotated, Sections 17-1-33, 17-1-35).

Nevada: Master plans for municipalities, counties, and regions are authorized to include a housing element, which must be based on and include an analysis of the existing housing stock, of the need for housing, and of the barriers to affordable housing (Nevada Revised Statutes, Section 278.160) The housing element is mandatory for counties with a population over 100,000 and municipalities in such counties (Nevada Revised Statutes, Section 278.150).

New Hampshire: Regional planning commissions are required to produce a regional housing needs assessment (New Hampshire Revised Statutes, Section 36:47), which a municipality is required to consider in adopting the ("shall include, if it is appropriate") housing element of their comprehensive plan (New Hampshire Revised Statutes, Section 674:2).

New Jersey: Local comprehensive plans must include a housing plan (New Jersey Statutes, Section 40:55D-28) that includes an inventory of existing housing, an analysis of existing and projected housing demand, an analysis of the community's fair share of affordable housing, and a designation of the land most appropriate for affordable housing development (New Jersey Statutes, Section 52:27D-310). See also the discussion of the New Jersey Fair Housing Act and the Council on Affordable Housing in Chapter 4 of this report.

New York: County comprehensive plans are authorized to address "existing housing resources and future housing needs, including affordable housing" and to consider "regional needs and the official plans of other governmental units and agencies within the county" (New York General Municipal Law, Section 239-d). Parallel provisions exist for regional comprehensive plans (New York General Municipal Law, Section 239-i).

Pennsylvania: Comprehensive plans must include a housing plan to "meet the housing needs of present residents and of those individuals and families anticipated to reside in the municipality," which is specifically authorized to include the preservation and rehabilitation of existing housing stock (53 Pennsylvania Consolidated Statutes Annotated, Section 10301).

Rhode Island: Municipal comprehensive plans must include a housing element "recognizing local, regional, and statewide needs for all income levels and for all age groups, including, but not limited to, the affordability of housing and the preservation of federally insured or assisted housing" that is based on analysis of the existing and projected situation and proposes specific responses and programs (Rhode Island General Statutes, Section 45-22.2-6).

South Carolina: Local comprehensive plans must include a housing element that specifically addresses "owner and renter occupancy and affordability of housing." The element must include an analysis of existing conditions, a statement of needs and goals, and implementation measures (South Carolina Code Annotated, Section 6-29-510).

Utah: The only reference to housing in the authorization for municipalities (Utah Code Annotated, Sections 10-9-301, 10-9-302) or counties (Utah Code Annotated, Sections 12-7-301, 12-7-302) is that the optional land-use element designates "housing" among the various land uses.

Vermont: Municipal plans must include a housing element that "includes a recommended program for addressing low- and moderate-income persons' housing needs as identified by the regional planning commission" (Vermont Statutes Annotated, Title 24, Section 4382). Regional plans must also include a housing element that "identifies the need for housing for all economic groups in the region and communities" (Vermont Statutes Annotated, Title 24, Section 4348a).

Washington: Local comprehensive plans are generally optional (Washington Revised Code, Section 36.70.320) but, if adopted, must include a land-use element that addresses "housing" among other uses and includes "standards of population density" and "estimates of future population growth" (Washington Revised Code, Section 36.70.330). Such plans may optionally include a housing element that includes surveys and reports to determine housing needs and housing standards to guide land development regulation appropriately (Washington Revised Code, Section 36.70.350). Under the growth management act, in counties over 50,000 residents or a 10 percent population increase over 10 years, the county and all municipalities must adopt and implement a comprehensive plan (Washington Revised Code, Section 36.70A.040) that includes a mandatory housing element "ensuring the vitality and character of established residential neighborhoods" (Washington Revised Code, Section 36.70A.070). The housing element must include an analysis of existing and projected housing needs, a statement of goals, identify land for housing, and make adequate provision for existing and projected housing needs.

West Virginia: Regional councils are authorized to make and disseminate studies of the region's resources in order to resolve existing and emerging problems, including housing (West Virginia Code, Section 8-25-8). Local comprehensive plans may addresses the uses of land, including "habitation" (West Virginia Code, Section 8-24-16) and "land utilization, including residence . . ." (West Virginia Code, Section 8-24-17).

Participants in APA Regional Planning
for Affordable Housing Symposium
October 29-30, 2000

Alex Amoroso
Senior Planner
Association of Bay Area Governments
Oakland, CA

William Baer
Professor of Planning
School of Policy, Planning and Development
University of Southern California
Los Angeles, CA

Caren Dewar
Director of Housing and Community Development
Metropolitan Council
Minneapolis, MN 55408

Tasha Harmon, AICP
Executive Director
Community Development Network
Portland, Oregon

Thomas Kemper
Builder Developer
Portland, OR

Roberta Longfellow, AICP
Housing Planner
Montgomery County
Dayton, OH

Rolf Pendall
Assistant Professor of City and Regional Planning
Department of City and Regional Planning
Cornell University
Ithaca, NY

Peter Reinhart
Hovnanian Builders
Red Bank

Jennifer Twombly
Research Director
National Low Income Housing Coalition
Washington, DC

Project Sponsors:
Dale Thomson, Social Science Analyst, HUD
Stephanie Jennings, Program Officer, Fannie Mae Foundation

APA Project Team:
Bill Klein, AICP
Stuart Meck, FAICP
Jim Hecimovich
Marya Morris, AICP
John Bredin

APA Project Team (not present at symposium):
Rebecca Retzlaff
Jim Schwab

Symposium Facilitator:
Joseph Whorton

A Bibliographic Research Note on Housing Forecasting and Fair-Share Allocation Formulas

This is a bibliographic research note on housing need forecasting for local and regional planning and on the formulation of distribution formulas for regional fair-share allocation plans. It is intended to direct the reader to some primary sources on the topic, but is not intended to work through the detailed mathematics or sophisticated methodological issues, which are beyond the scope of this report.

Housing Forecasting; Housing Market Analysis[1]

For the purposes of this research note, the terms housing forecasting and housing market analysis are interchangeable. A housing forecast projects the number of housing units that will be needed at some future time. A demand analysis is a reasonable projection of how the market is expected to perform based on population and economic growth.[2] The analysis includes a study of how many housing units currently exist, and an estimate of how many are likely to be removed from supply, and will thereby need replacement. For example, if high rise public housing is scheduled to be removed during the analysis period, it will need to be replaced by other forms of subsidized housing. The analysis then projects how many households will need housing.

As part of the demand forecast, need components are introduced. For example, if it is concluded that 25 percent of the existing public housing units are inadequate and will need to be replaced, then this number may be added to the supply requirement. However, it means that government will be responsible for demolishing and replacing these units, either through a public housing authority or some other vehicle. Similarly, if the analysis determines, through an analysis of census data and other sources, that 20 percent of the households are paying in excess of 30 percent of their gross income on housing, this can be identified as the number of units that need to be supported by subsidies, either by the provision of HUD Section 8 vouchers, or by the construction of housing that is affordable and subject to long-term affordability restrictions.

A housing forecast or market analysis for regional planning purposes involves the following steps: (1) defining the region or the market area, which can be a county, or a metropolitan area; and (2) identifying the components of change, which include the change in the number and composition of households, change in the number of vacant units, and change in the existing supply of housing. Assumptions about economic and population forecasts, household size (which can change over time), and the vacancy rate are key to the housing projections

Assuming that the analysis is begun sometime in the middle of the decade, a general and simple format for a five-year housing projection for 2006 to 2010 is shown in Table D–1.

(Note that this analysis does not further break down the housing demand or need into a variety of income subgroups. This topic is covered in some of the other technical publications on housing forecasting cited below).

Altering the assumptions of the forecasts will vary the outcomes. For example, increasing the desired vacancy rate will raise the number of units that need to be produced. Obviously, changing the rate of economic and population growth will also have an effect on the outcomes. In addition, if one has data for housing starts (and similar information on units lost to disaster, conversion, or demolition) for the first three or four years of the decade, that data may be arithmetically extrapolated to get to the middle of the decade.

Also entering into this analysis in some forecasts is the *jobs/housing balance*. Put simply, the jobs/housing balance is a ratio between the expected creation of jobs in a region or local government and the need for housing. The higher the jobs/housing ratio, the more the region or local government is generating jobs in comparison with housing, and is thereby exporting the need to create new housing units to other regions or other local governments.

TABLE D-1 HOUSING MARKET ANALYSIS FOR THEORETICAL MARKET AREA Steps	2000 Census	2005 Estimate	2010 Projection
Step 1: Collect and analyze population data			
a. Population	250,000	285,000	325,000
b. Group population	20,000	23,000	25,000
c. Household population (a-b)	230,000	262,000	300,000
d. Average household size–persons/household	2.8	2.7	2.6
e. Number of households (c/d)	82,100	97,000	115,400
Step 2: Collect and analyze housing data			
f. Total housing units	85,000	101,000	121,500
g. Occupied housing units	82,100	97,000	115,400
h. Vacant units (f-g)	2,900	4,000	6,100
i. Vacancy rate ((h/f) * 100)	3.4%	4.0%	5.0%
Step 3: Determine housing demand			
j. Change in number of households (e for 2010)– (e for 2000)	33,300		
k. Change in number of vacant units (h for 2010)– (h for 2000)	3,200		
l. Units lost to disaster	800		
m. Units lost to conversion	1,000		
n. Units lost to demolition	6,700		
o. Units lost that must be replaced (l + m + n)	8,500		
p. Total number of units needed 2000 to 2010 (j + k +o)			45,000
q. Housing starts (actual or estimated through interpolation), 2000 - 2005			19,000
r. Housing demand, 2006 - 2010			**26,000**

Source: Adapted from Constance Lieder, "Planning for Housing," in Chapter 12 of *The Practice of Local Government Planning*, 2d edition, Frank S. So and Judith Getzels, eds. (Washington, D.C.: International City Management Association, 1988), 390.

Here is a simple example (see Table D–2):

Assume that a regional planning agency is preparing a regional plan that includes a housing element. It develops four scenarios for different levels of economic activity and job creation.[3] It applies the jobs/housing (J/H) ratio to each:

In this comparison, the "jobs over housing scenario" has a J/H ratio of 2.0 and it means that job growth, while great, is accompanied by insufficient housing production levels that are resulting in a scarcity of workers living in the same region (or local government) in which the jobs are being created. A housing shortfall will be created. As a consequence, there will be a great deal of interregional or interjurisdictional commuting.

TABLE D-2
JOBS/HOUSING ANALYSES UNDER
THEORETICAL DEVELOPMENT SCENARIOS

Scenario Name	J/H Ratio	Jobs	Needed Housing Units
Base year (existing situation)1.625	1.625	455,000	280,000
Jobs over housing	2.0	900,000	450,000
Housing over jobs	1.25	750,000	600,000
Fast and balanced	1.5	900,000	600,000
Slow and balanced	1.5	600,000	400,000

Source: Montgomery County Planning Department and Maryland-National Capital Park and Planning Commission, *Comprehensive Growth Policy Study, Volume 2, Alternative Scenarios: Analysis and Evaluation* (Silver Spring, Md.: The Commission, July 1989) 2..

There are a number of useful works on housing forecasting, two of which were discussed in Chapter 2. One is the Federal Housing Administration's 1970 monograph, *FHA Techniques of Housing Market Analysis* (1970).[4] A second is *Regional Housing Planning: A Technical Guide*, published in 1972, and prepared by a consulting firm under the aegis of the American Institute of Planners.[5] It focused on the analysis and forecasting of requirements for new housing projection on a regional basis, and provided a series of worksheets to develop the forecasts. In contrast to the FHA manual, *Regional Housing Planning* was oriented to planners and public officials concerned primarily with evaluating and developing public policies, programs, and regulations to achieve housing goals.

A technical appendix to the New Jersey Administrative Code rules for the Council on Affordable Housing explains the basis for the housing forecasts used in that state's fair-share housing program.[6] Finally, the California Department of Housing and Community Development's state housing plan includes a detailed and well-illustrated analysis of its housing projection methodology, which is similar to that of New Jersey.[7]

C. Theodore Koebel authored a 1987 article on estimating housing demand and supply for local areas in the *Journal of Planning and Education Research*.[8] Koebel's work was based on efforts to produce an annual housing report for the State of Kentucky. The data are derived directly from administrative records or from estimation models that incorporate administrative data. Estimation models were developed for households (by age of householder and type of household), median family income, and mobile home shipments. No primary data collection is involved. These models may be used to monitor housing trends, conduct market analysis, and analyze housing affordability, shortages, and production patterns.

A 1997 article in the *Journal of the American Planning Association* set forth an approach used in Florida for the required housing needs assessment as part of a local comprehensive plan.[9] This article is notable for its discussion of the methodological issues related to projecting housing need and for translating need figures into a range of affordable housing prices and affordable rents.

Fair-Share Allocation Formulas

There are a number of monographs and plans that explain the technical aspects of fair-share housing allocation planning, which is discussed in detail in Chapter 4 of this report. The classic and early (1976) work is by Rutgers University researcher David Listokin, *Fair Share Housing Allocation*, where Listokin compares and contrasts fair-share formulae from a variety of jurisdictions.[10] Again, the New Jersey Administrative Code contains a technical appendix that describe the allocation system for that state's program.[11]

An excellent 1998 monograph by Sara McKay for the Community Development Network and the Coalition for a Livable Future in Portland, Oregon, looks at a diverse variety of formulaic and nonformulaic allocations techniques from around the country.[12]

Intended to help move the Portland Metro along in establishing a definition of fair share and an implementation policy for meeting fair-share standards (see below), it is a worthy update to David Listokin's pioneering work.

Finally, two regional housing plans, both described in Chapter 4, contain especially clear explanations of the allocation methodology. One is the plan for the Association of Bay Area Governments, which employs a variant of the jobs/housing balance ratio described above.[13] The second is the Portland Metro's 2000 Regional Affordable Housing Strategy, which includes a technical appendix describing how the affordable housing production goals for individual jurisdictions were derived.[14]

ENDNOTES

1. Portions of this discussion have been adapted from Constance Lieder, "Planning for Housing," in Chapter 12 of *The Practice of Local Government Planning*, 2d edition, Frank S. So and Judith Getzels, eds. (Washington, D.C.: International City Management Association, 1988), 388–391.

2. See generally Richard E. Klosterman, Richard K. Brail, and Earl G. Bossard, eds., *Spreadsheet Models for Urban and Regional Analysis* (New Brunswick, N.J.: Center for Urban Policy Research, 1993) (includes a variety of spreadsheet-based demographic and economic projection models).

3. These scenarios are adapted from Montgomery County Planning Department and Maryland–National Capital Park and Planning Commission, *Comprehensive Growth Policy Study, Volume 2, Alternative Scenarios: Analysis and Evaluation* (Silver Spring, Md.: The Commission, July 1989), 2–4. For a discussion of the impact of an increasing jobs/housing ratio on a housing shortfall in Alameda County, California, see Linda Wheaton, John D. Landis et al., *Raising the Roof: California Housing Development Projections and Constraints, 1997–2020, Statewide Housing Plan Update* (Sacramento: California Deparament of Housing and Community Development, May 2000), vol. 1, 147–149. Here, even in the face of a recession that reduced job growth, an increased jobs/housing ratio in the 1990s, 1.35, over the ratio of 1.26 in the 1980s, resulted in a production shortfall in the county of 21,750 units, equivalent to 45.5 percent of household growth during the 1990–1997 period.

4. U.S. Department of Housing and Urban Development, *FHA Techniques of Housing Market Analysis* (Washington, D.C.: U.S. GPO, August 1970).

5. Hammer, Greene, Siler Associates, *Regional Housing Planning: A Technical Guide* (Washington, D.C.: American Institute of Planners and U.S. Department of Housing and Urban Development, March 1972).

6. N.J.A.C. Ch. 93, Appendix A (Methodology). This methodology is also described in Chapter 4.

7. Linda Wheaton, John D. Landis et al., *Raising the Roof: California Housing Development Projections and Constraints, 1997–2020., Statewide Housing Plan Update* (Sacramento: California Deparament of Housing and Community Development, May 2000) (2 volumes). Chiefly responsible for the methodology was the University of Calforina at Berkeley's Institute of Urban and Regional Development.

8. C. Theodore Koebel, "Estimating Housing Demand and Supply for Local Areas," *Journal of Planning Education and Research* 7, No. 1 (Fall 1987): 5–14. See also C. Theodore Koebel, "Estimating Substandard Housing for Planning Purposes," *Journal of Planning Education and Research* 5:3 (1986): 191–202; L. Smith, "Household Headship Rates, Household Formation, and Housing Demand in Canada," *Land Economics* 60, No. 2 (1984): 180–88; J. Sweet, "Components of Change in the Number of Households: 1970–1980," *Demography* 21, No. 2 (1984): 129–30.

9. Paul F. Knoll, *et al.*, "Florida's Affordable Housing Needs Assessment Methodology," *Journal of the American Planning Association*, 63, No. 4 (August 1997): 495–508.

10. David Listokin, *Fair Share Housing Allocation* (New Brunswick, N.J.: Center for Urban Policy Research, Rutgers University, 1976).

11. N.J.A.C. Ch. 93, Appendix A (Methodology).

12. Sarah McKay, *Fair Share Housing Allocation Strategies: A Review of Methods and Approaches* (Portland, Ore.: Community Development Network and Coalition for a Livable Future, October 1998). This monograph is available from the Coalition for a Livable Future, 503–294–2884.

13. Association of Bay Area Governments, *Regional Housing Needs Determination for the San Francisco Bay Area* (Oakland, Calif.: Association of Bay Area Governments, 1999).

14. Portland Metro, *Regional Affordable Housing Strategy* (Portland, Ore.: Metro, June 2000), http://www.metro-region.org/metro/growth/tfplan/affordstrategy.html, (accessed Sept. 18, 2002). The methodology for the fair-share allocation appears in "Appendix B, Affordable Housing Production Goals," which is downloadable as a PDF file.

Excerpts from APA Growing Smart^{SM} Legislative Guidebook Containing Model Statutes on Fair-Share Housing Planning and State-Level Housing Appeals Boards with Commentary[1]

4–208   State Planning for Affordable Housing (Two Alternatives)

Alternative 1B A Model Balanced and Affordable Housing Act[2]

4–208.1   Findings and Purposes

The [legislature] finds and declares as follows:

(1) The primary goal of this Act is to assure the availability of a wide variety of housing types that will cover all income strata and accommodate a diverse population, including growing families, senior citizens, persons and households with special needs, single householders, and families whose children are of adult age and have left the household, with special emphasis and high priority on the provision of low- and moderate-income housing on a regional fair-share basis.

(2) The attainment of this goal of providing a regional fair share of the need for balanced and low- and moderate-income housing is of vital statewide importance and should be given highest priority by local governments. It requires the participation of state, regional, and local governments as well as the private sector, and the coordinated effort of all levels of government in an attempt to expand the variety of affordable housing opportunities at appropriate locations.

(3) Balance in employment and residential land use patterns should reduce traffic congestion, contribute to an improved environment through the reduction in vehicle-related emissions, and ensure that workers in this state will have available to them the opportunity to reside close to their jobsites, making the state more competitive and attractive as a location for new or expanded businesses.

(4) Balanced housing and employment opportunities at appropriate locations should result in reducing the isolation of lower income groups in a community or region, improving the safety and livability of neighborhoods, and increasing access to quality public and private facilities and services.

(5) State, regional, and local governments have a responsibility to use the powers vested in them to facilitate the improvement and development of a balanced housing stock that will be affordable to all income levels, especially middle-, moderate-, and low-income households, and meet the needs of a diverse population.

(6) The [legislature] recognizes that in carrying out this responsibility, each local government must also consider economic, environmental, and fiscal factors and community goals set forth in its local comprehensive plan and must cooperate with other local governments and state and regional agencies in addressing the regional housing needs for middle-, moderate-, and low-income households.

4–208.2   Intent

It is the [legislature's] intent to:

(1) ensure that local governments recognize their responsibilities in contributing to the attainment of the state's fair-share housing goal identified in Section [4–208.1] of this Act and that they endeavor to create a realistic opportunity to achieve this goal;

(2) ensure that local governments prepare and affirmatively implement housing elements in their comprehensive plans, which, along with federal and state programs, will realize the attainment of the state's fair-share housing goal identified in Section [4–208.1] of this Act;

(3) recognize that local governments may be best capable of determining which specific efforts will most likely contribute to the attainment of the state's fair-share housing goal identified in Section [4–208.1] of this Act;

(4)   ensure that each local government cooperates with other local and regional governments in order to address the regional housing needs of middle-, moderate-, and low-income persons;

(5)   assist local governments in developing suitable mechanisms and programs to promote and develop a variety of middle-, moderate-, and low-income housing types;

(6)   provide a mechanism whereby low- and moderate-income housing needs may be equitably determined on a regional basis and a fair share of such regional needs may be allocated to local governments by a state administrative agency [and by regional planning agencies];

(7)   encourage state agencies to reward performance by creating linkages between grant-in-aid programs and the provision of opportunities for low- and moderate-income housing by local governments;

(8)   implement programs that will encourage home ownership over a wide range of income levels, especially by middle-, moderate-, and low-income persons;

(9)   provide for a state administrative agency to review and approve local housing elements and provide state funding, when available, on a priority basis to those local governments with approved elements; and

[*or*]

(9)   provide for [regional planning agencies] to review and approve local housing elements under the general supervision of a state administrative agency which will provide state funding, when available, on a priority basis to those local governments with approved elements; and

(10) provide for a state administrative agency to prepare substantive and procedural rules to assist and guide [regional planning agencies and] local governments in carrying out this Act.

4–208.3   Definitions

As used in this Act:

(1)   "**Act**" means the Balanced and Affordable Housing Act of _____.

(2)   "**Affordable Housing**" means housing that has a sales price or rental amount that is within the means of a household that may occupy middle-, moderate-, low-, or very low-income housing, as defined by paragraphs (13), (14), (15), and (21), below. In the case of dwelling units for sale, housing that is affordable means housing in which mortgage, amortization, taxes, insurance, and condominium or association fees, if any, constitute no more than [28] percent of such gross annual household income for a household of the size which may occupy the unit in question. In the case of dwelling units for rent, housing that is affordable means housing for which the rent and utilities constitute no more than [30] percent of such gross annual household income for a household of the size which may occupy the unit in question.

It is the intention that the term "affordable housing" be construed throughout this Act to be synonymous with the term "middle-, moderate-, and low-income housing" and they are used interchangeably throughout this model. By contrast, when the term "low- and moderate-income housing" is used, the intent is to specifically exclude middle-income housing.

(3)   "**Authority**" means the entity designated by the local government for the purpose of monitoring the occupancy, resale, and rental restrictions of low- and moderate-income dwelling units.

(4)   "**Balanced**" means a recognition of, as well as an obligation to address, the need to provide a variety and choice of housing throughout the region, including middle-, moderate-, and low-income housing.

(5)   "**Council**" means the Balanced and Affordable Housing Council established by this Act which shall have primary jurisdiction for the administration and implementation of this Act.

(6) "**Density**" means the result of:

   (a) dividing the total number of dwelling units existing on a housing site by the net area in acres; or

   (b) multiplying the net area in acres times 43,560 square feet per acre and then dividing the product by the required minimum number of square feet per dwelling unit.

The result is expressed as dwelling units per net acre.

(7) "**Development**" means any building, construction, renovation, mining, extraction, dredging, filling, excavation, or drilling activity or operation; any material change in the use or appearance of any structure or in the land itself; the division of land into parcels; any change in the intensity or use of land, such as an increase in the number of dwelling units in a structure or a change to a commercial or industrial use from a less intensive use; any activity which alters a shore, beach, seacoast, river, stream, lake, pond, canal, marsh, dune area, woodland, wetland, endangered species habitat, aquifer, or other resource area, including coastal construction or other activity.

(8) "**Household**" means the person or persons occupying a dwelling unit.

(9) "**Housing Element**" means that portion of a local government's comprehensive plan, as identified in Section [4–208.9] of this Act, designed to meet the local government's fair share of a region's low- and moderate-income housing needs and analyze the local government's overall needs for affordable housing.

(10) "**Housing Region**" means that geographic area determined by the Council that exhibits significant social, economic, and income similarities, and which constitutes to the greatest extent practicable, the applicable primary metropolitan statistical area as last defined and delineated by the United States Census Bureau.

   [*or*]

(10) "**Housing Region**" means a substate district that was previously designated by the governor pursuant to [Sections 6–601 to 6–602, *or cite to other section of state statutes providing for substate districting delineation*].

(11) "**Inclusionary Development**" means a development containing [at least 20 percent] low- and moderate-income dwelling units. This term includes, but is not necessarily limited to, the creation of new low- and moderate-income dwelling units through new construction, the conversion of a nonresidential structure to a residential structure, and/or the gut rehabilitation of a vacant residential structure.

(12) "**Local Government**" means a county, municipality, village, town, township, borough, city, or other general purpose political subdivision [*other than a council of governments, regional planning commission, or other regional political subdivision*].

(13) "**Low-Income Housing**" means housing that is affordable, according to the federal Department of Housing and Urban Development, for either home ownership or rental, and that is occupied, reserved, or marketed for occupancy by households with a gross household income that does not exceed 50 percent of the median gross household income for households of the same size within the housing region in which the housing is located. For purposes of this Act, the term "low-income housing" shall include "very low-income housing."[3]

(14) "**Middle-Income Housing**" means housing that is affordable for either home ownership or rental, and that is occupied, reserved, or marketed for occupancy by households with a gross household income that is greater than [80] percent but does not exceed [*specify a number within a range of 95 to* 120] percent of the median gross household income for households of the same size within the housing region in which the housing is located.

   1. While the definitions of low-income and moderate-income housing are specific legal terms based on federal legislation and regulations, this term is intended to signify in a more general manner housing that is affordable to the great mass of

working Americans. Therefore, the percentage may be amended by adopting legislatures to fit the state's circumstances.

(15) **"Moderate-Income Housing"** means housing that is affordable, according to the federal Department of Housing and Urban Development, for either home ownership or rental, and that is occupied, reserved, or marketed for occupancy by households with a gross household income that is greater than 50 percent but does not exceed 80 percent of the median gross household income for households of the same size within the housing region in which the housing is located.

(16) **"Net Area"** means the total area of a site for residential or nonresidential development, excluding street rights of way and other publicly dedicated improvements such as parks, open space, and stormwater detention and retention facilities. "Net area" is expressed in either acres or square feet.

(17) **"Petition For Approval"** means that petition which a local government files which engages the [Balanced and Affordable Housing Council *or* regional planning agency] approval process for a housing element.

(18) **"Regional Planning Agency"** means a [*council of governments, regional planning commission, or other regional political subdivision*] with the authority to prepare and adopt a regional comprehensive plan.

(19) **"Regional Fair Share"** means that part of a region's low- and moderate-income housing units that is allocated to a local government by [the Balanced and Affordable Housing Council *or* a regional planning agency].

[(20) **"Regional Fair-Share Allocation Plan"** means the plan for allocating the present and prospective need for low- and moderate-income housing to local governments in a housing region that is prepared by a [regional planning agency] using regional need figures provided by the Balanced and Affordable Housing Council.[4]]

(21) **"Unnecessary Cost Generating Requirements"** mean those development standards that may be eliminated or reduced that are not essential to protect the public health, safety, or welfare or that are not critical to the protection or preservation of the environment, and that may otherwise make a project economically infeasible. An unnecessary cost generating requirement may include, but shall not be limited to, excessive standards or requirements for: minimum lot size, building size, building setbacks, spacing between buildings, impervious surfaces, open space, landscaping, buffering, reforestation, road width, pavements, parking, sidewalks, paved paths, culverts and stormwater drainage, oversized water and sewer lines to accommodate future development without reimbursement, and such other requirements as the Balanced and Affordable Housing Council may identify by rule.

(22) **"Very Low-Income Housing"** means housing that is affordable, according to the federal Department of Housing and Urban Development, for either home ownership or rental, and that is occupied, reserved, or marketed for occupancy by households with a gross household income equal to 30 percent or less of the median gross household income for households of the same size within the housing region in which the housing is located.

[*Commentary: Additional definitions may be needed as the Council develops procedures and programs to implement this statute. Some definitions may be incorporated into the Council's rules, thereby avoiding the need to amend the statute.*]

4–208.4 Creation and Composition of Balanced and Affordable Housing Council

(1) There is hereby established a Balanced and Affordable Housing Council.
(2) The Council shall consist of [15] members to be appointed by the governor. The members shall consist of the following:
    [(a) The commissioner or director of the Department of Housing and Community Development [*or similar state agency*];]
    [(b) The director of the State Housing Finance Agency;]

[(c) [3] members of a municipal legislative body [*or other elected chief officials of local governments, other than counties*];]

[(d) [3] elected chief county executives or legislators;]

[(e) [1] resident of low- or moderate-income housing or citizen designated as an advocate for low- or moderate-income persons;]

[(f) [4] citizens representing the various geographic areas of the state; and]

[(g) [2] representatives of professional and service organizations who are active in providing balanced and affordable housing, including, but not limited to, home building, nonresidential development, banking, construction, labor, and real estate.]

[**Commentary:** *A key to a successful balanced and affordable housing council is broad representation by both local officials and persons knowledgeable about building and managing middle-, moderate-, and low-income housing. While this model has the governor making all of the appointments to the Council, in some states, appointments could instead be made by the senate president and speaker of the house. Other designated appointments could include representatives of the state home builders association and/or a state chapter of the American Planning Association. While language has not been provided here, the Act may also indicate whether members should have term limits and how they may be removed.*]

4–208.5 Organization of the Council

(1) The Council shall elect its own chair and may create and fill such offices as it determines to be necessary. The Council may create and appoint advisory committees whose membership may consist of individuals whose experience, training, and/or interest in a program, activity, or plan may qualify them to lend valuable assistance to the Council. Members of such advisory bodies shall receive no compensation for their services but may be reimbursed for actual expenses expended in the performance of their duties.

(2) The Council shall meet at least [4] times each year.

(3) All actions of such advisory committees shall be reported in writing to the Council no later than the next meeting or within [30] days from the date of the action, whichever is earlier. The Council may provide a procedure to ratify committee actions by a vote of the members of the Council.

Alternative 1A B Strong Council with No Regional Planning Agency Involvement

4–208.6 Functions and Duties of the Council.

(1) The Council shall have the authority and duty to:

(a) determine, in consultation with affected agencies, and revise as necessary, housing regions for the state;

(b) estimate and revise at least once every [5] years the present and prospective need for low- and moderate-income housing for each housing region in the state;

(c) determine the regional fair share of the present and prospective need for low- and moderate-income housing for each local government in each housing region and revise the allocation of the need for each housing region in the state at least once every [5] years;

(d) review and approve housing elements submitted by local governments;

(e) establish a mediation process by which objectors to a local government's housing element may seek redress;

(f) hear and decide appeals on denials or conditional approvals from applicants seeking approval from a local government to construct an inclusionary housing project;

(g) adopt rules and issue orders concerning any matter within its jurisdiction to carry out the purposes of this Act pursuant to [*the state administrative procedures act*]; and

(h) prepare a biennial report to the governor and state legislature that describes progress in promoting affordable housing in the housing regions of the state.

(2) The Council may advise state agencies on criteria and procedures by which to reward local governments through the discretionary distribution of grants of state aid when their housing elements are approved pursuant to this Act.[5]

(3) The Council shall also take such other actions as may be necessary to carry out the purposes of this Act, including coordination with other federal, state, and local agencies.

Alternative 1A is appropriate in those states with either a weak (or nonexistent) county government and/or a weak (or nonexistent) regional planning organization. By contrast, in states that have strong county governments or strong regional councils of government, a regional planning agency can work in tandem with the Council in preparing the regional fair-share allocations and in reviewing and certifying local housing elements. These are discussed below.

Alternative 1B B Council and Regional Planning Agency Work in Tandem

4–208.6   Functions and Duties of the Council and [Regional Planning Agencies]

(1) The Council shall have the authority and duty to:

    (a) determine, in consultation with [regional planning agencies and other affected agencies], housing regions for the state, and revise such regions as necessary;

    (b) estimate the present and prospective need for low- and moderate-income housing for each housing region in the state at least once every [5] years;

    (c) review and approve regional fair-share allocation plans prepared by [regional planning agencies];

    (d) hear and decide appeals on denials or conditional approvals from applicants seeking approval from a local government to construct an inclusionary housing project;

    (e) hear and decide appeals of determinations by [regional planning agencies] pursuant to this Act and the Council's rules;

    (f) adopt rules and issue orders concerning any matter within its jurisdiction to carry out the purposes of this Act pursuant to [*the state administrative procedures act*];[6]

    (g) administer grants-in-aid to [regional planning agencies] to carry out their duties under this Act;

    (h) prepare a biennial report to the governor and state legislature that describes progress in promoting affordable housing in the housing regions of the state;

    (i) advise state agencies on criteria and procedures by which to reward local governments through the discretionary distribution of grants of state aid when their housing elements are approved pursuant to this Act; and

    (j) take such other actions as may be necessary to carry out the purposes of this Act, including coordination with other federal, state, and local agencies.

(2) [Regional planning agencies] shall have the authority to:

    (a) prepare and submit to the Council at least once every [5] years a regional fair-share allocation plan in accordance with Section [4–208.8] of this Act;

    (b) review and approve all local government housing elements that meet the requirements of this Act and the rules of the Council;

    (c) provide for a mediation process by which objectors to a local government's housing element may seek redress, subject to the rules of the Council;

    (d) provide technical assistance to local governments in the region in the development and implementation of local housing elements;

    (e) administer federal and state grant-in-aid programs to carry out the purposes of this Act; and

    (f) take such other actions as may be necessary to carry out the purposes of this Act.

4–208.7   Appointment of Council Executive Director; Hire by Contracts; Purchases and Leases; Maintenance of Public Records

(1) The Council shall appoint an executive director who shall select, hire, evaluate, discipline, and terminate employees pursuant to rules adopted by the Council. The executive director shall also be responsible for the day-to-day work of the Council, and

shall manage and supervise employees and consultants hired by contract, except for attorneys retained to provide independent legal counsel and certified public accountants retained to conduct independent audits. The executive director shall serve at the pleasure of the Council.

(2) The Council may hire by contract mediators and consultants for part-time or full-time service as may be necessary to fulfill its responsibilities.

(3) The Council may purchase, lease, or otherwise provide for supplies, materials, equipment, and facilities as it deems necessary and appropriate in the manner provided for in rules adopted by the Council.

(4) The Council shall keep a record of its resolutions, minutes of meetings, transactions, findings, and determinations, which record shall be public record.

[*Commentary: As an alternative, a Council may use the rule-making and contract authority provided for by the state's administrative procedures act or procurement laws.*]

Alternative 1A B Action by Council

4–208.8   Council Designation of Housing Regions; Determination of Present and Prospective Housing Need; Regional Fair-Share Allocations; Adoption of Need Estimates and Allocations

(1) The Council shall, within [18] months of the effective date of this Act, designate housing regions for the state, prepare estimates of present and prospective housing needs for low- and moderate-income dwelling units for each region for the next [5] years, and prepare regional fair-share allocations of those dwelling units to local governments in each region. The Council may, from time to time, revise the boundaries of the housing regions and shall revise the estimates and allocations at least once every [5] years hereafter. Revisions to the boundaries, estimates, and allocations shall be effected in the same manner as the original adoption.

(2) In developing the regional estimates, the Council shall consider the availability of public and private financing for housing and the relevant housing market conditions, shall use the most recent data and population statistics published by the United States Bureau of the Census, and shall give appropriate weight to pertinent research studies and reports by government agencies. The Council may utilize the assistance of the [state planning agency *or similar state agency*] in obtaining demographic, economic, housing, and such other data and in developing population, employment, and other relevant estimates and projections.[7]

(3) In calculating each local government's regional fair share, the Council shall consider, but shall not be limited to, the following factors:[8]

[(a) the number of vacant, overcrowded, or substandard housing units;

(b) the number of acres of:

1. vacant residential land;

2. residential land suitable for redevelopment or increased density of development; and

3. nonresidential land suitable, with respect to surrounding or neighboring uses, for residential use; in each local government presently sewered or expected to be sewered in the next [5] years;

(c) commuting patterns within each housing region;

(d) employment opportunities within each housing region, including the growth and location of moderate- and low-wage jobs;[9]

(e) the current per capita fiscal resources of each local government, defined by the total [nonresidential] real estate valuation of the local government, plus the total of all personal income, divided by current population;

(f) the relationship of each local government's median household income to the median household income of the region;

(g) the existing concentrations of low- and moderate-income households in each housing region;[10]

(h) the location of urban growth area(s) in an adopted regional comprehensive plan; and[11]

(i) the existence of an area of critical state concern[12] and any restrictions on development placed on it.]

(4) The Council shall adopt by rule, either individually or joined in one or more proceedings, designations for housing regions in the state, the estimates of present and prospective housing needs for low- and moderate-income dwelling units for each region for the next [5] years, and the regional fair-share allocations of those units to local governments in each region. At least [30] days prior to adoption, the Council shall transmit a copy of the proposed housing regions, as well as the estimates and allocations, to the legislative body of each local government in the state. Any interested party may submit written comments or may present oral testimony to the Council on the proposed rule. Such comments and testimony shall be incorporated into the hearing record. A copy of the adopted rule shall be transmitted by the Council to each local government's legislative body, to persons requesting a copy, and to the [state planning agency *or similar state agency*].

Alternative 1B B Action by Council and Regional Planning Agency

4–208.8   Council Designation of Housing Regions; Preparation of Estimates of Present and Prospective Housing Need; Preparation of Regional Fair-Share Allocation Plan by [Regional Planning Agency]; Adoption of Plan; Review and Approval of Plan by Council

(1) The Council shall, within [12] months of the effective date of this Act, designate housing regions for the state and prepare estimates of present and prospective housing needs for low- and moderate-income dwelling units for each housing region for the next [5] years. The Council may, from time to time, revise the boundaries of the housing regions and shall revise the estimates at least once every [5] years hereafter. Revisions to the boundaries and the estimates shall be effected in the same manner as the original adoption.

(2) In developing the regional estimates, the Council shall consider the availability of public and private financing for housing and the relevant housing market conditions, shall use the most recent data and population statistics published by the United States Bureau of the Census, and shall give appropriate weight to pertinent research studies and reports by government agencies. The Council may utilize the assistance of the [state planning agency *or similar state agency*] in obtaining demographic, economic, housing, and such other data and in developing population, employment, and other relevant estimates and projections.

(3) The Council shall adopt by rule, either individually or joined in one or more proceedings, the designations for housing regions for the state and the estimates of present and prospective housing needs for low- and moderate-income dwelling units for each region for the next [5] years. At least [30] days prior to adoption, the Council shall transmit a copy of the proposed housing regions and the estimates to each [regional planning agency] and the legislative body of each local government in the state. Any interested party may submit written comments or may present oral testimony to the Council on the proposed rule. Such comments and testimony shall be incorporated into the hearing record. The Council shall transmit a copy of the adopted rule to each local government's legislative body, to persons requesting a copy, and to the [state planning agency *or similar state agency*].

(4) The Council shall, within [12] months of the effective date of this Act, provide guidelines, data, and suggested methodologies to each [regional planning agency] in the state in order that each agency may prepare a regional fair-share allocation plan. In developing the guidelines, data, and suggested methodologies, the Council shall consider, but shall not be limited to, the following factors:

[(a) the number of vacant, overcrowded, or substandard housing units;

(b) the number of acres of:

1. vacant residential land;
2. residential land suitable for redevelopment or increased density of development; and
3. nonresidential land suitable, with respect to surrounding or neighboring uses, for residential use;

    in each local government presently sewered or expected to be sewered in the next [5] years;

(c) commuting patterns within each housing region;

(d) employment opportunities within each housing region, including the growth and location of moderate- and low-wage jobs;

(e) the current per capita fiscal resources of each local government, defined by the total [nonresidential] real estate valuation of the local government, plus the total of all personal income, divided by current population;

(f) the relationship of each local government's median household income to the median household income of the region;

(g) the existing concentrations of low- and moderate-income households in each housing region;

(h) the location of urban growth area(s) in an adopted regional comprehensive plan;[13] and

(i) the existence of an area of critical state concern[14] and any restrictions on development placed on it.]

(5) The Council shall adopt criteria for the review and approval of regional fair-share allocation plans prepared and adopted by [regional planning agencies] under this Act.

(6) Each [regional planning agency] in the state created pursuant to [*citation to statute creating or authorizing regional planning agencies*] shall prepare a regional fair-share allocation plan within [18] months of the effective date hereafter, and shall update and amend the plan at least every [5] years. In preparing the plan, each agency shall use the estimates of present and prospective need adopted by the Council for the region, and may use guidelines, data, and methodologies developed by the Council, or such other data and methodologies, provided that such data and methodologies are supported by adequate documentation, represent accepted planning techniques, and achieve an equitable allocation of need for low- and moderate-income housing to the region's local governments.

(7)[15] Each [regional planning agency] shall adopt by rule the regional fair-share allocation plan. At least [30] days prior to adoption, the [regional planning agency] shall transmit a copy of the proposed plan to each local government in the region, to the [state planning agency *or similar state agency*], and to the Council. Any interested person may present oral testimony to the [regional planning agency] on the proposed rule. Such comments and testimony shall be incorporated into the public hearing record, in accordance with the provisions of Section [6–105].[16] A copy of the adopted rule shall be transmitted by the [regional planning agency] to each local government's legislative body, to persons requesting a copy, to the [state planning agency *or similar state agency*], and to the Council. In transmitting the rule to the Council, the [regional planning agency] shall petition the Council for review and approval of the plan.

(8) Upon the receipt of a [regional planning agency's] petition for review and approval of a regional fair-share allocation plan, the Council shall undertake and complete a review of the plan within [90] days of submission of a complete plan. The Council shall approve the plan in writing if it finds that it is consistent with the requirements of this Act and with any rules of the Council. In the event that the Council does not approve the plan, it shall indicate in writing to the [regional planning agency] what changes should be made in the plan in order that the Council may consider it for approval upon resubmission.

(9) In the event that a [regional planning agency] does not submit a petition for review and approval of a regional fair-share allocation plan within the period specified in

this Act, fails to update the plan at least every [5] years, or fails to make changes as indicated by the Council within [90] days of the Council's decision on its petition and resubmits the plan for review and approval, the Council shall prepare a fair-share allocation plan for the region and shall adopt it in the manner provided for by paragraph (3), above. Upon adoption of the plan for a housing region, the Council may then also assume any duties of a [regional planning agency] as provided by Section [4–208.6(2)] of this Act for that housing region.

4–208.9   Contents of a Housing Element

(1) The housing element of the local government's comprehensive plan is intended to provide an analysis and identification of existing and prospective housing needs, especially for middle-, moderate-, and low-income housing, in its housing region and to set forth implementing measures for the preservation, improvement and development of housing. The housing element shall include all of the following, none of which may serve as a basis for excusing a local government from fulfilling its regional fair-share obligation:

(a) an inventory of the local government's housing stock by age, condition, purchase or rental value, occupancy characteristics, and type, including the number of units affordable to middle-, moderate-, and low-income households and the number of substandard housing units capable of being rehabilitated;

(b) a projection of the local government's housing stock, including the probable future construction of middle-, moderate-, and low-income housing for the next [5] years, taking into account, but not necessarily limited to, construction permits issued, preliminary as well as final approvals of applications for development, and all lands identified by the local government for probable residential development;

(c) an analysis of the local government's demographic characteristics, including but not necessarily limited to, household size, income level, and age of residents;

(d) an analysis of the existing and probable future employment characteristics and opportunities within the boundaries of the local government, especially those jobs that will pay moderate or low wages;

(e) an analysis of the existing and planned infrastructure capacity, including, but not limited to sewage and water treatment, sewer and water lines, and roads;

(f) a statement of the local government's own assessment of its present and prospective housing needs for all income levels, including its regional fair share for low- and moderate-income housing, and its capacity to accommodate those needs. The regional fair share as determined by the [Council *or* regional planning agency] shall form the minimum basis for the local government's determination of its own fair share;

(g) an identification of lands within the local government that are most appropriate for the construction of low- and moderate-income housing and of existing structures most appropriate for conversion to, or rehabilitation for, low- and moderate-income housing, including a consideration of lands and structures of developers who have expressed a commitment to provide low- and moderate-income housing and lands and structures that are publicly or semi-publicly owned;

(h) a statement of the local government's housing goals and policies. As part of the housing element, the local government can provide for its fair share by any technique or combination of techniques which provides a realistic opportunity for the provision of its fair share. The housing element should contain an analysis demonstrating that it will provide such a realistic opportunity. The local government should review its land-use and other relevant ordinances to incorporate provisions for low-and moderate-income housing and remove any unnecessary cost generating features that would affect whether housing is affordable. The model legislation provides, in (i) below, for the elimination or reduction of unnecessary cost generating features for all housing or affordable housing (on the theory that such action would reduce housing costs overall) or for only inclusionary developments (on the theory that it would ensure project feasibility).

(i) the text of adopted or proposed ordinances or regulations of the local government that are intended to eliminate or reduce unnecessary cost generating requirements for [all housing *or* affordable housing *or* inclusionary developments]; and

(j) the text of adopted or proposed ordinances or regulations of the local government that are intended to provide a realistic opportunity for the development of low- and moderate-income housing. Such ordinances or regulations shall consider the following techniques, as well as others that may be proposed by the local government or recommended by the Council as a means of assuring the achievement of the local government's regional fair share, removing barriers to and providing incentives for the construction of low- and moderate-income housing and generally removing constraints that unnecessarily contribute to housing costs or unreasonably restrict land supply:[17]

1. expanding or rehabilitating public infrastructure;

2. reserving infrastructure capacity for low- and moderate-income housing;

3. establishing a process by which the local government may consider, before adoption, policies, procedures, ordinances, regulations, or plan provisions that may have a significant impact on the cost of housing;

4. designating a sufficient supply of sites in the housing element that will be zoned at densities that may accommodate low- and moderate-income housing, rezoning lands for densities necessary to assure the economic viability of any inclusionary developments, and giving density bonuses for mandatory set-asides of low- and moderate-income dwelling units as a condition of development approval;[18]

5. establishing controls to ensure that once low- and moderate-income housing is built or rehabilitated through subsidies or other means, its availability will be maintained through measures such as, but not limited to, those that establish income qualifications for low- and moderate-income housing residents, promote affirmative marketing measures, and regulate the price and rents of such housing, including the resale price, pursuant to Section [4–208.22] below;

6. establishing development or linkage fees, where appropriate, authorizing such other land dedications or cash contributions by a nonresidential developer in lieu of constructing or rehabilitating low- and moderate-income housing, the need for which arises from the nonresidential development, generating other dedicated revenue sources, or committing other financial resources to provide funding for low- and moderate-income housing. Such development or linkage fees, land dedications, cash contributions, and dedicated revenue sources may be used for the following activities or other activities approved by the Council: rehabilitation; new construction; purchase of land for low- and moderate- income housing; improvement of land for low- and moderate-income housing; and assistance designed to render units to be more affordable;

7. modifying procedures to expedite the processing of permits for inclusionary developments and modifying development fee requirements, including reduction or waiver of fees and alternative methods of fee payment;

8. using funds obtained from any state or federal subsidy toward the construction of low- and moderate- income housing; and

9. providing tax abatements or other incentives, as appropriate, for the purposes of providing low- and moderate-income housing.

4–208.10   Submission of Housing Element to [Council *or* Regional Planning Agency]

(1) No later than [date], each local government shall prepare and submit to the [Council *or* regional planning agency] a housing element and a petition for approval in a form prescribed by the Council.

(2) The [Council *or* regional planning agency] shall complete the review of the housing element and determine whether to approve the element within [90] days after submission of a complete document. This [90] day period may be extended for an additional [60] days by the written consent of the local government and any objectors involved, or for good reason as determined by the [Council *or* regional planning agency].

[**Commentary:** *If a regional planning agency (such as a regional planning commission or council of governments) is in place, then approval of the local government's housing element would be undertaken by the regional planning agency.*

The initial years of the fair share program's operation will require closer scrutiny by the reviewing agency. However, as local governments gain experience with the program and demonstrate substantial achievement of goals, as an alternative, the reviewing procedures may be simplified and perhaps replaced by some type of self-certification by the local government. The self-certification process would have to be well-developed to allow for challenges by neighboring or affected jurisdictions and other third parties. In addition, the process would have to incorporate appropriate conflict resolution procedures.]

4–208.11   Notice of Submission

(1) At the time of submission to the [Council *or* regional planning agency], the local government shall provide notice of the submission to all owners of land whose properties are included in the housing element for the development of proposed low- and moderate-income housing.

(2) In addition, notice shall be provided within [1] week of the date of submission to a newspaper of general circulation in the area in which the local government is located and to all other persons who requested it in writing.

(3) The notice shall specify that the housing element has been submitted to the [Council *or* regional planning agency] for approval and that all persons receiving a notice shall have the right to participate in the agency's mediation and review process if they object to the plan. The notice shall also specify that copies of the housing element are available for purchase at cost, and shall indicate where they may be reviewed or copied.

(4) The notice shall also state that objections to the housing element, or requests to participate in the mediation, must be filed within [30] days of the date of the mailing of the notices.

(5) If the housing element is a revision of an earlier submission, notice shall also be given to any owners of land whose properties were included in the prior submission but whose properties were omitted from the one currently being proposed.

4–208.12   Objection to Housing Element; Mediation

(1) If any person or entity to whom notice is required to be given, or who requests notice, files an objection, the [Council *or* regional planning agency] shall initiate a mediation process in which it shall attempt to resolve the objections to the housing element voluntarily. Any such objection must be filed within [30] days of the date of service of notice of the filing of the petition for approval.

(2) Objections shall be filed with the [Council *or* regional planning agency] and the local government with as many copies as the Council shall by rule require. The objections shall state with specificity the provisions of the element objected to, and the grounds for the objection to each, and shall contain such expert reports or affidavits as may be needed for an understanding of the objection. In the case of objectors whose lands have not been selected in the element for consideration for low- and moderate-income housing, the objection may also set forth why the lands of the objector are more likely to produce low-and moderate-income housing and either why one or more of the sites proposed by the local government are not realistically likely to produce such housing during the period in which the housing element is in effect or why such sites are not suitable for same.

(3) The mediation and review shall be conducted by a mediator who is either selected by the parties and approved by the [Council *or* regional planning agency] or appointed by the [Council *or* regional planning agency] from its own staff or from a list of outside mediators maintained by the [Council *or* regional planning agency]. The mediator shall possess qualifications not only with respect to dispute resolution, but also with respect to planning and other issues relating to the siting and development of low- and moderate-income housing. The mediation process shall be confidential so that no statements made in or information exchanged during mediation may be used in any judicial or administrative proceeding, except that agreements reached during the mediation process shall be reduced to writing and shall become part of the public record considered by the [Council *or* regional planning agency] in its review of the housing element.

4–208.13 [Council *or* Regional Planning Agency] Review and Approval of Housing Element

(1) The [Council *or* regional planning agency] shall grant its approval of a housing element if it finds in writing that:

(a) the element is consistent with the provisions of this Act and rules adopted by the Council;

(b) the element provides a realistic opportunity for the development of affordable housing through the elimination or reduction of unnecessary cost generating requirements by existing or proposed local government ordinances or regulations; and

(c) the element provides a realistic opportunity for the development of low- and moderate-income housing through the adoption of affirmative measures in the housing element that can lead to the achievement of the local government's regional fair share of low- and moderate-income housing.

(2) In conducting its review, the [Council *or* regional planning agency] may meet with the local government and may deny the petition or condition its approval upon changes in the housing element, including changes in existing or proposed ordinances or regulations. Any approval, denial, or conditions for approval shall be in writing and shall set forth the reasons for denial or conditions. If, within [60] days of the [Council's *or* regional planning agency's] denial or conditional approval, the local government refiles its petition with changes satisfactory to the [Council *or* regional planning agency], the [Council *or* regional planning agency] shall grant approval or grant approval subject to conditions.

[(3) Upon denying, conditionally approving, or approving a local housing element, the [regional planning agency] shall provide a notice of its actions to the Council within [10] days. Where the [regional planning agency] has approved or conditionally approved a housing element, it shall transmit a copy of the approved element with the notice to the Council.]

4–208.14 Adoption of Changes to Development Regulations After Approval

(1) Approval of any housing element by the [Council *or* regional planning agency] shall be subject to and conditioned upon the adoption by the local government of all amendments to ordinances or regulations proposed in the housing element by the local government within [90] days of such approval.

(2) Failure to adopt such changes in the housing element as approved by the [Council *or* regional planning agency] shall render approval of the element null and void and shall subject the local government to the provisions of Section [4–208.16] of this Act.

[4–208.15 Quasi-legislative Review]

[(1) Review by the [Council *or* regional planning agency] of a local government's housing element shall be considered a quasi-legislative decision of general application, and not a decision in a contested case requiring an adjudicatory hearing with the calling of witnesses, cross-examination, or the use of sworn testimony.

(2) The [Council *or* regional planning agency] may appoint hearing officers to conduct such fact finding proceedings as may be appropriate in the event that the [Council *or* regional planning agency] in its discretion deems it appropriate to undertake more detailed fact finding prior to deciding whether to approve, disapprove, or approve a housing element with conditions.]

[**Commentary:** *The purpose of this Section is to avoid lengthy trial type administrative hearings with respect to the approval or disapproval of a housing element. This Section may be omitted if a more formal administrative hearing process is desired.*]

4–208.16 Appeal to Council of Decision Made by a Local Government Regarding an Inclusionary Development When a Housing Element is not Approved or is not Submitted

(1) In the event that the [Council *or* regional planning agency] denies approval of a housing element and the local government does not refile a petition for approval of a housing element, or the [Council *or* regional planning agency], upon reviewing a refiled petition, does not grant approval of the element, or a local government fails to submit a housing element for approval by [*date*], or a local government fails to update a housing element, an applicant seeking approval to build an inclusionary development shall have the right to appeal any denial or approval with conditions by the local government to the Council.

[**Commentary:** *The procedures in this Section could also be the responsibility of a separate appeals board or could be handled by a court. For an example of this, see Alternative 2 in Section 4–208, Application for affordable housing development; affordable housing appeals.*]

(2) Such an appeal may be taken to the Council within [30] days following receipt of a local government's decision of denial or approval with conditions of a proposed inclusionary development by filing with the Council a petition stating the reasons for the appeal. The petition for appeal shall be considered presumptively valid by the Council and the burden of proof shall be with the local government. Within [10] days following receipt of a petition, the Council shall notify the local government that issued the denial or approval with conditions that an appeal has been filed. The local government shall transmit to the Council within [10] days a certified copy of its decision, the application, and the hearing record for the application, if any.

(3) A hearing on the appeal shall be held by the Council within [45] days following receipt of the decision, application, and hearing record. The hearing shall be held on the record, consistent with the [*state administrative procedures act*]. The Council shall render a written decision on the appeal, stating findings of fact and conclusions of law within [30] days following the hearing, unless such time is extended by mutual consent of the petitioner and the local government that issued the decision. The Council may allow interested parties to intervene in the appeal upon timely motion and showing of good cause.

(4) In the case of a denial by the local government, the Council shall consider at the hearing on appeal, but shall not be limited to, the following issues:

   (a) has the local government previously authorized or permitted the construction of low- and/or moderate-income dwelling units at least equal in number to its regional fair share; and

   (b) the extent to which the project would cause significant adverse effects on the environment.

[**Commentary:** *Whoever promulgates rules for handling these appeals (i.e., the Council or a separate appeals board) should develop a list of evaluation parameters, perhaps in consultation with appropriate state environmental agencies and public health authorities, to determine whether a proposed project will cause "significant adverse effects" on the environment.*]

(5) In the case of approval with conditions by the local government, the Council shall consider at the hearing on appeal, but shall not be limited to, the following issues:

(a) whether the conditions are necessary to prevent the project from causing significant adverse effects on the environment; and

(b) whether these conditions render the project infeasible. For purposes of this Act, a requirement, condition, ordinance, or regulation shall be considered to render an inclusionary development proposed by a developer that is a non-profit entity, limited equity cooperative, or public agency infeasible when it renders the development unable to proceed in accordance with the program requirements of any public program for the production of low- and moderate-income housing in view of the amount of subsidy realistically available. For an inclusionary development proposed by a developer that is a private for-profit individual firm, corporation, or other entity, the imposition of unnecessary cost generating requirements, either alone or in combination with other requirements, shall be considered to render an inclusionary development infeasible when it reduces the likely return on the development to a point where a reasonably prudent developer would not proceed.

(6) In the case of a denial by the local government, if the Council finds that the local government has not authorized or permitted the construction of low- and/or moderate-income dwelling units at least equal in number to its regional fair share and that the project as proposed would not cause significant adverse effects to the environment, it shall by order vacate the local government's decision and approve the application with or without conditions.

(7) In the case of approval with conditions by the local government, if the Council determines that the conditions, if removed or modified, would not result in the project causing significant adverse affect to the environment and that such conditions would otherwise render the construction or operation of the project infeasible, it shall by order modify or remove such conditions so that the project would no longer be infeasible and otherwise affirm the approval of the application.

(8) The decision of the Council in paragraph (3) above shall constitute an order directed to the local government and shall be binding on the local government, which shall forthwith issue any and all necessary permits and approvals consistent with the determination of the Council.

4–208.17   Review of Decisions of the Council [and Regional Planning Agency]

(1) A review of a final determination by a [regional planning agency] shall be taken to the Council within [30] days of the determination and the Council shall conduct a *de novo* review of the matter.

(2) A review of a final determination of the Council shall be filed with the [*appellate court of competent jurisdiction*] within [30] days of the determination.

[**Commentary:** *The appeal should go to the state's intermediate appellate court. It would thereafter be subject to normal review by the state's appellate court of last resort.*]

4–208.18   Enforcement of Housing Element Requirements

(1) Subsequent to the approval of the housing element by the [Council *or* regional planning agency], any person with an interest in land or property that has been identified in a housing element pursuant to Section [4–208.9(1)(f)] of this Act may apply to the Council for such order as may be appropriate in connection with the implementation of the element, or the approval of any application for development of the property for low- and moderate-income housing.

(2) Such enforcement action may be taken where it is alleged that the local government has failed to implement the element or has conducted the process of reviewing or approving an inclusionary development on the land in such fashion as to unreasonably delay, add cost to, or otherwise interfere with the development of low- and moderate-income housing proposed in the element.

[*Commentary: Practical experience in New Jersey has shown that low- and moderate-income housing developments, even when included in a duly approved housing element that has dealt with the zoning of a development, become the subject of intense controversy at the time of site plan or subdivision review. To ensure that an approved element is carried out, the Council should have the power to order compliance with the element.*]

4–208.19   Assistance of Court in Enforcing Orders

(1) The Council may obtain the assistance of the [*trial court*] in enforcing any order issued by the Council pursuant to this Act. In acting on any such application for enforcement, the court shall have all powers it otherwise has in addressing the contempt of a court order.

(2) In a proceeding for enforcement, the court shall not consider the validity of the Council's order, which may only be challenged by a direct appeal to the [*intermediate appellate court of competent jurisdiction*], in accordance with the provisions of Section [4–208.17(2)] of this Act.

[*Commentary: An agency's power to enforce its order is important. The agency should therefore have the authority to ensure that its mandates are carried out.*]

4–208.20   Council as Advocate

The Council may act as an advocate for affordable housing developments in the obtaining of federal, state, regional, or local government development approvals or any other permits, approvals, licenses or clearances of any kind which are necessary for the construction of an affordable housing development.

[*Commentary: The development may need additional state permits for wetlands, sewers, etc. The agency ought to alert other permitting entities that the affordable housing project is in the public interest so that other permits and approvals may be expedited.*]

4–208.21   Designation of Authority; Controls on Affordability of Low- and Moderate-Income Dwelling Units

(1) Each local government whose housing element has been approved by the [Council *or* regional planning agency] shall designate a local authority ("Authority") with the responsibility of ensuring the continued affordability of low- and moderate-income sales and rental dwelling units over time.

(2) The Authority shall also be responsible for: affirmative marketing; income qualification of low- and moderate-income households; placing income eligible households in low- and moderate-income dwelling units upon initial occupancy; placing income eligible households in low- and moderate-income dwelling units as they become available during the period of affordability controls; and enforcing the terms of any deed restriction and mortgage loan.

(3) Local governments shall establish a local authority or may contract with a state, regional, or nonprofit agency approved by the Council to perform the functions of the Authority.

4–208.22   Controls on Resales and Re-rentals of Low- and Moderate-Income Dwelling Units

(1) The provisions of paragraphs (2) through (7) below, and the provisions of Section [4–208.23] below, shall apply to newly constructed, rehabilitated, and converted low- and moderate-income sales and rental dwelling units that are intended to fulfill a local government's regional fair share obligations, provided that one or more of the following conditions are met:[20]

    (a) The dwelling unit was constructed, rehabilitated, or converted with assistance from the federal, state, or local government in the form of monetary subsidies, donations of land or infrastructure, financing assistance or guarantees, development fee exemptions, tax credits, or other financial or in-kind assistance; and/or

    (b) The dwelling unit is located in a development that was granted a density bonus or other form of regulatory incentive in order to provide low- and moderate-income housing; and/or

Commentary: Controls on Resales and Re-Rentals

Affordability controls on resales and re-rentals are needed for several reasons. Affordable housing is often in short supply, so conserving the stock of new and rehabilitated affordable housing through controls serves an important public purpose. When government offers subsidies or other incentives to encourage the development of additional affordable housing, unless there are controls on subsequent future sales prices or rent levels, there could be profiteering in the short term on the difference between the below-market subsidized price or rent and the higher prevailing market value or rent of the unit. The controls assure that when the government gives a subsidy, the public in return will receive a benefit in the form of a lasting supply of affordable housing.

The need for affordability controls on resales and re-rentals will obviously vary by community and region of the state.[19] While some housing markets may call for minimal controls, other markets may require controls that are more stringent in terms of length of time and scope. In addition, it is important to re-evaluate the controls as they apply to individual developments on a regular basis to ensure that they remain relevant to market conditions. The imposition of controls could serve as a disincentive to the production of affordable housing because they may limit future flexibility, marketability, and return on investment. Consequently, it may be necessary to link controls on resales and re-rentals with incentives that might include: density bonuses, public contributions or subsidies of infrastructure or land, and expedited permit processing. Subsidies, as used in this model, are specific to the project and do not include such devices as federal home mortgage interest tax deductions. By contrast, a subsidy could include the public assumption of the cost of installing water and sewer lines to the site for a low- and moderate-income housing project or the write-down of land costs.

In imposing controls on rentals and for-sale housing, it is important to recognize the differences between the two types of housing. Rental housing is typically the best alternative for housing people in the very low-income groups and operators of subsidized housing are accustomed to accepting rent limits. However, rents should periodically be adjusted to reflect changing costs to assure economic and physical viability. In the rental case, the principal public policy objective is assuring an adequate supply of affordable units.

The for-sale case is complicated by a second public policy objective: helping families maintain their status as homeowners. Because homeownership entails many more elements of risk and expense than renting, it involves somewhat different public policy concerns. First, homeownership may not be the best choice for very low-income households. Second, there is a down payment and closing costs that are invested and put at risk. There is a longer lasting risk to good credit and a profound sense of personal failure for the foreclosed owners. There are also the financial burden and risk associated with maintaining a home, especially in facing large, unexpected maintenance items. In addition, locking into homeownership with long-term resale price controls constrains the homeowner's flexibility to respond to job or other life situations. These concerns, together with the public purposes served by homeownership, mean that resale price control terms should be more lenient in order to reward low-income homeowners with some measure of equity appreciation, if only to protect them from returning to renter status.

One way to temper the effect of resale price controls on the subsidized homeowner is to offer him/her the option of paying the subsidy back (either fully or partially). The purpose of such a payback of subsidy or "recapture" is three-fold: (1) to guarantee that housing remains affordable for a reasonable period; (2) to ensure that the stock of low-and moderate-income housing is not later depleted if the unit is sold at a higher price; and (3) to create a pool of monies that may be used to construct or rehabilitate affordable units. Once the subsidy has been recaptured by the public to be recycled into other assisted housing, the homeowner would be free to sell at market prices and to use the equity toward the next home purchase. Because of the complexity of recapture systems, their design is probably best done as part of an administrative rule-making process as opposed to a state statute.

An example of how recapture might operate: A homeowner buys a subsidized unit and signs a right of first refusal agreement with the local government that gives the government the right to buy back the unit for the subsidized price with adjustments for inflation, broker fees, etc. If the homeowner pays back the full subsidy, the government would not exercise its option and the house could be sold at market value. Alternately, the government could resell the house as an affordable unit to a qualifying low- or moderate-income homebuyer.

[*Commentary: Note that the various devices listed in subparagraphs (a) and (b) correspond to tools that are considered to be "subsidies," as defined in Chapter 3.*]

   (c) The dwelling unit was built subject to the terms of a local ordinance which requires the construction of low- and moderate-income housing as a condition of development approval.

(2) In developing housing elements, local governments shall determine and adopt measures to ensure that newly constructed low- and moderate-income sales and rental dwelling units that are intended to fulfill regional fair share obligations remain affordable to low- and moderate-income households for a period of not less than [15] years, which period may be renewed. The Authority shall require all conveyances of those newly constructed low- and moderate-income sales dwelling units subject to this Act to contain the deed restriction and mortgage lien adopted by the Council.[21] Any restrictions on future resale or rentals shall be included in the deed restriction as a condition of approval enforceable through legal and equitable remedies, as provided for in Section [4–208.23] of this Act.

(3) Rehabilitated owner-occupied single-family dwelling units that are improved to code standard shall be subject to affordability controls for at least [5] years.

(4) Rehabilitated renter-occupied dwelling units that are improved to code standard shall be subject to affordability controls on re-rental for at least [10] years.

(5) Dwelling units created through the conversion of a nonresidential structure shall be considered a new dwelling unit and shall be subject to controls on affordability as delineated in paragraphs (2), (3), and (4) above.

(6) Affordability controls on owner- or renter-occupied accessory apartments shall be for a period of at least [5] years.

(7) Alternatives not otherwise described in this Section shall be controlled in a manner deemed suitable to the Council and shall provide assurances that such arrangements will house low- and moderate-income households for at least [10] years.

4–208.23   Enforcement of Deed Restriction

(1) No local government shall issue a certificate of occupancy for the initial occupancy of a low- or moderate-income sales dwelling unit unless there is a written determination by the Authority that the unit is to be controlled by a deed restriction and mortgage lien as adopted by the Council. The Authority shall make such determination within [10] days of receipt of a proposed deed restriction and mortgage lien. Amendments to the deed restriction and lien shall be permitted only if they have been approved by the Council. A request for an amendment to the deed restriction and lien may be made by the Authority, the local government, or a developer.

(2) No local government shall permit the initial occupancy of a low- or moderate-income sales dwelling unit prior to the issuance of a certificate of occupancy in accordance with paragraph (1) above and with its zoning code and other land development regulations.

(3) Local governments shall, by ordinance, require a certificate of reoccupancy for any occupancy of a low- or moderate-income sales dwelling unit resulting from a resale and shall not issue such certificate unless there is a written determination by the Authority that the unit is to be controlled by the deed restriction and mortgage lien prior to the issuance of a certificate of reoccupancy, regardless of whether the sellers had executed the deed restriction and mortgage lien adopted by the Council upon acquisition of the property. The Authority shall make such determination with [10] days of receipt of a proposed deed restriction and mortgage lien.

(4) The mortgage lien and the deed restriction shall be filed with the recorder's office of the county in which the unit is located. The lien and deed restriction shall be in the form prescribed by the Council.

(5) In the event of a threatened breach of any of the terms of a deed restriction by an owner, the Authority shall have all remedies provided at law or equity, including the right to seek injunctive relief or specific performance, it being recognized by parties to the deed restriction that a breach will cause irreparable harm to the Authority in light of the public policies set forth in this Act and the obligation for the provision of low- and moderate-income housing.

(6) Upon the occurrence of a breach of any of the terms of the deed restriction by an owner, the Authority shall have all remedies provided at law or equity, including but

not limited to, foreclosure, recoupment of any funds from a rental in violation of the deed restriction, injunctive relief to prevent further violation of the deed restriction, entry on the premises, and specific performance.

4–208.24   Local Government Right to Purchase, Lease, or Acquire Real Property for Low- and Moderate-Income Housing

(1) Notwithstanding any other law to the contrary, a local government may purchase, lease, or acquire by gift, real property and any estate or interest therein, which the local government determines necessary or useful for the construction or rehabilitation of low- and moderate-income housing or the conversion to low- and moderate-income housing.

(2) The local government may provide for the acquisition, construction, and maintenance of buildings, structures, or other improvements necessary or useful for the provision of low- and moderate-income housing, and may provide for the reconstruction, conversion, or rehabilitation of those improvements in such manner as may be necessary or useful for those purposes.

(3) Notwithstanding the provisions of any other law regarding the conveyance, sale, or lease of real property by a local government to the contrary, a local government's legislative body may, by [ordinance *or* resolution], authorize the private sale and conveyance or lease of a housing unit or units acquired or constructed pursuant to this Section, where the sale, conveyance, or lease is to a low- or moderate-income household or nonprofit entity and contains a contractual guarantee that the dwelling unit will remain available to low- and moderate-income households for a period of at least [15] years.

4–208.25   Biennial Report of the Council to Governor and Legislature

(1) By [*date*] of each even-numbered year, the Council shall prepare a report to the governor and legislature. The Council shall report on the effect of this Act on promoting the provision of affordable housing in the housing regions of the state. The report shall address, among other things: local governments with housing elements that have been approved, with or without conditions, or that have not been approved by [the Council *or* a regional planning agency]; the number of low- and moderate income dwelling units constructed, rehabilitated, purchased, or otherwise made available pursuant to this Act; the number and nature of appeals to the Council on decisions of local governments denying or conditionally approving inclusionary developments and the Council's disposition of such appeals; [regional planning agencies with regional fair-share housing allocation plans that have, or have not been approved;] actions that have been taken by local governments to reduce or eliminate unnecessary cost generating requirements that affect affordable housing; and such other actions that the Council has taken or matters that the Council deems appropriate upon which to report. The report may include recommendations for any revisions to this Act which the Council believes are necessary to more nearly effectuate the state's housing goal.

(2) Every officer, agency, department, or instrumentality of state government, of [regional planning agencies,] and of local government shall comply with any reasonable request by the Council for advice, assistance, information, or other material in the preparation of this report.

(3) The Council shall send the biennial report to the governor, members of the legislature, state agencies, departments, boards and commissions, appropriate federal agencies, [regional planning agencies], and to the chief executive officer of every local government in the state, and shall make the report available to the public. Copies shall be deposited in the state library and shall be sent to all public libraries in the state that serve as depositories for state documents.

Alternative 2 B Application for Affordable Housing Development; Affordable Housing Appeals[22]

4–208.1   Findings

The legislature hereby finds and declares that:

(1) there exists an acute shortage of affordable, accessible, safe, and sanitary housing for low- and moderate-income households in the state;

(2) it is imperative that action be taken immediately to assure the availability of such housing; and

(3) it is necessary for all local governments in the state to assist in the provision of such housing opportunities to assure the health, safety, and welfare of all citizens of the state.

4–208.2   Purpose

It is the purpose of this Act to provide expeditious relief from local ordinances or regulations that inhibit the construction of affordable housing needed to serve low-and moderate-income households in this state. The provisions of this Act shall be liberally construed to accomplish this purpose.[23]

4–208.3   Definitions

As used in this Act:

(1) "**Affordable Housing**" means housing that has a sales price or rental amount that is within the means of a household that may occupy moderate-, low-, or very low-income housing, as defined by paragraphs (9), (10), and (12), below. In the case of dwelling units for sale, housing that is affordable means housing in which mortgage, amortization, taxes, insurance, and condominium or association fees, if any, constitute no more than [28] percent of such gross annual household income for a household of the size which may occupy the unit in question. In the case of dwelling units for rent, housing that is affordable means housing for which the rent and utilities constitute no more than [30] percent of such gross annual household income for a household of the size which may occupy the unit in question.

[*Commentary: Note that, for purposes of this model, the term "affordable housing" applies only to very low-, low-, and moderate-income housing and does not apply to middle-income housing.*]

(2) "**Affordable Housing Developer**" means a nonprofit entity, limited equity cooperative, public agency, or private individual firm, corporation, or other entity seeking to build an affordable housing development.

The inclusion of private developers, as well as nonprofit and governmental organizations, in this definition, is necessary to encourage a widespread participation in the development of affordable housing.

(3) "**Affordable Housing Development**" means any housing that is subsidized by the federal or state government, or any housing in which at least [20] percent of the dwelling units are subject to covenants or restrictions which require that such dwelling units be sold or rented at prices which preserve them as affordable housing for a period of at least [15] years.[24]

[*Commentary: The 20 percent standard for what constitutes lower income housing development has been used in New Jersey, particularly the Mount Laurel II case.*[25]]

(4) "**Approving Authority**" means the Planning Commission, Zoning Board of [Appeal *or* Adjustment], Governing Body, or other local government body designated pursuant to law to review and approve an affordable housing development.

(5) "**Development**" means any building, construction, renovation, mining, extraction, dredging, filling, excavation, or drilling activity or operation; any material change in the use or appearance of any structure or in the land itself; the division of land into parcels; any change in the intensity or use of land, such as an increase in the number of dwelling units in a structure or a change to a commercial or industrial use from a less intensive use; any activity which alters a shore, beach, seacoast, river, stream, lake, pond, canal, marsh, dune area, woodlands, wetland, endangered species habitat, aquifer or other resource area, including coastal construction or other activity.

(6) "**Exempt Local Government**" means:

    (a) any local government in which at least [10] percent of its housing units, at the time an application is made pursuant to this Act, have been subsidized by the federal or state government, or by a private entity, and in which occupancy is restricted or intended for low- and moderate-income households;

    (b) any local government whose median household income is, according to most recent census data, less than 80 percent of the median household income of the county or primary metropolitan statistical area as last defined and delineated by the U.S. Bureau of the Census in which the local government is located; or

    (c) any local government whose percentage of substandard dwelling units in its total housing stock, as determined by the most recently available census data, is more than 1.2 times (120 percent) the percentage of such dwellings in the housing stock for the county or primary metropolitan statistical area in which the local government is located.

[*Commentary: This definition of "exempt" local governments, found in various forms in the New England statutes, recognizes that certain communities may have already met their burden of providing low- or moderate-income housing. See, for example, Connecticut General Statutes Annotated, Section 8–30g(f). The county is suggested as a primary standard of comparison, but metropolitan areas may be substituted in place of a county. Use of an entire state would in most cases be impractical since entire regions of the state may have less than the statewide median income and use of the state as the base would thus exempt them from the applicability of the statute.*]

(7) "**Household**" means the person or persons occupying a dwelling unit.

(8) "**Local Government**" means the [county, city, village, town, township, borough, *or* other political subdivision] which has the primary authority to review development plans.

(9) "**Low-Income Housing**" means housing that is affordable, according to the federal Department of Housing and Urban Development, for either home ownership or rental, and that is occupied, reserved, or marketed for occupancy by households with a gross household income that does not exceed 50 percent of the median gross household income for households of the same size within the county or primary metropolitan statistical area in which the housing is located. For purposes of this Act, the term "low-income housing" shall include "very low-income housing."

(10) "**Moderate-Income**[26] **Housing**" means housing that is affordable, according to the federal Department of Housing and Urban Development, for either home ownership or rental, and that is occupied, reserved, or marketed for occupancy by households with a gross household income that is greater than 50 percent but does not exceed 80 percent of the median gross household income for households of the same size within the county or primary metropolitan statistical area in which the housing is located.

(11) "**Unnecessary Cost Generating Requirements**" mean those development standards that may be eliminated or reduced that are not essential to protect the public health, safety, or welfare or that are not critical to the protection or preservation of the environment, and that may otherwise make a project economically infeasible. An unnecessary cost generating requirement may include, but shall not be limited to, excessive standards or requirements for: minimum lot size, building size, building setbacks, spacing between buildings, impervious surfaces, open space, landscaping, buffering, reforestation, road width, pavements, parking, sidewalks, paved paths, culverts and stormwater drainage, and oversized water and sewer lines to accommodate future development without reimbursement.

(12) "**Very Low-Income Housing**" means housing that is affordable, according to the federal Department of Housing and Urban Development, for either home ownership or rental, and that is occupied, reserved, or marketed for occupancy by households with a gross household income equal to 30 percent or less of the median gross household income for households of the same size within the county or primary metropolitan statistical area in which the housing is located.

4–208.4   Local Government Action on Affordable Housing Applications

(1) An affordable housing developer may file an application for an affordable housing development in any nonexempt local government with the Approving Authority, in accordance with a checklist of items required for a complete application previously established by [ordinance *or* rule of *the* Department of Housing and Community Development *or other state agency authorized by statute*].

(2) The Approving Authority shall review the application in accordance with the standards set forth in Section [4–208.5(1)] below, and shall have the power to issue a comprehensive permit which shall include all local government approvals or licenses, other than a building permit, necessary for the authorization of the affordable housing development. The Approving Authority shall hold at least [1], but no more than [3], public hearings on the proposal within [60] days of receipt of the application and shall render a decision within [40] days after the conclusion of the public hearing(s).

(3) Failure of the Approving Authority to act within this time frame shall mean that the Authority is deemed to have approved the application, unless the time frame is extended by a voluntary agreement with the applicant.

4–208.5   Basis for Approving Authority Determination

(1) The Approving Authority shall grant approval of an affordable housing development unless facts produced in the record at the public hearing or otherwise of record demonstrate that the development as proposed:

   (a) would have significant adverse effects on the environment; or

   (b) would significantly conflict with planning goals and policies specified in the local government's comprehensive plan, provided they are not designed to, or do not have the effect of, rendering infeasible the development of affordable housing while permitting other forms of housing.

(2) The Approving Authority may condition the approval of the affordable housing development on compliance with local government development standards, contained in an ordinance or regulation, which are necessary for the protection of the health and safety of residents of the proposed development or of the residents of the local government, or which promote better site and building design in relation to the area surrounding the proposed development, provided that any such ordinances or regulations must be equally applicable to both affordable housing development and other development, and provided that such conditions do not render the affordable housing development infeasible. The Approving Authority shall waive such local government development standards where their application would render the provision of affordable housing infeasible, unless such waiver would cause the affordable housing development to have significant adverse effects on the environment.

(3) For purposes of this Act, a requirement, condition, ordinance, or regulation shall be considered to render an affordable housing development proposed by an affordable housing developer that is a nonprofit entity, limited equity cooperative, or public agency infeasible when it renders the development unable to proceed in accordance with program requirements of any public program for the production of affordable housing in view of the amount of subsidy realistically available. For an affordable housing development proposed by an affordable housing developer that is a private for-profit individual firm, corporation, or other entity, the imposition of unnecessary cost generating requirements, either alone or in combination with other requirements, shall be considered to render an affordable housing development infeasible when it reduces the likely return on the development to a point where a reasonably prudent developer would not proceed.[27]

4–208.6   Appeal to [State Housing Appeals Board *or* Court]

(1) An affordable housing developer whose application is either denied or approved with conditions that in his or her judgment render the provision of affordable housing infeasible, may, within [30 *or* 45] days of such decision appeal to the [State Hous-

ing Appeals Board *or other state trial court*] challenging that decision. The [Board *or* Court] shall render a decision on such application within [120] days of the appeal being filed. In its determination of any such appeal, the [Board *or* Court] shall conduct a *de novo* review of the matter.

[**Commentary:** *The New England housing appeals statutes are either silent on the burden of proof before the appeals board, or place the burden of proof on the local government.[28] Given the nature of the interests involved B municipal discretion vs. housing affordability B it is advisable to allow the appeal authority to conduct its own independent de novo review of the facts. Whether the applicant or the local government has the ultimate burden of proof is a question of policy for each state to determine as it balances the weight of affordable housing needs against local government planning discretion. Optional language on burden of proof is provided in paragraph (2) below.*]

(2) In rendering its decision, the [Board *or* Court] shall consider the facts and whether the Approving Authority correctly applied the standards set forth in Section [4–208.5] above.

[*add optional additional burden of proof language for (2)*]
[In any proceeding before the [Board *or* Court], the Approving Authority shall bear the burden of demonstrating that it correctly applied the standards set forth in Section [4–208.5] above in denying or conditionally approving the application for an affordable housing development.]

 (3) The [Board *or* Court] may affirm, reverse, or modify the conditions of, or add conditions to, a decision made by the Approving Authority. The decision of the [Board *or* Court] shall constitute an order directed to the Approving Authority, and shall be binding on the local government which shall forthwith issue any and all necessary permits and approvals consistent with the determination of the [Board *or* Court].

(4) The [*appellate court of competent jurisdiction*] shall have the exclusive jurisdiction to review decisions of the [Board *or* Court].

[4–208.7   Enforcement]
[The order of the Board may be enforced by the Board or by the applicant on an action brought in the [*trial court*].]

Where a housing appeals board rather than a court is selected, it must be given the authority to enforce its orders.

4–208.8   Nonresidential Development as Part of an Affordable Housing Development
(1) An applicant for development of property that will be principally devoted to nonresidential uses in a nonresidential zoning district shall have the status of an affordable housing developer for the purposes of this Act where the applicant proposes that no less than 20 percent of the area of the development or 20 percent of the square footage of the development shall be devoted to affordable housing, except that the applicant shall bear the burden of proof of demonstrating that the purposes of a nonresidential zoning district will not be impaired by the construction of housing in that zoning district and that the health, safety, and welfare of the residents of the affordable housing will not be adversely affected by nonresidential uses either in existence or permitted in that zoning district.

(2) For purposes of paragraph (1) above, the square footage of the residential portion of the development shall be measured by the interior floor area of dwelling units, excluding that portion which is unheated. Square footage of the nonresidential portion shall be calculated according to the gross leasable area.

4–208.9   Overconcentration Of Affordable Housing
In order to prevent the drastic alteration of a community's character through the exercise of the rights conferred upon affordable housing developers by this Act, the requirements to approve affordable housing developments by a local government as specified in this Act shall cease at such time as:

(1) the local government fulfills the requirements to become an exempt local government, as defined in Section [4–208.3(6)]; or

(2) where the number of units of affordable housing approved and built pursuant to this Act exceeds [__,000] dwelling units over a period of [5] years.

[*Commentary: Jurisdictions where there is faster growth may experience a rush of affordable housing proposals. To prevent communities from becoming overwhelmed by the prospect that developers may charge out to buy or option land within one community where there is ample vacant land, and seek zoning changes, there should be some upper limit on the amount of housing that can be approved under the special procedures contained in this statute. For example, in New Jersey during the 1980s, some towns were faced with as many as 11 lawsuits by developers.*[29] *In the Section above, this occurs when the local government meets the requirements for an "exempt local government" in Section 4–208.3(6) or when a statutorily established limit on the number of units of affordable housing over a certain period of time is met.*]

[4–208.10   Housing Appeals Board]

[(1) Composition [*describe composition of housing appeals board and terms of members*].]

[*Commenary: If a housing appeals board, rather than the courts, is selected to administer the statute, the state will have to determine its composition. There should be representation by local and, if appropriate, county interests, by private for-profit and nonprofit developers of affordable housing, by planning interests, and by the public at large. Provided that the interests are reasonably balanced, there is no single correct answer either to the size of the body or the precise breakdown of appointees.*[30] *If a court is chosen, it should be the trial court of general jurisdiction in the state.*]

[(2) Within [3] months after the effective date of this Act, the Housing Appeals Board shall adopt rules and regulations governing practice before it. The Board may adopt [subject to approval of the Department of Housing and Community Development *or other state agency*] such other rules and regulations as it deems necessary and appropriate to carry out its responsibilities under this Act.]

[*Commentary: The bracketed language in paragraph (2) gives the policy-making arm of the governor some input into substantive regulations. It is expected that general state administrative procedures acts will provide the procedural framework, such as notices, public hearings, publication, etc. for rule making, so that rule-making procedures need not be spelled out in this statute.*]

ENDNOTES

1. Excerpted from Stuart Meck, FAICP, Gen. Editor, *Growing Smart*[SM] *Legislative Guidebook, Model Statutes for Planning and the Management of Change, 2002 edition*, vol. 1 (Chicago: American Planning Association, January 2002). Bracketed references are to other sections of the *Guidebook*. The full document may be downloaded at http://www.planning.org/growing smart.

2. This model was drafted by Peter A. Buchsbaum, a partner in the law firm of Greenbaum, Rowe, Smith, Ravin, and Davis, in Woodbridge, New Jersey, Harvey S. Moskowitz, AICP/PP, a partner in the professional planning consulting firm of Moskowitz, Heyer, and Gruel, in Florham Park, New Jersey, and Stuart Meck, FAICP/PP, Principal Investigator, and Michelle J. Zimet, AICP, attorney and Senior Research Fellow, both of the Growing Smart[SM] project at the APA.

3. For sources of definitions for low-, moderate- and very low-income households, see 24 CFR, Section 91.5 (Definitions) and New Jersey Administrative Code, Title 5, Section 5:93–1.3.

4. See Section 6–201(5)(e), Alternative 2, of the *Legislative Guidebook,* which describes the components of a regional comprehensive plan, including a regional fair-share housing allocation plan. The definition of a regional fair-share allocation plan would only need to be included if the approach selected gives the responsibility of preparing the regional fair-share allocations to a regional planning agency.

5. For an example of a state-level policy that links the award of discretionary state funds with local government housing policies, see Commonwealth of Massachusetts, Executive Order No. 215, "Disbursement of State Development Assistance" (March 15, 1982).

6. For an example of language granting authority to a state planning agency to issue rules and orders, see Section 4–103 of the *Legislative Guidebook.*

7. For an example of housing need projections, see New Jersey Administrative Code, Title 5, Chapter 93, Appendix A (Methodology); see also David Listokin, *Fair Share Housing Allocation* (New Brunswick, N.J.: Center for Urban Policy Research, 1976), 48–51.

8. These factors are only intended to be illustrative. Compare California Government Code, Section 65584(a) (regional housing needs), where the factors are included in the statute, with New Jersey Administrative Code, Title 5, Chapter 52:27D–307(c)(2) (discussion of adjustment of present and prospective regional fair share). The allocation formulas must be tailored to each state. For an example of an allocation formula that is the result of rule making by a state agency, see New Jersey Administrative Code, Title 5, Chapter 93, Sections 2.1 et seq. (municipal determination of present and prospective need) and Appendix A. See also David Listokin, *Fair Share Housing Allocation* (New Brunswick, N.J.: Center for Urban Policy Research, 1976) for an early survey of allocation formulas.

9. Projecting the growth and location of moderate- and low-wage jobs is an important factor in assessing the need and approximate location for low- and moderate-income housing.

10. It is important that an allocation strategy and a local housing element seek spatial dispersion of low- and moderate-income housing opportunities since they should not add to the concentration of the poor.

11. See Section 6–201, Preparation of Regional Comprehensive Plan, Alternative 2, of the *Legislative Guidebook* for a treatment of urban growth area designation.

12. See Section 5–201 et seq. of the *Legislative Guidebook,* which addresses areas of critical state concern.

13. See Section 6–201, Preparation of Regional Comprehensive Plan, Alternative 2, of the *Legislative Guidebook* for a treatment of urban growth area designation.

14. See Section 5–201 et seq. of the *Legislative Guidebook,* which addresses areas of critical state concern.

15. Alternatively, the regional fair-share allocation plan may be publicly reviewed in the manner proposed in Section 6–301, Public Workshops and Hearings, and adopted in the manner proposed in Section 6–303, Adoption of Regional Plans.

16. Section 6–105 pertains to rule-making authority by the regional planning agency.

17. For an interesting and creative statute providing financial incentives to local governments for removing barriers to low- and moderate-income housing (as well as middle-income housing), see Florida Statutes, Section 420.907 et seq. (1995) (state housing incentives partnership), esp. Section 420.9076 (adoption of affordable housing incentive plans; committees).

18. While a local government may not want to designate specific sites for low- and moderate-income housing, it is nonetheless important to designate a sufficient supply of sites zoned at appropriate densities to assure an open, competitive land market.

19. Affordability controls may also be supplemented with other direct subsidies such as low interest loans to assist a homebuyer in making a down payment on a dwelling unit. Such a loan would be short term, such as five years, and would be recaptured in order to assist other future homebuyers of low- and moderate-income units.

20. If none of these conditions is present, then presumably the developer is operating outside of the local government's affordable housing program provided for under the Act. The developer would therefore not need any of the incentives or subsidies offered by the local government or other agencies.

21. A model deed restriction and lien for low- and moderate-income housing appears in New Jersey Administrative Code, Title 5, Chapter 93, Appendix I.

22. This model statute was drafted by Peter A. Buchsbaum, a partner in the law firm of Greenbaum, Rowe, Smith, Ravin, and Davis in Woodbridge, New Jersey, along with additional drafting and material by Stuart Meck, FAICP, Principal Investigator, and Michelle J. Zimet, AICP, Attorney and Senior Research Fellow, for the Growing Smart[SM] project.

23. The text of this model is drawn from Connecticut General Statutes Annotated, Section 8–30g; Massachusetts General Laws Title 40B , Sections 20 to 23; and General Laws of Rhode Island, Sections 43–53–1 to 53–8. These statutes, based on the original 1969 Massachusetts Affordable Housing Appeals Act, resemble each other.

24. For an excellent example of a deed restriction based on years of successful experience in New Jersey, see New Jersey Administrative Code, Title 5, Chapter 93, Appendix I, which contains the deed restriction for low- and moderate-income housing required by the State Council on Affordable Housing.

25. *Mt. Laurel II*, 456 A.2d 390 at n.37.

26. In some states where there a greater stratification of income and housing, a fourth category may be included entitled "middle-income" that would be defined as households with a gross household income that is greater than 80 percent but does not exceed 95 to 120 percent of the median gross household income for households of the same size within the county or metropolitan area in which the housing is located. See, e.g., 24 CFR, Section 91.5 (definition of "middle-income family").

27. For an existing statutory definition of "infeasible," see Rhode Island General Laws, Section 45–53.4(c), which provides:

> "Infeasible" means any condition brought about by any single factor or combination of factors, as a result of limitations imposed on the development by conditions attached to the zoning approval, to the extent that it makes it impossible for a public agency, nonprofit organization, or limited equity housing cooperative to proceed in building or operating low or moderate income housing without financial loss, within the limitations set by the subsidizing agency of government, on the size or character of the development, on the amount or nature of the subsidy, or on the tenants, rentals, and income permissible, and without substantially changing the rent levels and unit sizes proposed by the public agency, nonprofit organization, or limited equity housing cooperative.

28. See Connecticut General Statutes Annotated, Section 8–30g(c).

29. See, e.g., *Field v. Franklin Twp.*, 204 N.J. Super. 445, 449 A.2d 251 (1985).

30. Rhode Island General Statutes, Section 45–53–7 provides the following board makeup:

> Housing Appeals Board: (a) There shall be within the state a housing appeals board consisting of nine (9) members:

Housing Appeals Board

Represent:	*Appointed by:*
1 district court judge (chair)	Chief of district court
1 local zoning board member	Speaker of the house
1 local planning board member	Majority leader of senate
2 city and town council members	Speaker of the house
(plus an alternate) B representing	Majority leader of senate
municipalities of various sizes	(Governor)
1 affordable housing developer	Governor
1 affordable housing advocate	Governor
1 director of statewide planning or designee	Self-appointed
1 director of Rhode Island housing or designee	Self-appointed

> (b) All appointed [sic] shall be for two (2) year terms, provided, however, the initial terms of members appointed by the speaker of the house and majority leader shall be for a period of one year. A member shall receive no compensation for his or her services, but shall be reimbursed by the state for all reasonable expenses actually and necessarily incurred in the performance of his or her official duties. The board shall hear all petitions for review filed under [Section] 45–53–5, and shall conduct all hearings in accordance with the rules and regulations established by the chair. Rhode Island housing [sic] shall provide such space, and such clerical and other assistance, as the board may require.

Contact List

Affordable Housing Education and Development
Littleton, New Hampshire
tel (603) 444-1377, fax (603) 444-0707
161 Main Street, Littleton, New Hampshire 03561

Ames and Story County Housing Program
Ames, Iowa
tel (515) 239-5400, fax (515) 239-5404
P.O. Box 811, Ames, Iowa 50010
http://www.city.ames.ia.us/housingweb/

Association of Bay Area Governments
San Francisco, California
tel (510) 464-7900, fax (510) 464-7970
P.O. Box 2050, Oakland, California 94604
http://www.abag.ca.gov

Bay Area Council
San Francisco, California
tel (415) 981-6600, fax (415) 981-6408
200 Pine Street, Suite 300, San Francisco, California 94104
http://www.bayareacouncil.org

Central New Hampshire Regional Planning Commission
tel (603) 226-6020, fax (603) 226-6023
28 Commercial Street, Concord, NH 03301
http://www.cnhrpc.org

Columbus/Franklin County Affordable Housing Trust
Columbus, Ohio
tel (614) 372-1850, fax (614) 252-7261
1234 E. Broad Street, Columbus, Ohio 43205

Connecticut Department of Economic and Community Development
tel (860) 270-8000
505 Hudson Street, Hartford, CT 060105
http://www.state.ct.us/ecd/housing/

Cornell University
Ithaca, New York
Rolf Pendall, AICP
Assistant Professor of City and Regional Planning
Department of City and Regional Planning
tel (607) 225-5561, fax (607) 255-6681
106 West Sibley Hall, Cornell University
Ithaca, New York 14853
http://www.dcrp.cornell.edu

Council on Affordable Housing
New Jersey
tel (609) 292-3000, fax (609) 633-6056
101 S. Broad Street, P.O. Box 813, Trenton, New Jersey 08625
http://www.state.nj.us/dca/coah/

CountyCorp
Montgomery County, Ohio
tel (937) 225-6328, fax (937) 496-6629
40 West Fourth Street, Dayton Ohio 45402
http://www.countycorp.com/

California Department of Housing and Community Development
California
Department of Housing and Community Development
tel (916) 445-4728, fax (916) 327-2643
1800 3rd Street, P.O. Box 952053, Sacramento, California 94252
http://www.hcd.ca.gov/hpd/

Live Near Your Work
Maryland
Department of Housing and Community Development
tel (410) 209-5809, fax (410) 987-4660
100 Community Place, Crownsville, Maryland 21032
http://www.dhcd.state.md.us/lnyw/

Massachusetts Housing Appeals Committee
tel (617) 727-6192
One Congress Street, Tenth Floor,Boston, Massachusetts 02114
http://www.state.ma.us/dhcd/components/hac/

Metropolis 2020, Chicago, Illinois
tel (312) 332-2020, fax (312) 332-2626
30 West Monroe Street, Chicago, Illinois 60603
http://www.chicagometropolis2020.org/

Metro, Portland, Washington
tel (503) 797-1737, fax (503) 797-1797
600 NE Grand Ave., Portland, Oregon 97232
http://www.metro-region.org/

Metropolitan Council
Minneapolis, Minnesota
tel (612) 822-1016
1458 West 35th Street, Minneapolis, Minnesota 44408
http://www.metrocouncil.org/

Nashua Regional Planning Commission
tel (603) 883-0366
115 Main Street, P.O. Box 847
Nashua, NH 03061
http://www.nashuarpc.org

National Low Income Housing Coalition
tel (202) 662-1530, fax (202) 393-1973
1012 Fourteenth Street, NW, Suite 610, Washington, D.C. 20005
http://www.nlihc.org/

North Country Council, Inc.
tel (603) 444-6303, fax (603) 444-7588
107 Glessner Rd Bethlehem, NH 03574
http://www.nccouncil.org

Rhode Island Housing and Mortgage Finance Corporation
tel (401) 457-1285, fax (401) 457-1140
44 Washington Street, Providence, RI.

A Regional Coalition for Housing (ARCH)
Seattle, Washington
tel (425) 861-3676, fax (425) 861-4553
16225 NE 87th Street, Suite A-3, Redmond, Washington 98052
http://www.archhousing.org

Sacramento Housing and Redevelopment Agency
Sacramento, California
tel (916) 444-9210, fax (916) 441-1196
630 I Street, 2nd Floor, Sacramento, California 95814
http://www.shra.org

San Diego Association of Governments
San Diego, California
tel (619) 595-5343, fax (619) 595-5303
401 Broad Street, Suite 800, San Diego, California, 92101
http://www.sandag.org

Southern California Association of Governments
Los Angeles, California
tel (213) 236-1921, fax (213) 236-1963
818 West Seventh Street, 12th Floor, Los Angeles, California 90017
http://www.scag.ca.gov

Twin Pines Housing Trust
White River Junction, Vermont
tel (802) 291-7000, fax (802) 281-7273
106 Railroad Row, White River Junction, Vermont 05001
http://www.twinpineshousingtrust.com/

Vermont Housing and Conservation Board
Vermont
tel (802) 828-3259, fax (802) 828-3203
149 State Street, Montpelier, Vermont 05602
http://www.vhcb.org

The American Planning Association
Policy Guide on Housing (excerpt)

[**Editor's Note**: *The full text of this policy guide can be consulted at http://www.planning.org/policyguides/housing.htm. We are reprinting Section 3 of the guide, which specifically addresses affordable housing.*]

Adopted by the Chapter Delegate Assembly April 25, 1999
Ratified by the Board of Directors April 26, 1999

3. AFFORDABLE HOUSING

a. APA National and Chapters should collaborate with nonprofit and for-profit housing providers to educate citizens and elected officials about affordable housing and work to eliminate negative perceptions and stereotypes. Zoning requests for residential development affordable to low-income households should not be arbitrarily denied.

b. APA National and Chapters should encourage national, state, and local initiatives designed to preserve and expand affordable housing opportunities at a variety of income levels. Planners should work to ensure that scarce housing subsidies are used to provide long-term benefits to those in need of assistance. In general, capital subsidies for construction or acquisition of housing should also be accompanied by measures that ensure long-term affordability. (*See APA Policy Guide on The Supply of Public and Subsidized Housing, adopted 10/18/91*)

c. Planners should expand affordable housing opportunities by facilitating the development and preservation of accessory apartments, cluster housing, elder cottages, manufactured housing, mixed-income housing, shared residences, and single room occupancy (SRO) developments.

d. APA National and Chapters should work to preserve the federal Low-Income Housing Tax Credit, a critical tool for affordable housing finance, and to encourage accountability in the management of LIHTC projects.

e. APA National and Chapters should work to renew and expand the availability of federal funding for Section 8 Certificates and Vouchers or alternative models of direct rent subsidy to enable low-income households to afford decent housing in the private market. Alternative models should not be limited to federally supported initiatives but also embrace state and local programs.

f. APA National and Chapters should support, based on local conditions, controls on conversion of rental housing to condominiums where such conversion affects the availability of affordable housing; controls on unreasonable increases in rent; and requirements for just cause for eviction of renters. These tools should remain available to local governments for use in response to locally defined needs, and not preempted by state or federal legislation.

g. APA National and Chapters should work with state, federal and local governments to facilitate economic development strategies that will yield living wage jobs and enable families and individuals to afford housing without the necessity of additional public subsidies and incentives.

h. APA National and Chapters should support and promote a wide range of programs and incentives that encourage private and nonprofit development of affordable housing to supplement publicly owned and managed housing, and that complement local housing delivery systems. These measures include density bonuses, land donations, low-income housing tax credits, and commercial linkage impact fees.

i. APA National and Chapters should support, based upon local conditions, the provision of affordable housing for farm employees and their families, and other seasonal workers.

MAKING GREAT COMMUNITIES HAPPEN

The American Planning Association provides leadership in the development of vital communities by advocating excellence in community planning, promoting education and citizen empowerment, and providing the tools and support necessary to effect positive change.

461. Performance Standards in Growth Management. Douglas Porter, ed. January 1996. 44pp.

462/463. Modernizing State Planning Statutes: The Growing Smart℠ Working Papers. Volume 1. March 1996. 190pp.

464. Planners' Salaries and Employment Trends. Marya Morris. July 1996. 25pp.

465. Adequate Public Facilities Ordinances and Transportation Management. S. Mark White. August 1996. 80pp.

466. Planning for Hillside Development. Robert B. Olshansky. November 1996. 50pp.

467. A Planners Guide to Sustainable Development. Kevin J. Krizek and Joe Power. December 1996. 66pp.

468. Creating Transit-Supportive Land-Use Regulations. Marya Morris, ed. December 1996. 76pp.

469. Gambling, Economic Development, and Historic Preservation. Christopher Chadbourne, Philip Walker, and Mark Wolfe. March 1997. 56pp.

470/471. Habitat Protection Planning: Where the Wild Things Are. Christopher J. Duerksen, Donald L. Elliott, N. Thompson Hobbs, Erin Johnson, and James R. Miller. May 1997. 82pp.

472. Converting Storefronts to Housing: An Illustrated Guide. July 1997. 88pp.

473. Subdivision Design in Flood Hazard Areas. Marya Morris. September 1997. 62pp.

474/475. Online Resources for Planners. Sanjay Jeer. November 1997. 126pp.

476. Nonpoint Source Pollution: A Handbook for Local Governments. Sanjay Jeer, Megan Lewis, Stuart Meck, Jon Witten, and Michelle Zimet. December 1997. 127pp.

477. Transportation Demand Management. Erik Ferguson. March 1998. 68pp.

478. Manufactured Housing: Regulation, Design Innovations, and Development Options. Welford Sanders. July 1998. 120pp.

479. The Principles of Smart Development. September 1998. 113pp.

480/481. Modernizing State Planning Statutes: The Growing Smart℠ Working Papers. Volume 2. September 1998. 269pp.

482. Planning and Zoning for Concentrated Animal Feeding Operations. Jim Schwab. December 1998. 44pp.

483/484. Planning for Post-Disaster Recovery and Reconstruction. Jim Schwab, et al. December 1998. 346pp.

485. Traffic Sheds, Rural Highway Capacity, and Growth Management. Lane Kendig with Stephen Tocknell. March 1999. 24pp.

486. Youth Participation in Community Planning. Ramona Mullahey, Yve Susskind, and Barry Checkoway. June 1999. 70pp.

489/490. Aesthetics, Community Character, and the Law. Christopher J. Duerksen and R. Matthew Goebel. December 1999. 154pp.

493. Transportation Impact Fees and Excise Taxes: A Survey of 16 Jurisdictions. Connie Cooper. July 2000. 62pp.

494. Incentive Zoning: Meeting Urban Design and Affordable Housing Objectives. Marya Morris. September 2000. 64pp.

495/496. Everything You Always Wanted To Know About Regulating Sex Businesses. Eric Damian Kelly and Connie Cooper. December 2000. 168pp.

497/498. Parks, Recreation, and Open Spaces: An Agenda for the 21st Century. Alexander Garvin. December 2000. 72pp.

499. Regulating Home-Based Businesses in the Twenty-First Century. Charles Wunder. December 2000. 37pp.

500/501. Lights, Camera, Community Video. Cabot Orton, Keith Spiegel, and Eddie Gale. April 2001. 76pp.

502. Parks and Economic Development. John L. Crompton. November 2001. 74pp.

503/504. Saving Face: How Corporate Franchise Design Can Respect Community Identity (revised edition). Ronald Lee Fleming. February 2002. 118pp.

505. Telecom Hotels: A Planners Guide. Jennifer Evans-Crowley. March 2002. 31pp.

506/507. Old Cities/Green Cities: Communities Transform Unmanaged Land. J. Blaine Bonham, Jr., Gerri Spilka, and Darl Rastorfer. March 2002. 123pp.

508. Performance Guarantees for Government Permit Granting Authorities. Wayne Feiden and Raymond Burby. July 2002. 80pp.

509. Street Vending: A Survey of Ideas and Lessons for Planners. Jennifer Ball. August 2002. 44pp.

510/511. Parking Standards. Edited by Michael Davidson and Fay Dolnick. November 2002. 181pp.

512. Smart Growth Audits. Jerry Weitz and Leora Susan Waldner. November 2002. 56pp.

513/514. Regional Approaches to Affordable Housing. Stuart Meck, Rebecca Retzlaff, and James Schwab. February 2003. 271pp.